CRIME IN ENGLAND

VOL. I.

PATTERSON SMITH

REPRINT SERIES IN

CRIMINOLOGY, LAW ENFORCEMENT, AND SOCIAL PROBLEMS

PUBLICATIONS

No. 1. Lewis, Orlando F. *The Development of American Prisons and Prison Customs, 1776-1845.*

No. 2. Carpenter, Mary. *Reformatory Prison Discipline.*

No. 3. Brace, Charles Loring. *The Dangerous Classes of New York.*

No. 4. Dix, Dorothea Lynde. *Remarks on Prisons and Prison Discipline in the United States.*

No. 5. Bruce, Andrew A., Albert J. Harno, Ernest W. Burgess, & John Landesco. *The Workings of the Indeterminate-Sentence Law and the Parole System in Illinois.*

No. 6. Wickersham Commission. *Complete Reports, Including the Mooney-Billings Report.* 14 Vols.

No. 7. Livingston, Edward. *Complete Works on Criminal Jurisprudence.* 2 Vols.

No. 8. Cleveland Foundation. *Criminal Justice in Cleveland.*

No. 9. Illinois Association for Criminal Justice. *The Illinois Crime Survey.*

No. 10. Missouri Association for Criminal Justice. *The Missouri Crime Survey.*

No. 11. Aschaffenburg, Gustav. *Crime and Its Repression.*

No. 12. Garofalo, Raffaele. *Criminology.*

No. 13. Gross, Hans. *Criminal Psychology.*

No. 14. Lombroso, Cesare. *Crime, Its Causes and Remedies.*

No. 15. Saleilles, Raymond. *The Individualization of Punishment.*

No. 16. Tarde, Gabriel. *Penal Philosophy.*

No. 17. McKelvey, Blake. *American Prisons.*

No. 18. Sanders, Wiley B. *Negro Child Welfare in North Carolina.*

No. 19. Pike, Luke Owen. *A History of Crime in England.* 2 Vols.

No. 20. Herring, Harriet L. *Welfare Work in Mill Villages.*

No. 21. Barnes, Harry Elmer. *The Evolution of Penology in Pennsylvania.*

No. 22. Puckett, Newbell N. *Folk Beliefs of the Southern Negro.*

No. 23. Fernald, Mabel Ruth, Mary Holmes Stevens Hayes, & Almena Dawley. *A Study of Women Delinquents in New York State.*

No. 24. Wines, Enoch Cobb. *The State of Prisons and of Child-Saving Institutions in the Civilized World.*

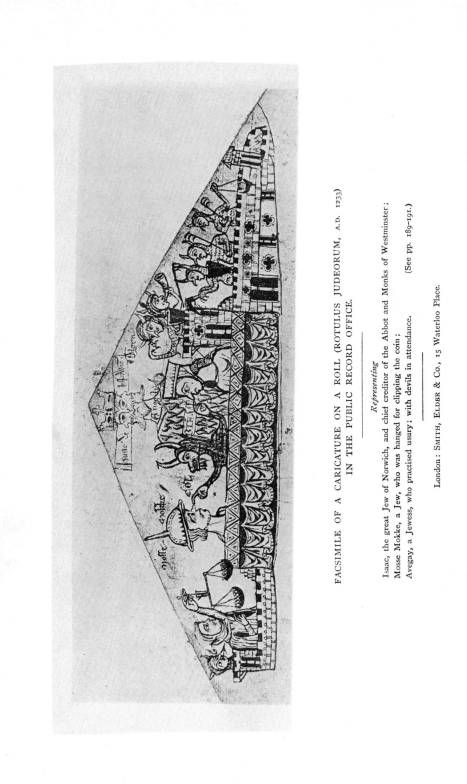

FACSIMILE OF A CARICATURE ON A ROLL (ROTULUS JUDEORUM, A.D. 1233) IN THE PUBLIC RECORD OFFICE.

Representing

Isaac, the great Jew of Norwich, and chief creditor of the Abbot and Monks of Westminster; Mosse Mokke, a Jew, who was hanged for clipping the coin; Avegay, a Jewess, who practised usury; with devils in attendance. (See pp. 189-191.)

London: SMITH, ELDER & CO., 15 Waterloo Place.

PUBLICATION NO. 19: PATTERSON SMITH REPRINT SERIES IN
CRIMINOLOGY, LAW ENFORCEMENT, AND SOCIAL PROBLEMS

A

HISTORY OF CRIME

IN ENGLAND

ILLUSTRATING THE

CHANGES OF THE LAWS IN THE PROGRESS

OF CIVILISATION

WRITTEN FROM THE PUBLIC RECORDS AND OTHER

CONTEMPORARY EVIDENCE

BY

LUKE OWEN PIKE, M.A.

OF LINCOLN'S INN, BARRISTER-AT-LAW

AUTHOR OF

'THE ENGLISH AND THEIR ORIGIN, A PROLOGUE TO AUTHENTIC ENGLISH HISTORY' ETC.

VOL. I.

From the ROMAN INVASION to the ACCESSION of HENRY VII.

Reprinted from the 1873-76 Edition

Montclair, New Jersey
PATTERSON SMITH
1968

Published by
Patterson Smith Publishing Corporation
Montclair, New Jersey

Library of Congress Catalog Card Number: 68-55779

PREFACE.

—◆◇◆—

SIR MATTHEW HALE, one of the many great lawyers who have shown an ardent love of history, and who have earnestly laboured to discover historical truth, bequeathed his manuscripts to the Honourable Society of Lincoln's Inn. I was not fully acquainted with the extent and value of his collection until I had drawn out the plan of the present work, and brought together the greater part of my materials. Fortunately, however, I ascertained, before I began to write, that there are in the Hale MSS. a considerable number of references to records, with abstracts conveniently placed under various heads, which have a direct bearing upon the History of Crime. According to the terms of Hale's will, not even a member of Lincoln's Inn is permitted to consult the MSS. without express permission, and for that permission I have to offer the Benchers my best thanks.

Some of Hale's references and abstracts are taken, word for word, from ancient calendars formerly in the Tower of London; others are apparently the result of independent research among the records themselves; but in every instance in which I have made use of the collection I have also consulted the original document. In my own notes, I have not only indicated the record from which any fact is taken, but wherever I was directed to it by Sir Matthew Hale, I have carefully acknowledged the obligation.

In the Library of the Inner Temple there is a great collection of transcripts from records, known as the Petyt MSS. ; and I am much indebted to the Benchers of that Honourable Society for the kindness and courtesy with which they granted me access to their historical treasures.

To the Librarians of both Inns I must also express my thanks for the ready aid given in answer to every question.

Except for the purpose of expressing thanks where thanks are due, a preface to a history is almost unnecessary. The book should speak for itself: for its method in its text—for its accuracy in its references. But, as I have indicated the sources from which I have drawn my materials, in a manner which has, I believe, not been previously adopted, a few words of explanation may, perhaps, be not altogether useless. The reader is in every case referred not from the text to the note, but from the note to the text, and the whole of the notes are placed at the end of the volume.

My reason for this innovation is not that I regard the references to original sources as of little importance, but that I regard them as of sufficient importance to be kept distinct from the narrative and the views of the Author. To know where the historian has sought his facts is to possess a very useful guide to his character as a historian ; and this knowledge, according to the plan of the present work, can be most readily attained by simply looking to the end of the volume. A very short time will suffice for any competent critic to learn whether the information upon which the history is founded is second-hand, or—as I venture to submit it should be in every history—first-hand.

Numbers of foot-notes are like the parentheses of one who relates something by word of mouth, and who frequently interrupts his narrative with such remarks as ' But I ought to have mentioned,' or ' I forgot to say,' or ' This is really a fact, as you may easily ascertain by reference.' It is difficult to understand why a habit which shows want of art in a story-teller has long been permitted to the historian, who should not omit to say that which, in his opinion, ought to be said, and who should, at least, possess the faculty of expressing in his text the distinction between an established fact and a mere possibility. Some authors have before adopted the expedient of placing their notes at the end, but so far as I am aware, they have all made their reference from the text to the note by attaching a number to some word in the text. This, though an improvement, still bears a likeness to a clumsy talker's repeated interruption of himself with the statement that he is telling the truth.

It seems better and more simple to announce, once for all, that no assertion for which there is not good warrant has wittingly been made in the text. All who wish to know what the evidence is have but to look in the side-notes of the Appendix, at the end of the volume, for the number of the page which contains the statement to be verified. They will there, I trust, find what will convince them.

In this volume it would have been almost impossible to follow the ancient plan of giving references by any kind of indication in the text. In many places, especially in the fourth chapter, almost every sentence in a paragraph has records adduced in its support, and the distraction of the reader's eye and attention by ever-recurring numbers would have been most tedious.

There is, too, an advantage in the method now adopted which seems to be very much in favour of historical truth. It is a very stringent check upon the writer. A number attached to a word in the text, and corresponding with the same number attached to a description of a manuscript or a book, is very apt to mislead, as all are aware who have verified the references of preceding authors. There is commonly nothing to show whether a reference applies to a sentence, a paragraph, or a series of paragraphs; and thus the real foundation of an important assertion often remains in obscurity. No such uncertainty can exist when the plan upon which the references are made involves a statement of the fact or facts established by every document mentioned.

To a reader who may cast his eye over the Appendix before looking at the text, there may possibly seem to be a disregard of chronological order. Every chapter, except the fourth, is, so to speak, a wide stage, on which the characters come and go—not, I trust, without good reason, but without regard to the method of annalists who make a mere inventory of the events which have occurred in each year. When a period displays a number of features which are little less marked at the end than at the beginning, it seems to be the historian's duty to show how and why they have this power of sustaining themselves, and how they are connected one with another. These remarks would, perhaps, be unnecessary if the references were suppressed, but are necessary as an introduction to the references considered by themselves. The Appendix is in support of a history in which the method is essentially chronological, but which advances period by period instead of year by year.

A very large portion of the text is founded on records which have never been published, and many of which have, in all probability, never before been consulted for any historical purpose. These are described in the notes by their technical names ; and anyone who chooses can inspect them for himself at the Public Record Office. In every case, too, in which I have availed myself of collections of printed records, as, for instance, Rymer's 'Fœdera,' I have given a reference not only to the printed book, but to the source from which the document is taken. A reference to Rymer with this precaution, is never, as it might otherwise be, a second-hand reference to a chronicle, but always a reference to an original record, made accessible by means of the printing-press.

A greater space than is occupied by the text would have been required to print in full all those hitherto unpublished evidences to which reference has been made. To reprint at length what is in print elsewhere, has not, in any case, appeared necessary, because no collection of mere extracts from chronicles will prove that the history

agrees in the main with the context of the extracts, as
well as with the extracts themselves.   A few remarkable
documents, however, will be found in the notes, and
among them the indictment of Oldcastle, as enrolled in
the King's Bench.   The important points in which this
original record differs from the transcript taken into
Parliament by the Chief Justice of England, and afterwards enrolled on a Roll of Parliament, have also been
indicated, and are well worthy of note.   A historian might
well believe, as historians seem to have believed hitherto,
that every Roll of Parliament is an original authority,
but this particular roll contains a reference to a King's
Bench record, which, upon verification, reveals a striking
discrepancy.   Such are the difficulties with which an
author has to contend who would arrive at historical
truth.

In full reliance upon records, I have, here and there,
departed from the account given of some matters in the
legal text-books ; and though I cannot hope to have
altogether escaped error, I trust I shall not be accused of
being in the wrong, simply because I have placed confidence in the best evidence I could find.

In order to avoid needless repetitions, I have pur-
posely reserved various matters for future treatment.
The records have been my guide in determining what
should be considered the chief characteristics of every
age.

The present volume ends with a well-marked period
of English history, and has been brought out by itself at
the suggestion of gentlemen who are far more able than

I am to judge how a work should be published. The materials for the rest of the history have, however, been collected ; the plan of the whole was drawn out before any of it was written, and some progress has already been made with the text of the second volume.

L. OWEN PIKE.

LONDON : *May* 1873.

CONTENTS.

———•◆•———

CHAPTER I.

INTRODUCTORY.

FROM THE ROMAN INVASION TO THE NORMAN CONQUEST.

CHAPTER II.

FROM THE NORMAN CONQUEST TO THE THIRD CRUSADE. ENGLAND
AT THE END OF THE TWELFTH CENTURY.

CHAPTER III.

FROM THE THIRD CRUSADE TO THE YEAR BEFORE THE BLACK DEATH.

CHAPTER IV.

ENGLAND IN THE YEAR BEFORE THE BLACK DEATH.

CHAPTER V.

FROM THE BLACK DEATH TO THE ACCESSION OF HENRY VII.

APPENDIX.

REFERENCES AND NOTES.

REFERENCES AND NOTES TO CHAPTER II.

REFERENCES AND NOTES TO CHAPTER III.

PAGE

REFERENCES AND NOTES TO CHAPTER IV.

Errata.

Page 23   5 lines from top, *dele* the second ' to be'
,,   31   12   ,,   bottom, *for* In *read* To
,,   173   5   ,,   ,,   *after* ' as ' insert a comma
,,   192   14   ,,   top, *for* objects *read* object
,,   210   12   ,,   bottom, *after* ' for ' insert a comma
,,   211   7   ,,   ,,   *after* Though *dele* it may be said that
,,   213   6   ,,   ,,   *after* as *insert* a
,,   226   14   ,,   top, *after* is *dele* the comma
,,   252   6   ,,   bottom, *for* and laid them waste *read* which they laid waste
,,   262   15   ,,   ,,   *after* ' that ' insert a comma
,,   301   7   ,,   ,,   insert the comma *after* ' that ' instead of *before*
,,   303   7   ,,   ,,   *after* ' relatives ' *dele* the comma
,,   346   second side-note, *for* erasures *read* erasure
,,   360   last line, *after* that *dele* the comma
,,   429   lines 20 and 23 from bottom, *for* the S in ' Signiferorum ' *read* L
,,   430   16 lines from top, *after* comparison *dele* the comma
,,   441   third side note, *for* Notes *read* Note
,,   445   10 lines from top, *for* Lives *read* Life
,,   490   6   ,,   ,,   *after* relate *insert* to
,,   495   22   ,,   ,,   *after* remains *dele* the comma

A HISTORY OF CRIME

IN ENGLAND.

CHAPTER I.

INTRODUCTORY.

FROM THE ROMAN INVASION TO THE NORMAN CONQUEST.

WHAT is Crime? Whence come the Criminals? Have we inherited from the darker ages a malady which is gradually becoming extinct, or The scope, are we ourselves indulging in new and more evil the sources, and the difficulties of the habits, which will corrupt still further the life- work. blood of posterity? Is it true that where wealth accumulates men decay, that our forefathers were better men than we, and that, as we strain our eyes back into the past, we can see in history that golden age of which poets in all countries have prattled? Savages who were noble, knights who were blameless in their lives and fearless in death, kings who lived only for their people, peoples contented with their rulers, plenty, happiness, and widespread virtue were, according to some philosophers, the blessings which the world once enjoyed, in spite even of the fall of Adam.

To such a picture as this our prisons and dockyards, filled by an ever-flowing stream of new offenders, or of criminals who are whirled back by successive eddies again and again to their former place, present a hideous contrast. There may be seen the deliberate murderer, with steel-blue eye and square jaw and set lips, patient as a beast of prey and not less cruel, marking with calmly vindictive glance all who come to see him in his cage, biding the time for his release, resolved that his next spring shall be at once more stealthy and more deadly than his last. There, with feeble frame and puny head, is he who sheds blood he knows not why, who is cursed with too much cunning to escape punishment as an idiot, blessed with too little sense to act discreetly. There is the thief by profession, with ears projecting outwards as though to catch the first sound of the pursuing thief-taker, and with unquiet eyes, which seem to dread detection even in the act of looking. There are the evil-doers of a higher class—each differing from his fellows because they have reached the same goal by somewhat different paths. But conspicuous among them all is the perjurer, from his resemblance to convicts of another stamp. With an unstable mien, like that of the habitual pilferer, he often has a bolder and more shameless air. His is often the massive neck, broad behind as the head itself, which is common to the most brutal among homicides, and which indicates a vigorous heart and a full flow of blood. He needs all his strength, even though destitute of feeling, to stand unabashed and be ever ready with a new lie when lie after lie has been detected and exposed. He may be observed only too often in every law-court, drawing himself together, with a characteristic but almost imperceptible gesture, for a new effort against truth as often as some unexpected shaft has grazed his impenetrable hide. Sooner or later he finds his way to gaol, which, however, he may enter for an offence of some other kind than perjury, and so become undistinguishable in the great mass of iniquity.

Such characters as these, and many others not unlike them, are unhappily within the every-day experience of the gaol-chaplain and the warder. They are often described as a reproach to our civilisation, and have baffled again and again the ingenuity of philanthropists. But can civilisation with justice be held wholly responsible for all that exists side by side with it ? Is civilisation in any respect a disgrace to the civilised ? Has its progress been only in a vicious circle ? Is its end to be suicide ? To such questions there is no answer except in history— not the history of a decade or a century, but the complete history of our nation. The causes must be studied in their operation through many long ages. To seek for them within the narrow limits of a modern period would be as vain as to judge whether the tide is ebbing or flowing from the marks of only two consecutive waves on the sea-shore. In that truth lies the justification (and with it some of the greatest difficulties) of the present undertaking.

In the attempt to write a History of Crime, a field is entered which has never previously been explored. The history of civilisation has been written again and again ; the manners and customs of past ages have been depicted by authors whose mastery of style compensated, so far as compensation was possible, for paucity of materials ; the changes in our laws, the development of our literature, the increase of our arts, and the growth of our science, have been narrated in almost every detail and discussed from almost every point of view. History has long ceased to be a bare chronicle of battles lost and won, of the rise and fall of dynasties, and of the intrigues of statesmen.   But in the reaction against that useless method of recalling the past which exalted a date as a thing to be remembered for its own sake, and appraised a man's intellect by the number of disconnected facts with which it was stored, there has arisen a danger of erring in an opposite direction.   The history which states the facts and omits the causes has been in some degree supplanted by the history which generalises upon causes where the facts are insufficient.   Civilisation is a great whole made up of so many different parts that unless workers can be found who will be content to investigate its constituent elements with some minuteness its progress can never be thoroughly understood.

It is surely a paradox that there have long been many ' Histories of Civilisation,' and not one ' History of Crime.'   The different opinions entertained at different times of similar actions, the varying amount of respect shown for human life and for property, the effects of ignorance and superstition upon the nature and the number of offences and upon the laws intended for their repression, the relation between political convulsions and social disorganisation belong essentially to the history of civilisation.   These and a variety of minor details connected with the history of crime have hitherto been either passed over in silence, or dismissed in a few dogmatic sentences, which might be true by chance, but were not founded on certain information.   An Oates has often been held up to execration as a disgrace to humanity, a Bacon alternately described as sinned against or sinning ; but none have set themselves to enquire what causes in the far-off past had aided in the development of a Bacon or an

Oates, how far they have now been modified, and whether it is possible that we may ourselves transmit any of them to our descendants.

We congratulate ourselves, not without good cause, upon improvements in the administration of justice. The integrity of our judges has long been so far above suspicion that we have almost ceased, for want of a contrast, to realise the value of a Bench without reproach, or the miseries of a country in which the interpreters of the law have lost the confidence of the people. It is only by a careful study of the past that we can know how immeasurably better, in this respect at least, is our condition than that of our forefathers. It is only by comparison of the past with the present that we can discern what grounds we have for hope in the future.

If Crime has received but little attention, even in histories of civilisation, it is probably because historians were not aware of the existence of sufficient materials to illustrate the subject. The subject could hardly have been considered either unimportant or uninteresting in itself. The means of effecting a comparison between one age and another, in their criminal and social aspects, cannot be found in sufficient abundance in printed books. Crabbed manuscripts, often dirt-stained and half obliterated by damp, written in a hand and in a language with which the classical scholar is not familiar, must be laboriously read by him who would fill up the gaps in the story of our English life. To omit this process is to be, in a great measure, at the mercy of mediæval chroniclers, who narrated that which seemed strange to them and passed over that which was familiar, and which is, for the practical purposes of our own time, best worth knowing. Records of inestimable value have, indeed, been published in more than one collection, in which learning and industry are seen to be combined with discrimination. But the earlier selections were made when the true functions of history were little understood ; and though those of later date display great judgment in the attempt to supply what was previously omitted, they are neces- sarily imperfect, because mere extracts cannot be other- wise. To depend solely upon such compilations, even when most excellent, is to adopt, unwittingly perhaps, the historical views of the compilers, whose professed object was not to suggest new subjects for history, but to illustrate history in the sense in which it had previously been understood. Thus, as the hill country often remains unsubdued when the plains yield to a conqueror, so the province which we are now about to enter has been without an owner in literature, because it has been exces- sively difficult of access. But, like the Alps, it abounds in rich pastures, and offers scenes not less picturesque than the deeds of great warriors, and the marriages and progresses of kings and queens.

There is another consideration which might well deter an author from undertaking so difficult a theme. He is almost certain to incur the imputation of presumption. It is impossible even to sketch the plan of such a work without collateral study of a very wide range, for crimes can never be exhibited in their true light without some knowledge of the surrounding social conditions. But in proportion as the design is comprehensive the chances of error increase, and the writer must sometimes appear in an unfavourable light to those who are better informed on some particular point upon which his scheme has compelled him to touch. Perhaps, however, some in- dulgence may be shown to one who freely admits that

mistakes are inevitable, and who asks that what is at
least honestly done may be leniently judged.

Of the customs which prevailed in Britain before it
fell under the dominion of the Romans we have but little
evidence, and that little of a not very trust- Teutonic
worthy character. To those who believe that the origin of our
earlier population was extirpated by the barba- Law.
rous tribes which succeeded the Romans as masters of the
soil, there will appear to be no cause for regret that the annals of an extinct race have perished—if, indeed, they ever
existed. Nor, for the purposes of this history, need the
loss be very deeply deplored by those who hold a contrary opinion. There is no doubt that the settlers who
crossed the German Ocean, and gave the name of England to Southern Britain, brought with them certain
customs which, with little modification, constituted for
many centuries the criminal law of the country. Municipal institutions and the tenure of land may, perhaps,
present more difficulties to the historian, but it seems
impossible that the rules for detecting and punishing crime
which the Normans found in England, and from which
a portion of our modern law has painfully emerged,
can have come to us from any but a Teutonic source.

There may, perhaps, after this admission, appear no
need to look beyond the Low German invasion of our
island for the history of its crime and of its civi- Advantage of
looking be-
lisation. Least of all may any such need be yond the Teutonic Inva-
thought to exist when the further admission is sion.
made that Race cannot, in modern times, be satisfactorily
weighed as one of the determining causes of crime in
this country. But as the subsequent history will hold
equally good whether we are or are not mainly of Teu-

tonic blood, and as our descent is at least a controverted
point, it may be excusable, if not absolutely essential, to
relate a few events and to describe a few customs which
seem to repeat themselves in later times, and which, if
they prove no more, prove how easily similar passions
may be stirred by similar circumstances.

It is, indeed, unnecessary to make any excuse for introducing a comparison of Roman culture with the bar-
General view barism which preceded it and with the barba-
of Roman
Conquest and rism which afterwards almost annihilated it.   If
Roman Cul-
ture.   it be true that the same causes produce the same
effects under the same conditions, there is a lesson to be
learned from the rise and fall of Rome—the most impressive lesson, perhaps, which is taught anywhere in
history.   Rome did her best to civilise her empire when
conquered, and it would be well if all conquering nations
could boast that they had succeeded as well as she.   But
her first contact with all tribes was made known to them
by the sharp edge of her sword, and recorded on their
soil in the burial-mounds of their bravest sons.   Could
the whole world have been united under her tolerant
sway, the whole world might have become like herself,
and the progress of mankind would not have been
retarded when the sceptre fell from her grasp.   But with
every new conquest she incurred a new danger; for what
she first asserted was not her superiority in mind, but her
superiority in brute force.   Those who had been last
brought under her yoke were always her most bitter
enemies, because they had lost independence, and did
not yet perceive how much they might gain in exchange.
As her frontier was extended the circle of hostile
barbarians grew larger, her own means of defence less
available.   The first art which she taught her new sub-

jects was the art of war, and they, in turn, taught it to their comrades beyond the border. Could their education have been completed, Rome might never have fallen, Christianity might long ago have been, in one form or other, the religion of every quarter of the globe, the inventions of the eighteenth and nineteenth centuries might have been anticipated in the seventh or eighth, and the nineteenth century itself might have been a happier time for mankind than mankind can even hope to enjoy in the thirtieth. It was because she had risen by her legions that her legions caused her, as she deserved, to fall. It was because she was a generous mistress that she became, as she deserved to become, immortal. To those whose chief thoughts were of blood and iron, she appeared only as the fortunate, but hateful, possessor of troops with iron which was a little better tempered, and with blood which was a little less easily to be shed than their own. By those who had learnt from her how much she had to bestow, she was regarded with pride as a part of themselves. Thus did she illustrate the truism, often repeated, and nearly always forgotten, that the empire of the intellect is higher than the empire of the strong hand. Thus did she show, as she fell, what is not less worth remembering, that the acquisitions made in the course of human progress are always in jeopardy so long as there is any section of humanity cut off from the enjoyment of them. Men must advance in a body, or those who lag behind will drag back those who are pushing to the front. Never was this great principle more terribly illustrated, never was the true origin of crime more conspicuously brought to view, than when Roman Britain became the prey of Teutonic hordes.

When we enquire what was the condition of those

Britons whom the Romans conquered we find no sources of information except some scanty notices by Roman authors, and even those notices are not always consistent one with the other. The absence of native records, however, goes far to show that the civilisation introduced from Rome was a great advance upon any which had previously been developed in Britain ; and there cannot be a doubt that Britain gained great benefits when she became a portion of the Roman Empire. It would be useless to discuss the manners and customs of the ancient Britons, except in those points which have a direct connection with the subject of the present history. But eighteen centuries ago the civilised world believed that there was in the far West of Europe a priesthood which exacted the penalty of death by burning, and as the exaction of the same penalty was sanctioned by another priesthood in another age, the belief is worthy of mention though it may not be unhesitatingly accepted as truth.

It is uncertain what was the condition of Britain before the Roman invasion.

Of one mode of punishment inflicted by the priests of ancient Gaul and Britain there is an account, which was current in Rome, but which may be true or false, like other travellers' tales. It was held, we are told, in those countries, as elsewhere, that the sacrifice of human beings was pleasant to the powers which ruled the universe, that the life of one human being could be given as the ransom for the life and welfare of another, and that the wrath of the gods could always be appeased, if not by one life, by many. This belief was shared by other tribes in every part of the ancient world ; but by them it was supposed that the most acceptable offering was a life only just matured and as yet unsullied by crime. In Gaul and

Alleged punishments and human sacrifices before the Roman occupation.

Britain, if we may believe the story which has been handed down to us, it was in the death of the criminal that the gods were thought to take the greatest delight. Elsewhere, in primitive times, it became a common custom to regard virginity as a type of sanctity and purity, and to sacrifice virgins to offended gods. In Gaul and Britain it was taught that the gods were made angry by crime, and relented only when the criminal had expiated his offence. There Iphigenia could never have raised that piteous wail, in which she bemoans her young life cut short for no fault of her own, the loss of all that woman holds most dear, the doom that denied her a husband and children. Had the gods demanded the sacrifice of only one human being, and had there been only one criminal, that criminal would have been selected, and the innocent maiden would have been spared.

The Gallic and British method of sacrificing criminals as described by the Roman author, is remarkable not only as an evidence of the sternness with which crime was said to be repressed by a priesthood, but also from the resemblance which it bears to the punishment inflicted on traitresses in England as late as the eighteenth century. The offenders were thrown into cages of wicker-work, made in the form of some well-known idol, and large enough to hold many human beings at once. Wood was heaped beneath and around them, and when all was ready the pile was kindled. The flames played about the fragile prison, and shot their forked tongues ever further and further into the mass of the writhing and shrieking victims. The semblance of the god was soon lost to view, but not before the crowd around had, as it seemed, seen the god himself deal death to the wrong-doers in its most appalling form. Then came one great blaze of the pile and the cage and the wretches who had been within it; and when that died out justice was satisfied, and the gods were content for a time. Had such scenes never been enacted in Smithfield, had women not been burnt in England a century and a half ago, the story of the Roman might be more easily disbelieved. Unhappily the similar horrors of a later time rest on evidence which is beyond all dispute.

If the Gauls and Britons were guilty of inflicting death by torture, the Romans appear at first sight to gain, in Roman punishments in the Arena. that respect, little by comparison. They not only burned Christians and slaves before Christianity was accepted in high places, but they made the exhibition of criminals battling with wild beasts in the arena one of the most prominent institutions of the Empire. To them, and to the inhabitants of their provinces, the death-pangs of the condemned, or, when none were condemned, of professional gladiators, became as familiar as the bull-fight is to the Spaniard, or as horse-races are to ourselves. While the baths were to the men what the clubs are to men of the nineteenth century, the amphitheatre was the public meeting-place for both sexes—the park, the opera-house, and the race-course in one. Beauties would bet sportively upon the issue of the struggle—eager for the death which would prove their judgment in the right. Sometimes the combat would be merely one of gladiator against gladiator; and so familiar was the Roman public with blood that there was an established signal—a mere motion of the thumb—by which the popular opinion bade the victor put the vanquished to death. A blow, perhaps a groan, a fresh layer of sand, a murmur of voices, such as we hear between the acts of a comedy, were the only indications that a life had passed away.

When so small a value was set upon human blood within the arena, it may seem hardly possible that homicide without could be regarded as one of the greatest crimes. Yet the suspicion is not fully justified by other facts, nor by Roman laws. Value set upon human life by the Romans. There have been handed down no statistics of the amount of crime committed throughout the Roman Empire, still less of its proportion to the population. The satirists, as many other satirists have done, mourn bitterly over the corruptions of the imperial city, over its murders, and its robberies, over the deceptions practised on the unwary, and the infidelities of married life. But there is little to be gathered from these vague declamations, except the fact that murder was regarded by certain ancient writers in Rome with almost as much horror as by ourselves in England at the present time.

The worst that can be said of the Roman criminal law, as it existed while Britain was Roman, is that it sanctioned torture for the purpose of extracting information, and the punishments of fire and of the arena for those offences which it pronounced most heinous, and that, in common with some The dark side of the Roman Criminal Law. barbarous laws, by which it was superseded, it magnified the offence in proportion to the littleness of the offenders. That which was almost venial in a man of high rank was a crime which brought terrible retribution upon a slave. Such distinctions are no more than an indication that authority has been won at the point of the sword, and that the conqueror belongs to a caste different from that of the conquered. But in this respect Rome may well bear comparison with the conquering nations which had preceded her and with many of those which followed her. She accepted that slavery which she found as an existing institution wherever she went, and with which she had grown familiar before she had conquered a province. But no nation could say of her that she had introduced slavery where it was unknown before. She conferred privileges, often amounting to equality, upon her subjects, and did not take away from them the privilege of keeping or of selling the slaves by whom they had always been served. In those points in which she placed the higher provincials on the level of slaves she placed the most favoured Roman on precisely the same level. In accusations of that crime alone which we should now call High Treason, she insisted that all men were equal in the eye of the law—to suffer the same torture—to die the same death.

Turn wherever we may in the immortal codes which Rome has bequeathed to us we find everywhere the same liberality, restrained only, but every-

The origin of the more cruel punishments.

where restrained, by the same military tradition, the same determination to acquire, and to hold what has been acquired, if necessary, by the strong hand. By fire and sword she won her way, and she did not survive long enough to banish the recollection of sword and fire from her laws. The slave who accused his owner of any crime, except treason, was, for the mere offence of committing such an act of insubordination, punished ' by the sword,' or, in other words, was condemned to a gladiatoral combat in the arena. The slave who, without his owner's knowledge, harboured a thief, the slave who committed adultery with a free woman, the coiner who brought discredit upon the currency of the Empire were, without mercy, given over to the flames.

What barbarism, it may be asked, could have been afterwards introduced more barbarous than such punish-

ments as these ? To that question a fitter answer may
be given in subsequent details than by a general statement. But any one who should regard only Brighter side
these blots upon the Roman code would have of the Roman
not the slightest conception of its general scope. Law : grada-
Nothing is more remarkable in it, nothing more ishments.
deserving of admiration, than the evident design to find
a penalty in just proportion to the offence, and to mark
out distinctly the various grades of crime. The old
Roman of the Republic could not imagine any sin
more revolting than to murder a blood relation—father,
mother, brother, sister, son, or daughter ; and the ancient
tradition survived through all the luxury of the empire.
Parricide was the legal name of this offence, and the different forms taken by the love of kindred among the
Romans and among those who succeeded them in Britain
are well worthy of remark. Among the Teutonic invaders of Britain, though the kin-tie was at the very root
of their institutions, we shall find the loss of a kinsman
regarded as an excellent opportunity for making a bargain ;
among the Romans the family-bond was considered so
sacred that a most extraordinary death was devised for
him who violated it. Not in the amphitheatre, not at the
stake, not on the cross was the parricide to perish. A
sack was to be his winding-sheet ; in that he was to be
sewn up alive, and venomous serpents with him. He
was to be thrown into the sea if the sea was near at hand,
and, if not, into a river, so that the heavens might be
hidden from him while still alive, and the earth deny him
a grave when dead.

A number of crimes were by special laws declared
capital — such as forcible entry upon land or house,
adultery committed by a free woman with a slave, and

infanticide. It should however be remembered that according to the Roman law a capital offence was not
necessarily punished by death, but was also a technical
description of those offences which were punishable by
loss of civil condition—by degradation from freedom to
slavery, or deprivation of the full privileges of citizenship.
A punishment analogous to the French galleys, or imprisonment in our own dockyards, was the compulsory
service in mines ; transportation, too, was by no means
uncommon ; and the precursor of our own tread-mill
may be found in the Roman hand-mill.

If the use of torture, the punishments inflicted on
slaves, and the punishments for witchcraft and parri-
Justice temp- cide, are left out of consideration, the Roman
pered with Criminal Law, as it existed during the later occu-
mercy under
the Empire. pation of Britain, is remarkable, even to modern
eyes, for the mercy which tempered its justice. Our
knowledge of it is derived from the ordinances which
the Emperors directed to various officers, and especially
to persons exercising authority in the Provinces. We
may, therefore, reasonably infer that, where the Roman
power was fully established, the Roman law became, in
all the more important criminal offences, the law by
which the provincials were judged. In the towns which
had an organisation of their own, some minor local customs may, in accordance with the liberal spirit of the
Romans towards their subjects, have been permitted to
survive, or even to grow up anew. But in cases of
treason or homicide, the imperial jurisdiction was asserted,
and the tenderness with which it was enforced is a remarkable contrast to the judicial murders of a later age.
The witnesses, if of low rank, might, it is true, be tortured
(as suspected persons might have been, many centuries

afterwards, by license of the King of England, and later still by virtue of an Order in Council), but in other respects the accused had every protection which human forethought could devise against an unjust judgment. Sentence of death was not to be pronounced unless either the accused confessed, or all the witnesses agreed ; the testimony of one witness alone, no matter what his rank, was insufficient ; and all evidence had to be given on oath. When the witnesses were not unanimous, the matter might be referred to the Emperor if the accused had sufficient confidence in his own case.

It is strange to find in the laws of a people which had always been familiar with slavery a regard for personal liberty such as was not to be discovered in Eng- Regard for personal lish laws before the Habeas Corpus Act was liberty. passed in the reign of Charles II. No one was in the eye of the law so much as accused until the accusation had been made, according to legal form, in writing ; still less could anyone be put to the torture upon the mere word of an enemy. Even when in gaol the accused were not to be subjected to any duress, nor were women to be imprisoned in the same room with men. The case of every prisoner was to be heard within a month, and, should either accused or accuser ask for a postponement, the judges were to make it as short as possible, and in no case allow it to exceed a year from the day of accusation. If the accuser did not appear to prosecute, or withdraw the charge within that time, he subjected himself to severe penalties, and the accused was of course set free. · It was, too, a rule worthy of remark, and perhaps of imitation, that the evidence of an approver should be entirely rejected. No man's freedom or reputation could be endan-

gered by the malice of one who confessed himself a
criminal.

Should it be asked whether the inhabitants of the
provinces had the full advantage of these beneficent laws,
Participation an answer may be found in a letter of the Em-
of the pro-
vinces in the peror Constantine directed to 'The Provincials
benefits of Ro-
man law. in General.' 'If there be any one,' he wrote,
'no matter what his dwelling-place or what his rank, who
can prove any mis-deed against judge, or count, or friend
of mine, or officer of my palace, let him lay the matter
before me; I will hold him harmless, I will see right
done, I will take care that he shall not suffer in standing
or in substance.' Constantine also denied to senators the
privilege of trial in their own country, and required that
they should be brought to justice in the province in which
they had committed a rape, or a forcible entry upon
another man's land, or any other serious crime. The
extortion of money by a provincial judge for his own
use was afterwards declared a capital offence.

There is no doubt that when condign punishments are
newly provided for any crime, the crime itself has been
recently brought into notice. There is no doubt that
when government is, in any sense, government by the
sword, the governed are to some extent oppressed and
plundered. Every classical scholar knows what Sicily
suffered under Verres, and will be inclined to believe that
Britain was not happier under any other Roman officer.
Yet if we admit that there were unjust and rapacious
governors sent from Rome, that military service was a
grievous burden, and that the strict letter of the law was
turned as much as possible against the native, rather than
in his favour, we shall still be forced to the conclusion
that life was in every way more tolerable in Britain for

every class in the fourth century than it was in the fourteenth.

It is not in one rescript, nor in two, but in the whole spirit of the Roman law after the accession of Constantine that we perceive what generous sentiments Compassion shewn under were beginning to prevail, and how rapid might the Empire to the children have been the advance of the civilised, could of criminals. the barbarians only have been kept out. It was most humanely provided that when any man was convicted of any offence except treason, the punishment should not extend beyond himself, and that his children should enjoy his goods without deduction. A comparison may with profit be drawn between this law and the law, upon which Englishmen acted within the memory of living persons, that not only conviction of felony involved forfeiture of everything, but the mere flight of the accused involved the loss of all his goods and chattels.

Even in the case of slaves, too, though the punishment of burning was not extinct, there was welling up a new stream of thought which must soon have extin- Improvement in the condi- guished it, had not the barbarians overwhelmed tion of slaves after the the Empire. The fourth century, it must be adoption of Christianity. remembered, was a time when Christianity was still young, when it had but just been adopted as the imperial religion in Rome, and when its priests could not act in direct opposition to the spirit of its Founder. There had been great moralists whom Greek Sophists had mocked, and whom Roman Epicureans had imitated, but none of them had enunciated the great principle—' It is not the will of your Father in Heaven that one of these little ones should perish.' In that sentence lies the great distinction between Heathen and Christian codes of morals ; and though Christians might easily enough disregard it when they had no longer to contend with opposing forms of faith, they were compelled, whether they would or not, to make much of it when the splendid worship of Jupiter, and the enlightened teachings of Aristotle were still competing for the approbation of mankind. Accordingly the first Christian Emperor forbade the practice of branding on the forehead those convicts who were condemned to the Games or to the Mines—punishments which involved the loss of freedom. It is true that the brand was to be placed on the hands or on the legs, just as it is true that slavery was not abolished. But the prohibition is none the less an indication that new views were beginning to show themselves in practice, and similar indications are by no means rare.

Constantine carefully limited the ' correction of slaves.' They might still be chastised with a slender rod or with the lash, but not, as in former times, with the cudgel. Among the prohibited punishments, too, were a mortal wound with any sharp weapon, the administration of poison, various kinds of torture, stoning, hanging, mutilation, and throwing from a height —' for these,' the Emperor added, ' are the cruelties of the ruthless barbarians.' Happy the provinces in the days of the Empire! The time was not far distant when those who had previously been free were to be made slaves, and all who had not the good fortune to be barbarians in Britain were to suffer those very atrocities which had excited the horror of Constantine—the mutilation, the fall down a precipice, and the stoning.

Treatment of slaves by Romans and by barbarians.

If we enquire what were, during the Empire, the ranks of men above the condition of slaves, we find in some respects a striking resemblance to the later feudal organisation, in others a striking difference. There was a class which tilled the soil, and which was in a position very like that of the villeins regardant under the Plantagenet kings.   When the land on which they were born was sold, they were handed over to the new owners by the same conveyance as the land itself; but like the villeins regardant, they could not be treated as mere chattels, and exported at the will of the landlord.   Like the villeins, too, they acquired, or began with, privileges very nearly approaching those of the copyholder of later times.   They paid a customary rent for the ground on which they lived, they could enjoy some at least of the profits of their own labours, and they could bequeath their property by will.   Directly or indirectly they contributed not a little to the revenues of the Empire.

Social grades under the Empire: the tillers of the soil.

Above these subject farmers, and in close relation with them was a class which corresponded in many respects with the knight, or land-holder, of the later feudal period.   These 'possessors' as they were called, were practically, however, the absolute owners of land, and could alienate it as they pleased, without the feudal restraints.   They could even grant a species of lease in perpetuity, reserving to themselves a rent to be paid at stated seasons.   In earlier times they were, like the feudal nobles, a military caste—men who had received a grant of land for good service, or who had inherited land through the good service rendered by their forefathers.   But city plebeians, who were described as of splendid fortune, were by no means unknown in the provinces; and the trader whose great grandfather had, perhaps, been a manumitted slave, could, under the Empire, meet patrician land-owners on terms not altogether unequal.

The land-owners.

The possessors were subject to certain burdens, from which, indeed, land has rarely been altogether free. To Duties of the repair the roads and the defences of the Empire, landowners: was a duty from which no men of substance the colonial courts. were exempt; and from the land-owner was exacted that kind of service which in later times was known as 'suit of court.' In the provinces there were courts which met in the principal cities to transact financial business, and to appoint certain magistrates. The members had each to render an account for a particular district, usually, no doubt, the territory which belonged to him. The accounts rendered by the whole of the members of all these local courts furnished the sum total of the land tax collected throughout the Empire. A brief, but precious document, tells us that this organisation existed in Britain as it existed elsewhere, and that the government of Roman Britain was, in all material points, like the government of the other provinces.

The members of these colonial courts, though they had certain onerous duties to perform, enjoyed, in com-Recognition pensation, both social distinction and valuable of personal property: privileges. Though themselves compelled to growth of commerce. serve, they had the power of compelling others to serve with them, and of deciding, in accordance with imperial rescripts, who were duly qualified, and therefore bound to sit in their court. They could not, like their slaves and dependents, be put to the torture, nor subjected to any humiliating punishment, and their position in their own district was equal to that of the senators at Rome. Nor were they in the fourth century all men of the same class—all favoured Italians, or successful military adventurers—meeting to compare notes concerning the money which might be extorted from a subject population.

Anyone, no matter what his origin, who possessed the property qualification, was nominated a member of the court which administered the affairs of his district. As wealth increased, too, the importance of personal property began to be recognised, and considered to be a sufficient qualification for a seat in the court. Other taxes began to approach the land-tax in value, and commerce began to improve the aspect of the whole Roman world.

In the towns there were bodies known as colleges, or, as we should now say, companies or guilds, which were under the supervision of the imperial government, and which had evidently attained a high position before the Romans quitted Britain. Known in the earliest days of Roman history, they survived all changes of political constitution, and seem even to have acquired a political power of their own. The imperial laws contain numerous provisions for determining the relation of the guilds to those local courts which have already been described. It became a common practice to plead membership of a guild as a ground of exemption from membership of the court. The validity of this plea was not admitted, and the guilds-men, if duly qualified, were compelled to serve in the court, and, perhaps, even to abandon their guild. But there can be no better proof of the progress made by corporations of various kinds than the fact that their members had the qualification for a seat in an essentially aristocratic court, and were yet by no means ambitious to occupy it.

As in the case of the local courts, so in the case of the Roman guilds, there is sufficient evidence to show that what happened in other provinces happened Britain enjoyed the full also in Britain. In various places inscriptions benefit of Roman civilihave been found which prove the existence sation. in Britain of those guilds which are mentioned in the

Theodosian Code, some of which were commercial and others religious. Nor, indeed, can there be any reasonable doubt that the Roman civilisation flourished at one time in all its splendour, not, perhaps, in the remote West, but from the Western Hills to the German Ocean, and from Hadrian's Wall to the Channel.

The loss to Britain, when she was deprived of all that the Romans had given her, is told not only in those laws Her loss towards which we have approached more nearly when the Ro- as we have risen above the succeeding law-mans aban- doned her. lessness, and which we know to have been established in our island, but in other monuments which not even ages of barbarism could wholly destroy. The ploughman still lights sometimes upon a store of coins which bear the image and superscription of men who ruled the civilised world. Busts which still bear traces of the sculptor's skill, pottery which still bears the mark of the factory where it was made, fragments of pillars and of mosaic pavements, the remains of roads built with such forethought and care as to command the admiration of modern road-makers, attest the combination of a great organisation with a knowledge which almost deserves to be called scientific. These silent witnesses rise year after year from the grave, to assure us that the ' Itinerary' of Antonine is no fiction—that there were no less than fifteen great roads in Roman Britain, each studded with growing towns, or with cities already magnificent. The peaceful arts leave behind them memorials more lasting than all the works of Agamemnon, or of the brave men who may have lived before him. They need not, like him, the inspired poet to sing their praises, but speak to posterity even after savages have destroyed them. It is not less easy to restore the design of a ruined temple, or to sketch the outline of a mutilated statue, than to represent to human eyes the form of beasts which lived before there were human beings upon earth. Those chapters in codes of Roman law which treat of public works, and prove how important they were in the mind of a Roman, need no commentary but the relics which accident or research has already brought to light in Britain. The pride with which each city was taught to regard its own works of art was, indeed, brought low, but is still to be read in the piteous lines of sculpture disfigured and buried for centuries, no less than in the law that the ornaments of one city should not be transferred to another. All that Rome had borrowed from Greece she lent in turn to the provinces which acknowledged her sway ; and we know, with as much certainty as we know any fact in history, that Southern Britain could boast of towns rich in public buildings, to which a long period of quiet and order had given all the grandeur of classical art.   And this was fifteen hundred years ago.

Fifteen hundred years ago Southern Britain was a land in which the most luxurious English gentleman of modern times, could he abolish the intervening centuries, would find life more to his taste than in that England which his great-grandfather thought marvellously civilised. When he rose in the morning some favourite slave would bring him his letters, one of which might, perhaps, be an invitation to stay with the Governor at a country villa. He would travel just as our grandfathers travelled, in a carriage, but by a better and a straighter road, and he would find relays of horses (provided only for men of rank) at convenient stages. If his journey was long, he would pass through at least one town in which the architecture of the court-house, and of many temples, could hardly fail to command his admiration. Perhaps, too, he might recognise a friend among the officers of a legion in garrison, with whom he might exchange a word or two while the horses were being changed, or he might inspect a mint in full operation. Further on he might meet another legion on the march—a legion of British soldiers destined for foreign service, or a legion from beyond sea brought over to do duty in Britain. Save these casual suggestions of the pomp and circumstance of war, he would encounter only indications of peace, of wealth, and of security. If he enquired what was yonder pile of buildings—a town in all but gates and towers of defence—he would learn that it was the villa perchance of some imperial officer, perchance of some Romanised Briton, descended from a line of petty kings, perchance of a merchant who had grown wealthy in trade. But, in a day's travel, he would see villa after villa, till the sight, like the sight of innumerable mile-stones, would cease to be a novelty, and he would cease to enquire for the owner.

At the moment when he began to be fatigued with a long day on the road, he might possibly be struck by the Splendour of beauty and convenience of the site chosen for a villa in Britain under some villa more imposing than any he had the Empire. passed. He would hear, perhaps, with agreeable surprise, that it was the country house or palace of Pacatian, 'Vicar of the Britains.' His carriage would be driven up a long and straight avenue, terminating in a flower garden in which box-trees and yew-trees were cut into innumerable fantastic shapes. The front of the house presented a long range of pillars, forming a continuous portico or covered walk, from which the grounds and the landscape could be seen to greatest advantage.

Beyond the portico was a hall, in which the guest would
be received, and which was unlike anything within the
ordinary experience of modern Englishmen.   It was a
square room of vast dimensions, roofed in· at the four
sides, but open in the centre.   It consisted of four
galleries enclosing a basin, into which the rain fell in wet
weather, and in which a fountain played when required.
The floors of these galleries were tessellated pavements
of no rude workmanship, and were, in fact, exquisite
paintings in mosaic, surpassed only by the still more
exquisite mosaic of the inner basin.   The walls were
relieved by statues representing all the favourite subjects
of the old mythology—Orpheus and his lyre, Naiads,
Satyrs, and Centaurs, Pan, and Triton, all the subjects of
classical romance, with, perhaps, a bust of the reigning
emperor.   From the great reception hall, unless his
chamber communicated with it immediately, he would be
conducted to another still greater hall, built in the same
fashion, and adorned with the same splendour.   A door
in this peristyle, as it was called, opened into a small
ante-room, or dressing-room, through which he would
pass to his bed-room.   If he asked for a bath, he could
enjoy it in any form he pleased, but most readily that
kind of bath which is now known as the Turkish.
Wherever he went some work of art would meet his
eye—paintings on the walls of his chamber, paintings
and sculpture in the passages which led to the bath-
rooms, paintings and sculpture in the bath-rooms themselves.   Nothing which could gratify the senses, or even
the intellect, was forgotten.   The very pavements, which
were worthy of study for their beauty and remarkable for
their exquisite cleanliness, were warmed, if necessary, by
an elaborate network of stoves and flues, watched by a

troop of unseen slaves, in the basement beneath the principal apartments.

When the guest returned to his chamber, he would find himself protected from chill by a glazed window, not unlike the lattices which are even now to be seen in England. When summoned to dinner, he would enter the dining-room through the greater hall, in which the fountains would be playing, and in which flowers and shrubs tastefully arranged would suggest the idea that the host or his wife had a love of nature as well as of art. If he paused a moment, to look more carefully around him, he would perceive that the leading conception of the architect had been to surround all that was most exquisite in art with the beauties of nature. If he turned his eyes to the portico by which he had entered, he could still see the garden and avenue by which he had approached the house, with green woods and sparkling streams in the distance; if he turned his back to the entrance, he could see, beyond the Corinthian pillars and brilliant frescoes in the midst of which he stood, another and more carefully tended garden, and, in the background, a bright landscape of hill and dale, rich with a golden harvest, and enlivened by a throng of harvesters.

It is needless to dilate upon the luxury of such a dinner as a Roman governor would have given to an honoured guest. The subject has been often handled, and has not, like the prosperity of the arts and the building of innumerable unfortified palaces in the open country, a direct bearing upon the general feeling of security, nor, therefore, upon the History of Crime.

Yet it may not be out of place to recall in imagination such a conversation as may have passed, at some time during a long visit, between the governor or his wife and a guest who was regarded as an intimate friend. The wife would have shown herself to be, like the governor himself, a person of culture and of taste.   Culture of its occupants.

Like a modern English lady, she held a high position, and was not, like the women of a savage or half-civilised tribe, placed on the level of a slave, forced to do the work which was beneath the dignity of a man, married by the ceremony of sale to a master. Both she and her children were secured against future poverty, so far as human circumstances permit security, by such settlements as are made in the present day. She had the command of waiting women, who were slaves, and she was respected both by the whole household and by her husband. If it pleased her, she could devote her time and her wealth to those feminine adornments in which the ladies of ancient Rome may almost be said to have set the fashion to the ladies of modern Europe. She could buy jewels and silk to her heart's content, and pile up false hair on her head as high as she pleased. But she could also (and many a Roman lady did) cultivate her mind as well as decorate her person. She had been taught in childhood by the same tutor as her brothers, and had access, after marriage, to her husband's well stored library.

With a lady such as might have been Pacatian's wife, or with Pacatian himself, a relative or friend of long standing might have discussed the politics of the day, and the position of Britain in the civilised world. It would have been hardly possible that such a question could have been asked as whether life and property were reasonably secure in the South Eastern, or truly Romanised part of the island.

General sense of security in Roman Britain.

Yet, had such a question been asked, it is not difficult to recall the easy and ready answer which would have been given. 'You have travelled the whole day in comfort, and have nowhere been robbed, or molested, or threatened. You have seen the natives peacefully gathering in their corn, which is more than sufficient for our wants, which can be easily carried from the very centre of the island to the sea, and some of which may be exported to less favoured lands. You have passed villa after villa standing alone in the open country, with no fortification, and with no protection save that which the owner's slaves would render without fail in case of need. You have met a legion of British soldiers, marching cheerfully to serve against the enemies of the Empire, of which they are proud to believe that they are not the subjects but the citizens. If you would know whether such human happiness as is possible anywhere is possible in Britain, you have but to trust the evidence offered to your senses every hour of the day.'

Though, however, the condition of his province might well have been a cause of pride to the governor, he *The dangers* might yet sometimes have seen, in imagination, *from without:* *the barbarism* a warning writing on the frescoed wall of his *which was to* *come.* palace. 'No land,' he might have argued, 'is so secure as Southern Britain—protected from the barbarians of the island itself by a continuous line of fortresses— protected from the barbarians of Northern Germany by the stronger fortress of the sea. But, secure as Britain seems, even she is in danger, and, perhaps, not least in danger where her strength seems greatest. The greed of gold has made us what we are, but well does it deserve to be called, as the poet has called it, accursed, when citizens of Rome give Roman arms and teach Roman arts of war to barbarians for a flock of sheep or a drove of oxen. Avaricious shipwrights have passed our Batavian frontier, and taught the art of ship-building to a brutal race which lives in the Northern wilds beyond. Our empire is the empire of the sea no less than of the land ; but these Germans, who have long lived by plunder on land, have already learned to seek plunder by sea. There will, no doubt, issue, ere long, an imperial edict forbidding Romans to do that which they have already done with too good effect. It will come, like many other edicts, too late.'

When the Empire was decaying, luxury was accompanied by a train of vices, very well known to savages, who enjoy a reputation for virtue only because they are unable to satirise their own misdeeds in writing. But the codes of Roman law are sufficient to prove that justice and mercy had kept pace with the advance of wealth and enlightenment. A Roman governor might have been, as might be even a modern Englishman, unjust and an extortioner, but he might also have been a man liberal alike in thought and in action, and delicately sensitive to the sufferings of others. In one of the better kind of Romans, the contemplation of such a possible event as the subjection of Britain to barbarous hordes from beyond the sea must have been intolerably painful. Yet, even a morbid imagination could hardly draw a picture more gloomy than the events of many succeeding centuries. The land which had been cleared was again to become waste and forest, the roads were to continue in existence not so much by rude attempts to repair them as through the skill with which they had been first constructed. The walls of the villas were to be demolished, sometimes out of mere wantonness, sometimes to build a hut for a contemptuous savage. Nothing was to remain of all the past splendour, save, perhaps, the towns which were impregnable to barbarians, some works too solid for barbarians to destroy, and some shattered tokens of the fine arts which, to barbarians, were meaningless. All this a Governor of Britain, who was familiar with the foreign affairs of his time, might have foreseen. He might have foreseen the day when the physicians, the secretaries, and the jesters of a future governor—nominally his slaves, in reality his friends—would be ruthlessly killed, or become the slaves of brigands who had never seen papyrus or parchment, and to whom writing was an unknown art. He must have had compassion for all who were to survive when military adventurers had sown dissension throughout the Empire, when Britain had, by intestine commotions, prepared her soil for an invader, and when the only invaders who could appear possessed hardly the rudiments of civilisation. 'There are few of my slaves,' he might have said, 'who have not more culture than a barbarian king. There are none for whom the future can be even tolerable, except, perhaps, the ploughmen and the grooms. The barbarians enjoy sport after their rough fashion ; they cannot live without corn ; and they may spare at least the lives of the men, who can feed them and keep their horses in condition. Yet it were better to kill a horse, or even a dog, than suffer it to be tortured by those merciless pirates, who are learning to sail on the Northern Sea.'

Before, however, we pass from the rule of the Romans to the rule of their successors, it is necessary to Roman and other superstitions. glance at some other matters which have their bearing upon the history, even if we assume that not one human being of British or Roman stock has

English descendants at the present day, and that no traditions survived the horrors of the Teutonic inroads. Superstition plays so prominent a part in the History of Crime, it asserts itself in so many different shapes—from the practice of the ordeal to accusations of witchcraft —that it is not altogether unworthy of study wherever it may be found. There are, therefore, two justifications for touching on the superstitions which must have had a footing in Britain during the Roman occupation. One is that subsequent events may receive some illustration from the wide realm of superstition in general, the other that, in the eyes of those who disbelieve the story of extermination by Teutonic swords, the continuity of our history may not be lost.

Fortune-telling in various forms, incantations, love-potions, magic, and many other appeals to human credulity are frequently mentioned, half laughingly, half seriously, by Roman writers of all ages. The Roman equivalent for witchcraft was a capital offence by the laws of the Twelve Tables. Horace gives a description of Canidia that would serve well enough for a witch of the seventeenth century. It was supposed that she had dealings with the powers of darkness below, and that she had some influence over the stars. She could deprive the body of its vigour, the complexion of its beauty, the hair of its colour. She could command sickness and pain to be present whenever she pleased. She could mount on the shoulders of her enemies and ride them whither she would.

The witches of Rome, like the witches in Macbeth, joined in hideous rites at midnight. Like the witches afterwards condemned in English courts of law, they were said to have made images of the persons whose destiny was to be influenced, and to have done to the images that which they wished to befal the living beings. The whole of the witch's apparatus was in the one age precisely what it was in the other, even to the infernal familiars in the shape of dogs and other brutes.

Later writers attributed to various priesthoods, and among them to that of the Britons, extraordinary powers of magic. Before the great British revolt, under Boadicea, it is credibly related that the Roman veterans were depressed by the supernatural manifestations which, as they supposed, threatened them with destruction. The statue of Victory which had been set up in Camulodunum (the modern Colchester) fell to the ground without apparent cause, and turned its back in token of defeat. Women, with the inspiration of madness, sang of death and destruction. Strange noises were heard in the court-house, and loud howlings in the theatre. The likeness of the town itself in ruins was seen in the estuary of the Thames. The very sea appeared to be stained with blood, and the shore to be strewn with dead bodies when the tide ebbed. The credulous Roman soldiers heard these stories and trembled.

The imported scepticism of such writers as Horace, the growth of the towns, and, with it, the promise of a higher civilisation, were influences operating during the Roman occupation of Britain, which had, perhaps, some tendency to eradicate these superstitions. But we know from many passages in the Theodosian Code that, in civilised Rome herself, after Rome had become Christian, it was thought right to torture and burn wizards and magicians. And when we reflect that so great a man as Sir Matthew Hale expressed his belief in witchcraft, we may feel certain that superstition had not been rooted out of Britain in the fourth century. The polytheism of the Romans had, before Christianity was the religion of Rome, practically, though not theoretically, degenerated into a kind of pantheism. In their empire there was no natural object which might not have its own divinity or genius, no human being who might not aspire to be Emperor, and after dying as Emperor, to live again as God. In the efforts to subvert the ancient beliefs Christians recognised witchcraft as a worship of devils; and if they recognised it at Rome we· may be sure that they recognised it in Britain. The stories that Peter the Apostle made a journey in person, and that St. Paul despatched Aristobulus to convert the Britons, are not found in any writings which will endure the test of historical criticism ; nor is there any evidence that Joseph of Arimathæa ever set foot upon this island. It is, nevertheless, tolerably certain that some form of Christianity, already infected with Gnosticism and with the old superstitions of paganism, was well known in Britain, if not generally accepted, before the Romans abandoned the island. A few sentences will suffice to show what was the character of that faith in its relation to the purposes of the present history.

It is possible by a train of reasoning which would be out of place in the text of this work, to show that Christianity was known in some portion of the British Islands, if not in that portion which is now called England, before the Council of Nice. This, however, it may be said, was not the Christianity of the Roman Church. So much the features of the subsequent controversies, in England, in the seventh century, upon the observance of Easter, and other matters, are sufficient to prove. In order, there-

Introduction of Christianity into Britain.

fore, to ascertain what was believed by the early British Christians it is necessary to consider what was believed by Christians in other parts of the world, as well as in Rome, before the fourth century. It happens that most of the writers who lived during that period were natives of the East—of Egypt, of Palestine, or of Asia Minor; and it is not a little remarkable that they give evidence of an almost universal belief in the same superstitions. The authors, as Christians, had an interest in the events and in the creeds of the whole Christian world, and they enable us to discover that many opinions passed current from Africa to the Alps, and from Asia Minor to the British Islands. They tell us, in fact, precisely what might have been inferred from passages in the Theodosian Code.

In almost all the countries of the Roman Empire the pagans believed that rocks, and woods, and springs, or the deities which presided over them, had the power of bestowing blessings or inflicting injuries. Wherever Christians dwelt among pagans they shared the same belief, but called the supposed powers by the name of 'demons,' and held everything connected with these evil spirits accursed. It is impossible to read the works of Tertullian, Origen, or Eusebius without perceiving that in their imagination the earth, and all that is upon or around it, must have been peopled with numberless invisible beings. Tertullian declared that Christians ought not to be present at those spectacles in which the Roman world delighted because they were ceremonies which had their origin in idolatry, because idolatry was equivalent to the worship of demons, and because all who had been baptised had promised to renounce the devil and his angels.   Origen

The super-stitions with which it was infected.

insists again and again upon the virtue existing in the names of Abraham, Isaac, and Jacob, which had only to be mentioned in order to put all demons to flight. He supposed that these enemies of mankind had taken up their abode in the dense air which hangs immediately above the earth, and that they were known by the names of Jupiter and of all the other heathen gods. He believed that they had light and volatile forms, which, like the wind, were unseen, but went where they listed, and that it was their malignant influence which produced famines, and blights, and droughts, and epidemics. The arts of magicians, and of all who practised sleight of hand, appeared to him to be the works of devils. But though the evil spirits had not the gross bodies of human beings, they could not, it was supposed, exist without food ; they delighted especially in blood, which they eagerly licked up when sacrifices were offered to idols. Sometimes even the liberty of the demons themselves could be restrained by the devices of magic ; and a devil could be chained to a grave or a building as surely as a horse could be held by his tether.

These doctrines, which developed in the East into the most charming of all romances degenerated in the West into the most grovelling superstitions. Their wide diffusion. The Teutonic adventurers perhaps learned nothing from the people they vanquished. Ideas, which, from their wide diffusion over the Roman Empire, must have been independent alike of race and language, might well have been shared by barbarians outside the circle of Roman conquest. That which was common to the Egyptian fellah and the Italian colonist might well have been common also to the German robber. A few sentences in Tacitus, which would be equally applicable to the beliefs of any uncivilised tribe, or even to the religion of the Romans, are all that remain to tell us of the creeds which came from Germany to Britain. Centuries afterwards the curtain is lifted again and we see mingled with Christianity in England, but deprived of all their beauty, those strange fancies with which the writings of the Eastern fathers teem, which have given names to imaginary crimes, and, age after age, have been put forward as the excuse for inhuman atrocities.

In Christian England, when it first becomes known to us under that name, one of the most striking features is the popular belief in the power of human beings to make contracts with demons. Special penances were provided for those who, by evil practices, acquired the art of sending forth tempests : in this and in similar cases it is always clear that the punishment is inflicted not for believing in the influence of the demons, but for making use of that existing influence to attain an end. The demons themselves seem commonly to be identified with the old pagan gods, who were held in honour many generations after Augustine's mission. Even as late as the beginning of the eleventh century it was thought necessary to enact that Christianity should be maintained and Heathenism expelled. The clergy during the whole of this time seem to have been most firm believers in the power of those who styled themselves magicians or enchanters ; and it was even decreed that if one of the clergy himself practised the forbidden arts he should be degraded. Witchcraft, as practised by women, already comes into prominence. A penance of one year's duration was considered sufficient for ordinary offences of this kind ; but when the woman succeeded, by her devilish devices,

Their appear-ance after the mission of Augustine.

in killing her victim, the amount of her punishment was
multiplied by seven.   The crime of seeking out a person
who professed to foretell the future, or of inviting such
person to enter a house, was not less heinous than
sorcery itself.   If a clergyman, the transgressor incurred
the sentence of degradation ; if a layman, he subjected
himself to a five years' penance.   It was a common
practice to make vows at particular spots which were
supposed to be favoured by supernatural powers, at
trees, at springs, and at stones, just as in the days of
Origen and Eusebius.   Love and hatred, fertility and
sterility, success and failure, health and disease, even
existence itself were believed to be, partly at least, in
the hands of the demons or pagan gods, who employed
the enchanters as their agents.

Almost indistinguishable from the belief in witchcraft,
as will be seen in later history, was the belief that
persons subject to epilepsy, mania, or any form of mental
weakness were possessed by a devil, which could be
expelled by the performance of certain religious ceremonies.   The Church sanctioned a form of exorcism,
and the exorcist was considered to hold the third rank
in the ecclesiastical order.   In England an attempt was
made to combine the forces of medicine with the forces
of religion, just as, many centuries afterwards, it was the
custom to consult a physician upon the cases of persons
bewitched.   Prescriptions were accordingly given, even
in these early days not indeed for the cure of madness,
but for the ejection of devils.   The remedies were
usually in the form of drinks.   Ale was always one of
the ingredients, mixed with various herbs.   Sometimes
twelve masses were sung over the mixture before it was
administered ; sometimes holy water was poured into the

ale. One recipe, however, was considered efficacious against the devil without any assistance from the Church ; it was an emetic, which, we may presume, was supposed to dislodge him bodily from his seat in the patient's frame.

In order to understand the prominence assumed by accusations of witchcraft in later times it is necessary to remember that the belief in the practice has descended from the most remote ages, has received in turn the stamp of many religions, and was unfortunately, though perhaps, inevitably, sanctioned by the successors of Augustine. The educated monks, who were the literary and scientific men of their day, have handed down in writing a number of charms which throw considerable light on the subject. To find cattle, to recover stolen goods, to heal the sick, to guard against 'every strange thing that cometh by air or by land,' were objects which, according to the ideas then prevalent, could be attained by certain collocations of words, and without incurring the sin of sorcery. Our forefathers, when they were converted, learned not to abandon their faith in charms, but to seek new charms in the ' Pater Noster ' and the ' Credo.' They were not brought face to face with a pure Christianity. At that time, when the Church discovered a stronghold of pagan superstitions, it fought not always for the demolition of the fortress, but for possession in its own name. Gregory himself suggested to Augustine that the buildings in which the ancient gods had been worshipped should not be destroyed but converted to the service of Christianity. The same principles pervaded every field of human life. The leech-books are not only full of pagan and of Christian devices for obtaining supernatural assistance, but show us the new creed marching boldly upon the

The crime of witchcraft and the Church.

ground of the diviner and the magician, and endeavouring to swallow them up as Aaron's rod had swallowed up the rods of the Egyptians. And thus, if the enchanters of the past had pointed out where that which was lost could be found by their arts, the Church was prepared with enchantments which were no less powerful, but which did not derive their power from the Devil. If the peasant discovered that his land was bewitched, he was assured that the priest could aid him as effectually and more safely than the sorcerer.

Thus far, only those beliefs and customs have been noticed which were, or, for all we know to the contrary, might have been, common to all the earliest in- *Customs in-* habitants of the British Islands, or which may *troduced by the Teutonic* serve hereafter as a measure of civilisation, or *settlers.* as materials for an instructive contrast. It now becomes necessary to follow the Teutonic settlers from their home on the continent, and to discover whether they brought with them any laws and customs which have a bearing upon the History of Crime.

The German tribes in general, according to Roman accounts, regarded homicide as a crime of little moment, hardly, indeed, as a crime at all. Bloodshed, *Setting a* and acquisition through bloodshed, are described *price upon human life:* as being the profession of the German ; and the *the blood-feud.* slaughter of a member of his own tribe was considered a less reprehensible action than a petty theft. The offence was easily expiated by the forfeit of a small portion of his wealth; and he had no wealth but horses, cattle, and sheep. A part of the fine was paid to the relatives of the deceased, who were supposed to be aggrieved by the loss of their kinsman and to receive an equivalent in a sufficient quantity of live stock. The remainder was paid to the chief, or became the common property of the tribe.

In this practice are to be found, on the one hand, the rudiments of our early laws relating to homicide, and, on Wide diffu- the other hand, a point of contact with the sion of the custom. usages of the savage in every part of the world. During the Homeric age the blood-feud was as fully recognised in Greece as afterwards in Germany; and one of the most prominent scenes on the marvellous shield designed by Hephæstus is a dispute concerning the payment of the fine. The institution prevailed in Ireland and Wales after the Teutonic conquest of Southern Britain, and probably even during the Roman occupation of this island. The progress of philological discovery suggests plausibly enough that this with other customs might have been introduced by the people which planted the Aryan group of languages over nearly the whole of Europe, and a great portion of Asia. Such a view, however, seems to be somewhat too narrow to embrace the whole of the facts. There is much to be learned from the study of philology, but still more from the study of human nature. Payment for human life is by no means simply co-extensive in its range with the diffusion of any group of languages. The ties of family have been recognised in this or a similar form in every nation or tribe of which the earliest history has been transmitted to us. The 'Avenger of Blood' appears in the laws of the Jews precisely as the obligation of the family to adopt the quarrel of the individual is found among the Germans described by Tacitus, and precisely as the next of kin prosecutes the murderer in England, both before and after the Norman Conquest. There are differences with

respect to the estimation in which the offence is held, and
the severity with which it is punished ; but from the
care with which compounding is prohibited in the Jewish
law there is good reason to believe that it was not unknown
either among the Jews themselves or among the nations
which surrounded them.   In short, the ties of blood are
so obvious that they have never escaped the notice of
the wildest savage in either hemisphere, and the cupidity
which will take goods in place of revenge is not the
heritage of one tribe more than of another.

The existence, however, of the blood-feud, combined
with the principle of compensation, where it has become
an established custom, indicates a particular stage   Stage of hu-
of human progress.   It shows that a chieftain   man progress
in which it
or governing body has perceived the advantage   exists.
to the community of preserving as many lives as possible
for the common good.   The primitive warrior's doctrine
is that there is nothing to be gained by diminishing the
available force of his battle-array, by inflicting death for
an offence which shows no lack of courage.   Better, he
thinks, to reserve ignominy and the last extreme of
punishment for those who will not or cannot fight.   Such
was the doctrine of the ancient Germans, such the doctrine of every tribe no further advanced in civilisation.
It is one step, and only one step, in advance of the most
savage form of life, in which compensation is impossible
because there is no property even in flocks and herds, in
which the whole world is supposed to be a hunting-
ground, and in which there is no right or justice but the
will of the strongest.   It is discovered only in a state of
society in which mercy, generosity, and that quality which
has been misnamed chivalry, have as yet found no place.
It belongs only to those who will slay the wounded as

they lie on the ground, and will, like Achilles, drag a fallen foe behind the victorious chariot.

Such a condition of society naturally endures a longer or a shorter time in accordance with the genius of particular tribes, or with their opportunities of improvement. It has been so well marked in the German-speaking nations, and it continued among them so long that it has often been described as one of their essential characteristics. The fact, however, that wherever a Teutonic tribe effected a settlement in a province of the Roman Empire it introduced the practice of compounding for homicide proves no more than that the whole of these tribes were in a state of extreme barbarism. Goths in Spain, Burgundians and Franks in Gaul, Lombards in Italy, and all those adventurers, whatever their true names may have been, who conquered a portion of Britain, showed themselves to be all on the same level of culture. They carried with them to their new homes those customs which—when writing had been taught them—they committed to writing, and dignified by the title of Dooms or Institutes. Sometimes they adopted either for themselves or for their subjects, a portion of the Roman Law which was drawn up for them in the form of a code; but in such documents as this they inserted a clause reciting, with a quaint air of wonder, and in a tone of some superiority, that the Romans had omitted to specify the tax upon murder. This flaw, as they supposed it to be, in the Roman system of justice, they invariably made good. With a superfluity of detail, and with an abundance of distinctions, they appraised the life of every human being in the land, from that of the king to that of the slave. From these crude beginnings it has been necessary to evolve the

It was inseparable from Teutonic conquest.

criminal law with respect to homicide in almost every country in Europe.

In that portion of Britain which was afterwards called England, there can be little doubt that the Roman Law had, in important matters, superseded all the native customs. And though even here the practice of compounding for homicide had pro- bably been in existence before the Roman occupation, there is not the least reason to suppose that it was re- vived, in the more civilised portion of the island, before the coming of the Teutonic settlers. To them, and to them only, must be ascribed the re-introduction of bar- barism in this form. As they were strong enough to impose their language, they must have been strong enough to impose their criminal rules upon those whom they did not slay. Wherever they were brought into contact with Roman civilisation, their course seems to have been uniform, and in this respect at least Britain could hardly have constituted an exception.

The history of human thought with respect to homi- cide can thus be traced continuously from its starting- point in savage life, through the very earliest forms of civilisation, through the conflict of ideas which arose when trade and letters asserted their right to exist against private and public wars, and robbery, and ignorance, through all our political convulsions, down to the present age of security and refinement. There is but one point which seems open to controversy—the question whether town life, with the results which it has produced, has descended to us from the Romans, or has been indepen- dently developed by the Teutonic conquerors. It will be seen in a subsequent page, that the partisan of either theory may hold his own opinion without prejudice to

It was intro- duced anew into Britain by the Teutonic invaders.

the general course of the narrative. The power of the towns to effect any advance beyond the first two or three stages of improvement was for many centuries in abeyance. If they continued to exist throughout the horrors which followed the evacuation of Britain by the Romans, they were in the end compelled to accept terms from the victor, and to adopt his usages with respect to crime.

When England first emerges into the light of history, about the end of the seventh century, the descendants of *It survived the re-estab-lishment of Christianity.* the pagan invaders and their subjects were nominally Christians. The process of conversion has been narrated by Bede, and his story is, to a certain extent, confirmed by the letters of some of the Popes ; but he lived so long after the events which he pretends to describe, and he has in other matters relied upon such worthless authorities, that it would be unsafe to give his statements implicit belief. The fact, however, that the inhabitants of Britain professed Christianity in his time may be considered undeniable ; it remains only to enquire what had been the effects of Christianity upon crimes and their expiation.

Except in one point, which will be considered in its relation to the influence of towns, there was, neither in the eighth century nor at any subsequent time before the Norman Conquest, any modification of the ancient Teutonic view with respect to murder. During this period the governing powers seem to have done more towards barbarising Christianity than Christianity towards softening the manners of its proselytes. The prelates were associated with the other ' wise men ' in framing rudimentary codes for the petty states, and finally for the whole of England ; but they appear to have adapted themselves to the society in which they lived. They

added the weight of their authority to various compilations of laws, but, except where the Church itself seemed
in danger, they succeeded in doing but little towards
infusing a Christian spirit into the laws themselves.
They not only sanctioned the principle of compounding
for murder, but established, side by side with it, the principle of compounding for penances.

The history of the latter custom shows how strangely
opposite causes may lead to similar results. The doctrine
of penance clearly arose out of the moral doctrine
that he who does wrong to his neighbour should
not only make compensation, but should himself
undergo a proportionate amount of suffering.
To mortify the flesh was very early considered meritorious by Christians, so far as any human action or conduct
could possess any merit ; and it was therefore natural
enough to believe that each particular sinful deed required
a particular act of mortification. Hence arose the practice of assigning fasts of greater or less duration for
various offences, including those of which the secular law
took cognisance. But the sick and the strong could not
sustain the pains of abstinence with equal powers of endurance ; and the penalty which was nominally the same
was seen to be very different in fact when applied to
different individuals. It therefore became necessary to
vary the form of punishment in order that the weak and
the aged might not suffer beyond their strength. The
substitutes for fasting were prostrations and genuflexions,
the singing of psalms, repetitions of the ' Pater Noster,'
' Credo,' or other prayers, and alms-giving. As soon,
however, as the principle of substitution was admitted it
led on to a system of equivalents. A certain number of
psalms or prayers was declared equal to a certain length

*It was asso-
ciated with
the practice
of compound-
ing for
penances.*

of fast.   If the language of modern finance may be applied to such a subject, the fast was the metal which, as the Mint adopts gold in the present day, was adopted by the Church for its standard ; the psalms, the prayers, and the alms were, like our notes, and silver, and copper, the tokens which were allowed to pass current for the sake of convenience.   Though, perhaps, the transition was inevitable, when the difficulties in the imposition of penances had been recognised, this principle of commutation at once effected a complete change in the character of penance itself as an institution.   To give alms as an atonement for a crime, though the name might disguise the true nature of the transaction, was in reality to escape by a sacrifice of worldly goods the personal suffering which had been regarded not only as an element of justice, but as a salutary moral discipline, for the wrong-doer. From first to last, perhaps, an attempt was made to inflict a real punishment—to adjust the payment to the means of the offender, and not simply, as in the case of the psalms and the prayers, to the length of the fast which had been enjoined.   At first, too, the privilege of compounding might have been rigidly restricted to those for whom it was originally intended.   But the seeds of corruption were sown, and when ambition found its way into the Church, alms were readily enough accepted from rich penitents, whether they were in sickness or in health.

One of the first effects of the introduction from Rome of confession and penance, together with the principle of commutation, was to strengthen those distinctions of class which were already only too familiar to the German - speaking conquerors. Those who had alms to give enjoyed a favour which was necessarily denied to those who were destitute, whose

Distinctions of class in the criminal laws.

bodies, and whose very souls were not their own. If ever it was distinctly manifest that there was one law for the rich and another for the poor in England, it was in the four centuries which immediately preceded the Norman Conquest. In those days men truly gave to him that had, and from him that had not they took away even that which he seemed to have. The noble could murder, and be quit for a fine to the Church and another to be divided between the kinsfolk of the slain and the king. He had the satisfaction of reflecting that, if murdered himself, his rank would be remembered in the sum to be paid as his price. The slave, however, not only incurred the penalty of death or of mutilation for the most trifling offence, but was not even entitled to the privilege of observing the ' mass days ' in that manner which was supposed to bring man nearer to God. These days, which all freemen were expected to keep holy, were very carefully enumerated, and were more than forty in number. But slaves had days given them only when it seemed expedient to their masters; the lord had it in his power to give or not to give; and the favour, when not withheld, was most contemptuously accorded.

These distinctions of class appear most prominently in all the criminal laws, for which the clergy are responsible jointly with the lay magnates. Homicide, regarded throughout with barbarous lenity, has a descending scale of payments in accordance with the rank of the slain ; other offences, regarded generally with a still more barbarous ferocity, have a scale of punishments varying with the rank of the offender, but always more savage in proportion as the criminal is more helpless. Wealth would usually purchase impunity for the thief who had offended but once. He could pay compensation and fine. A second offence, according to one set of laws, was punishable with death; but this does not appear to have been the ordinary rule—much less the provision once made that no one should be permitted to buy off his life even in the case of a first theft. It was for the free man of low estate, for the slave, and for women that the greatest atrocities were reserved. Men branded on the forehead, without hands, without feet, without tongues, lived as an example of the danger which attended the commission of petty crimes, and as a warning to all who had the misfortune of holding no higher position than that of a churl. The horrors of the Danish invasions had no tendency to mitigate these severities; and those who were chastised with whips before were chastised with scorpions afterwards. New ingenuity was brought to bear upon the art of mutilation, which was practised in every form. The eyes were plucked out; the nose, the ears, and the upper lip were cut off; the scalp was torn away; and sometimes even, there is reason to believe, the whole body was flayed alive. But in another form there was barbarism as great as this, not perhaps before the Danish incursions had commenced, but certainly before the Danish dynasty was established. It appears to have no immediate connection with the evil passions roused by the conflict of hostile races or factions, but it may, perhaps, throw some light upon the treatment of heretics and female traitors in later times. It is the condemnation to be burnt alive, which was sometimes passed upon a female slave who had been guilty of theft.

The laws in which this penalty was decreed belong to the first half of the tenth century. They seem to be less indulgent, even to free men of the higher grade,

than some of the similar compilations which precede
and follow them.   In savageness towards slaves and
women they have probably never been sur- Brutality cul-
passed by the practices of the wildest tribe in minating in the punish-
Africa.   They, perhaps, indicate a mad outburst ment of slaves and
against a state of lawlessness which, even in women.
that lawless age, seemed intolerable.   Among the punishments for theft are the very punishments forbidden
as barbarous in the Roman Code.   If the thief was a
free woman she was to be thrown down a precipice or
drowned (a precedent, without doubt, for dragging a
witch through a pond).   If the thief was a man and a
slave he was to be stoned to death by eighty slaves, and
if one of the eighty missed the mark three times that one
was to be whipped three times.   If the thief was a female
slave, and had stolen from any but her own lord, eighty
female slaves were to attend, bearing each a log of wood,
to pile the fire and burn the offender to death.

It would be impossible to estimate, at its true value,
the moral effect of such scenes as this, but they aid
in explaining the cruelties of later and comparatively
civilised ages.   It is only wonderful that any tenderness
or any mercy survived, and that the callousness of those
terrible days was not transmitted to all the descendants
of the men and women who were compelled to take part
in such horrors.   Fire, as an instrument of punishment,
was, as we have seen, not unknown to the Romans, nor,
perhaps, even to those whom they vanquished in Britain.
But to make women the special objects of this torture,
and, worse still, to teach them hardness of heart in the
office of executioner, were refinements of atrocity reserved for the barbarians who planted themselves in the
provinces of the Empire.

At the time when punishments for petty offences were worse than brutal, the methods by which criminals

Primitive Trials. were condemned were naturally not very refined. There was no distinction between offences against the Church, on the one hand, and offences against the State or the individual, on the other. Cases of theft and coining, like those of witchcraft, could be tried in a church. From the position of the clergy, as law-givers, it followed not only that the secular laws had the sanction of religion, but that religious observances were enforced by the secular arm, if enforced at all. Not only was it declared in secular laws that cheats, and liars, and robbers would incur God's anger unless they desisted, but it was made penal to eat flesh on a fast-day, or to buy, or sell, or pursue a handicraft on Sundays or feast-days. In later times there were attempts to separate the ecclesiastical from the civil jurisdiction ; but the Royal Proclamations against eating meat in Lent, and the prohibition of witchcraft by Statutes are curious instances of the persistence of an old tradition.

In these early times, if a thief was detected in the act of carrying off what he had stolen no trial was considered necessary ; if a poor man, who could not pay a fine, he was put to death with little ceremony. In more doubtful cases the punishment, upon conviction, seems to have been various, and guilt or innocence was ascertained, in the case of the layman, by one of two methods of procedure—by ordeal or by compurgation. Both would be simply ludicrous but that life and limb depended on the issue. The practical effect of the one was that the accused could be saved only by the aid of the priest ; the practical effect of the other, that he could be saved only by the oaths of a sufficient number of friends. The

repute in which man or woman was held, either by the
clergy or by the neighbours, decided the question of
innocence or guilt. The popular thief was certain to be
saved; the unpopular but guiltless prisoner was certain
to be condemned. Fortunately for the present time no
relic of these old practices survives, except the custom of
calling witnesses to prove general character.

The form of ordeal of which the best account has
been handed down is the three-fold ordeal by water.
When the test was to be applied the prisoner
was conducted into a church. The spectators
were divided into two lines, in which the numbers were
equal. One line was ranged on one side of the church,
the other on the other, one representing nominally the
friends of the accused, the other the friends of the
accuser. Between them, in the centre of the church,
blazed the fire which was to purge or to blacken. All
who were present were expected to be fasting and in a
state of chastity. The priest passed up and down,
sprinkling each with holy water, giving each holy water
to taste. To each he offered the Book of the Word,
and the Holy Rood, to kiss. Meanwhile the vessel of
ordeal, filled with water, had been set over the fire.
Four arbiters, two chosen from either side, pronounced
in due time that the water boiled—that the hour was
come. The rest of the congregation, who had hitherto
preserved a solemn silence, now joined in prayer to
Almighty God that he would make known his will in
the issue. The accused advanced to the place of trial,
his arm and hand swathed in fold upon fold of cloth or
linen. At the bottom of the vessel, at elbow-depth, was
a stone. This he had to snatch away unscathed himself,
if he could, when, perhaps, he was half blinded by the

The Ordeal.

smoke from the burning wood, by the steam from the seething caldron, and by the fears which must have oppressed him, whether innocent or guilty.   Here ended the first act of the drama.   After the expiration of three days came the final ceremony, when the bandages were unwound and the hand and arm exposed.   Then, if the flesh was uninjured, it was taught that God had declared for an acquittal; but if any trace of scald appeared, the anger of heaven, it was supposed, had marked out the wrongdoer for punishment, and he suffered a sentence in accordance with the magnitude of the crime and the ferocity of the age.

There was a minor ordeal by water, called the single ordeal, in which the only material difference was that the hand alone was plunged in as far as the wrist.   In the trial by hot iron, too, the ceremony was of a similar character, and the hand was protected in the same manner.   The accused had to lift a· piece of heated metal weighing, in the single ordeal, one pound, in the three-fold ordeal, three pounds.   The burn or the absence of a burn, after three days, proved guilt or innocence.   Another test, and one possibly more favourable to the criminal, was the 'corsnæd,' which appears to have been reserved for the clergy.   This was no more than consecrated bread or cheese.   He who could swallow it unharmed was innocent, he who failed was guilty.

In all these ordeals the clergy had the entire control not only of the final ceremonies but of the preliminary arrangements, upon which the issue must, in a great measure, have depended.   They prepared the 'corsnæd,' and it is quite conceivable that bread might have been so prepared as to prove guilt; they had the accused under their care for three days before the trial. The priest enjoined a fast of three days; the priest administered the Sacrament of the Lord's Supper; under the direction of the priest the hand and arm of the person to be tried were enveloped in the coverings which gave the only chance of acquittal by the hot water or the hot iron. The enemy of the Church or of the priest must have fared but ill in the proof by ordeal. But the priest was, in some cases, permitted to exculpate himself on far easier terms, by simply making oath on the 'housel' or sacramental bread.

In graver charges, however, it was necessary, even for an ecclesiastic, to find some fellow ecclesiastics who were willing to swear precisely as he swore. Compurgation. This process was extended to the layman, who, if not friendless, could escape the ordeal. He had but to find a sufficient number of compurgators, or fellow-clearers, who would make oath with him that he was innocent. The compurgation, like the ordeal, varied according to the nature of the accusation, and with the rank of the offenders. In some cases a greater, in others a less, number of compurgators was required; but in every case they called the Lord to witness that the oath of the person whom they had to support was clean and unperjured.

Of the two methods of trial perhaps the ordeal was the less demoralising to the laity. To them (whatever may have been its effect upon the clergy) it Its demoralising was only one form of superstition the more—a effects. matter of little moment where the forms of superstition were already numberless. But compurgation, on the other hand, could hardly have been better than organised and recognised perjury. It rarely happens to any one to

have certain knowledge of his own that another has not
committed any definite crime; never, indeed, except
when he has been present at the time of alleged perpetration, and has seen either that the deed was not of the
nature supposed, or was not done by the person to be
exculpated.   In some rare cases it is possible that all the
compurgators may have had this justification, and may
so have been by chance good witnesses for the defence.
But from the fact that a fixed number of compurgators
was always required it is obvious that the swearing was
a formality, and that the idea of evidence in our modern
sense was not entertained.   Sometimes, without doubt,
the swearers may have believed, from the general
character of the accused, that he must have been innocent of the particular offence with which he was charged.
This is the most favourable interpretation of which their
oath is susceptible, but is not the natural signification of
their words.   They verbally, at least, swore to the fact,
and not simply to their belief; in short, they swore that
which they did not know to be true.

    It has sometimes been supposed that out of the
system of compurgation sprang our Trial by Jury.   The
Its relation to opinion is not altogether without foundation,
Trial by Jury. but the relationship is not that of mother and
child.   There are various links which connect the jury
with the band of compurgators on the one hand, and with
the fellow-swearers, who were in certain cases called upon
to support the accuser, on the other.   This subject will
be discussed in a future chapter.   It is here only necessary to point out the ill effects produced by asking a
number of persons to swear that every statement made
by another person is true.   Bad customs are easily
handed down from generation to generation; and in the

system of compurgation is to be found the origin of those perjuries which, even in comparatively modern times, were the subject of most bitter complaint. It was long held an impossibility to obtain a true verdict even from a London jury.

With the practice of compurgation was intimately connected another institution which lies at the root of the whole of the early system of police in England. This was the Guild, which at various times assumed various forms, but which, in every form, involved the principle of association, either voluntary or compulsory. In the earliest form in which we have any notice of it under that name, it must have been compulsory—so far, indeed, as the law had any power to compel. The payment of a sum of money in cases of homicide, according to the rank of the person slain, has already been noticed as a prominent custom among the Teutonic settlers in Britain. The person liable, in the first instance, was of course the slayer, and, in accordance with the importance attached to the family tie, his kin were also liable with him. The death, in fact, constituted a family feud between the relatives of the slayer and the relatives of the slain, who were to satisfy or be satisfied by blood or by money. Sometimes, however, it happened that the relatives of the slayer were unable to find the sum necessary to exculpate him; sometimes he was kinless, and sometimes the person slain had no kin who were entitled to receive compensation. To meet these contingencies, which in the one case would have led to further bloodshed, and in the others would have rendered the law nugatory, there was enforced a species of artificial family bond which completed the circle of mutual liability. Certain sections

Police system. The Guild compulsory and voluntary. The Peace-pledge.

of the population were joined together in guilds, which aided the homicide who had no kin to pay his penalty, and which received a portion of the fine when one of their own body was the victim.

It is not, indeed, quite certain whether, in the first instance, guilds of this kind were associations to one of which every free man was compelled to belong, or were merely subsidiary to the great family bond, and applied only to those whom no family owned. There would, however, have been great practical difficulties in bringing the kinless together; and it is more probable that the guild, in this sense, was an association which the law directed every one of a certain rank to join, either in his own person or by his representative—the head of the family. This it certainly was eventually, when it appeared as the tithing, in which all free men below a certain rank, whether in town or country, were compelled to be numbered.

The Tithing consisted of ten men, who were collectively responsible for the good behaviour of every The Tithing, member. A crime perpetrated by any one of and the Hundred. them rendered the whole liable to that form of punishment which, next to mutilation and death by torture, is most prominent in all Teutonic laws—a payment of goods or money. The Hundred, though in all historical times a territorial division, was, perhaps, originally a guild of a hundred freemen, just as the tithing was a guild of ten. The distinction between responsibility shared by the inhabitants of a district, because they were its inhabitants, and responsibility shared by a definite number of persons, who of course inhabited a definite district, is far too fine to have any persistence in barbarous times. Speculation on this subject would,

however, be profitless. The essential fact is perfectly
well established, that when any offence had been committed, there was a responsibility incurred in the first
instance by the offender, but ascending, so far as the
pecuniary penalty was concerned, from individual to
family and association, until the means of bearing the
burden had been found.

Each of these associations had its head man or president; and, even after the Norman Conquest, each particular tithing or 'frank-pledge' was known by the name of
its chief. There was also for the hundred a kind of court
which, so far as matters of police are concerned, was identical with the Court of the Manor. Indeed, if it were not
clear beyond all dispute that private jurisdictions existed
before the Norman Conquest, it might almost be inferred
that some lords of manors soon after that time usurped
the power and the functions of the hundred-man. Theoretically, the right of inspecting the tithings, or, in other
words, ' the view of frank-pledge,' with the various incidents of that ceremony, belonged at one time to the hundred; practically, it was, not very long after the Norman Conquest, an ordinary appurtenance of a manor.
The tithing, however, in its relation to the hundred and
to the territorial division, which in the end was called a
manor, left not a single person in the realm (outlaws
excepted) who did not, either directly or indirectly, give
some kind of security to the state for his good behaviour.
The landed magnate, it is possible, was, to use modern
phraseology, only bound in his own recognisances—gave
no security but the stake which he held in the country
for himself and his household. The rest were not only
compelled to find bail for themselves, but themselves to
be bail for their own sureties.

Such was the institution which went by the name of the Peace-pledge. It was, perhaps, not established in

Full develop-
ment of the
system under
the Danes. full force until the Danes became masters of England, in the beginning of the eleventh century. But the responsibility of the guild is mentioned in laws as early as the end of the seventh century, and can be traced downwards to the time when it had become an elaborate system of police. It is true that, in the intermediate period, the simpler plan of exacting bail when a particular offence had been committed was not unknown. The custom of reciprocal warranty may, therefore, have been put in force and abandoned alternately in a series of vain attempts to reform the criminal tendencies of the population. Nor is it impossible that the law may have required specific bail for each person accused of a particular crime, in addition to the responsibility already incurred by the guild or tithing to which he belonged. The necessity, however, which the Danes felt very keenly, of having some security against assassination by their subjects, caused them to define the law of Peace-pledge with clearness, and to enforce it with rigour. The free-man who could not name his tithing and his hundred was then an outlaw ; his kin had no claim to compensation if he was killed ; if accused himself he could not be exculpated by compurgation.

In the penalty attached to the neglect of this law may be discerned a clue to the weakness of a system

Its inherent
weakness. which, at first sight, appears to render crime impossible. There is evidently a connexion between the compurgators and the tithing or hundred. The man who will not take upon himself the responsibilities of the peace-bond forfeits all the advantages of the family-bond, and, of course, of the peace-bond itself. One of the advantages of the latter, there can be little doubt, was, that the fellow tithing-men, or fellow hundred-men could, upon occasion, make oath for a comrade. If they swore to his innocence, or their belief in it, the effect was that the accused person escaped, and that his peace-union did not pay. If they declined to swear, they not only exposed him to the dangers of the ordeal, or worse, but they practically taxed themselves for his offence. Thus, the Peace-pledge, though it apparently constituted every man a constable, had really the opposite effect of setting a reward on perjury.

It is not, however, necessary to suppose that any man's compurgators, as a body, were strictly identical with any particular peace-union, though his peace-union The Guilds and the Com-must almost certainly have furnished some of purgators. his compurgators. If the tithing and the hundred were guilds in which men were associated by compulsion, there were others in which they were associated by choice. The rules of some of these, as they existed before the Norman Conquest, are still extant. Like the others, they exhibit the principle of mutual insurance, which, however, is developed into the principle of mutual aid in times of trouble. The brothers, as the members were called, contributed to bear the burden when the house of one of their number was burnt. They helped to pay the fine when one of them had committed a homicide. They all had an affectionate interest for one who had the misfortune to find himself in prison. They met at stated seasons for convivial entertainments; and there can be little doubt that they were held together by a tie only less strong than that of the family itself. They professed, it is true, to respect the law, and to draw a distinction between accidental or justifiable homicide, and that which in modern times would be called murder. But as they would probably not have been permitted to enjoy their organisation if they had not shown this apparent spirit of obedience, there is little importance to be attached to it in the face of other well-established facts.

The effect of this double system of guilds upon the system of compurgation may readily be imagined, especially when the country was in the hands of the foreigner. To screen an offender would be, according to the social code, an act of good fellowship, according to the political code, remunerative. Thus two of the strongest motives by which human beings can be influenced were brought into action, not, as the law-givers intended, for the repression of crime, but for the escape of the criminal. The results will be made apparent, not only in the history of the time at which these institutions were most prominent, but unfortunately also in the history of many subsequent centuries.

In the present age—when the use of the dagger is called in ordinary speech un-English, when assassination The Guilds is described as the crime of the foreigner or of and the Assassins. the Irishman—it is difficult to realise the fact that England itself was once considered almost a land of assassins. In the year 1002 the massacre of the Danes in cold blood, in time of peace, gave the subsequent Danish dynasty good reason to fear the temper of their subjects and to look well to the perfection of the Peace-pledge. Even if it were possible to disbelieve the chronicle in which this terrible event is narrated, and to assume that the words were written half a century after the date assigned to them, the story would still be a monument of the morals which rendered those times hideous. In this year, calmly reports the annalist, on Saint Brice's Day, by the King's command, the whole of the Danes in England were slain. There is a feeble attempt to justify the deed by reference to some plot which the victims might otherwise have carried into execution. But not one expression of reprobation, or even of regret, is there to soften the hard outline of the tale ; there is reason, on the contrary, to believe that the act of murder could not have been so general as the chronicler represents, and that he deliberately exaggerated its magnitude in order to make it appear more creditable to his country !

No wonder, then, that when retribution came, and England fell under the yoke of the Danes, the new rulers strained to the utmost the responsibility of the hundred, in which they might well have believed some security was to be found. But the Dane, like the Norman, must have discovered that the system of guilds was a stronger support to the homicide than to the arm of the law. He did not, like the Norman, draw a distinction between those who were akin to the victors and those who were akin to the vanquished, nor provide that the hundred should be responsible for deaths by violence in one class only. At most, therefore, he could but have obtained for his fellow-countrymen a protection from murder as great as that which was enjoyed by the native popu- lation. How great that was it is not difficult to infer even from the meagre annals of the time. As the petty kings of earlier days commonly perished by assassination, so the magnates of the eleventh century, when obnoxious to their rivals, were killed with little hesitation and with little blame to the slayer. A fine and a temporary

banishment satisfied the law and appeased the anger of
the king. Respect for human life is a sentiment which
had no place in the tenth century or the eleventh. Nor
when the Englishman remembers the deeds which his
forefathers did, not only before the Norman Conquest
but long after, has he any reason for the Pharisaical
belief that his nature is not as the nature of an
Irishman.

Thus far the guild has been regarded in only two
of its aspects—as the police-guild and as the social guild.
Trade-guilds It has, however, another, and in later times,
and the
Towns.   more familiar aspect—as the trading-guild.
How one sprang from another, or which was the first
in origin, it would, perhaps, be impossible to determine
with certainty. The trading-guild appears in more
forms than one—as the guild merchant, which it is
difficult to distinguish from the town-corporation, and
as the guild of craftsmen. The craft-guilds do not come
into notice before the Norman Conquest, but, on the
other hand, they show themselves soon afterwards, and
there seems to be no good reason for denying them any
previous existence. An antiquity, extending at least
as far back as the time of Edward the Confessor, is
claimed for the guild merchant, and allowed, in the later
charters to some of the towns; the Guild-hall of the
burgesses at Dover, and the Guild of burgesses at Canterbury are mentioned in Domesday-Book. In the earliest
record of the Exchequer after Domesday, the guilds of
weavers appear to be regularly constituted and perfectly
familiar to the revenue officers. Rude as were the
earlier times, it is certain that even gold-workers attained
some skill in England, and it can hardly be supposed
that the country was destitute of weavers. And if it

be admitted on the one hand that there were handi-
craftsmen, and on the other hand that guilds were
established for various purposes, it is very difficult to
believe that the guild principle was not applied to the
trades. If so much be conceded the priority of any of
the three forms of guild becomes a mere matter of conjecture, and the source of the whole system must necessarily remain doubtful. Regarded from one point of
view, the guild has a strong resemblance to the family
tie of the Teutonic and other barbarous tribes ; regarded
from another, it is a species of bail, which involves a
principle too universally applied to be considered
characteristic of any one people ; regarded from a third,
it is strikingly like that institution of colleges or companies which was always familiar to the Romans, and
which we know from inscriptions to have existed in
Britain during the Roman occupation, both in the form
of the religious guild and in the form of the craft-
guild.

It would be possible, indeed, to elaborate a very
plausible argument for the development of the whole
guild system out of Roman institutions rather than out
of the family tie of the Germans. This, indeed, might
have come to pass by two wholly distinct processes—
either through a tradition handed down by the ancient
Roman townsmen, or through a new introduction at the
time when Roman missionaries came to restore Christianity in that part of Britain which had become pagan
England. The second process would fully account for the
existence of guilds in parts of Germany never conquered
by the Romans. Human nature, however, whether
civilised or barbarous—Greek, or Roman, or Teutonic—
has everywhere some kind of social instinct; and the

common historical blunder of attributing to a race, or a country, or a language that which belongs to humanity shall, in this place at least, not be repeated. The truth is that the guild system existed before and after the Norman Conquest, but that there is no historical evidence of its beginning. It is, however, a fact of too much importance to be forgotten that the guilds afterwards became, for a time, in one form at least, the vital principle of the towns.

In the History of Crime, and of its varying forms, the history of towns and of commerce must play a *Importance* conspicuous part. In the occupations of the *of the history of Towns in* people lie their temptations; by those occu- *the History of Crime.* pations, in a great measure, the moral standard of society is formed. With the growth of the peaceful arts crimes of violence disappear; when government is unsettled, and men are familiar with war, life falls in value, and murder ceases to be regarded as a heinous offence. To the Englishman, who lives securely in the greatest cities which the world has seen, the small beginnings of modern civilisation have a special interest and importance. The struggle of the warlike spirit against the trading spirit, of ignorance against know-ledge, of brute force against the inventive faculties, might be described as the struggle of crime against social order, had social order, in the modern sense, existed when the conflict was at its height.

Those who believe that the Roman towns survived the Teutonic invasion will date the beginning of the *Disputed* campaign from that all-important event. They *origin of Towns in* will see in the contempt of the lord for the *England.* trader the inherited contempt of the victor for the vanquished. They will see in the persistence of the townsmen a stubbornness inherited from the time when townsmen drove back the invader from the walls, and yielded at last only to the necessities of hunger. But it is the duty of the historian not to put forward as fact that which is mere possibility. There is no evidence that the towns were destroyed. There is a statement made by a monk that a few were at a particular time deserted. There is the fact that at no period of history had towns ceased to exist or to be inhabited in any of the great divisions of England. Beyond this all is conjecture. There are, however, some materials upon which an opinion may be formed, and which, if they are not conclusive upon the question of origin, are not without their value for the main objects of this work. The towns, as they existed before the Norman Conquest, must be regarded in their relation to the known customs of pure Teutonic tribes, as well as to the territorial divisions, and to the tenure of land which prevailed in England when Southern Britain had acquired that name.

From the northern walls to the Straits of Dover, the names of Roman stations were adopted by Roman names: the the conquerors. Where the Roman had raised Chesters. walls and dug trenches the new possessor of the soil described the fortress in language more Roman than that of the Roman himself. The legions of the Empire, when they settled in a British town, accepted commonly enough the British designation. To them Isca, Venta, and Glevum were enough ; to their successors it seemed necessary to add the Roman word ' castra,' or chester ; and the same places became Exanceaster or Exeter, Wintanceaster or Winchester, Gleawanceaster or Glou- cester. Of these chesters nearly sixty have survived to the present day.   Bath and St. Albans were chesters centuries after the departure of the Romans, the first being called Bathanceaster, or Acemannesceaster, the second both Verlamacaestir and Vaetlingacaestir.   Other chesters again, of which the sites cannot now be indenti- fied, are mentioned in various writings between the eighth and eleventh centuries.   Some important places, however, retained their Roman names. without the addition of chester, or, as in the case of Bath, without a fixed and permanent addition.   Among these were York (sometimes called Eoforwic-ceaster), and Dover.   Lin- coln, or Lindocolonia, is the Roman 'colonia' of Lindum. London was known as London in the time of the Emperor Claudius, and as London it has always been known, except when the Romans honoured it, for its magnitude, with the additional title of Augusta.

The persistence of the word 'chester' in every part of England is the more remarkable from the fact that when Britain returns again into the light of history the land is not in the power of a single chieftain or tribe, but is divided into many independent kingdoms, which long continued to wage war one against another.   They had no tie but that of a common language, which, however, exhibits some variations of dialect in the different districts.   It has been believed, from the days of Hume to our own time, by historians whose works entitle them to respect, that, when South Britain was conquered by the Low German tribes, the process was one of complete extermination.   Others, and among them Gibbon, have entertained a very different opinion, have admitted that the evidence upon which the belief is founded is wholly unworthy of credit, and that all the analogies to be found in Europe point to a different

question which involves a long train of scientific reasoning. Even a summary of the arguments upon either side would be out of all proportion to the value which any result would possess for the objects of this history. A critical examination of the historical authorities, a careful estimate of the value of language as a criterion of race, a discussion of various anatomical and psychological problems, an investigation of the length of time required to effect a change of physical characteristics by means of climate and soil are all necessary branches of such an enquiry. This is, therefore, not the place to deny that although the German barbarians, when they had but the Rhine to cross, failed to extirpate the Gauls, they could cross the German Ocean in sufficient numbers to extirpate the Britons. Still less would it be worth while to enquire by what means the invaders discovered the names of the Roman stations after they had slain the only persons who could give them the information. Least of all would it be profitable to combat the opinion that we should attribute to mere coincidence such facts as the existence of a chief city, at the time of the Norman Conquest, upon the site and with the name of a chief city known to the Romans, and the apparent identity of Winchester, the city of second importance, with a Roman city which bore a British name.

There is, however, one point upon which those who regard the Teutonic wave as a deluge may agree with those who regard it as a wave and nothing more. Even if it be supposed that the invaders, after putting the inhabitants to death, left not one stone upon another in any town which they found in the island, it must nevertheless be admitted that the towns were sooner or later rebuilt. One of three possible cases must be accepted as fact : new towns were built with the ancient name on or near the ancient site, or new inhabitants occupied the towns, of which the former possessors were slaughtered, wholly or in part, or the original possessors retained their hold after the new comers had settled round about them. These are the limits of conjecture; history gives but one fact to aid it:—towns bearing their Roman names existed when Bede, the first historian, began to write, nearly three hundred years after the date which has commonly been assigned to the mythical voyage of Hengist and Horsa. Every one may imagine the events of the intervening period according to his own wishes or prejudices, for it may be shown that the history of our towns begins at the same point whether we accept the Roman or the Teuton as the founder.

The marauders who commonly gave the name of 'chester' to the walled towns, which excited their wonder, sometimes substituted 'byrig' or 'burh' (the modern borough) for that term. Thus, London was sometimes called Lundenbyrig; and while Kent retained its ancient name its capital became Cantwara-byrig. In early times the word borough was borne by few towns as a portion of their names, but it became, as it could hardly fail to do when the language of the Romans ceased to be spoken, the generic term for every walled town. It started from very humble beginnings. It seems at one time to have denoted a hill, or a rude earthwork such as the primitive Teuton threw up as a defence against a hostile tribe. Afterwards it was used to express a more solid and permanent fort or tower, of which the Burghs in the Shetland Islands may be mentioned as specimens. Later still its signification was extended to that of a castle or walled town of any

Teutonic names : the Boroughs.

extended to that of a castle or walled town of any dimensions. And finally, in the long conflict with feudalism, it gained the complex meaning which we now attach to it.

The history, therefore, of the Teutonic Borough and the history of the Roman Chester are one. Both alike carry us back to the most primitive form of society. A savage tribe has a quarrel with a neighbouring tribe, and makes its first step towards civilisation when it imitates artificially the natural mound behind which it has found shelter. Out of the mound grows the idea of systematic intrenchment on the one hand and of turret-building on the other. From the savage tribe with its 'pah' grows the military nation with its 'castra.' The 'castra,' at first only a temporary camp, must of necessity develope in time into the permanent camp, with all its wants and its offers of employment. Out of the permanent camp grows the walled town ; out of the walled town the city with its civilisation. Such must have been the history of Rome, such the history of London. This fact has a far more direct bearing upon the History of Crime than the question whether our blood is British, or Roman, or German. And there is not a doubt that if the Teutonic invaders learned the art of building towns and castle walls from the Romanised Britons, they had, before the Norman Conquest, applied it to new sites and modified it according to their own rude ideas.

The origin of the Roman Chester and of the Teutonic Borough the same.

The condition of the towns before the Norman Conquest is involved in much obscurity. We have no means, except where walls still exist, of ascertaining their magnitude during the Roman occupation ; but the remains of temples, baths, pave-

Relation of the Town to the Shire.

ments, and amphitheatres, with innumerable coins, indicate that all the civilisation of the empire had been imported into Britain.   Such as the municipal constitution was elsewhere the Theodosian Code tells us it was in this island ; but whether this constitution was handed down to the Teutonic invaders, or the invaders created a municipal organisation of their own, is a question which cannot be decided with historical certainty.   It is easy to represent the borough as the counterpart of the shire, with similar officers and a similar system throughout.   It is easy to represent the shire as the equivalent of the ' Gau ' found elsewhere—as an aggregate of Teutonic tribes—and to trace the whole pre-Norman Government, by a series of analogies, back to the primitive barbarism in which the Germans lived according to the account of Tacitus.   But it would be no less easy to represent the officers of these boroughs as officers of the Roman city, called by a Teutonic translation of their Roman name. The counterpart of the town would then be found in the shire ; the officers and the organisation of the shire could then be represented as borrowed from the town, and the men who owed suit to the County Court, as imitators of the Roman decurions.

While, however, it is thus easy to heap conjecture upon conjecture, there is one fact in the relations of town to shire which may, perhaps, afford an indication of the power possessed by towns at a very early period.   In the midst of all the disputes of antiquaries it is certain that the shire did not commonly give its name to the town, and that, in a very large number of instances, the town gave a name to the shire.   York, Lincoln, Leicester, Chester, Worcester, Gloucester have not only preserved in their names the recollection of Roman influence, but have extended them to the shires which constitute a very large portion of England. Even where the name of the town is not Roman, whatever may have been its origin, the same principle is seen in operation ; and the only exceptions to the ordinary rule of nomenclature are found in the few shires retaining the name of some settlers who at one time enjoyed an independent government.

The German of the time of Cæsar and of the time of Tacitus hated the very thought of living in a town. His ideas of life, virtue, and happiness were simple. To fight an enemy and carry off plunder, to make himself drunk when the battle was over, to remain drunk so long as the spoils affoded him the means, and then to fight and drink again—these were the objects of existence, and to attain them in perfection was to be a good man and true. Work of any kind he considered degrading to his noble nature, fit only for slaves and women and children. He dwelt sometimes in a cave, sometimes in a hut plastered over with mud. He despised architecture ; and mortar and tiles were unknown to him. A shapeless log of timber for a wall when he built a hovel, dung to keep him warm when he descended into his cavern, some flocks and herds, out of which he might pay a fine when he had committed a murder, a horse and arms, with which he might go to battle, were all the luxuries which he desired. This, according to Tacitus, was a human being of a far higher type than the civilised, but corrupt, Roman ; this, according to others, was the builder of our towns, the founder of modern society. It matters, however, but little whether it is to him or to the Roman that we are to look for the beginning of our civilisation ; it is but a question of a few centuries. The Roman himself did

Contrast between the primitive Teuton and the Town-builder.

but pass a little earlier through the stage of barbarism in which he found the Teuton.

One of the most important points in which the rulers of England before the Norman Conquest differed from The Teuton the primitive Germans of Tacitus was the use in possession of a coinage. of coin. Among the scanty notices which we possess of the towns during this period not the least important are those which show that they had the privileges of the Mint, or were compelled to undertake its duties. Thus it happens that in the early Institutes of England we find human life appraised not in horses and cattle, but in shillings and pence. This, perhaps, may be regarded as the second stage of civilisation. But, though in itself only one step above the custom which it succeeds, it is a step which could hardly have been made without the operation of causes wholly distinct from any which are known to have existed in the social or political organisation of the Teutonic tribe itself. There is no need for coins where there are no towns and no commerce ; and to the primitive Teuton town-life seemed to be nothing less than pollution. It is true, that wherever he was brought into contact with Roman civilisation he immediately abandoned his prejudices and possessed himself of money as often as opportunity offered. There is no doubt that on the continent the great change in the conditions of life which is implied in the adoption of a coinage was effected for the German through the influence of the Roman. Analogy points to a similar process in Britain ; and there must have been either a similar process or one which it is far less easy to comprehend. But in the absence of all documents which deserve to be called historical, it would be unsafe to make a definite historical statement. The facts which are known with certainty are few in number and separated by wide intervals of time. They may be summed up in a sentence. The Germans when free from external influence had no cities, no trade, no objects of barter except flocks and herds, nothing but live stock with which they could even pay a penalty; the Romans left Britain with numerous towns, with flourishing arts, and with a coinage; some centuries later the governing powers used a Low German dialect and paid their penalties, sometimes at least, in money coined in towns, which were still numerous, and many of which were still more or less Roman in name. The art of coining was not introduced by Augustine or by his foreign successors, because there are in existence coins belonging to the period between the Teutonic invasion and the coming of the Roman missionaries.

In Britain, as elsewhere, the possession of towns and of money was necessarily accompanied by another element of civilisation—a tax for the common good. The Teuton in Wherever the Teuton gained possession of a possession of walls, bridges, fragment of the Roman Empire, a species of and roads. tenure began to prevail which was not only unlike any known to the ancient Germans, but founded on a principle altogether opposed to their primitive ideas. Having been previously a hater of towns, he imposed upon all the lands which he acquired the burden of maintaining town-walls or castles as well as the bridges and roads which sustained the communication from one town to another. It is, indeed, difficult to understand how the roads could have continued to be used if the towns which they connected had been destroyed. The fact, however, that the Roman roads were adopted by the successors of the Romans is not to be disputed; and in that fact lay, during many centuries, almost the only hope that civilisation might one day be revived in Britain.

The discordance which may be observed between these indications of a more advanced civilisation and the barbarity of the criminal law assumed also a variety of other forms, and affected both town and country. When the Teuton began to permit the existence of towns, and even to live in them himself, he began to understand that an individual might possess, in addition to horses, cattle, and sheep, some property of his own as distinguished from the common stock, and that such possession might extend to land as well as to manufactured goods and coin. But the traditional method of dividing land, which has been acquired by force, could not be at once thrown aside ; and thus when England first appears in history, after the Teutonic conquest, her soil is divided in a manner which shows a conflict still hardly decided between the primitive notion that land belongs to no one, or to the tribe, and the notion that one man may hold a portion of it if he can.

Change in his views with respect to land-tenure.

That land, which has been acquired by an unsettled tribe through a common effort, should be held in common is a natural consequence of the mode of acquisition. The custom has existed among the Aryan-speaking nations from the Indian Ocean to the Atlantic. But it has been by no means restricted to a race or a language. When the Israelites entered the Promised Land a division was made into as many portions as there were tribes to claim a share ; and in America, before it was conquered by the European nations, it is said that the Aztecs held their land in common, tribe by tribe. In the village-communities of India little or no progress has, even now, been made

Land held in common by every primitive tribe.

beyond this primitive state of society. Elsewhere it has been followed by a complete or partial subdivision, among individuals, in the first instance of arable land and afterwards of grass-land and wood-land. But the original barbarism has seldom failed to leave a trace in the practices of civilised life; and thus common of pasture was an institution familiar alike to Italians and provincials who lived under the Roman Empire, and to the churls and serfs who lived immediately before the Norman Conquest, as it is to the peasants of our own day.

The Germans, in early times, constituted no exception to this general rule. Among them a ' mark ' was a ring of waste or forest surrounding a community, The Teutonic which tilled, by means of its slaves, as much 'Mark' and arable land as was sufficient for its own support. Over the waste or forest the families constituting the tribe or clan had common rights. In the central arable land each had a severalty, or individual proprietorship, which was apparently shifting, rather than permanent or hereditary, in the time of Tacitus. It is probable, however, that each head of a family had, as soon as tillage became a recognised institution, a right to a certain definite measure of arable land for the support of himself and those who were dependent on him. But the fertility of any particular plot would, when the principles of agriculture were unknown, soon be exhausted; he would thus be compelled to occupy different spots at different times.

This species of shifting severalty is the intermediate stage between possession in common and hereditary possession by private persons. It is, from the Stage between tenure nature of the case, excessively difficult to pro- in common and tenure in nounce where one begins and the other ends. severalty. The line which distinguishes the right to a particular section of land of a particular size from the right to a section of land of a particular size but not in a particular spot is so dimly drawn that it cannot be followed in its whole length. It is probable, however, that when men discovered the advantage of letting lands lie fallow, and when there was an abundance of land to divide, the head of the family received an allotment sufficiently large to support him and his, not only for one year, but permanently. As soon as this was done, whenever it may have been, the shifting severalty had given place to a severalty in permanence, and a blow, apparently slight but really severe, had been struck at the whole principle of tenure in common.

In England, after the Teutonic invasion, there seems to have been recognised a common property in land in two different senses. There was a common right of mast, turbary, and pasture in the unenclosed lands ; and there were, at the same time, lands called ' folc-land,' which belonged to the state, but which, before the Norman Conquest, the state could grant for a life or lives, and even in perpetuity, as the reward of good service. By degrees, however, the common land diminished in quantity as parts of it became the property of individuals; and with the land the allodial lord acquired many of the privileges and functions which had previously been entrusted to the elect of the tribal assembly.

Common land in England.

For this reason, as well as others, it has been suggested that the great land-holder—the lord of the manor—was developed out of an elected, and afterwards hereditary, head man of the tribe or clan. In some instances it is probable enough that this was his origin, but the principle must not be carried too

Origin of the private land-holder.

far. The early existence of towns, whatever their origin, and the adoption of the Roman roads preclude the possibility that the system of living in isolated tribes, surrounded by a mark, could have been universal. There were, without doubt, waste lands and forests in abundance, yet their continuity had been broken by the Roman engineers and the builders of the Roman towns. The great lord, therefore, though he may sometimes have been no more than the hereditary head man of his tribe, may also have sprung sometimes from a different source. When the invaders from Germany effected a settlement in Britain it is not improbable that some of the chieftains, with their select companions, may have imitated the customs of those whom they dispossessed in taking a share of the soil, and perhaps even a villa to themselves apart from their followers of a lower grade. This, however, is a matter of little moment. The ancestors of the Romans had, no doubt, once been nomad tribes, enjoying their hunting grounds in common. They had passed through phases of life to which the Teuton was yet a stranger, but which seem inevitable in the existence of every people capable of civilisation.

Acquisition by force, in one form or another, either by individuals or by communities, constitutes the first title to all land in England. And where all inherited the traditions of those who believed that acquisition was meritorious, and not least meritorious where most violent, community naturally became no less jealous of community than lord of lord, or petty king of petty king. The spirit of invasion, handed down from the past, infected the whole of society from its greatest divisions to its least. War was its normal condition—if not the war of the little, the

war of the great.   Where the local customs of one place
differed from those of another in all respects but one,
they at least agreed in recognising the rule of the
strongest; and though the idea of peace throughout the
realm did somehow become possible to the rulers, and an
attempt was made to secure order by the peace-pledge
or system of mutual bail, nature and habit proved far
stronger than law.   The very mode of settlement
adopted by the invaders and their descendants must
have given increased energy to the old love of combat.
The great owners became the natural enemies of those
who held state lands for a term, or who had common
rights, and those who had common rights the natural
enemies of the great owners.   All were alike ready to
encroach or to resist an encroachment; and even in far
later times it will be seen that a township would sometimes assert a petty privilege by force.   Out of these
conflicting elements grew many of the anomalies of land-
tenure which have descended to our own time, and
especially the manor, with the various common rights
claimed by the tenants.

It has been well remarked by one of the greatest
admirers of Teutonic institutions that the right of private
Connexion   war was the foundation of Teutonic (he might
with the right
of private   have added of all semi-barbarous) laws.   That,
war.   together with the blood-tie, produced the system
of compensation for murder.   That was, in theory, asserted equally by the lowest freeman and the greatest
lord.   That, however, it was which took the little power
they possessed from the weak and gave it to the strong.
That, represented as the free-man's inheritance, was precisely what converted the free-man into a dependent.
That was long the greatest obstacle to personal liberty,

the support of slavery, the greatest discouragement to industry, the enemy of all order, and even of strict military discipline. But that was the privilege which the great holder could assert on a great scale. He could insist on the appeal to arms against a neighbouring lord, or against the king. He would accept a grant of the public land or folc-land from the King and Witan, and consent to have it elevated to the rank of book-land, or land of which the ownership was certified in writing. But he trusted little to the security of books; and long after the Norman Conquest he would take by violence his neighbour's land, and the parchments which proved his neighbour's rights. He would submit to the decision of that which has been called a court—if it happened to be in his own favour. But the strong arm gave a better title than any deed of grant or court of thanes ; and the primitive mode of taking possession was neither forgotten nor allowed to fall into disuse for many centuries after the time now under consideration. It seems indeed that out of the first barbarous seizure of the soil grew one of the maxims of the common law—that actual entry is necessary to possession. Thence came the forcible entries of later times, which statutes long failed to repress, and which would never have been repressed had not a power stronger than legislation come to its aid.

Thus, sooner or later, the descendant of the rude marauder began life as a great landholder, prepared to retain by the sword that which the sword had won for him, and by the sword to win still more if he could. Thus the smaller holders were, in those lawless times, altogether swallowed up by the greater, or only permitted to exist by a sacrifice of independence. Thus it came to pass that there were king-makers before the Earl of

Warwick, and even before the Norman Conquest—that a Godwin was not less powerful in relation to the king than any of the strictly feudal barons.   The power which could be used to raise or depose a king was, in fact, only the territorial power which a lord, or a combination of lords, could wield against another lord, or another combination.

Within a society such as was the clan within its mark, such as are village communities in India, there were Origin of Private Jurisdictions. necessarily, as indeed there are in every savage tribe, the rudiments of a court of law.   If the chief did not treat all his inferiors as slaves, and exercise absolute power over limb and life, there was an elected head-man who presided at certain assemblies in which matters affecting the community were discussed.   The disputes of those who held adjoining plots of land, and such petty thefts as it was possible to commit in a society so little advanced, were brought before him.   In this, of course, it is easy to point out an analogy not only to the hundred court, but also to the manor court of later times. Not the least important, indeed, of the powers acquired by the private landholder was that of private jurisdiction. Little is known of its history before the time of the Norman Conquest.   But the technical terms which the conquerors were compelled to adopt, which belong to the language of the vanquished, and which remain untranslated in the Latin treatises of the Norman lawyers, give sufficient evidence of the institution.   The gallows for hanging men, and the pit for drowning or half-drowning women, were among the most cherished appurtenances of the manor, or of its prototype, as it existed before the year 1066.   The lord set great value upon his privilege of holding his own court, and not less upon his privilege of hanging his own thieves. Even when the offender had committed a theft without the limits of the land held by his lord, it seems to have been in some places an established custom that he was to be brought back and hanged upon the gallows which his lord had provided for him.

These private jurisdictions were so numerous as to form a conspicuous feature in Domesday Book, which shows not only that the lord of the manor had his equivalent before the Norman Conquest, but that the principle which he exemplifies had extended itself even into the towns. Stamford and Lincoln had each twelve magistrates with power (in the case of Lincoln at least hereditary) to hold their own courts. In Norwich, Canterbury, Huntingdon, Hereford, and other towns, private individuals had a still more independent authority. The two largest towns, London and Winchester, are not mentioned in the record, but their subsequent history indicates that they were not, at the time of the Norman Conquest, free from the curse of little lords with their little tribunals. A right of trying criminals was attached to the ownership of Baynard's Castle in London in the time of John, and claimed long afterwards by the descendants of Robert Fitz-Walter. Not the least of the privileges which he enjoyed was that of drowning in the Thames all traitors taken within the limits of his territory.

Their diffusion in town and country.

It cannot be satisfactorily decided by direct evidence how far the towns themselves, in their municipal capacity, possessed jurisdiction before the Norman Conquest. There was, however, in every borough a moot or court which probably resembled that of the hundred, and had power at least to give judgment on

Municipal Jurisdictions.

minor offences.   In the towns, as in the rural districts,
the peace-pledge was rigorously exacted, and there must
have been some power similar to the hundred court to
inspect each union of ten.   The towns, like the counties
and hundreds, had their reeve, a part of whose functions
was, in all likelihood, to preside, or at least to take a prominent place, in some kind of court.   It is worthy of
remark, too, that in London, the wards, of which the constitution must have been long anterior to the Norman
Conquest, act afterwards precisely as the hundreds act in
criminal enquiries.

None of the courts of which there is any trace before
the Norman Conquest afford any indication that they were
Feebleness of governed by fixed principles, that they observed
the higher
jurisdictions. uniformity of procedure, or that any legal knowledge was required in the persons who presided over
them.   To the last, every shire was a little kingdom in
itself, jealous of its own local privileges.   The Bishop,
with the chief lay officer in each, sat twice a year to transact the chief judicial business of the district.   Their court
was called a meeting, which certain inhabitants of the
shire were expected to attend.   They had, in a certain
sense, cognisance of the greater criminal offences, and
decided civil causes, so far as it can be said that civil
causes were legally decided at all in those primitive times.
Beneath the court of the shire was the hundred court
which had final jurisdiction only in minor cases.   Above
it was a higher jurisdiction, corresponding in constitution,
perhaps, to the King's Court under the earlier Norman
kings, but acting apparently only as a court of appeal.
These matters are, however, excessively obscure, and the
scanty details here given are barely established by a
comparison of the few contemporary documents with the

institutions of a better known period. But the actual feebleness of all higher jurisdictions may be inferred from the number of persons who had private jurisdictions of their own.

We who live in the nineteenth century, though we may have as much, have no more in common with the men who lived in Britain between the sixth General view century and the eleventh than an accomplished of Society in England from and humane gentleman has with the rough and the sixth century to the cruel and ungovernable boy whose existence eleventh. may have been continued in his person. We have all been taught, in the nursery, to regard Alfred as a hero, and to set before his name the epithet Great. Popular vene- For the age in which he lived he was truly ration for Alfred " the great—great in comparison with the excessive Great." littleness around him. But nothing could be more unjust to his memory than to judge him by a modern standard, for that would be to compare the inches of an infant with those of a full grown giant. We need not believe all the dubious stories said to have been told by a Welsh monk, the biographer of this king of the West Saxon line— the stories of a monarch turned minstrel and spy in the camp of the enemy, of a warrior turned baker in the hut of a peasant. But we may well believe there was an Alfred who stood, like one of Homer's heroes, a head and shoulders higher than his fellows, an Alfred who had a dim perception that knowledge was better than igno- rance, an Alfred who had the good sense to import the literary culture in which his subjects were wanting. Still all the efforts of an Alfred served but to throw a flicker- ing and unenduring light upon the dark deeds which were characteristic of the age, and to which no one individual

could have put an end had he been an Alexander, an
Aristotle, or a Justinian instead of an Alfred.

It is a remarkable fact that in the laws which bear
the names of Alfred, of Canute, and of Edward the
Confessor—names more familiar than those of
any other kings who ruled in England before the
Norman Conquest—the same ferocious spirit is
to be observed as in laws of an earlier date, as
in the customs attributed to barbarians by the
Roman Emperors.   In one respect, indeed, a collection of
laws attributed to Alfred differs from those of other kings,
and perhaps affords an indication of his literary tastes. It
is not, like the rest, a repetition, with slight variations, of
ancient maxims belonging to Western barbarism, but a
selection, from the Old Testament, chiefly of those passages which sanction the demand of an eye for an eye, of
a tooth for a tooth, of an exact equivalent for every injury.
All such precepts are of course laid down with the simplicity
of a school-boy who has with some difficulty mastered the
mere letter of the text, and who has no suspicion that the
spirit may be somewhat different, or that any allowance
is to be made for the hyperbolical expressions of an
eastern language.   Alfred perceived some sort of resemblance in words between the ancient laws of the
Jews and the laws which his predecessors or their councils
had drawn up for the people of England.   What could
be more natural than to add, as he supposed, the
authority of Scripture to the penalties which were in
those days believed to deter man from crime in proportion to the cruelty with which they were enforced ?

If the laws of Alfred were not more merciful than
those of his predecessors, the laws of Canute were not
more merciful than those of Alfred, nor the laws in force

Ferocious spirit in the laws of Alfred, Canute, and the Confessor, as in the laws of an earlier date.

under the Confessor than those of Canute. Alfred may
have attempted to reform the manners of his subjects by
severities which themselves needed reformation Persistence of
and taught the too easily-learnt lesson of cruelty. the same general con-
Canute may have striven for empire, and dreamt ditions of life through six
of a military supremacy of which the seat centuries.
should be in London and the power extend beyond the
sea, while his subjects in England were to be ruled by
the sword, and rendered less dangerous than their wont
by employment in war. Edward the Confessor may have
believed that the piety shown in neglect of his wife, and
the polish shown in the encouragement of French adventurers could aid him in the government of the country ;
but punishments under him were as brutal as they had
been under Ethelbert, king of Kent, or Ine, king of
Wessex, or any of the leaders who had brought Teutonic
customs across the German Ocean. During the whole
period from the coming of the barbarians to the coming
of the Normans the chief conditions of life must have
been nearly the same. They are most aptly described in
the speech which Bede attributes to a pagan chieftain.
' Our existence,' he said, ' seems but a moment in the life
of a bird. In the stormy winter-time when the wind is
howling, and rain or snow is falling thickly without, but
when the hearth within is warm, and the table is spread,
a sparrow flutters into the hall. It enters at one door
and departs by another. For a moment only it remains
in the warm and tranquil air. It flies out of the wintry
blast ; in the wintry blast again it is lost to sight. Such
appears to be the life of man, for we know not what has
gone before or what shall follow after.'

These words were used as an argument in favour of
Christianity, which offered certainty beyond the term of

natural life, but they tell a tale of the life itself which
suggested the comparison. They tell that the Roman
civilisation had been extinguished in the rural districts,
that glass had ceased to be applied to the private houses
of men who were styled nobles, that there was not even
a rough substitute for glass in the depth of winter, and
that the chieftain with his followers bivouacked in a rude
building—his chief idea of luxury a blazing fire, his chief
idea of pleasure an abundance of food and drink. To this
condition were the inhabitants of Britain reduced, and in
this condition, or one but little better, they remained save,
perhaps, here and there in a monastery where some monks
had been taught to write and to illuminate, and in the
towns which were struggling to revive commerce, and,
with commerce, civilisation.

To present the aspects of life in England before the
Norman Conquest as a harmonious whole would be to deprive them of their great distinguishing character

Partisanship
the only bond
which held
men together.

—want of harmony. Conflict prevailed everywhere—even in principles, if principles could
be said to exist. Every man who had power was a law
unto himself. Of the towns some were strong and others
weak, and that which would be true of one would be false
of another. There were state laws, but the state had no
power to enforce them, and the great state jurisdiction of
the king and his "wise men" could not have given any
greater security than that which is to be found in a party
struggle. Partisanship was in fact the only bond which
held men together, the only feeling which prevented the
whole population from being a population of Ishmaels,
each with his hand against every man, and with every man's
hand against him. Jurisdictions and courts have been
mentioned in these pages for want of better names; but

it must be remembered that there were practically no courts and no jurisdictions for the decision of matters of fact. The accuser and his party came before a certain assembly ; if the accused had a party sufficiently strong he also appeared and was saved by his friends. Even in the ordeal the theory at least of party and party was maintained. The guild-tie, the family-tie, and the land-tie were, in a sense, all elements of union, but in practice were, still more, elements of discord. Justice in the abstract was an unknown idea ; the only recognised obligation in matters of dispute was to be true to the bond— whichever bond it might be. Family was the enemy of family, guild of guild, domain of domain. Each of these unions possessed a kind of collective freedom, but gave no freedom to its members. Contradiction reigned here, as everywhere else ; and when men united to escape some form of mediæval tyranny they sacrificed the last shred of individual liberty.

The position of the slave with respect to punishments has already been described. This human chattel might be sold at the pleasure of its owner, with the The Slave sole restriction that a Christian was not to be Churl. made over to a pagan ; but boat-loads of man-flesh were despatched from the ports of England, and it would be difficult to discover who became the purchasers. The position of the slave, however, was only one degree worse than that of the churl, who always stood in need of some powerful protector, and who could not safely refuse to do that which his lord commanded him. The boundary which divided the free from the unfree was so slight that the churl was always in danger of passing over it. The infliction of a penalty which he could not pay, and which none would pay for him, rendered him utterly

bankrupt in freedom. His limbs were not his own to
carry him whither he wished to go. If he left the place
assigned to him it was held that he had stolen his own
body. He could be summarily hanged when caught,
and his life was worth nothing to his lord, or even to his
kindred, unless they redeemed him. This was the fate
which was continually impending over the free man of
low estate if he had the misfortune to make enemies
among those who had the power to save or condemn
him. In such a condition of society he was naturally
reckless. In the time of Tacitus the German lover of
freedom would stake the precious gift in some game of
chance. The custom probably survived in England ;
and as every man's life had a fixed price his liberty may
well have been a negociable commodity. It has often
been assumed that had Teutonic institutions never been
introduced into Britain we should never have been a free
people. As a matter of fact, the Teutonic invaders were
at least as well acquainted with slavery as the Romans :
they valued independence just as much as the young
spendthrift values money when he goes drunk to the
gaming table and flings his wealth upon the cloth.

With slavery in its worst form the barbarians, who
became masters of Britain after the Roman power was
The custom of wife buying. broken, introduced also the custom of wife
buying. An unmarried woman was, among
them, in the position of a chattel, for the sale of which
the owner was entitled to make as good a bargain as
possible. It was only natural that in a community in
which it was necessary to pay for taking a man's life
it should be considered equally necessary to pay for
permanent possession of a woman's person. The payment represents, in each case, a rude attempt to super-

sede a primitive condition of universal violence. The
two subjects have, however, not been treated together,
because, in the one case, the law remained unchanged
for many centuries, in the other, the law, if not the
practice, appears to have undergone an important modification before the Norman Conquest.

In the laws of the first Christian King of Kent the
provisions for the transfer of money or cattle, to be given
in exchange for the bride, occupy a prominent
place. The principle was carried out with the   Its nature.
utmost consistency when the wife proved unfaithful to
her owner. Nothing was then considered but the market
value of the woman; and the adulterer was compelled
to expend the equivalent of her original price in the
purchase of a new bride, whom he formally delivered to
the injured husband.

The Church was compelled to accept this, with many
other discreditable institutions, when it first made converts in England. In the laws of a King of The Church
Wessex, who lived at the end of the seventh was at first
compelled to
and beginning of the eighth century, the pur- accept it.
chase of wives is deliberately sanctioned; and it is stated
in the preface that the compilation was drawn up with
the assistance of the Bishop of Winchester and a large
assembly of 'God's servants.'

The policy of the Church, however, was to persuade
mankind that no civil contract was of any avail to
constitute marriage, that the cohabitation of a The Clergy
afterwards
man and a woman was in itself unholy, and that used their
influence to
nothing but a religious bond or sacrament, abolish it.
accompanied by the blessing of a priest, could render it
inoffensive in the eyes of God. It was impossible, therefore, that wedding by purchase could long be recognised

by religion as a binding contract (even though weddings
by purchase might continue to be made) when Christianity was firmly enough established to be above all
danger of subversion.   The provisions for bride buying
accordingly disappear from collections of laws of a later
date.   The daughter of the free-man seems then to have
been allowed, by law at least, some choice before matrimony.   She even became capable of holding property in
her own right, though the strong arm of husband or
kinsman must always have been necessary for its security.
The marriage of priests, too, which was at one time
very common, must have had considerable influence in
changing the national custom, for though the accusations
brought against them were innumerable, they were never
accused of buying their wives, and could never have
performed a public act so inconsistent with their professions.   When the monastic party. gained a partial
ascendancy, and marriages among the secular clergy
became less frequent, it was more than ever the interest
of the Church to secure the independence of women.
Virginity and liberality to religious houses were then
extolled as the greatest of womanly virtues; and though
it may be doubted whether the persuasion of the priests
was always for the benefit of the person persuaded, it
cannot be denied that they rendered a service to the
country when they taught men that a wife was not to be
regarded in precisely the same light as a sheep, or even
as a slave.

Thus was effected a distinct modification of a most
barbarous custom.   A great price was paid for it when
celibacy was extolled as a virtue; but perhaps no price
could be too great for the establishment of the doctrine
that the strong have not necessarily the right to enslave

the weak; and the abolition of purchase in marriage was the first step towards that end—the only step, to all appearance, which was made before the Norman Conquest. The change of law was probably not accompanied, at first, by any change of sentiment, or even by a complete change of practice, but rendered a gradual change of sentiment and of custom possible in later times. For this, at least, we have to thank the Christianity of that remote age. But the pagan superstition and the pagan barbarism in which it was imbedded were, in other respects, immoveable.

In theory, of course, the clergy set up a standard of morals which was opposed to most of the worst faults of the age. But the theory was by no means in accordance with the practice. "Peace on earth, good-will towards men" might serve as the text for some of the Ecclesiastical Institutes of the time when there was no peace and but little good-will. A simple industrious life, in which the priest, himself a workman, was to educate his flock, was the ideal which has been handed down in writing. In reality, the priest took to money-getting and wenching, and was frequently rebuked by his superiors for his own ignorance. Priest became the rival of priest for tithes, bishop of king for worldly dignity. The bishop who had begun by washing the feet of the poor and by teaching the gospel in court and council remembered that his life was appraised at regal value, and that he had a seat in the 'Meeting of the Wise'; but he forgot the rest. Thus even in the eleventh century it is possible to discern the germ of discontent which made Wycliffe popular in the fourteenth, and the orthodox clergy, both secular and regular, unpopular. The continuity of those causes which finally led to the 'Reforma-

Character of the clergy.

tion' receives, as will hereafter be seen, a strange illustration from the History of Crime.

Such was the age immediately preceding the Norman Conquest. To the greed of the savage for flocks or for hunting-grounds had been added the thirst of the trader for wares and for coins; but the townsman had done little, as yet, to soften the manners of the rustic marauder, and force was the ruling principle within the walls not less than without. There were restrictions, and police, and punishments in abundance, watch and ward upon the highways, and watch and ward at the gates. Even to entertain a guest for more than one night in a town was to be responsible for his good conduct. But all these laws served only to show by contrast the lawlessness, violence, and recklessness of the people. Life continued to be bought and sold; property was secure only to him who had the power to hold it. A permanently settled government, which, whatever may be its form, is the truest friend to civilisation and the greatest enemy to crime, was a blessing of which the idea was as yet hardly conceivable. The curse of the barbarian conquest still weighed heavily on the land; and when Lanfranc, an Italian monk accustomed to the manners of Norman nobles and Norman clergy, became Archbishop of Canterbury, he was appalled by the manners and customs of his flock. To him a war between lord and lord, between town and town, could not, after his experience of life, have appeared an extraordinary event. To him it might have seemed wrong, but not strange, that a bishop should assert territorial or even spiritual rights by violence. To him slavery was not an unknown nor, perhaps, even an indefensible institution. But beyond all this there were features in the English life of his time

Description of the inhabitants of England by Lanfranc.

which almost drove him to despair. To be the Primate, and to be the friend of the Conqueror seemed to him no compensation for the necessity of living in a country so uncivilised as England; and he addressed the Pope, in no hesitating language, with a request to be relieved from the intolerable responsibilities of his position. Let me, he said, retire again to a monastery ; better that than be the religious ruler over these godless tribes of barbarians.

CHAPTER II.

FROM THE NORMAN CONQUEST TO THE THIRD CRUSADE :
ENGLAND AT THE END OF THE TWELFTH CENTURY.

I N an age when chivalry was almost a synonym for
brutality, the relations of the Normans to the Englishry
led inevitably to acts of cruelty on the part of the victors
First effects and of treacherous assassination on the part of
of the Con-
quest.   the vanquished.   The actors, indeed, in the
events which were immediately consequent on the battle
fought near Hastings had neither the will nor the power
to give accurate descriptions of the scenes before their
eyes.   The weaker minds were stunned ; the more active
became blindly vindictive.   Even the native annalists
who lived at the beginning of the following century were
still dazed by the shock of a battle no longer recent.
With a strange mixture of resignation and spite, they
magnified the extent of the disaster and attributed it to
the will of God.   He, they said, accomplished in the year
1066 a design which He had long conceived, and
delivered over the English race to be exterminated by the
merciless and crafty Normans.   That mediæval tone of
thought, according to which a thunderstorm was a miracle,
and a fever was caused by witchcraft, naturally enough
represented a successful invasion and a change of system
as the annihilation of a people by fire and sword.

The continuity of our history from the time which preceded the Conquest to later ages has, however, long been made clearly manifest by the industry and skill of eminent lawyers and scholars. Nor is it less easily to be traced in the crimes of either period than in the uncouth terms for which the Normans could find no French or Latin equivalent. The mass of the population hated its Norman as it had previously hated its Danish rulers, but it was in no sense altered in character. The degradation of a new foreign yoke was, indeed, added for a time to all the evil influences which had long retarded the growth of civilisation ; but England was neither better nor worse in moral tone at the end of the eleventh century than she had been in the middle of the tenth. A change, most beneficial to later generations, was effected indirectly by the army of William the Norman, but it was a change so slowly brought about and so little perceived during the time of its progress that there need be little wonder if the English regarded the establishment of a new dynasty as a misfortune beyond redemption, and vaguely clamoured long afterwards for the Laws of the Confessor.

For many a year the insolence of the oppressor and the hatred of the oppressed produced their natural fruits, which are independent of race, or climate, or even of civilisation. It would, however, be most unfair to hold the Conqueror or his successors responsible for the brutal punishments inflicted during their reigns. Mutilation in every form had long been the recognised penalty for trivial offences. William the First and William the Second, perhaps, availed themselves of it to preserve their forests in a manner unknown to their predecessors ; but it was in itself as familiar to the English as any institution

Continuity of History.

which they possessed. The first object of the Conqueror was without doubt the security of himself and of his followers ; but he was hardly less anxious to provide for the good government of his realm in the only sense in which it could be understood in that semi-barbarous age. He rigorously enforced the responsibility of the hundred, in order to prevent the loss of French lives at the hands of English assassins ; and the English themselves were not allowed to enjoy the same protection against murder. But the assassination of the Danes under similar circumstances may, perhaps, serve as some justification for this severity ; and in other respects the English seem to have been gainers by the systematic repression of crime to which they had never been accustomed. They confessed with astonishment, in the year 1087, that murder had become comparatively rare, and that a traveller had been known to arrive at the end of his journey without having lost his money.

If deeds of violence and robberies had diminished at this time, it would be difficult to exaggerate the lawlessness of earlier years. It must have been not long afterwards that Lanfranc wrote to Robert de Limesey, then styled Bishop of Chester, in terms which show the scant respect entertained even by the clergy of those days for authority and for property.

The Normans and the Englishry.

' I sent you, not many days ago,' says Lanfranc, ' a letter, which, as I am informed, you barely read before you threw it from you in a passion. I now send you another, on the part of the king and of myself. I command you to put an end to those grievances which it is said you are inflicting on the monastery of Coventry, and to restore, without delay, what you have carried off from it by force. The abbot and monks have complained to

me that you entered their dormitory by violence, broke
open their chests, and seized all the goods which they
possessed. You pulled down their buildings and ordered
the materials to be conveyed away for use in your own
diocese.' Lanfranc concludes with a rebuke, of which
the practical value may be estimated from the fact that
this very Robert de Limesey continued to be a bishop all
the days of his life, and removed his see from Chester to
Coventry, the scene of his former exploit, where he was
buried with the honours due to a great and good man.
Such deeds, so easily condoned, may receive some explanation from the contempt with which a foreign bishop,
perhaps, regarded native abbots and monks. But the
spirit of the age still proclaims itself, after all allowance
has been made for the special circumstances.

If, however, rude Normans believed themselves to be
not only the conquerors, but also the superiors, intellectu-
ally and morally, of the conquered, there can be no doubt
that they had some justification in facts. The practice of
exporting slaves had never been abandoned in England,
and William, much to his credit, sternly repressed it.
There is some reason also to believe that the improvement in the marriage laws which had been gradually
effected by the influence of the Church had been in-
operative upon the masses of the populace. Even after
the Conquest, a letter from Pope Gregory VII. to Lanfranc, contains evidence that the barbarous custom introduced by the settlers from Northern Germany still
continued to exist. He had heard, he said, that, in
Scotland, men commonly deserted their wives, and sold
them too ; and he desired the Archbishop to forbid such
wickedness, both there and elsewhere ' in the Island of
the English.' It may be inferred from his description

that the old practice had not yet become obsolete, that
it was still possible, though, perhaps, not legally, to
purchase a bride, and that if she proved unfaithful, the
seducer was still compelled, probably by threats or by
violence, to make restitution in the shape of another
woman bought at the same price.

It is, too, but justice towards the Italian appointed by
William, as the successor of the native archbishop, to
Humanity of acknowledge that he aimed at the establish-
Lanfranc. ment of a far less brutal rule than that which
contented the Norman knights. If the king, or his
council, enunciated the principle that malefactors so
debased as those of England should not suffer death—
only because it was better that they should, as cripples,
serve for a warning to the ill-disposed—it is not less
true that, in the synod held at London under Lanfranc
in 1075, the assembled bishops and abbots expressed
their disapprobation of the maxim. It is true that there
were, in later times, bishops who had no more humanity
than savages, but it is not less true that gentleness and
mercy were, as far as he had the power, introduced into
England by Lanfranc.

The amiable character of this Italian priest stands
out in strong relief not only against the brutal manners
Lanfranc, of his native flock but also against the some-
and the   what less brutal manners of the king and his
scenes
around him. followers. The Normans added the trial by
combat to the other barbarous methods of deciding
matters of fact already existing in our island. To them
the duel seemed the fairest and most chivalrous way of
settling all disputes ; and it may be admitted that the
duel conducted on certain established conditions, in the

presence of spectators, was not inferior to the similar
recognition of the blood-feud, to the practice of composition, to the ordeal, or to compurgation. But the
whole course of Lanfranc's life, and the whole tenour of
his letters show what weariness of spirit he endured
when he reflected on the scenes around him. He was
unfortunate, so far as his own happiness was concerned,
in being the most liberal, and probably the most learned,
prelate of his age. He stands almost alone in the great
waste of mediæval bigotry as a bishop who possessed at
once erudition, discretion, genius, and charity. He
may be regarded as the impersonation of the good effects
which were ultimately consequent upon the Norman
Conquest He was one of the first leaders in the great
literary revival, in which the most acute intellects were
led on from the study of the poets and historians of
Rome to the study of the philosophers of Greece. The
stream of Greek thought thus poured into Christian
minds, created, as is well known, a new school of
Christian metaphysics, which, though it did not itself
produce great results, was of great service in the development of European intellect. One of the first of those
thinkers who attempted to strengthen religious doctrines
by scholastic arguments was Lanfranc, Archbishop of
Canterbury. It was a happy augury for future ages, that
he was distinguished from those who surrounded him not
less by moral worth than by mental energy. The dawn
of learning was attended by the morning star of that
mercy which is often the truest justice. Both, indeed,
were obscured almost as soon as they appeared; but in
the end, increasing obedience to improving laws kept
pace with the growth and diffusion of knowledge.

Though the progress of learning, and with it the

diminution of crime, must in any case have been slow, it was retarded in England by the rigour with which the prelates, under the new dynasty, insisted upon the celibacy of the clergy. In the eyes of Lanfranc a priest's wife was a living evidence of barbarism, no less than ignorance of the Latin language ; and thus he could not attempt to improve the minds without offence to the sentiments of English ecclesiastics. To them it seemed that he offered metaphysics as a substitute for matrimony, but not that they would profit by the change. They would have been willing to accept instruction as a gift, but the price demanded was far too high. They thought it better for a man to be illiterate and the father of a family than learned and a monk. One of Lanfranc's earliest letters to Rome contains a complaint that there existed, both among the laity and among the secular clergy, a feeling strongly adverse to the monastic life ; and he related, with horror, that the Bishop of Lichfield had not only a wife but children, and made no attempt to conceal his iniquity. The Pope's legates excommunicated this incontinent Englishman, who was at last persuaded to end his days in a monastery. Thus the Church took away with one hand while it gave with the other, and added a new element of hostility between conquerors and conquered.

It was not, perhaps, only a coincidence that the Conquest was effected at a very critical period in the history of the Church. The time at which it is commonly said that England became feudal was the time at which the Church attempted to make all earthly kings the feudal vassals of the Pope. It was not without ulterior designs that Alexander sent to William the consecrated banner which encouraged the French

Feudalism and the Church.

adventurers on the field near Hastings. The change which the papal court hoped to effect in the tenure of thrones was far greater than any effected by the Conqueror in the tenure of lands. The churls were dependents on military chiefs before the Norman set foot on the soil; they would afterwards have found difficulty in showing any real difference in their condition. The new superiors spoke a strange tongue and perhaps called their domains by a strange name; but the manor had long existed, in fact if not in word, and its lord continued to be called lord in the vernacular speech whatever the title which he had adopted himself. It will hereafter be seen that the traditions of the earlier time were handed down to reigns long subsequent to the Conquest, and account for much of the lawlessness which prevailed. It is, therefore, unnecessary to discuss the effects of that great revolution upon the theoretical position either of the land-holder or of his subordinates. Regarded from another point of view, the feudalism introduced by the Conqueror differed from the feudalism previously existing in England by its superior organisation and completeness. This had a beneficial effect, in a manner which will be explained in another page, but not simply because it was feudalism. So far as the mere relation of inferior tenant to superior lord is concerned, the effort made at the same time by the Church to usurp the supreme power is of more importance in the History of Crime and of its punishments.

Gregory VII., who succeeded Alexander as Pope, assumed over the Conqueror, as over other monarchs, the authority of a superior lord. He perceived that the organisation of the feudal system must inevitably thwart the ambition of his order

Separation of ecclesiastical and secular jurisdictions.

unless the Church could adapt that very organisation to her own purposes. Bishops and abbots already did homage, and swore fealty to kings, before they could enjoy their lands ; but if kings could have been brought to swear fealty to the Pope the relative positions of Church and State would have been reversed, and there would have been but a single ruler, at once spiritual and temporal, of Christendom. William, like all but the very weakest of his successors, firmly resisted the attempted encroachment, and declined to recognise the Pope as his superior lord, on the ground not only that he had never promised any such submission, but also that none of his predecessors had sworn fealty to the predecessors of Gregory. Though, however, the Court of Rome did not attain complete success, it did, even in the reign of the Conqueror, make a great advance towards the end which it had in view. The ecclesiastical jurisdiction was at this time formally divided from the civil by charter. The line of demarcation, it is true, was never very clearly defined ; but the mere fact that courts Christian were thus established was regarded by the ambitious clergy as a proof of growing power and independence, and gave a sort of colour to the appeals, and other recognitions of Roman authority, which for many generations embarrassed our kings. Closely connected, too, with this distinction of courts spiritual from courts secular was the strange feature in our criminal jurisprudence, subsequently known as Benefit of Clergy.

The exemption, however, of ecclesiastics from secular jurisdiction, never quite complete in England, had not
Growth of its origin in the reign of the Conqueror. His
the Privilege
of Clergy. regulations had for their object the discrimination of offences, and the increase of ecclesiastical authority

over offenders of a particular kind. But it had long been usual for men in orders, when accused of any crime, to assert the right of clearing themselves in a manner different from that prescribed for laymen ; and the priest, when reduced to the necessity of escaping by compurgation, had fellow-priests for his fellow-swearers. Thus much was firmly established when the Danes were masters of England, and probably as soon as Christianity was itself firmly established in the country. The ancient immunity developed into benefit of clergy, as the barbarous customs which preceded the Conquest developed or were changed into legal processes ; and there can be little doubt that the extension of clerical power about this time gave new strength to the privileges which the clergy had previously enjoyed. In this way an anomaly, which had sprung up in the rudest times, gained force enough to survive through ages of a very different complexion, and expired almost recently when everything was changed except itself.

Among the more direct consequences, not of the feudal system, but of the Conquest itself, was the erection of fortresses in every part of England. The Normans — superior to the subject race in mechanical knowledge as in military skill — naturally protected themselves by strongholds, which would be impregnable in the eyes of any native chief, while no native chief would have so secure a place of refuge in case of need. These castles exceeded, both in magnitude and in solidity of construction, all similar buildings with which that generation of Englishmen was acquainted. They had, as was intended, the effect of overawing the rebellious spirits of the neighbourhood in which they were planted ; they had also other effects, not

Religious and Military ferment throughout Europe.

perhaps foreseen, but of considerable importance in the history of our manners and customs.   If they exalted the baron they also depressed the burgher ; if they gave strength to that military discipline which is in some degree a check upon criminals they also weakened those forces to which towns give nourishment, and which have a far wider and more important operation upon crime by diminishing the tendency to commit it.   Military ardour received a new impulse from the success of the Norman invasion and of the policy by which its results were rendered permanent.   At the same time the flame was fanned by the feudal aspirations of the Church, eager that all Christian kings should rank as captains fighting under her banner.   There was nothing of which men could speak or think but wars and rumours of wars, from the Irish Sea to the walls of Jerusalem.   Not only Britain but the whole of Europe was in a state of change, from which it would have been impossible for the wisest to predict the issue.   It is, indeed, at first sight, a marvel that England escaped as soon, and on as easy terms as she did, from the fires that blazed upon and around her ; and, before describing the many long centuries of misery which the circumstances of the Norman invasion and the antecedent causes rendered inevitable, it is necessary to dwell a little more in detail upon the advantages directly attending the Conquest.

Even in the reign of the Conqueror himself it is possible to discern the beginnings of order, of system, of unification in matters of finance, and as a neces-sary consequence in matters of law.   Before this time it does not appear that there was any central authority which could demand an account in writing from subordinates at a distance.   Domesday

Policy of the Conqueror ; Domesday-Book.

Book is at any rate the earliest of the returns to writs
issuing from the king or his court in England. The idea
of making this compilation has of course been attributed
to Alfred just as the absence of thieves and the safety of
gold and silver hung upon hedge-rows have been attributed to his reign in works written for children, or
chronicles forged by monks. But the conception of one
England held in a firm grasp under a single king was
hardly possible to Alfred—much less a scheme, such as
that which was carried into execution by the Conqueror,
for showing the value and tenure of all the lands in the
country.

In the plan according to which Domesday was put
together lies the nucleus of the plan according to which
justice was administered in subsequent reigns. The King's
Local functionaries and local testimony were Court; the
Exchequer;
subordinated to that higher power which, if not Fines for
Crimes.
in this reign, was subsequently known as the King's
Court. As the first of the Public Records relates chiefly
to finance, though it incidentally illustrates various other
matters, so the second (if mere charters be excepted)
belongs to that department of the original King's Court,
which was soon afterwards called the Exchequer. This
roll which was written at the end of the reign of Henry I.
is hardly less precious than Domesday itself, as showing
the continuance and progress of the policy by which an
attempt was made to consolidate the kingdom and to give
it what it had never possessed before the Conquest—
uniformity in its fiscal system, in its laws, and in the
method of administering them. The revenue was then
to a considerable extent dependent upon the fines paid
by hundreds, for offences committed within their limits, as
well as by individuals. The criminal jurisdictions which

were not private had therefore an intimate connexion with
that branch of the central authority which had to deal
with receipt and expenditure.   In the Great Roll, as it
was called, the accounts of the sheriffs of the various counties were entered, and, among them, the profits to the
Crown from legal proceedings.   From the time of Henry
II. downwards, the Great Rolls were made up year by
year and preserved in the Exchequer.   Before this time
only the one Great Roll of the thirty-first year of Henry I.
exists.   But whether this is or is not the first of a once
continuous series, it is, with its successors, a great monument of the new notions of order and responsibility for
which we are indebted to the Norman dynasty.

In this Roll, too, are some indications of the system
of eyres or circuits definitely established in the reign of
First indi- Henry II.   It is apparent that the old custom
cations of still survived, and that the local magnates were
the Eyre or
Circuit. judges in their own districts not only in the
ancient shire-moots but also in the courts introduced by
the Norman kings.   Yet it is also apparent that in the
latter they had the assistance of men possessing some
little pretensions to legal training.   One at least of those
who hold the pleas travels over no less than twelve
counties.   The names of others appear in as many as six
counties ; and though in some cases it is not difficult to
perceive that the possession of land has conferred the
judicial qualification, the beginnings of a most salutary
change are sufficiently manifest.   National life, national
organisation existed as yet only in idea ; they cannot be
brought into existence by an edict ; the earliest efforts to
foster them must of necessity be only rude experiments.
But the first crude conception of a plan with those results
for its object marks the starting-point of a new era.   The

unity of the realm is the leading principle in the scheme of the Conqueror and of Henry the worthiest of his sons ; and the principle is not restricted to the barren regions of abstract speculation, but displays itself in such action as was possible to the limited intelligence of the period.

It is difficult, under the trammels of our modern language, and in the midst of our modern civilisation, to describe the difference between the successive _{Attempts to} stages of mediæval society. That which is but _{effect improve-ments continu-} an incipient glimmer through the darkness, if it _{ally thwarted.} is not passed over in silence, is apt from the force of contrast to appear as a glare of strong light. The promise of improvement which showed itself in the reign of Henry I., was only a promise of improvement upon the disorganisation and barbarism of the age which preceded the Conquest. It was followed by disorganisation and barbarism of a similar character during the civil wars between Stephen and the Empress. It re-appeared under Henry II., but it long remained a promise with little fulfilment, and was thwarted again and again by the persistence of those influences which came into operation upon the fall of the Roman empire.

To deny that Henry I. or his advisers had better ideas of government than any which existed in England under the West Saxon dynasty would be to ignore all _{Good govern-ment in the} the scanty evidences of either period. To sup- _{modern sense} pose that any approach towards good govern- _{impossible.} ment in the modern sense was then possible would be to misapprehend the whole character of the times. Rough distinctions between what was crime and what was not crime, rough punishments, rough and even tyrannical methods of enforcing them throughout the kingdom might be described as the ideal of perfection to which the

best even of the Norman monarchs aspired. William the
Red was a tyrant, unredeemed by any higher aims than
the secure enjoyment of his rough tyranny. Henry I.
was a tyrant hardly less rough, but endowed with a certain
rugged sense of justice. He would not have hacked and
chopped the limbs of his subjects for mere sport; but
still less would he have been deterred by any sense of
pity from hacking and chopping any low-born transgressor of the law.

Crimes in those days, and for many a generation
afterwards, were committed wholesale. When anarchy
Henry I. and was not superior to monarchy, punishments
the Coiners. were necessarily wholesale also, and brutal to
boot. Apart from mere crimes of violence which were so
common and so essential a characteristic of the age that
no attempt can be made to estimate their number, the
offence which comes into greatest prominence is that
of false coining. So imperfect was every rude attempt
at commerce that, even in the reign of the Conqueror,
live stock might legally be offered in payment instead
of money. Before the reign of Henry I. the coinage
had been so little developed that the silver denarius or
penny was commonly broken into halves or fourths
when the sum due involved fractions of the whole
coin; and this, it should be remembered, was at a time
when the purchasing power of the piece of silver must
have been far in excess of that possessed by our modern
shilling. Moneyers were, as they had been before the
Conquest, numerous, but their art had so fallen into decay with the Roman Empire that money was scarce.
The population, not familiar with the current coinage as
we are, were easily deceived by spurious metal or light
weight. Henry I. attempted to provide a remedy for

some of these evils by coining round half-pence and by
increasing the severity of the laws relating to the mint.
Under the kings of the West Saxon dynasty the loss of
the right hand had been the common sentence against
the coiners of false money who appear to have been
generally the authorised moneyers of the various towns.
Henry detected the same class offending in the same
manner and, without introducing any cruelty unknown to
the ancient constitution, applied to their transgression a
penalty formerly restricted to offences of a different nature.
The chief moneyers throughout the whole of England
were convicted of making pence in which there was base
metal illegally alloyed with the silver. By the king's
command they were all brought to Winchester, and there
suffered in one day the loss of their right hands and of
their manhood.

The stern and pitiless rule, of which this punishment is
a fair example was probably the best which it was possible
either for king or for subjects to conceive in Anarchy dur-
England at the beginning of the twelfth ing Stephen's reign; private
century. The choice lay between that and mints.
anarchy in a greater or less degree, with the not
uncommon accompaniment of a civil war. The reign
of Henry I. presents a somewhat greater contrast to
that of his successor than it would have presented had
Stephen possessed a better title to the throne. But the
dispute concerning the succession gave no more than free
play to the pent-up brutality of all classes, which centuries
of gradual progress alone could soften. From the time
when the Romans abandoned the island, there had never
been internal peace of any long duration ; lawlessness, if
partially hidden for a few years, was always ready to
burst forth when any temporary restraint was in the least

degree weakened. The very claim of Stephen was, in itself, an indication that government according to established law, on the one hand, and obedience to established law, on the other, were not the recognised principles of action. Even the order of inheritance had not yet been settled : and when the son of the Conqueror's daughter asserted his title, the daughter of the Conqueror's son could prove her title preferable only by a resort to arms. The question which had been undecided before the Conquest—whether a brother should inherit in preference to a son—was undecided still ; and the more complicated question which arose when Matilda and Stephen asserted each a right to succeed could be set at rest in only one way.

The disruption of the kingdom, which was the consequence of the inevitable civil war, was rendered more disastrous by the castle-building tastes of the Norman knights. Neither claimant of the crown was strong enough to refuse a licence to fortify if asked, or perhaps even to insist upon the right of granting it. Every noble who had the means built a castle; every holder of a castle was a petty sovereign ; each of these petty sovereigns proved himself a tyrant. Bishops and counts and barons usurped the royal authority ; each of them set up a mint of his own. Thus in a few years all the good effected under Henry I. was turned to evil. The punishment inflicted on the false moneyers lost all its terrors when every local magnate became a false moneyer for his own purposes. The improvements in the law, of which there was fair promise in the first of the Great Rolls, were checked, and for the time, almost forgotten when the kingdom was divided against itself and there was no central authority to dictate harmony in the administration. Records, without which justice is a mockery, ceased to be written, or were destroyed; the king's court sat no longer; men forgot even to solemnise the principal festivals. The chiefs among the clergy and laity alike forswore themselves again and again, as their interests inclined them, and carried their followers from side to side as opportunity offered. Government, indeed, no longer existed, and there was no security for life or property but the will of a capricious lord, or the mercy of a merciless man at arms.

Such anarchy as this, continued partly from the love of independence, which was the heritage of lords and barons both of English and of Norman blood, had almost its only antidote in the policy which had become traditional in the family of the Conqueror. The unification of the kingdom, by making the central authority visible throughout its length and breadth, was an object of which the monarchs given to us by France never lost sight; and, though they may have had selfish ends in view, the effect upon the laws was in the end none the less beneficial. When the articles of peace were drawn up between Stephen and Matilda's son Henry, both contracting parties were equally anxious to secure effectually the interests of the crown, which were at that time almost identical with the interests of the people. Unless the sense of the treaty has been very much perverted by the mediæval chroniclers, it might have been taken as the expression of a most earnest desire on both sides to save the country from bloodshed, oppression, extortion, and injustice of every kind. Even the popular superstitions were treated with deference, and a prophecy said to have been uttered by Merlin, the enchanter, was carefully explained, in such a way that

Unification of the kingdom the traditional policy of the Conqueror's family.

no disaster might be apprehended from its supposed fulfilment in the compromise between Stephen and Henry.
Good laws, prosperity, and peace within the realm, if not
without, were to follow this happy agreement. In the
expression of all these good intentions there was some
sincerity, but there was also a strong desire that loss of
power by the Conqueror's family should not be the consequence of the family quarrel. Much was promised to
the classes which suffered most when most the great
barons could overawe the crown; but the crown had every
prospect of being more blessed in giving than the subjects
in receiving.

The class which in the end profited most by the
troubles of Stephen's reign was the clergy. The interests
of ecclesiastics as feudal nobles were, in some
This policy was distaste- respects, identical with those of the barons : but
ful to the clergy. the clergy also constituted a party with interests
of its own. As always happens when there are many
parties in the state, that which holds together most firmly
is best able to carry its point by taking advantage of
weaknesses in the others. Thus, though in grasping at
privileges for themselves, the clergy sometimes incidentally secured a new liberty for the people, it was impossible
for them to look with favour on the policy by which the
Norman kings wished to consolidate the kingdom. Their
hostility to it was less apparent on the surface than that
of the lay nobles, but was at bottom even more dangerous.
That uniformity in the administration of the law which
was beginning to be regarded as the outward and visible
sign of the royal authority was never the end and aim of
a spiritual lord, even though he might hold the office of
Chief Justiciary. While the object of the sovereign was
always unity, the object of the bishops was duality.

When they acted most faithfully as ministers, they were still more faithful to their order; and, for that reason, when justice became something more than a mere name, it was clogged with the strange encumbrance called Benefit of Clergy.

The power acquired and exercised by the clergy during the troubled reign of Stephen led almost inevitably to quarrels between the King and the Church. Most conspicuous, from the crime which followed it, was the quarrel between Henry II. and Thomas à Becket. The clerical dignitaries were eager to uphold their dignity; the royal authority was not yet secure. The law was so unsettled that insolence on one side or tyranny on the other might be speciously represented as a desire to do right. Henry had not been many years on the throne when an Archbishop of Canterbury of his own selection opened the campaign against him on behalf of the Church. The story is differently told by different narrators, according to their prejudices or their different sources of information. There is, however, no doubt that Becket wished to carry out one leading idea, which it is easy to discern in the most contradictory accounts. Wherever the Church was concerned, or ecclesiastics asserted that it was concerned, in respect either of property claimed or of persons accused, there, according to his view, the ecclesiastical courts alone had jurisdiction.

The quarrel of Becket with Henry II.; the rival jurisdictions.

The cases first brought into dispute were apparently certain ecclesiastical claims to land and advowsons; but the chronology of the chroniclers is somewhat confused, and as the records of the period do not supply what is wanting, it is vain to look for a perfectly accurate version. It may suffice, however, to state that in these matters the archbishop asserted a final right of appeal to Rome as well as the primary jurisdiction of the ecclesiastical courts in England, and that the king denied one no less than the other.

About the same time a similar battle was fought on another field. Some members of the ecclesiastical body had been accused of various offences, including rape and murder. A canon, too, had spoken ill of the king's Justiciary. Sentence of degradation had been passed in courts Christian, but, as the king believed, no sentence proportionate to the crimes. He therefore wished that clerical criminals should be punished by secular judgment. But this, the archbishop maintained, would be contrary alike to precedent and to the canon law. The king and his party maintained that, whether contrary to the canon law or not, it was in accordance with precedent. The royalists probably had in their minds the fact that the Church had not enjoyed the advantage of an actual division of jurisdiction before the Conquest, nor, perhaps, during part of the reign of Henry I. The clergy could have pointed, with no less justice, to the custom according to which the clearance of accused persons belonging to their order had long been effected by compurgation, and according to which, in the most ancient times, the compurgators were not laymen. Here, as elsewhere, the law was in a state of transition, or, to speak more correctly, principles of law were but just coming into existence. It was impossible to give clear definitions when the first rude attempts were being made to evolve order out of a chaos: and had consciences been more tender than they were in that age, either the king or the archbishop might safely have declared that if they erred they erred in ignorance.

The ill-feeling engendered between the king and the archbishop increased from day to day, and could not be allayed by any apparent reconciliation. As in many similar cases, the most terrible effects were in the end brought about by the most trivial causes acting upon minds already irritated and ready to disregard all the dictates of reason. Henry II., sensible of the insecurity of all order in his realm, determined to associate his eldest son with him in the sovereignty. The younger Henry was solemnly crowned, but not by Becket, who, as Archbishop of Canterbury, claimed the right to officiate. In consequence of this slight the primate obtained from the Pope letters of excommunication against certain bishops who had been present at the ceremony. In spite of an apparent renewal of friendship, this last act seems to have rankled more deeply in the king's breast than all the archbishop's previous arrogance. He allowed, in a moment of anger, certain expressions to escape him, which were construed by some members of his household into a desire that Becket should no longer exist to trouble him. They quitted the king's court in Normandy, sailed by stealth for England, met at Saltwood, the seat of one of Becket's greatest enemies, and there deliberately matured their designs.

It was but a few days after Christmas Day when four knights unceremoniously entered the primate's chamber, and seated themselves unbidden in his presence. They had, they said, a very simple request to make—absolution for the excommunicated prelates. Becket raised some technical objection—and it probably was not in his power to do that which was asked precisely as the knights asked it. They were retiring in a manner which caused him to enquire whether they intended to threaten him in his own house, and for answer they said only that they would do more than threaten.   The fact, however, that they went out seems to indicate that they had entertained some hope of gaining their request by intimidation, and that they had not yet finally decided upon the deed which followed.

In those days few men had faint hearts for crime.   To consult in hot blood after such a refusal as they had met, and with their recollection of the king's words in their minds, was to take the worst resolve.   They soon returned, but found that the primate was now in the Church, at vespers.   They gave him his choice—either to absolve the bishops or to die.   His answer did not satisfy them, and they laid hands upon him to drag him out of the Church.   He clung with all his strength to a pillar, and it became difficult to remove him without bloodshed.   To one who was more persistent than the rest he applied the epithet ' Pimp.'   This was the signal for a blow.   His head was injured, though an attendant suffered in attempting to save him.   The knights struck him again and again on the crown till it was severed and he fell, a corpse, before the altar.   One of their ruffian attendants who, it is said, had taken orders, gloated over the deed in a manner which was only too consonant with the tone of the age, and was permitted by these noble companions of the king to pick out the brains of the victim with his sword, and to spread them, in grim triumph, over the pavement of the cathedral.

With the action of the king and of the Pope in consequence of this atrocious deed the present history has

Plans of legal
improvement
under Henry
II.

no concern.   The crime itself has been described as an apt illustration of the acts which were possible in those times, and of which the

'chivalry' of England was capable. It will be seen that
the knights or 'chivalers' of later times were little more
merciful, little more refined. The only marvel is that in
the reign of Henry II. there were any intellects sufficiently advanced to perceive the need of great reforms,
and to design, however roughly, plans of legal improvement. In this respect the advantages of the Norman
Conquest were beginning to show themselves; and
had Henry's immediate successors possessed his genius,
or been fortunate enough to discover advisers as
skilful as his, they might, perhaps, have hastened by a
little—by a very little—the progress of English civilisation. The quarrels with the archbishop and with the
Pope do not appear to have had the effect of retarding
the legislation upon which the king had resolved; and he
persevered consistently in the course which he had
marked out for himself as most likely to lead to the complete consolidation of his kingdom. It was not in his
power to see the whole of the obstacles in his way; nor
could men in those days discover the gradual operation
of causes through long periods of time. To devise a
present remedy for a present evil was the most that could
be expected of the most enlightened lawyers ; it was not
given to them to discern the causes of present evils in
past ages of brutality, or to attempt a mitigation of crime
by a mitigation of ferocity in the law. Nothing that
the king's advisers could have contrived would have
effected a great and immediate change in the manners
and moral tone of the people ; but all that it was possible
for men to do in such an age they did.

Exactly a century after the battle near Hastings, a
judicial system was promulgated in the 'Assise of Clarendon.' In this document occurs the first mention of

a body which, so far as criminal matters are concerned, can be directly compared with the juries of modern times. Origin of the This and the Laws of the Conqueror afford Grand Jury. the connecting links between the fellow-swearers of old and the jurors of to-day. According to the Assise, enquiry was to be made respecting murder, robbery, and theft, by means of the oaths of twelve lawful (free and not outlawed) men of every hundred, and four lawful men of every vill, in every county in the realm. Anyone whom they charged before the Justices or before the Sheriffs, either as principal or as accessary, was to be apprehended and tried by the ordeal of water. The nearest approach to this scheme which can be discovered in any reign before the Conquest is to be found in the ' Laws of King Ethelred,' which, in the clause now under consideration, certainly refer only to the northern part of the realm. It is there provided that in every wapentake the reeve and the twelve elder or superior thanes shall swear to accuse none who are innocent, and to conceal none who are guilty. But the mention of the reeve is sufficient to prove that the institution, whatever it may have been, was of a more permanent character than a mere jury.

It is, however, by no means improbable that the old custom of the northern wapentake may have contributed one of the elements to the constitution of the jury on which the whole nation has been accustomed to pride itself. A combination of some attributes possessed by the reeve and thanes with some attributes possessed by the fellow-swearers on the side of persons accused or on the side of individual accusers will give, in a rudimentary form, nearly all the characteristics of the grand jury. The fellow-swearers were brought together, as required,

to take oath upon one particular charge. The same reeve
and thanes, on the contrary, 'presented' charges of unlimited number from time to time, and probably during a
whole year at least. If the element of permanence be
taken from them, they are hardly distinguishable from
the ordinary supporters of the prosecution ; if the fellow-
swearers have the element of permanence added to them,
they are hardly distinguishable in function, though they
may differ in rank, from the reeve and thanes. The
latter, too, had every inducement to exculpate natives of
their own hundred, though it was legally their duty to
send suspected persons to trial. They have, therefore,
a resemblance to the swearers on either side. The
modern petty jury is as temporary in its nature as the
ancient band of fellow-swearers. The modern grand
jury is neither so temporary as the ancient band of
fellow-swearers, nor has it, like the reeve and thanes,
any of the permanence of a court. Like the latter, it
presents a number of charges for subsequent trial ;
but, like the former, it dissolves, never to meet again, as
soon as the objects for which it is summoned have been
attained.

The intimate connection of the grand jury, as it
developed itself after the Assise of Clarendon, with the
ancient fellow-swearers and with the reeve and thanes,
may also be inferred from a passage in the Laws of the
Conqueror, which would be absolutely unintelligible if
there were no explanation in the previous and subsequent writings. It is provided that a person accused in
the hundred by four, is to clear himself by the 'hand of
twelve.' Hand upon holy things were the twelve thanes
to place when they swore ; hand upon holy things was
the rule whenever oath was made. As the twelve in the

one case were to swear that they would truly present for
trial those who by common report were criminals, so the
twelve in the other case were to swear that a particular
charge was falsely made against a particular person.
Twelve, it is to be observed, is a number which, before
the Conquest, appears only as an exception, and in the
northern shires.   Immediately after the Conquest it is
the favourite number in the selection of bodies which
have to give a verdict of any kind.   As both Normandy
and the north of England had been conquered by Scandinavian chiefs, it is by no means improbable that some
old Norse or Danish superstition lurks under the modern
preference of the number twelve for a jury.   Twelve and
multiples and fractions of twelve are, of course, treated
with favour in laws of Germanic origin on the continent;
but the number twelve is certainly by no means prominent in our own earlier laws, and as certainly comes
into prominence in the reign of William I.   In the most
important of all matters—the compilation of the laws in
existence under his predecessors, which his new subjects
called the Laws of the Confessor—it was decided by
him and his council that the work should be accomplished by twelve men in each county, sworn to omit
nothing, to add nothing, and to change nothing.

The Assise of Clarendon was recast, and in some
matters extended, ten years later, by the Assise of
Northampton, which supplies another connecting link
between the ancient reeve and thanes mentioned in the
'Laws of King Ethelred,' and the compurgators mentioned in the Laws of the Conqueror.   At Northampton
it was provided that the twelve men of the hundred were
to be, if possible, knights; but that twelve other free and
lawful men would suffice.   The knights correspond most

clearly with the elder or superior thanes ; the other free men are only such as might have been ordinary fellow-swearers to clear a particular person under William I. The reeve and thanes, reappearing as knights, have lost the character of a permanently constituted body; free men of the lower class, who, in the wager of law, might still act as mere fellow-swearers for a particular occasion, are permitted also to participate in the higher functions of those who make a general report upon the crimes of the district.

The change which was gradually effected by the growth of juries receives also some illustration from the later history of compurgation as applied to laymen. The old practice, under a new name, survived, half-hidden, in its original shape, long after its blood-relations had almost ceased to resemble it. The Wager of Law, as it was called after the Conquest, to distinguish it from the Wager of Battle, was not formally abolished by statute till the reign of William IV. This, as is well known, was long a recognised mode of procedure in civil cases though the extent to which it was in use can only be established by reference to unpublished records. Centuries after the Conquest it was the custom in some manors for those who were accused of such petty trespasses as killing a neighbour's sheep or pigs to declare themselves innocent and offer the wager of law. Their exculpation was still, as before, by a certain number of 'hands,' and twelve, in the north at least, reappears as the number most favoured. Such as was provided for the hundred in the Laws of the Conqueror was the rule of law for some manors even after the invention of printing. Common repute in the district was in all cases the nearest ancient approach to the modern testimony of

[side note:] Compurgation and the Wager of Law.

witnesses, and the modern verdicts of juries. Between
the courts of the manor and the courts of the hundred,
there is, indeed, no real distinction, and from the customs
observed in them, there can be little doubt, has been developed the whole system of trial by jury. But both
the grand jury and the petty jury differ alike from the
court of thanes and from the fellow-swearers, and have
assumed features peculiar to themselves of which, in the
case of the petty jury, even the rudiments are hardly
discernible in the features of their ancestors. The wager
of law, buried among the rolls of manor courts is
like those fossil species of animals but recently extinct,
which, as naturalists tell us, show the descent of crea-
tures still before our eyes and point the moral that
modifications of organisation are necessary when the conditions under which we live have themselves become
modified.

The jury-system was, however, during the reign of
Henry II., beginning to develope itself in various direc-

Development
of the jury-
system under
Henry II. ;
the Grand
Assise.

tions. The Grand Assise for the settlement of
disputes respecting land is described by Glanville as a boon accorded by the king to the
people on the advice of the nobles. The lawyer
contrasts it with the duel, for which it was the alternative,
in somewhat extravagant terms of laudation. He draws
a picture of a trial by battle in such a way that it seems
to possess some features more like those of the unre-
formed Court of Chancery than those of the primitive
resort to force. The parties could not appear in person,
but were compelled to send each a champion to maintain
his cause. Before the actual combat was begun there
might be innumerable delays caused by excuses on either
side. The poor man's substance was eaten up while he

was waiting for a decision; and Glanville admits, as an educated man could hardly fail to admit, that the issue was not always in accordance with justice. With a regard for human life which few except himself possessed in that age, he regrets that in this legal encounter one man must either be slain, or bear the name of "recreant;" and to be a craven was to be dead in the eyes of all who could distinguish between manhood and the want of it. Each champion he regards as a single juror sworn to maintain the truth, and insists that the testimony of a greater number must necessarily have greater weight.

In the constitution of the grand assise, as well as in the fact that it was looked upon as a concession, there is an indication that its origin must be traced to native institutions. The old appeal to common repute, the old mention of the shire and of the neighbourhood, even the old family tie are impressed more or less clearly upon the grand assise. Four lawful knights of the county and of the neighbourhood, chosen by the sheriff or, perhaps, by his county court, are to elect twelve other lawful knights of the same neighbourhood, who are to declare upon oath which of the litigants has the better right to the land in dispute. If, perchance, none of those first nominated have any knowledge of the matter, they are to make oath in court to that effect, and others are to be brought in until some are found who are acquainted with the facts. If some have knowledge and others not, those who are ignorant are to be excluded and substitutes are to be summoned until the number of twelve at least is made up. Should some declare for one party, and the rest for the other, more must again be called in until at least twelve are unanimous on one side or the other. All must swear

that they will not knowingly declare what is false or conceal what is true ; and nothing is held to be within their
knowledge for which they have not the evidence of their
own eye-sight, or their own hearing, or the words of their
own fathers, or words which they feel bound to consider
as trustworthy as their own.

Enthusiasm for such legal machinery as this will raise
a smile on the face of a modern lawyer.   The jury or
Partisanship recognitors, though they have the final decision
and Perjuries
of Jurors.   in their hands, are in one sense witnesses, and
in another judges ; but they are also counsel and attorneys
in the cause which they decide.   They practically have
the power to collect evidence outside the court and to
give it effect by their judgment inside.   There is no
check upon them except their oath to tell the truth, and
no check whatever upon those from whom they may have
obtained information.   The jurors themselves, indeed, were
punished, if they were found guilty of perjury or if they
confessed it, by forfeiture of goods, by imprisonment for not
less than a year, and by the infamy of incapacity to make
oath again in any court.   But the prospect of conviction
had little terror for a juryman who had sworn falsely.
The old spirit of partisanship had lost little or none of its
strength, and even Edward I. was unable to eradicate it
though his laws most vigorously denounced it.   The
guild or the neighbours would hang together, and the
danger of conviction would be not for him who had sworn
falsely in concert with his comrades, but for him, if any
such could be found, who had sworn truly but had not
been supported.   The threat, nevertheless, of prosecution
for perjury is an important addition to the institution of
the grand assise—perhaps even more important than the
assise itself.   It recognises far more distinctly than had

previously been recognised, the distinction between truth
and falsehood, and is a step towards breaking down the
superstition that whatever is stated upon oath must
necessarily be accepted as true. This is an advance
towards the later plan of listening to evidence on both
sides and giving a judgment after comparison. But it was
not until the evidence, which the jurors of the grand assise
could acquire for themselves in the district, was brought
into court, and there sifted, and until jurors were forbidden to consider facts within their own previous experience that there existed, even for civil causes, a true jury
in the modern sense.

A connecting link between the jury of the grand
assise and the later jury for the trial of criminals is to be
found in the jury summoned to decide whether Link between
a Christian had died in the crime of usury. This the Grand
Assise and the
offence, it seems, could not yet be made the later jury in
criminal
subject of a direct accusation. But if it was cases.
commonly reported that any one had practised usury
there followed upon his death an inquest to ascertain
whether he had repented and abandoned the practice
during his life.   If not, his goods and chattels were forfeited to the king and his lands to the lord of whom he
held—as in cases of felony.   The question was decided
by twelve lawful men of the neighbourhood, who, like the
twelve knights in the grand assise, made oath concerning the facts of the case, and possessed complete control
over the possible inheritance of the usurer's representatives. Here, as elsewhere, partisanship must have determined the issue; and usury was regarded with such
superstitious horror that all who were suspected of
profiting by it must have left their families almost
destitute of friends.   In this method, however, of trying a

suspected person when his body was in the grave, may, in spite of its injustice and its defects, be discerned a step towards the jury of the coroner and the jury of the criminal court.   The advance was just as great as that made by the grand assise in civil cases, but no greater.   In both there are indications of an attempt to ascertain truth by evidence, but they are so slender that they might pass unnoticed if they were not seen by the light of later history.

The complicated scheme for the selection of the jurors to form the grand assise was, probably, drawn up with the object, long unattainable, of checking the prevalent tendency to swear in favour of persons rather than in accordance with facts. The interposition of the four knights between the sheriff, to whom the king's writ was directed, and the twelve who were to decide the cause, there can be little doubt, was a device to counteract the partiality of the chief administrative officer in the county.   A very similar piece of legal machinery came into operation elsewhere, in the reign of Richard I., or perhaps before.   The twelve jurors of each hundred, who had to make their presentments to the Justices concerning its crimes, according to the Assises of Clarendon and Northampton, were afterwards chosen on a plan obviously imitated from the form of civil procedure which had been extolled by Glanville.   In the first place, there were to be selected, probably by the sheriff, possibly in full county-court, four knights out of the county at large.   These four were to select two lawful knights out of each hundred or wapentake, who were in turn to select ten more knights or lawful freemen, and so to make up the jury of twelve.   Here, perhaps, may be seen another attempt to apply a filter, and a vain hope that partiality

Attempts to counteract the evils of partisanship.

might be left behind in one of the many layers of men through which justice was made to pass.

Conspicuous above all things in these legal reforms, of which the idea belongs to the reign of Henry II., is the growing uniformity of procedure. The parts of the kingdom are brought up to the *Attempts to secure uniformity of procedure.* level attained is by no means high, but all parts of the kingdom are brought up to the same height; and in the application of similar processes to civil and criminal cases is to be discerned the germ of an important principle, which was in the end developed into our modern system of determining matters of fact by evidence given before jurors in court. It is from this period that the growth of trial by jury can be historically traced; it was after this period that were effected the important distinctions between grand jury and petty jury, and between jurors and witnesses. There is, indeed, some temptation to trace the descent of the petty jury from the band of compurgators, and of the grand jury from the reeve and thanes—to find for each only one parent in a single institution; but the legal formalities existing at the end of the twelfth century forbid the acceptance of so simple a pedigree for either. The old customs, indeed, survived the Conquest; but they were barren till French or Italian lawyers and ecclesiastics settled the terms of their union, married them in a fashion previously unknown, and taught their offspring to tread in new paths. The English juries of modern times—a somewhat numerous progeny—are all descended from a common ancestry, and, though their walks in life are different, are all partakers in a family likeness.

The Assises of Clarendon and Northampton, however, are remarkable for other most important articles besides those which relate to the primitive jury. So far as the criminal law is concerned these two documents differ little, except in the greater severity shown in the latter, which was drawn up after the suppression of a troublesome rebellion.

General design of the Assise of Clarendon, the Assise of Northampton, and the Inquest of Sheriffs.

The general scope of both was to provide for the apprehension of criminals, for their safe custody before trial, and for their punishment when found guilty. But the difficulties which impeded the execution of this design are painfully obvious in every detail. In the first place it appears that some of the counties possessed no gaol or prisoner's cage. The deficiency was to be made good at the king's expense, and, if possible, out of the king's wood. It may easily be imagined how much the brigands of the time were impressed by the authority of the law, when they had long been accustomed to roam over whole shires in which they could not be imprisoned by the king's officers. These cages were to be constructed within the king's castles, or fortified towns, and were, probably, designed with a view not less to the prisoner's discomfort than to his safe-keeping. The sheriffs had authority to apprehend suspected persons, and to enter the liberties of those who enjoyed private jurisdictions in order to discharge their duties. But if they attempted to act upon their instructions it was by no means improbable that they would be insulted and violently expelled. The king's writ was thrown in the face of its bearer long afterwards; and a clause in the Assise of Clarendon shows that the privileges of local magnates had been upheld against the royal power long before. The law was good, but to make a law is one thing, to enforce it another; and that which was difficult to the first three Edwards must have been impossible to the first three Henries. The mode of trial was to be what it had been before the Conquest, with the difference that compurgation was no longer permitted in those cases which were of sufficient importance to be brought before the Justices in Eyre. Compurgation, indeed, would have been inconsistent with the action of the twelve men who presented the accused for trial, and who would, under the ancient system, have been fellow-swearers, either on the side of the accuser or on the side of the accused. Ordeal, therefore, stood to the twelve men of the hundred in the relation in which the petty jury afterwards stood to the grand jury. It finally decided the facts of the case. He whose innocence was denied by the hot water, in a case of murder, robbery, arson, or offence against the coinage, lost a foot, and after the Assise of Northampton, a hand in addition. He was also compelled to abjure the realm; and, by a strange provision, even those who were acquitted by the ordeal were also banished, if they were of ill fame. This is, perhaps, another faint indication of an attempt to weigh evidence, and to act upon it.

The ancient system of Peace-Pledge was fully recognised in these Assises. The sheriffs were directed also to register the names of all those who fled from their own counties so that they might be sought throughout the whole realm. As in the age before the Conquest, no stranger was to remain more than one night in a town, unless his host would be responsible for him. Finally, all the inhabitants of England were strictly forbidden to give either lodging or sustenance to any unfortunate person who had been branded on the forehead as a heretic; and any house which had been polluted by the presence of one of the renegades was to be carried beyond the walls and burnt. In those cruel times, perhaps, the last inhuman clauses were but a natural corollary of the early institutions which had survived the change of dynasty.

Conspicuous above all other provisions in these laws is that Norman policy of unification which was dear to all the Conqueror's successors. The subordination of the sheriffs, in their judicial capacity, to the higher judicial authority, is made apparent in many of the articles. In one, the duties of the sheriffs upon receipt of a summons from the travelling justices, are expressly regulated, and it is fully apparent that the intention was to reduce the local potentates from the position of independent judges to that of officers carrying the law into execution under the direction of the King's Court, as represented in the Eyres. In the interval between the time when the Assise of Clarendon was drawn up, and the time when it was confirmed and extended by the Assise of Northampton, a severe blow was dealt against the territorial magnates by means of an 'Inquest of Sheriffs.' In the majority of the counties new sheriffs were appointed, and this was no slight change at a time when their office did not ordinarily terminate with the year. Those who were displaced, and all who had held the shrievalty, since the king's last voyage to Normandy, had to find sureties for their appearance in the King's Court to answer for their past conduct. The 'Inquest' also affected those barons who administered justice either in their own franchises or in the royal demesne, and was, without doubt, intended to serve the double purpose of strengthening the royal power, and of allaying the bitter complaints which were now, and for many centuries afterwards, raised against all the ministers of the law. The contemporary authors from whom it is possible to gain some knowledge of the actual state of society, show only too clearly, that the general dissatisfaction was by no means ill-founded, and that if the Inquest of Sheriffs did not greatly improve the moral tone of the kingdom, it was, at least, justified, and demanded by the existence of wide-spread corruption.

The reign of Henry II. is a historical stand-point from which the past and the future may be conveniently surveyed and compared.   The local and private jurisdictions which had grown up after the fall of the Roman empire were yielding slowly and sullenly to the institutions which men who had studied the Roman civil law believed to be better alike for king and people.   It was not, indeed, because a copy of Justinian's Pandects had been discovered at Amalfi in 1130, that new ideas had travelled to England, and that Oxford had begun to instruct her pupils in the legal lore of a civilised people.   The Roman traditions had never been entirely lost on the continent, and they could not fail to produce their effect upon our island when the Norman rule brought it under the influence of French lawyers and Italian ecclesiastics.   The civil law, however, was not yet applied in practice, for it could not easily be harmonised with the feudal tenure of land, or with the native methods of trying and punishing criminals ; and commercial contracts had not yet assumed sufficient importance to demand a special mode of procedure. But it was no small gain to the country when a school of law was established, and when men trained by the study of the Roman jurist began to deal with the hideous conglomeration of inconsistencies, which, under the name of local customs, had survived the Norman Conquest.

Improved legal education.

The subject people, always petitioning for the Laws of the Confessor, were not unnaturally opposed to any innovation. They understood perfectly well that a visit of the Justices was attended by fines which were, in many cases, unjust, and were engines of extortion; they could not understand that out of the plans put in operation by Henry II. there would one day be developed a system of justice under which impartiality would be a matter of course, and under which not a Judge upon the Bench could even be suspected of corruption. To them a new tribunal seemed only a new torment; the reason was not that the new tribunal was not better than the old, but that the old had been so bad as to appear worse than none. The robbers and outlaws, a very numerous class, were averse to any institutions which might render robbery more difficult; the barons, accustomed to hold little king's courts of their own, had no wish to see their power swallowed up by the greater King's Court at Westminster, which was putting forth suckers in all directions; the under-tenants, not too well content with the exactions of their superior lords, perceived in the eyres only a device for making them subject to two masters instead of one— for flaying them after they had already been shorn. In those days it does not seem to have occurred to any one that he could individually be the better for law and order firmly established throughout the country. The old legal formula by which jurisdiction was conferred, was incomplete without the word 'tol'; and with toll the idea of jurisdiction had become inseparably associated. To be left to himself, to take what he could, and to hold what he had, as best he might, by his own strong arm, or by the aid of his friends, was still the Englishman's ideal of life.

General aversion to changes in the law.

For the past he had all the stolid reverence of ignorance ;
for any attempted change he had no feeling except suspicion ; for reforms designed by a foreign dynasty he had
but one epithet, 'outlandish' ; and that was sufficient to
stamp them as prejudicial to his interests.   The re-introduction of civilisation was thus beset with almost
insuperable difficulties.   The best devised measures, if
they effected a benefit in one direction, could not fail to
do harm in another.   The law-giving class, while improving its own intellect, was rousing the evil passions of those
whom it was attempting to govern.   Those for whom a
blessing was intended obstinately regarded the blessing
as a curse.   The barbarism of the past was considered an
inheritance to be carefully preserved ; and he who
attempted to remove it seemed, in the eyes of the English,
to be a Jacob attempting to deprive them of their birthright.

It is only the persistence of this habit of thought,
fostered by almost ineradicable traditions, which can
explain the anomalies of later times.   It was not Opposition to
simply because Henry III. was a feeble king the eyres.
that he had to limit the visits of the travelling justices for
the trial of criminals to one in seven years ; it is easy
enough to perceive that they were equally unpopular in
the time of his grandfather Henry II., whose force of
character was insufficient even to carry out the eyres as
intended after the Assise of Northampton.   The Great
Rolls of the Exchequer, if studied with a little patience,
show how very different were these early eyres from our
modern circuits, and how feeble the institution was in its
early growth.   An eyre, indeed, followed immediately
upon the legislative decisions of Northampton, when it
may be assumed that the king's appetite for judicial

reform was strongest. But even at this favourable
stage, it was two years before the justices travelled the
country again with full powers; and at the end of the
reign of Henry II., the interval between eyre and eyre
had already become nearly, if not quite, three years. If
in the next two reigns the judicial visitations for holding
pleas of land became more frequent, judicial visitations
for investigating crime did not become more popular.
Thus local obstructiveness held its ground against central
authority, until it gained its great, though temporary,
victory over the King's Justices, and excluded them from
every county for seven years at a time.

The meaning of this persistent hostility to the
authority of the crown in the higher criminal jurisdiction
Meaning and was that the perpetration of crime in any degree
effect of this
hostility. was not, according to the popular opinion of the
time, an evil so much to be dreaded as the extortion of a
judge. Its effect was that the greater the crime, the
greater was the probability of the criminal's escape.
Minor offences, such as larceny, fell under the cognisance
of the Sheriff, whose courts were held at reasonable intervals throughout the year. Cases of homicide, and all
other Pleas of the Crown were reserved for the king's
Justices, the time of whose circuits was uncertain, and
commonly so remote as to have little terror for the evil-
doer. But it must be remembered that these rare visits
of Justices trained in the king's court were instituted as a
remedy for still greater laxity in the administration of the
law, and that if the murderer commonly escaped after the
Assise of Northampton, he had still more commonly
escaped before. From the fact that an eyre set in motion
not more than once in two years was regarded, on the one
hand, as a powerful engine for the repression of crime, and,

on the other, as an un-English attack upon the liberty of the subject, may be inferred the state of society which the king or his advisers wished to supersede ; and the inference will be strictly in accordance with the sketch which an attempt was made to draw in the first chapter of this history. It will hereafter be seen that subsequent legislation and subsequent records point to precisely the same conclusion, and that the barbarism introduced by the Teutonic invaders of the Roman empire possessed a vitality which only the operation of antagonistic causes through many generations could thoroughly soften.

In the meantime, the retarding effect of that subjection to a foreigner, which must have been felt with bitterness during the reign of Henry II., and long after- Position of wards, should not be forgotten. It is true that the Englishry in the rural an eminent official of the Exchequer is said to districts. have compiled a work concerning that department, from one passage of which it might be supposed that the distinction between English subject and French ruler had disappeared at the end of the reign of Henry II., except among the rustics of the lowest grade. But the author of this treatise—whose name, and the time of whose existence are only matters of inference—must, if he really lived at the period assigned to him, have been extraordinarily ignorant of the legal proceedings and of the records with which he should have been familiar. Nothing is more apparent in the Great Rolls of the Exchequer and in the records of the King's Court than the rigorous observance of that distinction between Englishman and Frenchman which had been sternly drawn in the laws of the Conqueror. The hundred has still to pay for the murder of a Frenchman, is still excused when the person murdered is an Englishman, still

bears the humiliation conveyed in the principle that
whoever cannot be shown to be English shall be considered in the eye of the law as worthy as though he
could be shown to be French.   Nor has the Conqueror's
law degenerated into a mere form, according to which the
hundred is liable for the violent deaths of those who
cannot be identified, or for the omission of the hue and
cry.   The Englishry is, like the Jewry, still a term of
contempt; the life of the Englishman is of less value
than the life of a Jew.   Not only has the hundred to
make its ' presentment of Englishry,' when the name of
the Englishman secretly slain is known, not only is it
fined when the parentage of the dead is unknown, or for
concealing the death altogether, but sometimes it is
detected in falsifying the facts, and incurs an additional
penalty for declaring that a murdered Frenchman was an
Englishman.   The law-book compiled by Bracton in the
reign of Henry III. shows that the old institution was
still in force, and that the first point for the hundred to
establish in a case of murder—or slaying without witnesses
—was, whether the person murdered was English or
not.   Though the reign of Edward I. was one conspicuous above all others for legal reforms and for improvements which affected the whole legal system, the
presentment of Englishry still survived, and was not
abolished till it had indeed grown out of date in the reign
of Edward III.—a full century and a half after the time
now under consideration.   To a courtier, indeed, who
knew that the royal blood of England was already compounded of the blood of the West Saxon kings, and the
blood of the Norman dukes, it may have seemed that the
difference between conqueror and conquered was effaced ;
it was, no doubt a common topic of conversation that if

descendants of those who had held land under Edward
the Confessor held the same land under Henry II., the
intermediate generations had been prudent in their
marriages ; and it was obvious that English birth was no
longer an insuperable obstacle to promotion in the
Church. But the recognition of no class except the king,
the clergy, and the great landholders on the one hand,
and the serfs on the other, is, in itself, an indication of the
subjection in which the bulk of the English people was
held. The division of classes was, perhaps, still as nearly
as possible what it had been before the Conquest, but the
serf had exchanged a master speaking his own language
for one who was very commonly ignorant of it. The
small freeholders had certain rights according to law, but,
when viewed from so great a height as the Exchequer,
they seemed indistinguishable in the great mass of
English humanity, to which the official gave the common
name of villeins.

The position of the rural population naturally suggests
an inquiry concerning the condition of the towns during
the first century after the Conquest. As, how- The towns
ever, they had not yet come into marked not yet able
                                              to exert their
prominence it will be convenient to defer the influence for
                                              good.
consideration of their growth, and of their influence upon
crime, to another chapter. In this place it is only necessary to remark that they were beginning to receive
charters, which seem to have had two distinct effects —
one good the other evil. It was, in the end, most beneficial to the country that they acquired power, and exercised their power in a direction opposed to the barbarism
which had long retarded their increase. But the early
mode of acquisition was, in accordance with the prejudices
of the time, adverse to those improvements which the

king's advisers wished to introduce into the administration of justice. The ancient practice of compurgation had no place in the Assise of Clarendon; and the intention obviously was to abolish it throughout the realm, and to give uniformity to the criminal mode of procedure in every county. One of the privileges, however, which the towns-men were most anxious to secure, and most successful in securing, was that of independent jurisdiction, or, as it was commonly expressed in their own charters, that they should not be compelled to plead outside. It is thus apparent that the dread of the judge, and of his extortions, was as deeply-seated in the towns as in the country—that the word 'justice' had become a by-word for that which all were anxious to avoid. Thus while the towns-men were, unconsciously perhaps, laying the foundations of a far higher civilisation, they were, unconsciously also, propping up those remains of barbarous customs which were the greatest obstacles to progress of every kind. They were supporting the principles of private jurisdiction and compurgation—the one the great obstacle to the existence of a strong and united England—the other the very essence of opposition to that free and fair inquiry, without which all intellectual advancement is impossible. Yet for this mistake, which they could not have avoided, they made at last a splendid compensation, by converting their petty individual independence into national liberty, and the barbarism which had been forced on them by successive conquerors into widespread order, security, and refinement.

The purpose, however, of the legislation which has been described, and the task which remained to be per-

General state of society. formed in the future, cannot be fully understood without the aid of a more comprehensive sketch

of the general state of society than has yet been given. The actual amount of crime, and its proportion to the population, at the end of the twelfth century, cannot indeed be stated with any accuracy, but materials are not wanting for a description of the manners and customs, and of the general tone of thought, which prevailed in England.

The universal want of respect for human life is shown in all the chronicles of the period. In London, where Jews were frequently massacred by hundreds, the streets were, after sunset, given up to rapine and murder. That which would now be called crime became the favourite pastime of the principal citizens, who would sally forth by night, in bands of a hundred or more, for an attack upon the houses of their neighbours. They killed, without mercy, every man who came in their way, and vied with each other in brutality. On one occasion a band of these distinguished murderers and burglars marched to the house of a merchant. It was strongly built of stone, but the assailants were well provided with the implements of house-breakers, and forced a passage through the solid masonry with their iron wedges. They supposed that they could then easily satisfy their thirst for plunder and blood. But the occupant of the house had been forewarned of the attack, had collected his servants, and had invited his friends to aid him. The leader of the robbers, who was known as Andrew Bucquinte, was, perhaps, related to a sheriff of London who bore the same name. Bucquinte advanced with a lighted torch and with a brasier full of burning coals ; but while an attempt was being made to increase the light, by the aid of some candles which the practised robbers had had the forethought to bring with them, the master of the house suddenly sprang out from his place of conceal-ment. Bucquinte attempted to stab him, but he wore a cuirass, which resisted the blow, and in another moment he had struck off Bucquinte's right hand with his sword. The rest of the band, surprised at the resistance, fled and left their leader a prisoner. In return for this desertion, and to save his own life, Bucquinte betrayed his accomplices. Among them was one John Senex, or John the Elder, who was known as one of the richest and most influential men in London. He was tried by the water-ordeal, but failed to clear himself. He then offered five hundred marks to the king for a pardon, which was refused, either because the sum was too small, or because the scandal was too great; and he was hanged like thieves of a lower grade.

It might be almost safely assumed, without evidence, that, when the chief merchants of London were in the habit of practising burglary and murder, the inferior traders were not scrupulously honest. There is, how-ever, no necessity to rely upon conjectures when contem-porary documents afford sufficient proof of the fact. False weights, false measures, and false pretences of all kinds were the instruments of commerce most generally in use. No buyer could trust the word of a seller, and there was hardly any class in which a man might not with reason suspect that his neighbour intended to rob, or even to murder him.

The morals of the court were no better than the morals of the shop. There was no subject in which the best writers of the period took a greater delight than in the vices of the court of Henry II. Walter Mapes Archdeacon of Oxford, himself

The Court as described by an Arch-deacon.

a courtier and wit, has described, with sarcasm but with evident enjoyment, the scenes of which he was a witness. He would not, he said, undertake to prove that the court was hell, but he had no fear of contradiction when he stated that the court bore as great a resemblance to hell as a mare's shoe bears to a horse's.   Hell had been described as a place of torment, but there were no torments imagined by the ancient poets which were not realised in the court.   If Tantalus was doomed to thirst for waters which flowed before his eyes, but which he could never taste, the courtiers were always thirsting for their neighbour's goods, which were always eluding their grasp.   If Sisyphus was condemned to roll a huge stone up the side of a steep mountain, and to see it always bounding away from him when he reached the summit, the courtiers were always falling back into the valley of avarice as soon as they had scaled the mountain of wealth.   If Ixion was bound to a wheel destined to revolve for ever, the courtiers also were bound to the wheel of fortune ; and no day passed in which they were not alternately elated by some worthless success or depressed by some ridiculous mishap.

As there were birds of ill omen and of prey in the infernal regions described by the classical writers, so, said Mapes, there were birds of ill omen and of Venality of prey in the court. These were the Justices, the Justices, Sheriffs, and Sheriffs, the Under-sheriffs, and the Bedels, other courtiers. whose eyes were everywhere, and who were always careful to punish the innocent.   The acceptance of bribes was the great sin of these officials, in whose behalf the Archdeacon quotes the saying of Ovid, that 'giving is a proof of good sense.'   Mapes confesses that the clergy were not more merciful or more just than the laymen, and relates a story of an abbot who became a justice, and who exceeded all his colleagues in extortion because he hoped to buy a bishopric with the spoil. The avarice of men in authority, and the eagerness of place-hunters, became a favourite theme of invective. The Foresters, especially, whose duty it was to discover and punish all offences committed upon the king's hunting-grounds were held in the utmost detestation. The subordinates of the king's chief officers were so numerous, and bore such a character, that they were compared to swarms of locusts which devoured everything in their course, and which if by chance they left a single leaf untouched left it only to be devoured by succeeding swarms.

The chief qualification for success at court was the power of making and appreciating mirth. The mental gifts which earned for our country the name of 'Merrie England,' and which afterwards displayed themselves in the writings and sayings of humorists and play-wrights were not without cultivation at the end of the twelfth century. The royal favour might be earned by a pun or a witty retort almost as certainly as by service in the field—far more certainly than by upright and honourable conduct. The courtiers who wished to distinguish themselves in the king's presence made collections of amusing stories. Geoffrey of Monmouth, the founder of historical romance, had recently died, and had bequeathed to posterity a rich mine which poets have not even yet exhausted. The deeds of Arthur and his British knights became familiar to all the frequenters of the royal palace; but Geoffrey's tales alone could not suffice for the great and ever increasing demand for amusement The camp in the Holy Land, and the city of Rome became the two great marts for the interchange of social wealth; every traveller and every Crusader added new anecdotes to those which were already in circulation; and every country began to learn the favourite tales of its neighbours.

The infidelities of women were commonly the narrator's theme, and an exhortation to avoid matrimony was the most common form of advice given by a man to his friend. War and intrigue were regarded as the two principal amusements in life, the acquisition of wealth the only object worth serious consideration. A consequence of this creed was that the husband frequently set a price upon his wife's virtue, and made a profit of his own dishonour. Fathers were ready to sell their daughters, and excused the iniquitous traffic on the ground that the end would be the same whether they received the money or not. The unnatural procurers avenged themselves by seducing the wives and daughters of their acquaintances and employers; they studied every art by which a mean advantage might be gained, and thought themselves most fortunate when they could fawn themselves into an office which gave them opportunities of extortion and oppression.

When the courtiers grew weary of the minstrel's songs and the jongleur's pranks, when they were not occupied in making love or discharging the office of pander, they beguiled the lagging Loaded dice. moments by the dice, and by gaming in every form then known. Before the third Crusade there was in England no check upon the vice and no limit to the stakes. The gamester who, when young, had been defrauded of his patrimony, preyed in turn upon unsuspecting youth. He lived upon the weaknesses of human nature, watched with pleasure the trembling fingers and flushed cheeks of

his victims, led them on by apparent carelessness to risk
a larger sum after losing a smaller, and left them only
when they could no longer call even their clothes their
own.   The dupes often discovered, when it was too late,
that they had never had a chance of winning, but had
been ruined by the dishonesty of their adversary.   They
then began to practise the arts of deception for their own
advantage, lured their friends into the snare in which
they had themselves been caught, and made themselves
independent of fortune by loading the dice.

It was from such courtiers as these that Henry was
compelled to select the officers whose duty it was to
carry out his legal reforms.   His own court was
the greatest impediment to his own best designs,
for the more scrupulous a man was, the more
difficult he must have found all access to the king.
Henry made various experiments, seeking, now among
the laymen now among the clergy nearest to him, for
that honesty which he never made remunerative.   But
he could neither discover nor create an honest Justice.
Driven almost to despair by the condition of his kingdom,
he selected, in 1179, the Bishops of Winchester, Ely, and
Norwich to be his Chief Justices, in the hope that they
might check the iniquities of their subordinates.   But if
it was the function of the courtier bishops to see that the
law was impartially administered, they must have been
somewhat slow in learning their duty, for the whole
country continued to suffer from the abuses against
which their learning and purity were considered a safeguard.   The whole clerical body, indeed, if they grew no
worse, could certainly not have grown better between
this time and the end of the century.   Even the amorous
Richard I. was astonished at the profligacy of the men

Character of the Clergy according to contemporaries.

whom he expected to set an example to his subjects. It was the custom of the secular clergy, he said, to spend the alms extracted from the laity not upon the poor, for whom they were intended, but in vice and debauchery, to pass their days in guzzling and drinking, and to deck their mistresses in gay attire, while they gave no thought to their own vestments or the books of their church. All this he could have endured, had they not carried their lust into the homes of the laymen, and added adultery to their other offences. He did not even know where to choose a bishop or an archdeacon whose character befitted a preacher of God's Word.

In such sweeping denunciations as this there is, of course, some exaggeration. The art of telling the simple truth was not cultivated in the age of chivalry; but the simple truth was that, though the social condition of England gave better reason for hope than at any time since the Romans had quitted the island, it was, according to modern ideas, almost incredibly depraved. There is difficulty in realising a state of society in which one archdeacon considers it a good joke to trace the resemblance between the infernal regions and a court consisting in great part of ecclesiastics, and in which another archdeacon devotes energies and abilities by no means contemptible to scurrilous attacks upon his superiors, and afterwards descends to the most abject supplications. Peter of Blois, Archdeacon of London, had no hesitation in describing a certain prelate as a monster of iniquity. This bishop, he said, hated honest men, took the prudent by surprise, lured the unwary into his toils, robbed the rich, oppressed the poor, never did a good action, and was a nuisance to all mankind. He would never listen to what others had to say; he would only

consider what others had to give. He had no pity for
the afflicted and no indignation against the cruel or
unjust. He regarded every event as a pretext for the
extortion of money by fair means or by foul. He made
his demands with a shameless face ; he felt no gratitude
to those who gave, he showed no mercy to those who
refused. There was no human tie which could bind him,
no appeal which could move him, no hope of his improvement. Hated by all who knew him, he was himself a hater of law and order, a despiser of good faith, a
breaker of his word, slothful in action, and furious in
anger. At table he rendered himself disgusting by his
gluttony, his drunkenness, and his filthy language. He
had no moderation in prosperity, and no courage in
adversity. He cared nothing for the sanctity of his
office, and had lost all capacity for friendship, all regard
for honesty, and all sense of decency.

It will be seen, from this specimen, that the language
of the most cultivated writers of the period was as violent
as the spirit of the times, for the letters of Peter
of Blois do not, except perhaps in superior literary skill, differ in character from those of his contemporaries. Nor indeed was it only in words
that the clergy conformed to the manners of their age.
Like their predecessors of earlier days, they would resort
to main force when they saw no other means of attaining
an end. Thus, it had long been maintained by the
Archbishops of York, that an Archbishop of Canterbury
could never justly claim the Primacy of all England by
virtue of his see, but only by virtue of his prior consecration when he happened to have been consecrated before
the existing Archbishop of York. When Thomas à
Becket was succeeded by Richard, Prior of Dover,

*The Clergy of the two pro-
vinces ex-
change blows
at Westmin-
ster.*

Roger the Archbishop of York became the senior Metropolitan, and asserted his claim to the Primacy. Richard strenuously opposed his rival. A council was summoned by the Papal Legate, to meet at Westminster. The usual seat of the Primate was on the legate's right hand, and the Archbishop who could occupy that position would exhibit himself to the assembled ecclesiastics as the head of the English Church, while the Archbishop who failed to secure it would appear to have yielded to his rival. Roger, being the weaker of the two disputants, was the first to appear in the council-chamber, and lost no time in seating himself in the place of honour. Richard, when he entered, refused to take any seat but that which was occupied by Roger. Loud and angry words were followed by blows, and a hand-to-hand fight ensued between the clergy of the two provinces. Numbers in the end prevailed, and Canterbury proved itself superior to York in physical prowess. Roger was ignominiously dragged from the chair which he had appropriated, and was trampled in the dust by his victorious enemies. Pointing to his tattered robes, he asked redress of the Cardinal-Legate, who dissolved the council, and announced that the dispute must be decided at Rome. It does not, however, appear that the Pope expressed any displeasure at this tumult, or that either of the Archbishops lost any of that respect which he had previously won.

When the two chief ecclesiastical dignitaries of the realm were not ashamed to engage in a furious brawl, it may well be believed that the inferior clergy were not on all occasions respecters of the law. *Value of relics.* Their ambition, combined perhaps with their superstition, led them into some remarkable crimes, which it is difficult to narrate with becoming gravity. The miracles

which were supposed to be wrought by the bodies or by
any relics of saints invested the burial places of holy men
with extraordinary sanctity. Not only did Henry II.
make pilgrimages to the tomb of the murdered and
sainted Becket, but Louis VII. of France crossed the
Channel to beg the intercession of Saint Thomas of
Canterbury in favour of his afflicted son. Fortunate,
indeed, was the monastery or the church which possessed
any wonder-working remains, and strange the means by
which they were obtained. So great was the value set
upon them that, like the wealth of this world, they
tempted men to be dishonest.

In the Abbey of Bodmin rested the bones of Saint
Petroc, the virtues of which, it may be supposed, had

Stealing of
Relics sanc-
tioned by a
Religious
House. grown famous in the dialects of Britanny and
Cornwall. Martin, one of the canons of Bodmin,
was persuaded to escape from the house, to carry
off with him the remains of the Saint, and to bestow them
upon an Abbey in Britanny. He succeeded perfectly in his
design ; the Breton monks received the treasure with exultation, and without remorse for the theft of which they
rendered themselves the accomplices. The Prior of Bodmin, as soon as he discovered the loss which he and his
brethren had sustained, presented himself to the king, and
related his misfortune. Henry promised his aid, and directed
a letter to the Justice of Britanny, in which authority was
given to enforce the restitution of Saint Petroc's body.
The justice placed himself at the head of his retainers, and
rode to the doors of the Breton abbey. The abbot and
monks were at first obstinate in their refusal to give up
their ill-gotten prize; but the justice warned them, with
an oath, that unless they delivered it to him without
further delay, he would take it by force, as the king had

bidden him. This argument at last prevailed, and the justice received from them, as he supposed, the remains of the saint. When, however, the Prior of Bodmin received again the object of his monastery's veneration and pride, he was seized with a horrible suspicion that his dishonest enemies were still defrauding him, and that they had substituted another and less holy body for the body of Saint Petroc. Nor could he be satisfied that the remains had been really restored in their integrity until the Breton abbot and monks had confirmed their protestations by an oath taken on the relics of their own house. He must have had a remarkable faith in the power of such things to give honesty and veracity to thieves.

The possession of holy relics, however, was but one of the many sources of wealth enjoyed by the religious houses. The monasteries derived immense revenues from lands which supported the dignity and contributed to the pleasure of the Abbot or the Prior. They furnished, perhaps, an entertainment for the king when he travelled through his realm, and their doors were not always closed against more humble wayfarers. But they were not, as might be supposed, so many fountain-heads of charity devoting their riches to the relief of the poor. The clergy did, without doubt, distribute alms, but they first received the alms, not in the shape of rents from their own manors, but in the shape of gifts, certainly from the Royal Exchequer, and probably also from private individuals. It is in no sense true that the burden of supporting those who could not support themselves was first thrown on the laity or on the State when the monasteries were dissolved. Even as early as the time of Henry II. provision out of the royal income was made for

The Clergy and the Poor.

the sick in all the chief cities and in many of the smaller
towns.   Persons who were disabled by blindness or by
other permanent infirmity received special grants.   The
task of distribution was naturally enough entrusted to
those members of the clerical body who preferred a life of
active charity to the excitement of the court or the useless
misery of an anchorite's cell.   Many of the religious
houses also received, year after year, sums of money for
which they alleged some special need.   The payments,
however, to monasteries, by virtue of the king's writ, are
rare in comparison with remissions of payments due from
the monasteries to the Crown.   It is difficult to conceive,
when all these advantages are borne in mind, that the
disbursements of abbeys or priories, under the head of
public duties, could have exceeded their receipts in one
form or other from the king's sheriffs.   Almost all the
alms either to religious houses or to the sick became established as annual payments and were deducted in each
county from the total sum due to the Treasury; the temporary exemptions also were soon established in like
manner by a kind of prescription, though they were not
officially classed under the same head.

In these facts, and in the ancient rule that a share of
the tithes was for the poor, are perhaps, to be found the
first rudiments of the doctrine that the State should help
those who are otherwise helpless—in short, of our modern
poor-laws.   The poor, indeed, are frequently mentioned
in the laws or dooms antecedent to the Conquest; but
bare precepts, without records of the mode of working,
though they may be used to build up a theory, give but
little aid in the narration of facts.   It must of course be
remembered, that long before and long after the Conquest
those classes of the laity which were nearest to the con-

dition of paupers had, except perhaps in the towns, and among the numerous hordes of brigands, a superior lord, who, with all his brutality, would, for obvious reasons, be reluctant that a dependent should starve. The poor, in the modern sense of the term, could hardly have had any existence, except as poor townsmen or as poor ecclesiastics. Before the Conquest, the man who had no lord was regarded as a thief ; after the Conquest, the same principle is apparent in those regulations by which a stranger was forbidden to remain more than one night in a town and the sheriffs of each county were commanded to register the names of all fugitives from other shires. The burden of relieving the poor must, therefore, have been but light, and was distributed in effect as nearly as possible in the manner in which it is distributed at the present time. It was borne not by the Church, but by the public—in part by the great land-holders, in part by those other classes which could afford to pay taxes. The king's revenue was the revenue of the State ; and it was therefore practically at the expense of the State that all grants were made, and out of taxes upon the people that all deficiencies were repaired.

It is pleasant to dwell for a moment on this one bright spot in the desert of mediæval cruelties : to see that there was one form in which compassion was not wholly extinct—to know that a cripple, Charity. if he did not chance to be also a heretic, was sometimes supported by his more fortunate fellow-countrymen. It is pleasanter still to reflect that this charity—this higher conception of Christianity—prevailed, in the end, over that bigotry which made orthodoxy almost a synonym for ferocity. But any one who banishes from his mind those exhibitions of inhuman hatred which were called forth by the very name of a heretic cannot realise to himself the condition of society at the end of the twelfth century.

At this period numerous sects had arisen, and come into prominence in the south of France. In spite of persecution at home, they succeeded in making numerous converts abroad. One of them, known as that of the Publicans or Paterines, sprang up, or was revived, in Gascony, spread thence through France, Spain, Italy and Germany, and at last appeared in England. The preachers of the new doctrines in England were, it is said, not very numerous, and were Germans by birth. The contemporary writers differ very materially in their accounts of the success attained by these missionaries, but unite in attributing to them the most revolting doctrines and practices. In the nineteenth century, it is hardly necessary to remark that the tenets held by heretics in the twelfth century are not to be correctly ascertained from the writings of their adversaries; and the heretics have not been permitted to address posterity for themselves. It was, however, commonly believed that these Paterines scoffed at the Sacrament of the Lord's Supper, and abjured baptism, matrimony, and the unity of the Catholic Church. It was their custom, as reported, to meet in the evening in order that they might celebrate the rites which they declared to be essentially Christian and strictly in accordance with the teaching of the Apostles. The only positive doctrine which was enunciated was that true charity consisted in doing or suffering what any Christian brother or sister might desire. After certain hymns had been hummed, rather than sung, the lights were extinguished, and the brothers and sisters indulged their passions as

Appearance of heretics in England.

they pleased. So, at least, says Walter Mapes, afterwards Archdeacon of Oxford.

The Paterines, however, may be considered to have cleared themselves from the charge of mere reckless depravity by their conduct in the time of trial. Inhuman treatment of them. They might have preserved their lives and found opportunities for the gratification of their lusts had they been without real faith and willing to recant. But, though their converts wavered, the heretics who had come from beyond the sea, adhered stubbornly to their creed. A council of Bishops assembled at Oxford in the year 1160. The Paterines were bidden to do penance for their opinions and to be reconciled with the Church, but they were deaf both to persuasion and to threats, and they cried out, in the words of the Saviour, ' Blessed are they which are persecuted for righteousness' sake, for theirs is the kingdom of heaven.' The Bishops, without further delay, delivered the heretics to the civil arm for punishment. The Paterines displayed as much firmness as the martyrs of earlier times. Their foreheads were seared with a hot iron so that every passerby might know the men who had committed the crime of thinking for themselves. Their garments were torn off from the waist upwards, and they were whipped publicly through the streets. They raised no cry in their anguish, they invoked no curses upon their tormenters, but they repeated again and again the words of their Master : ' Blessed are ye when men shall revile you, and persecute you, and shall say all manner of evil against you falsely, for My sake.' Every Englishman was forbidden to give them food or shelter, and the brand on their faces marked them out as objects for the exercise of cruelty. An English ecclesiastic, who lived at the time, has related, in a tone of exultation, that it was winter when these un-happy foreigners were driven from the principal seat of English learning into the open country, that the frost was intense, that no honest English heart was moved to com-passion by the harshness of the sentence, and that the enemies of the Church died in the torments of cold and starvation.

Cruelty begets cruelty as certainly as animals beget their like. When the Church slew her enemies in a manner which was not brutal only because brutes are more merciful, when ecclesiastics exhorted one another to inflict such punishments upon heretics that no human being might in future become heretical, the heretics themselves began to imitate their oppressors. Forbidden to worship as their consciences taught them, forbidden to enter the houses of orthodox believers, for-bidden even to purchase the necessaries of life, the per-secuted who survived their persecutions were compelled to join communities of outlaws. There were many such bands, each numbering many thousands of persons in various parts of Europe. They served as mercenary soldiers under any prince who could afford to hire them or could promise them booty. They were known as Routiers or Brabazons, and it was said that some of them at least had been originally formed in Brabant. In their ranks any man was well received who could add to their strength, and any woman who could contribute to their pleasure. They never enquired too curiously into the faith of their associates, and they demanded no virtue except fidelity to their own body. When monasteries were sacked and the inmates murdered or ravished, when towns and even cities were burnt to the ground, and when it was discovered that there were at least some

Brigands described as heretics.

heretics among the offenders, the Church began to regard the Brabazons as one of the heretical sects. It does not, however, appear that they held any positive doctrine in common, or any sentiment except hatred of the constituted authority. In their body every class was represented, and every form of discontent was permitted to exist. They received with equal favour heretics of all shades of opinion, ecclesiastics who had incurred the censure of superiors, fugitive monks, robbers, and men who were in peril of death for political offences.

Mercenaries, such as were the Brabazons, and the Brabazons themselves were employed in the civil wars between Stephen on the one side, and the Empress and her son on the other. Henry II. as soon as he · was firmly established on the throne, sent the Brabazons out of the kingdom, probably at the instigation of the clergy. It does, not, however, appear that any great good was achieved by this attempt to abolish heresy and brigandage at one blow. The evil did not lie in a single sect, or a horde of robbers bearing a single name, or even in paying mercenaries to secure the throne. It was far more deeply seated in the barbarism of the times, and was inherited from those sad days when the Northern plunderers had torn the Roman Empire to pieces. It was not to be eradicated for many another generation, and has had its effect even upon the present age. Not all the legal reforms of Edward I. could do more than slightly modify it—much less the reforms of Henry II.

The position of the Jews, like the position of the heretics, illustrates at once the fanaticism and the lawlessness of the age. The heretics proscribed by councils could find refuge only among robbers less cruel than lawgivers. The Jews, under the king's

Source of the prevailing barbarism.

Position of the Jews in England.

protection, were never secure from attacks made by the whole Christian mob of any town in which they might have licence to dwell.   Before the reign of John, at least, it must have been the real wish as well as the expressed intention of the kings to keep the Jews harmless.   They contributed in no small measure to the royal revenue, and diverted from the royal officers some of the odium which commonly falls upon the tax-gatherer.   They became an important body in the country soon after the Conquest.   A charter, confirmed by John, was said to have been granted to them by Henry I.   The effect was that they might reside in England as free men, might travel from town to town, might claim redress if molested, and might even hold lands in pledge until a loan had been repaid.   The benefits conferred by the Norman monarchs were, however, only an indication of services demanded in return.   The Jews became, in fact, if not in name, officers of state, bearing a very close resemblance to those Publicans of the Roman Empire whom their forefathers had hated and shunned.   In every town in which they settled they sat continually at the receipt of custom.   The genius and traditions of their race rendered them, in all commercial knowledge, infinitely superior to the Englishmen by whom they were surrounded, and they practically farmed from the king a monopoly of the money-market. For the sums which they lent upon the security of land they sometimes gained sixty per cent. per annum, and they were at one time allowed by law to gain forty.   The king, who exacted service of some kind from all his subjects, exacted a return for the privilege which he conferred of taking usury from his subjects.   The accounts of the 'Jewry' thus became of great importance in the Exchequer, and as the nature of the transaction was not perceived in those rude times, the tax upon borrowers went ungrudged to the king. All the hatred of ruined men towards those who have ruined them, and all the jealousy which can be excited by superior skill and wealth were thus combined with a religious frenzy against the Jews, whose avarice certainly was not all their own.

When a London merchant hoped that the profits of bargains made in the morning might be increased by burglaries effected in the night, the life of a Jew must have been a life of ceaseless apprehensions and horrors. The trials which he was compelled to endure, not only in England, but elsewhere, excite wonder that his race survived, and invite admiration for the patience and for the tenacity with which it remained true to its faith under a martyrdom lasting for ages.

The treatment suffered by the Jews is, perhaps, best illustrated by the events to which the coronation-day of Richard I. gave birth. The whole of that day's doings were most characteristic of the age. The ceremony was one of more than ordinary magnificence, and all the most distinguished men in the country were present. From the king's chamber to the altar in Westminster Abbey, the way was covered with woollen cloths. In front of the procession, as though to proclaim 'Peace on earth, good will towards men,' marched the inferior clergy, who bore aloft the cross and the candles, sprinkled holy water right and left, and waved censers of burning incense while they sang in full chorus. They were followed in due order by the priors, the abbots, and the bishops, intermixed with whom were four barons holding four golden candlesticks. Next came earls and barons, each entrusted with some of the

[side note: Scene on the Coronation-day of Richard I.]

insignia of royalty—the sceptre, the dove, the golden-hilted swords in sheaths of cloth of gold, the robes, and the jewelled crown. Close behind the crown walked Richard himself, with a bishop on either hand, beneath a silken canopy, supported by four barons on four lances. A crowd of nobles and privileged officials brought up the rear. In the Abbey, Richard took the coronation oath, was anointed by the Archbishop of Canterbury, robed, crowned, and enthroned according to custom. All seemed happy in Westminster that Sunday morning, all prepared to make merry. From the palace to the Abbey, and from the Abbey back to the palace, bright faces and gay colours seemed to betoken nothing but joy. The king and the nobles took their seats in the palace-hall, glad to exchange the restraint of the past solemnity for the freedom of a royal banquet. But in the midst of the feast, high above the loud voices and loud laughter of the rough king and his rough guests, were heard the sounds of strife in the outer court.

When the king had re-entered his palace, some of the leading members of the Jewish community, laden with costly gifts, attempted to make their way into the royal presence. The Jews had been expressly forbidden to show themselves at the coronation, for it had always been considered a profanation for a Jew to enter a Christian church, or to be present at a Christian ceremony. The intruders, for so they seem to have been considered by reason of the prohibition, were instantly known by their features to be Jews, and were expelled with insults and blows. The cry of ' The Jews' was raised, and that cry sufficed to rouse the whole populace to fury. It was Sunday, and every inhabitant of the city had been free to join the crowd at Westminster,

Massacre of the Jews in London.

to gain, perhaps, a glimpse of the procession, and to indulge himself in every pleasure within his reach. It was Sunday, and all London was making holiday in honour of the new and popular king. It was Sunday, and this was the day on which the Jews had dared to pollute the approaches to the royal court. It was Sunday, the Lord's day, the day on which the Redeemer had risen from the dead, after he had been crucified according to the wish of the Jews. 'The Jews!' cried the mob, bent on enjoying the day, and determined to have vengeance at once for all past iniquities, and for this new insult to the Christian faith and the Christian king. Irresistible numbers marched to the Jews' quarter in the city. They killed every Jew who came in their way. They broke into every Jewish house which was not strong enough to resist their blows. They passed all the afternoon of that Sunday, and the whole of the following night, in murder, robbery, and destruction. They set fire to the houses which they had sacked, and the flames spread to the dwellings of the Christians. They laid the richest part of the capital in ruins in showing their loyalty to Church and King. Such was the London of the twelfth century.

The news of this riot became the signal for attacks upon the Jews in many of the other principal towns. York was the scene of an outrage even more *At York.* horrible than that which had disgraced London. The Jews became alarmed at the menaces of the popu-lace, and fled for refuge to the Castle. The Constable promised them his protection and, for a time at least, kept his word. One day, however, he left the castle, and the Jews suspected that he intended to betray them, in order that he might secure for himself the greatest share of their wealth. In the extremity of their fear they closed the gates, and excluded the Constable from the castle in which he had given them shelter. Not only the mob, but the officers whose duty it was to hold the mob in check, were exasperated by this defiance of the king's authority. The castle was besieged, and the Jews had no hope either of succour or of escape. They saw that death was inevitable, and the greater portion of them resolved to disappoint the wrath of their enemies by committing suicide. With their own hands they killed their wives and children, set fire to the castle, and put an end to their own lives. When the Christians of York stormed the walls, they found no defenders, no human beings but a few wretches who had lacked the courage to anticipate their fate, or whose religious scruples had restrained them from following the example of their comrades. Upon these miserable suppliants for mercy the assailants were not ashamed to wreak their vengeance; and the last of the Jews in the castle was put to death by men who lived around the cathedral of an archbishop, and by men who displayed the Cross as soldiers devoted to the service of Christ.

At Lynn there was a riot, in which fire and sword were carried into the Jewish quarter; and while the At Lynn, Stamford, and Lincoln. houses of Jews were blazing, and the corpses of Jews were strewn about the streets, the wealth which these enemies of Christianity had accumulated was carried on board ship. At Stamford, during the great fair, the Jews were compelled to take refuge in the Castle; and the Crusaders, who had been exhibiting their crosses to the wondering crowd, sacked the deserted houses, carried off their booty, and escaped all punishment. At Lincoln, too, there were outrages, of which the chroniclers have not preserved a full account, but which the Rolls of the Exchequer show to have been not less violent than those perpetrated in other towns. No adequate retribution overtook the offenders. A few only were hanged in London; in York thirty-nine, and in Lincoln no less than ninety-four were amerced for participation in these deeds of bloodshed. The lists of names are not without their interest; they show clearly that the mobs were not composed solely of common thieves or soldiers eager to practise those vices for which an indulgence had been proclaimed, but that the better classes of the population—the traders, the householders, and even the nobles—displayed zeal for the coming Crusade by attacking the Jews.

At this time—at the accession of Richard I.—all the chivalry of Europe affected to live for the single purpose of wresting the Holy Sepulchre from the Infidel. The whole of Christendom had been *The Crusades according to romance.* excited to a fervour such as had been unknown since the days of the early persecutions. It might, therefore, be supposed that, if the necessity for laws continued to exist in the midst of such religious enthusiasm, the existing laws were, at least, cheerfully obeyed, and that there could but rarely have been occasion for the infliction of punishment. As the imagination travels back through the long centuries of the past, it is tempted to raise a picture of the purest innocence animated by a spirit of the most holy self-denial. It sees heroes, absolutely without fear and without reproach, battling for no earthly honour, but fighting their way to the kingdom of heaven at the gates of Jerusalem. It hears the prayers of the sick, of the women, and of the little children for the success of the Christian arms. It has no eyes for the foulness of mediæval iniquity. The external aspect of a Crusade is

M 2

not unlike a painting of some rich tropical scene, in which
the artist bids us remember only the luxuriance of vege-
tation, the brightness of the sky, and the plumage of the
birds—in which he makes us forget that disease is inhaled
with every breath, and that corpses lie rotting in the
jungle. Romance has made the Crusades her own, has
exhibited to all the world the beauties which she has discovered in them, and has hidden away, where she could,
the horrors of the age.

To the strength of the first two Crusades, the British
Islands contributed little; but nothing, perhaps, better
illustrates the moral condition of Northern
Europe during the eleventh and twelfth centuries than the history of those expeditions.

Historically
they illustrate
the moral
condition of
Europe.

The forces which had received a plenary indulgence for
all crimes, and which had been excited to more than
ordinary ferocity by the language of preachers, commonly
displayed the cruelty without the discipline of brigands.
If they had devoted themselves to the service of God,
they convinced the inhabitants of the towns on their line
of march that they had ceased to respect the laws of man.
They considered themselves privileged to gratify every
wish and every lust as it arose. They recognised no
rights of property, they felt no gratitude for hospitality,
and they possessed no sense of honour. They violated
the wives and daughters of their hosts when they were
kindly treated, they devastated the lands of friends whom
they had converted into enemies, they resorted to wanton
robbery and destruction in revenge for calamities which
they had brought upon themselves. They believed that
they proved their superiority to Mahommedans by
slaughtering the defenceless Jews; and this was the only
exploit in which the first divisions of the Crusaders could

boast of success. The bodies led by Walter Sans-Avoir, by Peter the Hermit, and by Gottschalk, suffered defeats almost as disgraceful as their previous conduct. After three years, however, of toil and suffering, and after a loss of lives which the chroniclers estimate by hundreds of thousands, the object of the first Crusade was attained, and the Christians were in possession of the Holy Sepulchre. Soldiers displaying conspicuously the Cross of the Prince of Peace burst in all the pride of war through the gates which He had entered meekly riding upon an ass. Where He had taught love, and pity, and tenderness, where they believed that He had healed the sick and raised the dead, they gave vent to all the passions of savages, they refused all quarter to their enemies, they caused torrents of blood to flow through the streets. On the very spot where Joseph and Mary had found Him instructing the Doctors, and where He had overthrown the tables of the money-changers in the Temple, one of the highest Christian generals eagerly seized, as his spoil, the treasures which had been stored in the Mosque of Omar.

In less than half a century it was discovered that a second Crusade had become necessary, in order to secure the gains of the first; and in the year 1147 Treacheries of Conrad III. of Germany, and Louis VII. of the Crusaders. France took the cross. But the sins of the first crusaders were visited on the soldiers of the second Crusade. The court of Constantinople had not grown more friendly to the western adventurers in the interval between the two expeditions; it regarded them with well-merited suspicion, and thwarted them by every device which could be brought into play without an open exhibition of hostility. After much loss and many defeats, they made their way to Palestine, when the sovereigns consulted together and resolved to attack Damascus. When the siege had been carried on with so much success that the garrison saw no hope of safety, some of the Christian leaders accepted bribes from the enemy, and deserted. The two monarchs, perceiving that their enterprise must be fruitless, left their followers to straggle home as best they might, and made their way with all speed to their own dominions. The kingdom of Jerusalem which had been established as the result of the first Crusade was, perhaps, maintained in existence for a few years by the second. There ended the advantage ; honour there was none. The treachery which had rendered the siege of Damascus fruitless was imitated by a Christian commander in the year 1187. It was not difficult for the Count of Tripoli to dispose the Christian forces to the advantage of Saladin, when the chiefs of the Christians had more jealousy of each other than zeal for their cause. A great defeat of the Christians at. Tiberias was followed by the fall of the Holy City itself. Saladin, with a generosity which his adversaries might have won credit in imitating, granted the possession of the Sepulchre to his defeated enemies. But neither policy nor passion would permit the court of Rome to acquiesce tamely in such a loss as they had sustained, or to recognise any virtue in an unbeliever. A third Crusade was immediately proclaimed, and this time the frenzy extended itself in full force to England. It was checked, indeed, by the war of Henry II. with Philip of France, and with his own son. But upon the accession of Richard, a prince so virtuous and valorous that, if he could not use his sword elsewhere, he was glad to wield it against his father, the smouldering fire burst into flame.

The young Richard seemed in popular estimation to be the incarnation of all that is kingly and chivalrous. He fought, as his contemporaries proudly Character of boasted, with the heart of a lion ; and he seems RichardCœur de Lion. to have possessed as much courage, as high a sense of justice, as tender a regard for the helpless, as the noble beast of the forest. The expedition to the Holy Land appealed to the popular imagination ; and all classes were agreed that there could not be a braver commander or one more fit, according to all precedent, to bear the name of Crusader. What mattered it that he had leagued himself with his brother to undo his father, if he was willing, like a true knight, to league himself with the French king to undo the infidel Soldan ? If he sold bishoprics and offices, it was no more than his predecessors had done before him, and if he had declared that he would sell London itself to raise money, did not the end sanctify the means—did not the expression itself show a generous nature?

To those who are familiar with the characteristics of the age handed down through many centuries of barbarism, it will not seem strange that the young His popularity. king was popular—that his cheerful mien and his brawny frame atoned, in the eyes of the populace, for the absence of qualities which they had not learned to miss. His army was an army of Crusaders little if at all less savage than the hordes which Peter the Hermit had brought together nearly a century before ; and these Crusaders were the picked men among the masses of our forefathers, carrying with them the sympathies of their fellow-countrymen. They were Crusaders fit to serve under the Prince of Crusaders—ready, indeed, to risk their lives in fair fight, but not less ready to murder an

unarmed Jew, or to break any one of the last six com-
mandments. The admiration of Richard, which long
survived and still survives in song, shows how completely
he represented the popular notion of a good king, and
how indifferent men were to any qualities except mere
physical courage and that gay and careless temperament
which often accompanies it.

The embarcation of Richard's army, however, was
a great event in the history of England. The men who

Remote ad-
vantages of
the Cru-
sades. sailed were unconsciously helping to destroy
the distinction between Normans and English-
men, and to weld the two classes into one
nation, in accordance with the policy of the Conqueror
and his successors. Their enterprise, hopeless in a military sense, was full of promise to anyone, had such there
been, who could have looked beyond the range of
mediæval bigotry and mediæval aspirations. But the
benefits which the Crusades were to confer not only upon
England but upon Western Europe were not yet, and
could not for many years become, apparent. Regarded
apart from the results which could not have been foreseen, they were the crowning effort of barbarism animated by superstition.

The ordinances for the voyage to the Holy Land
show, in a few unambiguous sentences, the character of

The Age of
Chivalry
illustrated by
the ordinan-
ces made for
the Crusa-
ders. the soldiers who sailed, and of the knights who
commanded them. Whoever killed a man on
board ship was to be tied to the corpse and
thrown with it into the sea. Whoever killed a
man on shore was to be tied to the corpse and buried
alive with it. Drawing blood with a knife was to be
punished with the loss of a hand ; a mere blow, with
three complete duckings in the sea. A thief was to be

shaved, to have boiling pitch poured upon his head, and a cushion of feathers shaken over it, so that his misdeed might be known to all; and he was to be put ashore at the first place at which the ship touched.

Such was the age of chivalry some time after its beginning; such the rules by which Christian kings attempted to enforce discipline among Christian heroes of romance. To the leaders, who could not write their own names, deception and treachery were as familiar as force; to their followers rapine and murder were so congenial that, in the absence of Saracens, Jews, or townsfolk, it seemed but a professional pastime to kill or to rob a comrade in arms.

CHAPTER III.

FROM THE THIRD CRUSADE TO THE YEAR BEFORE THE BLACK DEATH.

THERE is probably no period in history so strongly marked by glaring contrasts as the thirteenth century and the first half of the fourteenth. During that time many towns rose from a condition very nearly approaching serfdom to the dignity of sending representatives to Parliament, the laws were greatly improved and developed in every branch, the strength of the kingdom was increased by the conquest of Wales, and the distinction of race between Norman ruler and English subject ceased to exist. But, on the other hand, the ferocity of the barbarians who had over-run the Roman empire had struck root so deeply that it could not yet be eradicated from the masses of the population, and often overshadowed the more enlightened law-givers. The right of private war lost its legal sanction, and the exaction of revenge by an individual began to be a crime against the state. But, on the other hand, individuals continued to value their own privileges far more than the common weal ; and the lords of every manor, and the seamen of every port, were still reluctant to abandon the appeal to force when they believed the issue would be in their own favour. To one who studies

The period exhibits remarkable contrasts.

only the history of the constitution, it will appear that marvellous progress had been made at the end of the reign of Edward I. ; to one who studies only the history of the people, it will appear that but little progress had been made even when Edward III. was in his prime ; to one who studies both, it will become manifest that civilisation is, like a forest tree, easily cut down by a few strokes of the axe, but slow of growth, and not to be matured by the mere will of kings or legislators. The extinction of Roman civilisation in Britain may be related in a few sentences ; volumes barely suffice to show how England became civilised in later times.

The growth of the towns, which was freer and fuller after the disorganisation of feudal society consequent on the Black Death, seems to have been previously confined within certain well-marked limits. London, always held in respect by kings, *The Towns become quit of the murder-fine.* even before the Conquest, was the model to which the other towns attempted to assimilate themselves. It had received a general confirmation of its ancient privileges from the Conqueror ; but not until the reign of Henry I. did it become, in the legal language of the day, quit of murder. Before this time the towns, like the rural hundreds, or, perhaps, in some cases, as part of the hundreds, must have been compelled to make presentments of Englishry, and to pay for a Frenchman slain within the walls. It was no small advance towards escape from the reproach of subjection to a foreign yoke when the Englishman was promoted to equality with the Norman in the city of London. But the majority of the towns do not appear to have obtained exemption from the murder-fine earlier than the reign of Richard I. ; nor had they all obtained it at the end of the reign of

John. The royal favour had to be purchased for money;
and it was not until the Crusades had caused property
to change hands, and had stimulated intercourse with the
Continent, that the burghers were able to pay for new
privileges, or the kings were willing to grant them. The
townsmen, when their opportunity came, seem to have
thought first of securing some position which had been
lost or imperilled at the time of the Conquest. If they
are not exempted from the murder-fine in so many words,
they receive a confirmation of their ancient liberties and
customs ; of the ancient liberties and customs which they
enjoyed in the time of King Edward ; of the privilege of
clearing themselves, in the Pleas of the Crown, according
to the ancient custom of their city. To the citizens of
London is expressly granted the ancient right of compurgation by the charter of Henry I. ; and the inhabitants of many other towns regain it indirectly by
clauses in later charters, which place them, in criminal
matters, on the same footing as the capital.

The Londoners maintain that their ancestors hunted
on the Chiltern Hills and throughout the counties of
They obtain Middlesex and Surrey; the king allows their
other privi-
leges.   claim, and, though sport is a pleasure almost
exclusively royal, permits them to enjoy it as freely as
their forefathers. Similar indulgences are afterwards
granted on a smaller scale elsewhere, and probably for
similar reasons. Thus Richard I. allows the burgesses of
Colchester to hunt the fox, the hare, and the cat. The
grant of a borough to its inhabitants is sometimes made in
the same form as a grant of land to a favoured noble or
to a religious house. They are to hold their liberties well
and in peace, freely and quietly, wholly, fully, and with
honour, in woodland and in clear-land, in roads and in

paths, in meadows and in pastures, in fees and in demesnes, in waters and in mills, in fish-ponds and in fisheries, in moors and in marshes—as well without the walls as within, as far as their free customs extend.

It would be of no practical use to enquire, in this place, what was the origin of such claims as those which were successfully asserted by London. In the absence of sufficient historical testimony, a con- Their guilds. clusion, however ingeniously drawn, has to struggle for existence against rival conclusions or rival prejudices, and the matter is left in the end precisely where it was before the discussion began—in doubt. It is impossible to give at once a clear and a trustworthy description of the precise political position of any town as existing before the Conquest, and for that reason it is most difficult to estimate at their true value the town-charters of the twelfth and thirteenth centuries. The curt sentences of Domesday are not less prone to excite an appetite for the information which they withhold than gratitude for the information which they impart. They tell us that a brewer of bad ale in Chester was exposed, whether male or female, on the seat of filth ; but they do not tell us that there was a guild merchant at Lincoln. Possibly there was not; but the charter granted to the citizens of Lincoln by Henry II. allows them their guild merchant, as enjoyed by them in the time of his predecessors, including Edward the Confessor. There is not complete uniformity in the returns from the various counties entered in Domesday ; and, as according to the book itself, there were guilds of burgesses at Canterbury and Dover before the Conquest, it is by no means impossible that the claim of Lincoln may be founded on fact. When King John gives a charter to Gloucester, the guild mer-

chant is mentioned as already existing, and the burgesses
who belong to it are exempted from certain imposts.   In
many other charters, including one granted as early as
the reign of Henry I. to Beverley, the guild and the
guildhall or hanse-house are introduced in such a manner
that they seem rather to gain a new legal recognition than
to be newly established.   In none of those granted to
English towns are the words identical with the words
employed towards the burghers of Niort, who obtain a
licence not simply to have a guild or commune, but to
establish one which they may afterwards enjoy.

In the reign of Henry I. the citizens of London
obtained, or regained, the privilege of electing their own
They recover sheriffs, and took the county of Middlesex to
from the ef-
fects of the farm.   In other words, the elective sheriffs of
Conquest
sooner than London were thenceforward sheriffs also of
the rural dis-
tricts. Middlesex, and paid a fixed annual sum into
the Exchequer in satisfaction of all ordinary payments due
from the county.   The position of the city after this concession was not only stronger than that of any town, but
stronger also than that of any shire in the country, for
there is no doubt that after the Conquest the sheriffs were
usually nominated by the king.   Before the end of John's
reign the principal towns had so far followed the example
set them by London, that they could choose their own
chief magistrate, subject only to the king's approval, and
were independent of the jurisdiction claimed by the
sheriffs of the counties in which they stood.   Individual
townsmen could now hold their lands in burgage—a
tenure as free as socage, which was the freest lay tenure
known in the shires.   The villein who could escape the
observation of his lord, and remain in a chartered town
for a year and a day unmolested, could be a member of

the guild, commune, or corporation, and become a free man ever afterwards. It is not, indeed, probable that until the Black Death had taught the labourer his value, freedom was often acquired, in this manner, by the bondsman fleeing from his lord. It may be, too, that the towns collectively gained by the third Crusade nothing which some towns, at least, had not enjoyed before the Conquest; but it is quite certain that if they had not yet raised themselves to a level absolutely higher than any attained under the West Saxon dynasty, they had been the first to recover from the effects of the disaster near Hastings. Their fellow-countrymen in the rural districts were contemptuously regarded as mere Englishry long after the burgesses were known simply as burgesses. The relative positions of classes thus underwent a change, at the time almost imperceptible, but in the end of no little importance to English civilisation.

The advantages secured by the towns were, however, not free from certain adverse influences, springing in part from the very sources of benefit. If the towns-man became more wealthy through the increase of commerce, if he learned from the Crusaders how the towns of Italy could dictate terms, instead of accepting them from feudal chiefs, and was animated by a spirit of emulation, the traditions of the past were continually directing his energies into the groove which led back towards the old forms of barbarism. If he freed himself from the duel, he reverted to compurgation; if he excluded the Sheriffs and Hundred-men he also excluded the King's Justices ; if he strengthened his town-organisation he retarded the unification of the kingdom. Even if he took the Italian cities for his models, he would always have in his mind the fact that each of them fought

They are in danger of reverting to the old forms of barbarism.

under its own leaders for its own benefit, and preferred
its own right of making war to such an abstract idea as
that of national unity.

It is necessary to bear well in mind this continual
conflict of causes, this atavism of the barbarous wherever
They begin to barbarism has once been introduced among any
be represen- population. The excessively slow growth of
ted in the le-
gislative body. civilisation in England at a time when legislation
was specially favourable to its progress, cannot otherwise
be easily understood. Before the end of the thirteenth
century, the principle of representation in a national parliament had been accepted by the land-holders, by the
clergy, and by the townsmen. This was a most important step towards that consolidation which had always
been the aim of the Norman or French sovereigns, though
it had been made in the manner least agreeable to their
ideas of government. It would be foreign to the purposes of
this history to describe at length the conflicting efforts of the
different estates of the realm. They have left their marks
in Magna Carta and its many confirmations, and in the
Statutes passed after Simon de Montfort had set the
great precedent of summoning a truly national assembly. But there are some points in the great constitutional
struggle which cannot be dismissed without notice.
Before the Conquest the king was assisted by a council,
styled, when it assembled, the Meeting of the Wise, at
which the bishops and chief land-holders held seats. Immediately after the Conquest there was a council of a
very similar character, of which the members were also
lay and ecclesiastical. It cannot be stated with certainty
on what occasions the king summoned his council either
before or immediately after the Conquest, because the
writs of summons are not in existence. For similar
reasons it is impossible to decide whether the council

filled vacancies in its own body, or the king had unlimited power to select new councillors as he pleased. Nor indeed is it necessary to suppose that there was any abstract theory of constitutional government, or even any consistency of practice at a time when king and nobles were alike ready for an appeal to arms on the slightest provocation. Of representatives freely elected by the people, or a considerable portion of it, there was no trace. As soon, however, as the towns began to have a recognised corporate existence they began also to send representatives, elected by the members of their corporation, to Westminster. In the charters in which their various liberties and immunities are secured there is commonly a provision that their common council shall elect two of their more lawful and discreet men and present them to the Chief Justice at the Treasury with a statement of accounts. This is a most important advance towards parliamentary representation and towards the constitutional doctrine that the right of granting supplies belongs to the Commons. The two burgesses, at this early stage, have, it is true, no discretionary power given them by their electors ; they do not meet the burgesses of other towns, nor any knights from the shires ; they are simply entrusted with the care of certain documents which they are prepared to explain and to justify on the part of their fellow-townsmen. But on the other hand they are the means of communication between the king (or his representative, the chief justice) and their constituents in all matters of finance; they become familiar examples of the representative principle in combination with free election ; they suggest an expedient for future use ; and in the struggle which calls forth a national assembly they are naturally transformed into members of parliament.

A combination of three antagonistic principles was effected in that stage of national growth in which a national parliament became an established insti-tution. Unification, the great leading idea of the Conqueror and his house, was realised in a central legislative body; local independence, dear alike to the shires and to the towns, found its expression in local representation ; representation, the enemy alike of local-isation and of despotic rule, took both by the hand and reconciled them to each other by means of a compromise.

Fusion of opposing principles.

The townsmen, brought into contact with representa-tives from the shires, now began to exert an influence, at first very slight and not in all respects beneficial, upon the lives and occupations of other Englishmen. England seems at this time and long afterwards, to have grown, on the average, only sufficient corn for home consumption. Permissions to export corn alternate, in the Records, with prohibitions, apparently according to the abundance of the harvests near the coast. The greater part of the land, where it was cleared, must have been grass land. The chief commerce was the export of wool to Flanders where better and finer cloth could be made than any of native manufacture. A cloth, however, of coarser quality was made in England and even exported to Norway, and there were at least as early as the twelfth century guilds of weavers in London, Oxford, York, Nottingham, Huntingdon, Lincoln, and Winchester. One of the great objects of the townsmen when they acquired a little power, was to prevent the import of foreign manufactures and even the export of English wool, and they sometimes succeeded in obtaining a proclamation favourable, as they supposed, to their interests. The export duties on wool were, however, too

First effects of town in-fluence.

fertile a source of revenue to be abandoned; and a far better plan was carried into execution when a colony of Flemings was introduced into England by Edward III. in order that they might teach his subjects the art of which they enjoyed the sole possession. A most favourable impulse was thus given to an important branch of national industry, but its full effects do not yet become perceptible.

Perhaps, a more certain indication that commerce had already begun to exercise an influence over the thoughts and actions of men is to be discovered in certain changes of the law. In the reign of Edward I. land was, by two statutes, made liable for debts contracted in trade—a most convincing proof that the trading classes were beginning to show some power in the House of Commons, and possibly also that the land-holders were beginning to engage in commerce.

The proportion of the trading or town population to that of the country will, however, probably afford a better gauge of the strength of commercial interests *Proportion of* than any isolated facts to be gleaned from the *town popula-*
tion to rural Statute Book. Thus much it is possible to *population.* ascertain with some approach to accuracy, even though it may be impossible to discover what was the total population of England. Fortunately there exists a roll on which appears the number of men demanded by Edward II. (when he intended to make an expedition to Gascony) from every county except the palatinates, and from almost every town except the Cinque Ports. There can be no doubt that the force required from each place bore a certain ratio to the total of males between the ages of sixteen and sixty, who were at this time all liable to military service, and whom it was the duty of the Commissioners of Array to muster and inspect.

The first demand upon the shires (afterwards considerably reduced) was for 410 'hommes d'armes,' 1,020 hoblers, 2,190 archers, and 19,220 ordinary foot soldiers—making a total of 22,840. The first demand upon the towns (afterwards reduced in only three instances) was for 1,950 men, who were all to be ordinary foot soldiers. The towns were therefore held capable of supplying less than a twelfth part of the whole national army; or, in other words, it was supposed that the males between the ages of sixteen and sixty were distributed, in country and town, in about the proportion of eleven to one. Nor was this a mere supposition, for the views of frank-pledge, and the rolls relating to the Assise of Arms, must have given our forefathers a very clear insight into the population of every district; and the levies were, no doubt, made in accordance with well-ascertained facts. The proportion of women and children to adult males may of course be assumed as identical in all parts of the country, and it therefore seems reasonable to believe that the town population has been fairly estimated, and been set in its true place in the whole population of the kingdom. When the result is compared with the figures given in the census of 1811, it is possible to arrive at some idea of the great social revolution through which the country had passed in the interval. At the beginning of the nineteenth century, only 32 per cent. of the whole population were engaged in agricultural pursuits; the 32 per cent. had diminished to 25 per cent. in 1841; and the time seems now to be approaching when the rural districts will contain as small a fraction of the whole English population as the towns contained in the reign of Edward II.

In the roll from which these details have been gathered

may be discovered also some other facts which show a little more minutely the distribution of the population, and aid in defining the true position of the towns. London was credited with three times as many inhabitants as any other city or town in the realm. Next in rank, and all equal, were the towns near the chief seats of the worsted manufacture and woollen trade—Norwich, Lynn, and Great Yarmouth. York and Bristol were the only two others which were each expected to send a hundred men—as many as each of the three chief towns of the eastern counties. Lincoln stood next, and was asked for eighty men. Then came Winchester, Exeter, Shrewsbury, Hereford, and Oxford, which were each to send sixty. Canterbury, Ipswich, Northampton, Salisbury, Southampton, Bury St. Edmunds, and Beverley were each set down for fifty. Kingston-on-Hull was at first asked for forty, but the number was, as in the cases of Beverley and York, afterwards reduced. The demand upon Coventry was for thirty; upon Nottingham, Wells, Gloucester, Worcester, Chichester, and Boston, for twenty men each; upon Derby and Bath, for sixteen each; upon Rochester, Warwick, Stafford, Grantham, Stamford, and Huntingdon, for fifteen each. Maidstone, Southwark, Cirencester, Newark, and Ely, were required to muster no more than ten each; Somerton and Bedford, no more than six each. Barton-on-the-Humber, Grimsby, Scarborough, and Ravensrode are entered on the roll, but the scribe omitted to place the number of men opposite their names. The other towns which may have been in existence outside the counties palatine, and exclusive of the Cinque Ports, were apparently of too little importance to receive a separate summons, and their men were included in the general force of the counties.

[margin note: Relative magnitude of the towns.]

The most populous county was Lincolnshire, which
was required to send twelve hundred men of all arms;
First effects
of Commerce
upon the
distribution
of the popu-
lation. Kent and Norfolk hardly fell behind it. Yorkshire, in spite of its great area, held only the
fourth rank, and was set down for a thousand
and eighty men. Elsewhere there was nothing
specially worthy of remark except that the counties on
the sea-coast were considerably more populous than those
inland. This fact is, however, of importance, as showing
the first effects of commerce upon the distribution of the
population. The defective condition of the roads forbade
inland traffic of any magnitude; there was no considerable inland manufacture, and the district nearest to the
sea was therefore of necessity the first to feel the beneficial effects of trade. Goods could be carried a few miles
to the nearest port, but, as will hereafter be seen, it would
have been impossible to convey them in any great quantity any great distance. No one would have attempted
even to find a market for corn a hundred miles from
home; and the inhabitants of one county might be in the
enjoyment of plenty, while the inhabitants of another were
starving. It was, no doubt, the difficulty of internal communication which caused the chief seat of trade to be in
the eastern counties, whence it was easy to sail for
Flanders with wool and wool-fells, or to Norway with
worsteds. The branches of agricultural industry which
were connected with the production of these exports
naturally flourished in the immediate neighbourhood; and
thus it came to pass that if the sea-board generally was the
most populous part of England, the eastern counties were
the most populous parts of the sea-board.

London was the only city which was more populous
than its surrounding county; and from the fact that

its inhabitants numbered more than those of Middlesex may, perhaps, be inferred the general scantiness of the population throughout England. The London of those days was not the London of ours, but the 'City,' and nothing more. The proclamations against building in the suburbs, for which the reigns of the Tudors are remarkable, were yet to remain for many generations unnecessary. It is, therefore, most significant that the comparatively small area on which old London stood sent three hundred men to battle, when Middlesex sent only two hundred and forty. The only possible ·inference is that the rural houses and hamlets were few and thinly scattered, even in the district from which the capital was supplied with the necessaries of life.

Scantiness of the population as a whole.

In the important document from which these details have been gathered, the antagonism of burgher and baron is reflected from the description of the forces. From the shires are summoned men of all arms —cavalry, archers, and ordinary foot-soldiers ; from the towns only foot-soldiers, who constituted, indeed, the bulk of the army, but who were held in the lowest estimation. In every class there was a struggle for privilege. The old spirit of partisanship survived in all its narrowness. The feudal aristocracy, already perhaps jealous of the progress made by the townsmen in freedom and wealth, attempted, though not always so successfully as in the present instance, to retain in their own hands all the higher military duties. The townsmen, striving to free themselves from the extortions and the insolence of aristocratic sheriffs and justices, were no less anxious to assert their rights in opposition to the townsmen of a rival borough than against the knights who

Narrowmindedness among the townsmen and other classes.

affected to despise them.   Sympathy extended as yet no
farther than the guild commercial or the guild social.
Inherited barbarism prompted every man to regard his
neighbours as enemies; to take from others what others
could not keep ; to exclude others from advantages which
he had secured for himself or his guild.   In such an age
it was inevitable that all who engaged in commerce should
attempt to secure monopolies in the pettiest form—that
they should attempt to expel others from fields of commercial enterprise, in the same manner as their knightly
neighbours expelled weaker knights from coveted lands.
Thus the citizens of London, being more powerful than
other citizens, obtained commercial privileges throughout
England, which were reserved when charters were granted
to other towns.   Thus townsmen of other boroughs
showed at least as much anxiety to exclude rivals from
the rights which they acquired as to acquire those rights
for themselves.   Thus were introduced such clauses as
that which appears in the charter to Hereford, after the
guild-merchant had been legally recognised :—' We have
granted that no one who is not of that guild shall buy or
sell in the city or its suburbs without the consent of the
citizens.'

This narrowness of spirit, which, in spite of many
improvements in legislation, was common to all classes,
This was
illustrated in
the treatment
of the Jews.
was sometimes rendered doubly injurious by an
alliance of one class with another for the purpose
of destroying a third.   If it could be said with
strict precision of language that a nation can commit a
crime, it would be true that one of the greatest national
crimes ever committed, was committed in England when
the Jews were expelled through the combined influence
of the clergy, the traders, and the barons.   But that is not

a crime which is in accordance with law, and it was by law that the Jews were compelled to leave the country. This most remarkable episode in English history is specially worthy of note in a History of Crime both because it is in itself an illustration of the bigotry, jealousy, and contracted partisanship through which barbarism has to pass in its progress towards civilisation, and because there is good reason to suspect that it has a very close connection with one of the most audacious robberies ever perpetrated.

The principles of commerce, nowhere very well understood in the thirteenth century, were best understood by the Italians and the Jews. In all the chief Envy excited by them: their towns of England there was a Jewish quarter, superior knowledge of only too often the object of such attacks as commerce. those which followed the coronation of Richard I. The inhabitants were allowed to possess a certain organisation which was in later reigns designated, like that of a chartered town, a commune. It will be readily understood by all who realise to themselves the character of the age that these aliens were regarded with the most bitter hatred by the traders who were less successful in trade, by the land-holders whose patrimony was consumed in satisfying the demands of the usurers, and by the clergy, who, like the land-holders, fell into debt, and who were as implacable in their faith-feud as their ancestors had been in the blood-feud. Envy was added to other causes of animosity, and the Jews who had grown rich were commonly supposed to have gained their riches by every kind of crime which can be applied to the acquisition of property.

It was, therefore, no doubt, partly in accordance with popular feeling, though principally, as before explained, to secure a very important branch of revenue, that certain clauses were introduced into the regulations for the Jewry promulgated soon after the return of Richard I. from the Holy Land. Every Jew was to make oath that he would cause all his debts, securities and possessions of every kind to be registered, and that he would not only be guilty of no concealment himself, but would give information to the Justices of any concealment attempted by others, of all forgeries, and of all clippings of the coin. In these last provisions were embodied the popular belief concerning the practices of the Jews—a belief, indeed, not wholly unfounded, but at least equally true when applied to other classes.

They have various frauds attributed to them.

During the first nine years of John's reign the Jews lived in prosperity. But, when the necessities of the weak and treacherous king increased, the smallest loss of revenue became a danger to his throne, and he discovered or suspected that the Jews were in the habit of concealing their wealth and sending a false account to the Exchequer. This offence, it must be remembered, legally subjected them to the loss of all non-registered possessions and must have been in the king's eyes an unpardonable violation of the agreement according to which their rights of person and property were secured.

There is a famous story of a Jew of Bristol which proves that John's suspicions were not altogether unfounded. This man, had been guilty, perhaps, of some other offences, but certainly of attempting to defraud the king. He was required to pay ten thousand marks and the result shows that his accusers were well informed of his hidden treasures. The money-lender protested that he did not possess in the whole world so much as was demanded of him, that he was an

The story of the Jew of Bristol.

honest man, and much poorer than he was supposed to be. He was sternly bidden to make his choice—either to obey the king's command or to lose a tooth every day until his jaws were toothless. He still refused, he still denied his riches, he still asserted the truthfulness of his accounts. The king's officers began to execute their threat, and one of the Jew's teeth was drawn. His fortitude was not less remarkable than his wealth. He still maintained that he was innocent and poor; he still argued that he could not give what he did not possess. A second tooth was drawn, and still his resolution was unshaken. He submitted for seven successive days to the cruel torture, and then his courage gave way. He confessed his dishonesty and paid the money. Though it is difficult to repress a feeling of pity for the Jew, whose money was extorted from him in a most lawless fashion, who preferred the loss of seven teeth to the loss of his wealth and the loss of his wealth to the loss of an eighth tooth, it would be unjust to regard him merely as the helpless victim of a tyrannical king. He lived in a lawless age, in which little was thought of any mutilation, and he had grown rich by a succession of dishonest practices. His sufferings would have been averted had he rendered a true account of his wealth. The documents kept in the Common Chest of the Jews would have been accepted as sufficient evidence of his possessions, and a reluctance to pay on his part would have been met simply by a seizure of his goods and chattels on the part of the king.

After this time the kings were less able and, perhaps, less willing to protect the Jewry against its enemies. The royal authority was growing weaker—especially in all matters connected with the

Hostility of the Clergy to the Jews.

revenue. The privileges of the Jews were somewhat curtailed by Magna Carta. The influence of the Church began to make itself felt in opposition to the enemies of its faith. The ecclesiastical policy had long been to render the life of a Jew intolerable in every Christian community. During the earlier years of the reign of Henry III. a plan devised at Rome was adopted in England. It had the merits of great simplicity, and some ingenuity, but was hardly inferior in cruelty to the most cruel tortures of the Inquisition. At a time when a Jew was a mark for the blows of every ruffian and every Crusader, an order was obtained under the king's seal that all male Jews should wear a badge. They were forbidden to appear outside their houses, without two strips of white linen or parchment fastened conspicuously on the upper garment. Stephen Langton, then Archbishop of Canterbury, would gladly have distinguished the Jewesses in the same manner as the Jews, and have caused the fingers of all good Christians to point at them in scorn, A decree to that effect was passed at a synod held at Oxford, but was not enforced by royal authority till a later period.

About seventy years before the expulsion of the Jews from England the animosity of the clergy against The Clergy them begins to be most conspicuous, and desired their expulsion. another cause for it appears in addition to religious fanaticism. In the third year of Henry's reign, Pandulf, the Pope's Legate, was Bishop Elect of Norwich and placed himself at once in the van of persecution. The moment was most opportune for the execution of every clerical design. The king was but a child. Peter des Roches, Bishop of Winchester, and Hubert de Burg were joint guardians of the realm. Pandulf wrote a letter to them in which he declared that he could no longer bear with patience the continual clamourings of the Christians against the wicked ways of the Jews. This perfidious people, he said, was always extorting immoderate and oppressive usury from Christians in direct opposition to the decree of the Lateran Council. The victims were so exhausted that they could hardly breathe. His indignation was specially excited by the misfortunes of his dear sons the Abbot and Monks of Westminster. A Jew, named Isaac of Norwich, vexed them unceasingly with suits to be pleaded before the justices of the Jews. Pandulf therefore, requested, or rather commanded the Bishop of Winchester and Hubert de Burg to give instructions to the justices of the Jews for the postponement of the hearing of a cause, in which the abbot was defendant, until the legate could himself be present. It would then, he added, be time to consider, how an end could be made of these evil practices, and how the great stumbling block could be cast out of the kingdom.

This is the first indication of any design to expel the Jews ; and it is worthy of remark that, although Pandulf begins his epistle by expressions of deep com- The clergy were in debt to them. miseration for all believers who may be suffering from Jewish extortion, he ends it by asking a special indulgence for his own friends. The abbot and monks of Westminster were in debt ; the scandal of their case and others like it suggested to the legate not that the debt should be paid and that the debtors should be more prudent in future, but that the debt should remain unpaid and that the creditors should be exiled beyond the seas. The Abbey of Westminster, however, was in no worse case than many other religious houses which had mortgaged their lands to the Jews. Tithes, too, which were originally destined for the benefit of the poor, the repair of the church and the support of the minister, became the security of the Jewish capitalists ; and in the smallest of the English counties there were at least three parsons at one time who had given bonds to the money-lenders—the parson of Luffenham, the parson of Whissendine, and the parson of Morcott.

Isaac of Norwich, who roused the wrath of the legate by demanding his interest from the Abbot of West-A contempo- minster, was one of the wealthiest and most rary carica-
ture of them. powerful of the Jews, and therefore excited the jealousy of all classes in the highest degree. He was not only a money-lender, but a merchant. He possessed a quay at Norwich, at which his vessels could lade or unlade their freights. Whole districts were mortgaged or otherwise pledged to him at once. Letters were frequently addressed to him in the king's name. He was probably the richest man among the Jews of Norwich, and, no doubt, infinitely richer than any of his fellow-townsmen who were Christians. He appears as the principal figure in a cartoon, with which a satirical clerk in the Exchequer adorned the head of a roll. The drawing, though rude, is full of life and spirit. The scene is laid on the walls of a castle. Isaac stands in the centre of a group, with his head and shoulders above all the surrounding figures. He presents three faces, one in the centre looking to the front, and one on each side in profile. Surmounting the three is a crown, and it is perhaps to be supposed that there is a fourth face concealed from the spectator, and that the Jew is a monarch surveying his possessions in every quarter from which the wind can blow. On the right of Isaac stands Mosse Mokke, another Jew of Norwich, and on the left Avegay, a money-lending Jewess. A horned demon

touches each of these two on the nose—one with the right fore-finger, the other with the left. On the right of Mosse Mokke is a figure holding a pair of scales heaped up on each side with coins. On the left of Avegay is Dagon, the god of the Philistines, who is seated on a turret, and has evidently become the faithful subject of the Jew. Further still to the left are three demons in armour, one of whom holds another pair of scales with more coins. Though six centuries have passed away since the sketch was made, there are many of the allusions which it is impossible to mistake. The castle of which the Jew is master tells of the jealousies which were roused by the acquisitions of the usurers, and shows that popular feeling was already prepared for the decree which subsequently forbade the Jews to hold land. The coins and scales point to the means by which it was commonly supposed that all the Jews grew rich—to the devices of clipping and counterfeiting. As Mosse Mokke was subsequently hanged, it may be reasonably inferred that he was at last found guilty of the crime of which he had long been suspected. All the principal figures may be considered not only as caricatures of real persons, but as types of a class. Isaac represents the greatest men among the Jews who, in wealth at least, were the equals of proud barons ; Mosse Mokke represents the commoner sort of Jews, who were, perhaps, in some instances not content with sixty-five per cent. per annum as the interest for their money. Avegay represents the Jewesses who were usurers, who were so numerous and who so frequently bore the same name, that it is impossible to determine which of them the draughtsman intended to portray.

The wealth accumulated by the Jews had long

excited the covetousness and the wonder of every class;
The Jews and the Pope's money-changers. but about the year 1235 the appearance of the Caursins, who were permitted to style themselves 'the Pope's Money-changers,' produced a ferment throughout England. The spectacle of Christians practising all the Jewish devices, and growing as rich as the Jews themselves, excited the cupidity of all ranks. Every man was eager to have his neighbour in his debt, and to receive sixty pounds per annum for every hundred which he lent. The field, however, seems in the end to have been divided between the Caursins and the Jews—the only two classes which had sufficient knowledge to make their trade permanently successful. The objects with which these Pope's Money-changers were sent into England was no doubt to aid in expelling the Jews—an object never lost from view from the time when it was first set forth in Pandulf's letter. An attempt had already been made to deprive the Jews of food, by an injunction of the Archbishop of Canterbury that no Christian should supply their wants—though this had been superseded by the king's writs. According to the spirit of the age, the possession of a privilege by any class naturally excited a desire in another class not to participate in it, but to seize it. That which had been granted to the Jews the clergy, therefore, naturally enough wished to appropriate for the Caursins.

The Jews were, however, for some time successful in preserving their wealth. They had the means of doing The Jews bribe the Justices. that which was now and long afterwards done by all who wished to retain property or increase it. They could at least bribe the Christian Justices of the Jews, as those officers were entitled who had

to decide causes between Jews and Christians, and to
enquire what revenue could be extracted from the Jewry.
If all property in the hands of the Jews was registered,
and if they could not recover by law either the interest
or the principal of any debt which could not be proved
by reference to the Common Chest, it was manifestly
impossible for them to defraud the Government, except
by hiding coin or other valuables in their houses. But
to put away his talent in a napkin, to let his money lie
idle without a hope of increase, would, in the eyes of a
Jew, be to dry up the fountain of his riches. His plan,
therefore, was bold, simple, and effectual; he gave the
Justices as much as was required to secure their support.
Thus it became necessary to issue writs of inquisition
into the concealments of the Jewry. Thus Philip Lovel
was convicted of receiving presents to further the interests of Jews, and Robert de la Hoo of affixing his seal
to a forged bond, and both were deprived of the office of
Justice.

The Pope's money-changers nevertheless grew gradually richer, and the Jews gradually poorer. In the
civil wars of the reign of Henry III. the Jews Their privi-
fared even worse than the rest of the popula- stricted.
tion, and were robbed and massacred in riot after riot.
The Jewry, in the sense of the revenue to be derived
from taxes on the Jews, was mortgaged again and again,
until at last it was pledged to their rivals the Caursins.
With the right of exacting payment was commonly given
the right of distraining; and there can be no doubt that
during some of the later years of the Jews' sojourn in
England many of their goods and of their securities, in
the shape of bonds, passed into the hands of the Pope's
money-changers. In the year 1270 it was ordained that

no Jews should in future possess any freehold in England, except the dwellings which they occupied, or which they let to other Jews in the towns where they had licence to reside. All previous conveyances made to them were to be held null and void, and the lands were to be given back to the Christians who had formerly been in possession, on repayment of the purchase money without interest.

Soon after the accession of Edward I. was enacted the Statute of the Jewry, in which it was recited that many honest men had lost their inheritances through the payment of usury to the Jews, and that many sins had been committed from the same cause. It was therefore ordained, for the honour of God and for the common benefit of the people, that no Jew should in future practise usury. In this it is not difficult to perceive a desire to conciliate the landholders and the townsmen. In another document it is no less easy to detect the influence of the Church. The king was informed that certain Jews were in the habit of blaspheming the Catholic faith, the Crucifix, the Blessed Virgin Mary, and the Sacraments. He considered it his duty to repress such iniquity by virtue of his office as a Catholic prince; and the Justices appointed to investigate crimes affecting the coinage of the realm were commanded to punish all Jews guilty of insults to the Christian faith by death or mutilation. The letter concluded with a command, long desired by the clergy, that every Jewess should wear a badge on the upper garment in the same manner as the male Jews.

We who live in an age in which half-civilised countries Absurd   still afford instances of attacks upon the Jews,
accusations
against them. and of absurdly false charges made against them, can, while we congratulate ourselves upon our own

progress, estimate at their true value some of the accusations made by our forefathers. The Jews of Lincoln, it was said, had stolen a Christian child, hidden it away in one of their houses, fattened it on milk, and then crucified it in mockery of the Christian faith. It was reported that a general invitation had been issued to all the Jews of England, who had journeyed from every city in order that they might be present at the ceremony. A jury of course convicted those Jews who were accused, and they were hanged for an offence which it may be considered certain that they did not commit. At Oxford, one Ascension-day, the Chancellor, the Masters, and the scholars were marching in procession through the streets of the city with the cross borne before them. Suddenly, none knew from whence, a man was seen to throw himself upon the bearer of the holy symbol, to seize it in his hand, to hurl it to the ground, and to trample it in the mire. The surprise was so great that he had escaped before an attempt could be made to capture him, and the consternation was increased by the discovery that the cross was broken. Every one said that the author of this outrage must have been a Jew, and that, if he could not be taken, the community to which he belonged must be made to suffer. The Jews of Oxford were therefore compelled to provide a new cross of silver to replace that which was broken, and to set up a cross of marble as a memorial of the event.

Such were the offences against Holy Church of which the Jews were suspected in the time of Edward I. Whether there was any better foundation for the accusation that they were in the habit of clipping or counterfeiting the coin it is not easy to decide. But the previous convictions of moneyers employed at the author-

Two hundred and eighty of them hanged in London.

ised mints are at least sufficient to show that the Jews were no worse in this respect than their neighbours.   The result, however, of an enquiry into the state of the coinage, in the reign of Edward I., was that two hundred and eighty Jews were hanged in London alone.   After this wholesale execution, a great number of persons, who in the records are styled Christians, adopted the profession of informer, and threatened with prosecution those Jews who had never been convicted or even suspected.   The object was simply to extort money ; and as conviction was followed by death, the price of silence was high in proportion.

Suspected of every crime, deprived of their synagogues, some of which were converted into Christian churches, forbidden even to pray after their own fashion within the walls of their own houses, the Jews still lingered a few years in England. But in the year 1289, the clergy, supported no doubt by the popular feeling both of the townsmen and of the landholders, made a final and successful effort to banish the infidels from the country—or, as they expressed it, to separate the goats from the sheep.   The Exchequer had ceased to draw a considerable income from the Jewry.   The king had less control over the revenue than his predecessors, and had therefore but little interest in opposing the general wish, and he was persuaded to name a day, after which no Jew was to be found in England on pain of death.   Cruel as such an edict would be at any time, it was doubly cruel when there was hardly a country in Europe in which the exiles could seek refuge.   The Jews had already been expelled from France as they were now expelled from England, and there was no Christian nation which would clothe the naked and feed the hungry when the hungry and the

Cruel expulsion of the Jews from the kingdom.

naked were Israelites. But the order had gone forth that the Israelites were to depart ; there was to be a new Exodus, in which they could not spoil the Egyptians, but must be despoiled in turn.

More than sixteen thousand Jews sailed from England, in the year 1290, in quest of new homes. So sad a banishment as this has never been narrated by historian or conceived by poet. Men who have been driven into exile for political offences have, in all ages, been consoled with political sympathy abroad. Even the Phocæans when they abandoned their hearths were not without hopes of a glorious future. The Jews were compelled to embark on frail vessels with their families and with those moveables which they were allowed to retain. They were at the mercy of seamen who bore them no good will, and who thought it rather a good deed than a crime to injure a Jew. Their most difficult task was not, as the Roman had said of other exiles, to ecape from themselves, but to escape from Christians. They were uncertain where they might be permitted to land, and certain only that if they escaped death they were doomed to persecution. Their fate was not very unlike that of the Paterine heretics, whom all true Christians were forbidden to feed, a century earlier, and was hardly less cruel than that of other heretics who were burnt in England a century later.

Both the king and the Church profited by the expulsion of the Jews. The king became master of all their houses and all their debts. The latter he appropriated Its advantage to the king to satisfy his own needs ; the proceeds of the and the former he promised that he would devote to clergy. pious uses. The Letters Patent by which he granted the houses, the synagogues, and the burial places of the Jews to his Christian subjects are still extant, and show that the greater portion of the synagogues and burial-grounds, at least, fell into the hands of the clergy. If the Jews possessed any friend in England who would write a letter to them in their exile, they must have suffered a new pang in learning that their cemetery near Cripplegate, where the bones of their ancestors had reposed nearly two hundred years, had been bestowed, as a mere piece of waste land, upon the Dean of St. Paul's.

Whether the monks of Westminster had, in the seventy years which had elapsed since the time of Pandulf and Isaac of Norwich, succeeded in freeing them- selves from the debts with which they were burdened, it is now impossible to discover. The difficulty of paying off money borrowed from usurers at a high rate of interest is proverbial ; and it is, therefore, by no means improbable that there was still embarrassment in the monastery, and that bonds, in which the corporation was held liable, were still out- standing. When the Jewry began to be impoverished, the Pope's money-changers, and, after them, the Lombard merchants or bankers, must, in the ordinary course of business, have become possessed of many securities previously held by the Jews ; and the clergy, who had disliked the Jews as creditors, complained no less bitterly of their creditors the Caursins. These con- siderations may, perhaps, afford some explanation of a crime which was attributed to the Abbot and monks of Westminster, a few years after the banishment of the Jews, and in which some members of the House were almost certainly implicated.

Edward I. had not many days left Westminster for a campaign against the Scots. The whole available force of the kingdom was on its march northwards to crush the

Its bearing upon a crime attributed to the Abbot and Monks of Westmin- ster.

brave Wallace. In the king's absence there was no body-
guard at the Palace ; every soldier who could be spared
was in active service in the field. On the twenty- The Great
sixth of April, and succeeding days, great num- Robbery at
                                                 the Royal
bers of precious stones, and all kinds of gold- Treasury.
work and silver-work were offered for sale to the goldsmiths of London, and bought by them with a readiness
which did them no credit. A rumour soon travelled from
mouth to mouth that the Royal Treasury, which was
within the Abbey, but close to the Palace at Westminster,
had been entered and robbed. Nearly all its contents had
been carried off, and some of them had been found in the
burial-ground near the Abbey. The loss to the king was
afterwards declared to have been no less than a hundred
thousand pounds. It is not easy to state the modern
equivalent of such a sum ; but materials for an estimate
may be found in the fact that the whole revenue of the
kingdom amounted to no more than forty thousand
pounds about thirty years before the time of the robbery,
and that the customs of the chief ports of England were
farmed to a company of foreign merchants, about thirty
years later, for an annual payment, not exceeding eight
thousand pounds.

The king was in Scotland when his loss was
announced to him, and it was not until the sixth of June,
when he was at Linlithgow, that he found an Commission
opportunity to appoint a commission of enquiry. of Enquiry.
The mode of proceeding is a curious illustration of
the ancient jury-system, in which there was no distinction between jurors and witnesses. A jury was
empanelled for every ward of the city of London,
and for every hundred of Middlesex and Surrey—and
in addition to these there was a jury of goldsmiths

and a jury of aldermen. The separate findings of the
juries are the sum of the evidence in the case. On
the chief points there was a remarkable agreement in
the verdicts ; on others, the jurors of some of the
hundreds were silent. It was not disputed that access
had been gained to the Treasury from within the walls
of the Abbey, that an aperture had been made in the solid
masonry for the purpose, and that the person most actively
concerned was one Richard Podelicote, who was described
as a travelling merchant. Some of the juries found that
he had the assistance of masons and carpenters, and most
of them, including the aldermen, that he was insti-
gated by certain of the monks, who had planned the
whole scheme. The Sacristan of the Abbey had, according to some accounts, offered a portion of the jewels to a
girl to induce her to become his mistress. He and the
Sub-prior had, according to the aldermen and other jurors,
been the principal framers of the design. The Sub-prior,
too, had been seen by the Keeper of the Palace in the very
act of carrying off some of the spoil.

Abbot and monks were alike under grave suspicion
when these facts were brought to light. The Sacristan,
Indictment Sub-prior, and others were imprisoned in the
and Trial of Tower. The Abbot, however, was held to bail.
the Sacristan
and Monks. A petition was then sent to the king, in which
it was represented that the abbot and monks and other
persons accused were innocent, and that they were suffering great injustice in being detained in the Tower.
Though the abbot was really in the enjoyment of freedom,
the king's sympathy was, perhaps, excited by the picture
of an abbot and all his monks confined on a charge of
robbery. But whether this was so or not, he lost no time
in appointing justices to hear and determine the case.

Juries were summoned from the various hundreds and wards, as in the preliminary enquiry, and their recorded verdicts were in all material points identical with those of their predecessors. The correctness of their finding was to a great extent confirmed by the subsequent confession of Podelicote. He did not directly implicate any one except himself, but he admitted that he had been at work upon the wall, through which the Treasury had been entered, night after night, from the seventeenth of December to the twenty-fourth of April. On the night of the twenty-fourth he succeeded in making his way through. He spent the whole of the twenty-fifth in the Treasury, and occupied himself during the day in selecting jewels. In the course of the following night the treasure was carried away,

It is quite evident that an enterprise which required more than four months for its accomplishment could not have been successful had there been no collu- Conduct of the monks sion within the Abbey-gates. The findings of before and after convic- the various juries point to a deep-laid conspiracy tion. between some persons in the Abbey and others in the neighbouring Palace. There was a path from one to the other which was frequented up to a certain hour in the evening, after which the gates were closed and no one could pass. It was remembered, when the robbery had been committed, that these gates had for some time previously been closed at an earlier hour than usual. This could hardly have been done without the consent of persons in authority in both buildings, and the object was obviously to give Podelicote an opportunity of working without fear of interruption. It is not, indeed, clear that the abbot was cognisant of what was done by his monks, or that the keeper of the Palace connived at what was done by his subordinates. It is, however, quite certain that, after all the accomplices had been paid, the booty would have been sufficient to pay even such a debt as might have been due on a bond transferred from the Jews to other merchants or money-changers. It is also quite certain that charters were commonly forged in religious houses, and that when the fraud was detected the abbot did not commonly suffer. There is, therefore, no antecedent improbability in the supposition that this audacious crime of the fourteenth century was planned by those who would not have hesitated to secure land for their House by means of a false deed. So, no doubt, thought the judges, who sentenced some laymen, against whom verdicts were found, to be hanged, and detained the convicted monks in prison more than two years. The monkish writers exclaim loudly against the iniquity of the Justices, but adduce not a particle of evidence to show that the juries were deceived, and do not even accuse them of taking a false oath. Nor is it even denied by these partial historians that the abbot and monks of Westminster were guardians of the treasure which was stored within their walls. Nevertheless, when the king returned in triumph from Scotland, the Church had sufficient influence to procure the liberation of the monks— partly, no doubt, in celebration of his victories. But this act of clemency seems to have had indirectly the effect of increasing the suspicion against all the inmates of the monastery. An irreconcileable discord arose between the abbot and his monks; charges and counter-charges were made; words were uttered and acts were done which the monkish chronicler describes as too paltry for repetition; and the king, the nobility, and the members of other religious houses were utterly disgusted at the scandal to religion.

It is only in the inner life of the nation—in the life which lies beneath pomp and pageantry and ceremony— that progress can be measured, only by the readiness with which laws are obeyed that the success of legislation can be fairly appreciated. During this period, when the towns were be- ginning to enjoy their civic organisation according to charter, when the assertion of rival interests was developing, as it were, by a happy chance, the English constitution, when commerce was feebly groping its way to the light in the midst of such dark deeds as the oppression and expulsion of its best friends, the Jews, the criminal law was undergoing a change wholly out of proportion to any change effected in the manners of the people. The only conclusion to be drawn from this strange contrast is that the general tone of society is at any time a stronger force than the provisions of the most brilliant law-giver, though, of course, as his thoughts are made known to the masses, he may in the end improve the general tone. In proportion as education is more widely diffused, the good effects are more easily produced ; but, when barbarism has held its own for centuries, a mere improvement in criminal procedure long remains little more than an improvement in writing. How much progress there was in the law, a slight sketch will suffice to show ; how little progress there was in refinement may be made apparent by some of the deeds done in the period between the Third Crusade and the Black Death, and still more by a picture of England as it was in the year before that terrible plague.

Contrast between the improvements in the laws and the lawlessness of the people.

We have seen what was the trial by ordeal in the dreary age which preceded the Conquest; we have seen

The Ordeal abolished through the influence of the Church. what was the action of the Church in persecuting heretics and Jews ; the beneficent influence of the Church in abolishing the ordeal yet remains to be told.   Soon after the establishment of the Norman rule, the ancient practice of conducting the ceremony within the walls of a church was abandoned. The scene of ' God's Judgment' was removed to a trench or pit, and numerous entries on rolls of the reign of Henry II. refer to payments made for the preparation of the pits, and the consecration of the apparatus.   The ordeal by water still continued to be the more common, though in the reign of John a number of persons of ill repute were allowed the alternative of the water or of ' carrying the iron.'   The exclusion of the hot water and the hot iron from churches was, however, but the prelude to their exclusion from the office of detecting guilt by order of the Church.   By a decree of the Lateran Council in the year 1215 the ordeal was forbidden, and in the year 1219 it was formally abolished in England ; and there is no doubt that to the clergy is due the credit of putting an end to this particular form of barbarism.

As compurgation in cases of felony was now no longer permitted, except in some privileged towns and in

The judicial duel: an instance. ecclesiastical jurisdictions, the abolition of the ordeal left the accused without any means of exculpation except the duel.   This does not seem to have been repugnant to the ecclesiastical opinion of the time, and the wager of battle was yet to remain an established institution during many long ages.   It was in use as a form of trial for civil no less than for criminal matters, and it was applied even to such a purpose as the decision of the right to an advowson. A case, indeed, in which an advowson was in dispute affords a better insight into the nature of the judicial duel than any other which a laborious search has brought to light. Outside the walls of Northampton a plot of ground was marked out for the trial, and was kept by soldiers. The Justices in Eyre sat as they would have sat in a grand assise or in an assise of novel disseisin. The parties to the suit appeared, as was the law in civil cases, not in person, but each by champion. A great crowd surrounded the field of battle, or court of law, but the partisans on one side were in far greater number than those on the other. After the signal had been given, the combatants began to struggle, each bound to conquer or die, or to bear for ever afterwards the most disgraceful of all names—recreant. At length both fell at the same moment. The friends of the deforciants, fearing that the issue might be adverse to them, drew their swords, broke through the line of soldiers, and surrounded the two fallen men. Some were mounted, others on foot, and the force at the disposal of the judges was wholly unable to cope with them. They held the ground and kept off both the soldiers and the justices. The champion of the plaintiffs was unable to raise himself, the horses were made to trample upon him, and when he was quite helpless he was proclaimed a recreant. The sheriff raised the hue and cry, and the judges left the ground, without any attempt to bring the proceedings to a legal termination. A complaint was afterwards laid before the king in council, when it was held that the attack upon the justices and the champion tended to the subversion of the royal dignity, peace, and crown, and that the

champion should not incur the infamy and the disabili-
ties of recreancy, but should enjoy his free law as fully as
before the duel.

To such a trial alone, subject to such interruptions,
could a person accused of felony be brought, after the
The Petty
Jury taking
the place of
the Ordeal,
and, in part,
of the Duel.
abolition of the ordeal; and even this method of testing the truth or falsehood of a
charge could not be applied unless the accusation was made by an individual as distinguished from the ' country' or the jury of the hundred.   It
was at this time that a form of proceeding which was
developed into our modern trial by petty jury crept into
the place left vacant by the hot iron and the hot water.
The presentment made by the jury of the hundred was
no more than the story of a body of accusers, which was
commonly denied by the person accused.   The judges
soon discovered that unless some other means of arriving
at the truth could be found, either every indictment
would be equivalent to a conviction, or every criminal
would escape through the want of some final process by
which he might be tried.   They therefore enquired of
each juror of the twelve who had presented the charge
upon what information he believed it.   They also asked
the accused whether he suspected any juror of malice,
and removed those to whom he objected.   It often happened that eleven of the jurors had taken the word of the
twelfth for the facts, and that the twelfth, when closely
pressed, could not assign any reasonable ground for his
statements.   After this examination, and, when necessary, the substitution of unchallenged for challenged
jurors, the jury, which might still consist entirely of the
men who had preferred the indictment, found a second
verdict which decided the fate of the prisoner.   This

was a step made at once towards our modern system of
examining and cross-examining witnesses, and towards
the creation of a second jury to consider the charge of
the first. As soon as this second verdict had become a
recognised stage of the criminal proceedings instituted
'by the country,' it naturally suggested an alternative for
the duel in prosecutions instituted by individuals. Thus
it became the custom to ask the accused in what manner
he would be tried, and thus arose the form of answer
'by my country.' The jury in this case, though chosen
in precisely the same manner as the jury which made
indictments, or as we should now say, the grand jury, yet
gave a final verdict upon a particular case in the same
manner as the modern petty jury. But when the precedent had once been set, when once a jury had been
summoned for the simple purpose of deciding the guilt
or innocence of a particular prisoner, it was inevitable
that a distinction should sooner or later be drawn
between the jury which accused and the jury which tried
—that where an indictment was preferred the final
decision should sooner or later be by the verdict of a
second jury, not by a second verdict of the first.

In the reign of Edward I. some progress had been
made towards the division, into two classes, of the juries
summoned to give verdicts upon criminal affairs.
Nothing could better illustrate the practice of the time
than the proceedings which followed the great robbery
at the Treasury. The juries of the various hundreds
and wards, summoned in obedience to a special commission, found that certain persons were implicated in
the crime. After the indictment, five justices, of whom
only two had been engaged in the preliminary investigation, were directed to try the prisoners. Juries were

summoned from the same hundreds and wards as before, but in obedience to a different commission. There was only one reason why the individual jurors who sat upon the second occasion should not have been in every instance men who had not sat upon the first. The existence of each of the first set of juries, taken as a whole, had as much come to an end after the committal of the monks to the Tower as the existence of a grand jury which sat at the Old Bailey ten years ago has come to an end at the present moment. But as the first set of juries were expected to give a verdict according to their own knowledge, so also were the second. In both cases the jurors were witnesses ; and, unless disqualified by their conduct in the first stage of the proceedings, they would be required to repeat their evidence in a final verdict. Thus, though the abolition of ordeal caused in a very short time a formal separation of the trying jury from the accusing jury, the whole system of trial was, so far as criminal affairs were concerned, long afterwards vitiated by the inherent defect which allowed the same person to exercise at once the functions of prosecutor, of witness, and of judge. It cannot, indeed, be shown with any certainty that, even in civil causes, witnesses distinct from the jurors were examined in court before the time of Henry VI. ; and centuries afterwards the jurors were, in theory at least, supposed to have been summoned because their testimony was of value upon matters of fact.

In the next chapter it will be shown that when convictions were obtained, they followed almost always upon indictments, and hardly ever upon appeals— which were accusations made by individuals. For this there were many reasons. One was that when jurors had in the first instance given an accusatory

Indictments and Appeals: Party-swearing.

verdict, they could not afterwards give a verdict of acquittal without imminent danger of a prosecution for perjury. Another was that the old habit of fellowship in swearing had contributed not a little to the growth of trial by jury. If the reeve and thanes accused a man, before the Conquest, his friends made a party to swear that he was innocent; if a private person was the accuser, his oath also was supported by those of his friends. Though these ancient institutions had gone through many changes, there was still sufficient resemblance to the old forms for the old spirit of party-swearing to continue in full vigour. Though the indictment was a species of compromise between the accusation by reeve and thanes and the accusation by the oaths of a fixed number of private persons, the obligation to injure as much as possible the adversary of a friend was considered as binding as ever; and if it would not ensure a conviction, there was no motive which would. On the other hand, compurgation, though no longer a part of the common law of the land, was by no means forgotten. The recollection of it was kept alive by the wager of law which, though now applicable only to minor trespasses, was identical with the ancient mode of escaping punishment for great offences. In appeals, in cases in which a charge was made by one person against another, the juror who, it must be remembered, had taken no part in the accusation, could hardly fail to look upon himself in the light of a compurgator. His simple reasoning would be that he must be on one side or other, that he was not on the side of the prosecutor, and that he must therefore be necessarily on the side of the prisoner. He had probably acted often enough as one of the 'hands' in the wager of law, and it must have been impossible, in an age of such dense ignorance, to make him see, in an appeal of rape or murder, that he was not simply one of the 'hands' whose office it was to swear, without hesitation, that the person appealed was innocent.

In the confusion which followed upon the abolition of the ordeal the judges seem to have been thrown into some perplexity by the refusal of prisoners to submit themselves to any kind of trial. In the reign of John an accused person who 'went to' the fire or water, and failed to clear himself, was hanged. Only two years after these tests had ceased to be applied in England, some criminals made the experiment of standing mute when brought before the justices, and their fate was precisely what it would previously have been if they had been convicted by the 'Judgment of God.' Early in the reign of Edward I. a number of malefactors were surrounded and attacked by the Sheriff of Yorkshire. Some were killed in the struggle, some were made prisoners, and some were beheaded on the spot, because they would not consent to be tried 'according to the law and custom of the realm.' This, however, does not appear to have been considered satisfactory, for a year or two later, a statute was passed to the effect that when notorious felons were accused at the king's suit, and refused to stand to the law, they should be sent to the 'prison forte et dure.' About the reign of Henry IV. the 'prison forte et dure' was transformed into the 'peine forte et dure,' or torture of the press, which was not indicated in the Statute of Edward I., and did not for many generations form a portion of the judgment pronounced upon mute persons. Before the additional horror was inflicted, to be adjudged to the 'prison forte et dure,' was to be adjudged to penance and perpetual

Standing mute : the 'prison forte et dure.'

imprisonment; but the penance was confinement in a narrow cell and absolute starvation. The gaolers, however, when their prisoners were their friends, found in the credulity of the age a ready aid to their friendship; and it is possible that some distrust of their fidelity may have suggested the hideous cruelty by which an attempt was afterwards made to draw speech from the silent. A pardon granted by Edward III. shows with sufficient clearness both what was the intention of the law with respect to those who would not plead, and how it was sometimes thwarted. 'The King to all his bailiffs and faithful men to whom these presents shall come, Greeting. Whereas Cecilia, widow of John Rygeway, lately indicted concerning the death of her husband, was adjudged to her penance because she held herself mute before our Justices of Gaol delivery at Nottingham; and whereas she afterwards sustained life without food or drink, in close prison, during forty days, after the manner of a miracle, and contrary to human nature, as we have been informed on trustworthy testimony ; We, moved by piety, to the praise of God, and of the glorious Virgin his mother, from whom, as is believed, this miracle has proceeded, have of our special grace pardoned unto the same Cecilia the execution of the judgment aforesaid, and do desire that she be delivered from prison and be no further impeached of her body.'   ✦

Though it may be said that the abolition of ordeal led indirectly, after many generations, to the institution of the torture by press, it seems nevertheless to have had collateral effects which more than compensated for this perpetuation of barbarism in a new form. The horrible punishment of mutilation which was characteristic of the centuries immediately

Effects of the punishment of mutilation.

preceding the Conquest and had been adopted into the laws of the Conqueror, as best fitted to impress the native mind, gradually became extinct. The brutalising effect which it had had upon the whole population can hardly be conceived in the modern age of refinement. In the midst of the general lawlessness every man was, when he had the power, a law unto himself, and inflicted upon his enemy the punishment which the law of the land destined for the evil doer. Maiming, that is to say, depriving a human being of a member, was consequently one of the commonest of offences—for which the law provided a wholly inadequate remedy in the appeal of maihem. The

An illustra- subject can hardly be better illustrated than by
tion.   an act which has been recorded among the rolls
of the Court of King's Bench. One Guy Mortimer was rector of the church of Kingston-on-Hull. He bore some grudge against William Joye, one of his parishioners, whom he instructed another clergyman and some of his followers to attack. When the man was prostrate and helpless, Guy appeared, drew a knife, and with his own hand deliberately cut off the upper lip of his enemy. The sufferer estimated his loss at a hundred pounds—a considerable sum in those times—and instituted a suit. The two chief offenders appeared in court, but maintained that as they were clerks they were not bound to answer, and persistently refused to answer in the absence of their Ordinary. The court, however, held that this was a case in which no Benefit of Clergy could be claimed —not indeed, because the offence was too heinous, but because it was a mere trespass and no felony. Judgment was accordingly given against the rector and his assistant, who were each required to pay a hundred pounds, and were committed to prison until they should have

satisfied the complainant and the king. The deed which
Guy Mortimer had done was simply one of the deeds
familiar to the executioner from time immemorial, and
familiar in its results to all Englishmen who, if they were
not thoroughly accustomed to see lipless criminals, had
heard 'many a time of the sights seen by their fathers.

It was, however, one of the most agreeable features
of the age that such acts were ceasing to have the sanction of the law, and were reserved for occasions Gradual sub-
in which it seemed expedient to execute a more stitution of
other punish-
than ordinarily impressive sentence. It was, as ments.
the laws of the Conqueror show, considered more merciful to hang than to cut off an important member, and to
this extent justice had grown more humane towards
thieves. Even in the reign of Edward III. the ancient
terrors were brought to bear upon the too prevalent habit
of brawling in court. A tailor of London was convicted
of this act of contempt, of which he had been guilty in
the presence not only of the justices, but of the king
himself at Westminster. He was condemned to imprisonment in the Tower of London for life, and to the loss
of his right hand. He had, however, the good fortune
to be pardoned ; and the rolls of Gaol Delivery of this
period show conclusively that the ordinary punishments
were hanging, the pillory, and the tumbrel or dung
cart.

There is so close a connexion between the disuse of
mutilation as punishment and the mitigation of the
Forest Laws that the consideration of the one The Forest
naturally suggests the consideration of the Laws.
other. It will be remembered that, before the Conquest,
certain lands were known as folc-land or people's land,
which was, perhaps, unenclosed, even during the Roman

occupation, and that certain common rights existed on portions even of those lands which were afterwards designated manors. The wood-lands had been regarded by the invading Teutons in nearly the same light in which the American Indians used to regard their hunting-grounds. Tribes, to which cities were an abomination, had advanced but very little beyond that view of life according to which the whole world is a free forest, where the first comer may take whatever he can find. Other notions concerning property were with difficulty fostered in the towns ; princes and kings, though recognised as the heads of their clans, were long before they could impress upon their followers that they ought to enjoy any exclusive rights over the haunts of the partridge, the hare, or the deer. Traditions, handed down from the time when land was held in common, found their expression in attacks on parks, and chaces, and in the life of the forest brigand many a century after the Conquest. They survive, even now, in the sympathy often enjoyed by poachers, and in the antipathy often shown to the game-laws. But long before the Norman Conquest private individuals had asserted their exclusive rights to hunting over their own woods and fields, and king Canute had issued an impressive warning to trespassers upon the royal forests which were probably a part of the folc-land. Under the Conqueror the folc-land became in name, as it was already in fact, the king's land, over which the forest laws were exercised with a rigour often described as execrable. The truth, however, seems to be that if any change was really effected in this respect under our first three kings of the French line, it was only a part of that vigilant severity which pervaded the administration of other laws and was necessary for the security of foreign

invaders. The forest courts or moots have both in their
names and in their mode of operation the marks of an
age anterior to that of William I. The policy of de-
vastating whole tracts of country, which afterwards
became forest land, was suggested, in part, at least, by
military considerations. The doctrine, that hunting was
a royal privilege to be enjoyed of right by the king
alone, and to be granted to subjects only as a favour, was
no more than an expression, in another shape, of the
doctrine that the king was the superior lord of all
land. It was, at most, only feudalism in a more systematic form than had been previously known. No new
punishment was introduced, and if men lost life or limb
for killing or stealing a deer they had long before been
horribly mutilated for thefts as petty, and, probably
enough, for the very same offence.

When, however, mutilation ceased to be a punishment
in common use it ceased to add horror to the administration of the forest laws. By the Forest Charter Mitigation of them.
of Henry III. it was provided that for the
future no one should lose life or member for the king's
venison. Any one detected in taking it was to pay a
heavy fine, or to be imprisoned for a year and a day, and
after that time to find sureties for future good behaviour.
If none would be responsible for him when his term of
imprisonment expired, he was compelled to abjure the
realm. The penalty was still out of all proportion to the
offence, but it had ceased to be disgracefully brutal ;
and the only remnant of sheer cruelty which was left
in the forest laws after this time, was the practice of
mutilating dogs.

The diminished frequency of the more brutal forms
of punishment had, no doubt, sooner or later an effect

upon the national character ; but no greater error can
be committed by statesman or historian than is involved in
the supposition that manners, customs, and sentiments, handed down from generation to generation, can be suddenly altered by the promul-
gation of a law.   The true history of a nation is
not so much a history of the laws which have been
made for its governance as a history of the motives
which have guided the individuals composing it.   Laws
are nothing unless they are obeyed, and they are worth
little unless obeyed in the spirit as well as in the letter.
When they are far above the level of popular feeling they
are practically valueless; when they descend low enough
t) lift a population by easy stages to higher views they
attain their greatest value.   The gradual withdrawal of
legal sanction from the practice of mutilation was one of
those happy reforms which imperceptibly improve the
moral tone of a people, and which are not followed by
less important results because little is expected from
them.   The cruelty inherited from ages of barbarism
could not be eradicated in a year or a century ; but when
the subtle influence of a bad example was removed there
was a clearer field for the operation of more favourable
causes at a future time.   It was long, indeed, before that
time came.   Burning at one period took the place occupied by chopping at another ; but there were not so
many stakes for heretics as there had been amputating
instruments for thieves ; and human tenderness was not
quite so effectually blunted by the occasional execution of
Lollards as by the ever-recurring sight of men rendered
cripples according to law.   The whole history of crime
tells how slow was the progress towards a sympathy with
human suffering, but it tells also that progress was made,

Slow effects of legislation upon the tone of society.

and bids us not to despair when we find some new enactment apparently useless, nor to form hasty theories
concerning any subjects of our empire, when we fail to
effect a miracle by the magic of a statute.

We, who have long enjoyed the blessings of a settled
government, can only with the greatest difficulty throw
ourselves, in imagination, back into a period when a
settled government was as little expected by Englishmen
as Shakspeare expected, when his Puck bragged of
putting a girdle round about the earth in forty minutes,
that a girdle would one day convey a message round the
earth in forty seconds.   In that reciprocal action which
makes a cause appear to be sometimes an effect, and an
effect at other times a cause, it is not easy to discover
at what point a greater willingness to obey laws produces a more settled government, or at what point
a more settled government produces a greater tendency to obey laws.   Men's interests are the prime
movers of their actions ; and, as commerce and education
enlarge their views, they perceive that their true interests,
no matter what their class, are best advanced by well
established laws peacefully obeyed.   But there was no
such enlightenment in the troubled times of the thirteenth
and fourteenth centuries ; and it is but too evident that
barons then excited commotions in order to become individually their own lawgivers, and that the compromises
which they effected with kings became recognised at last
as constitutional principles.   The Manor Court, which
still possesses vitality, is a memorial of a time when a
baron possessed a prison, into which he could throw
' hand-having ' or ' back-bearing ' thieves before he hanged
them, when he took advantage of a civil war to seize his
neighbour's goods on pretext of distraining by virtue of

his own jurisdiction, and when his chief object in opposing the king's authority was that he might be a little king himself. A statute which restricts these privileges by no means implies a state of society in which they are restricted; nor does the abolition of a needlessly cruel punishment render men at once averse to needless cruelty. If consonant with the tone of the age a good statute effects in time a proportionate good; but it is not now an immediate panacea for all evils, and still less was it such a panacea before the Black Death. The laws, indeed, of that early period which at first sight appear to mark the truest advance were but a bitter mockery of the every-day life of an Englishman.

In a writ for the Conservation of the Peace bearing the date 1233, may be seen an attempt to develope and enforce the ancient system of police which had existed before the Conquest. It will be remembered that there was a certain apparent completeness in this system even in the tenth and eleventh centuries. The mutual responsibility of the Peace Pledge seemed to find all that was required to render it effectual in the watch and ward provided for the highways and within the town walls. Its real use, as amended under Henry III., was only that of handing down to posterity a summary of the inconveniences to which our forefathers were subjected by futile attempts to give a little security to their lives and property. Any stranger attempting to pass through any town at night was to be arrested and kept under guard until the next morning; if he escaped he was to be followed with hue and cry. No one was to entertain a stranger within his house more than one night, except on condition of finding sureties and incurring the same responsibility as for a member of his own

Provisions for the Conservation of the Peace.

household. All who possessed private jurisdictions were to be answerable to the Justices in Eyre for any neglect of these provisions. The sheriffs and foresters were to use all diligence in attempting to preserve the peace, and, if they heard that malefactors made any wood a place of shelter, they were to summon the whole neighbourhood to aid in effecting a capture. The sheriffs or their bailiffs were to receive into their custody any malefactor taken by a private person, and were not to exact a fee for the performance of this duty. Any one unknown, and found travelling with arms, was to be lodged in gaol until he could produce sureties for his good behaviour; and in the same manner all found in possession of property of which they could not give a satisfactory account were to be imprisoned for a year and a day, and if they were then unable to produce sureties they were to abjure the realm.

Similar provisions are repeated in the year 1253, when the armed watch at every gate of every town is somewhat more minutely described, and when the connection between the old system of police and the assise of arms is rendered more apparent. All the males, between the ages of fifteen and sixty, in town and in country, are to be ‘sworn to arms’—all, that is to say, are to prove that they possess arms of the kind suited to their condition of life. All are to be ready, when called upon, to take part in the hue and cry, and to aid in the capture of malefactors; none are to carry their arms except when specially summoned to preserve the peace. In these regulations we see that every man was under the obligation of military service, as in the old days before the Conquest, and that military service implied police duties in time of peace as well as field duties in time of war. It seems, too, that a merchant or other traveller could claim an escort from the mayor and bailiffs of any city or borough, if he chose to show that he had a considerable sum of money in his possession.

In the famous statute of Winchester (A.D. 1285) the ancient law with respect to watch and ward, to hue and

The Statute of Winchester. cry, and to the assise of arms, was again declared. Some further provisions, however, were added. A space of two hundred feet was to be cleared of all bushes on either side of every highway, and there were to be no dykes within the same distance, in which malefactors could lurk. The whole hundred, with the franchises which might be included in it, was to be answerable for every robbery committed within its limits, as it was already answerable for the murder of all persons who were not English. The meaning of this was that the hundred must either produce the offenders and indict them, or pay a fine. The reason for making the neighbourhood responsible was plainly enough expressed in the statute, and will not excite any surprise in those who have followed the course of our criminal law from the days of the peace-guild and of compurgation. Felons, according to the preamble, could not be convicted by the oath of jurors, who would rather that strangers should be robbed with impunity than that their own neighbours should be indicted either as robbers or as receivers. Perjury, in short, was not in popular estimation considered a crime; and it appears from another statute, not less famous than that of Winchester, that Englishmen had in the reign of Edward I. as little hesitation in swearing falsely to deprive a man of his land as to screen a brother brigand from punishment.

With the attempt to render the ancient system of police effective was combined a change in the method of administering justice. After Magna Carta, in which it was provided that Common Pleas should not follow the king's person, the King's Court branched out gradually into the Courts of King's Bench, of Common Bench or Common Pleas, and of Exchequer, which three Courts, however, did not absorb quite the whole of the functions of the original stem. The Justices in Eyre continued their circuits, but in the reign of Edward I. the commissions by virtue of which they sat began to be more clearly defined. In this reign the distinction between the Commission of Nisi Prius or Assise and the Commission of Oyer and Terminer was well marked, and Justices of Assise became also Justices of Gaol Delivery. In the first year of the reign of Edward III. good and lawful men in each county were appointed to keep and maintain the peace ; and our modern Justices of the Peace seem to have been developed out of these ancient guardians. In short, nearly the whole of the machinery by which justice is administered in the present day was, nominally at least, in existence early in the reign of Edward III.

Changes in the method of administering justice.

The difficulty of repressing crime, however, caused some fluctuations in the criminal law, especially with respect to the issue of Commissions of Enquiry and of Oyer and Terminer. The assignment of special Justices to enquire what persons had committed offences of special magnitude, or to try offenders mentioned by name, begins early in the reign of Edward I. ; and the practice is continued long afterwards—sometimes in the appointment of Justices of Trailbaston, sometimes in the appointment of Justices who, if not so designated, had the functions of the Justices of Trailbaston. Trailbaston seems to have been a term for which brigandage is the nearest modern equivalent—to have designated the crimes perpetrated by armed bands which either had a fixed rallying-point or wandered about from county to county, murdering, pillaging, making prisoners, and setting fire to houses. The extent to which the evil prevailed, even in the comparatively tranquil reign of Edward III., will be described in another chapter. For the present it may suffice to mention that the special commissions were as unpopular as the earlier eyres had been on their first institution. The statutes contain numerous references to abuses, and attempts to provide a remedy. A petition was presented in Parliament on behalf of persons who had been concerned in indicting offenders before the Justices of Trailbaston, and who had obtained convictions. They complained that, after payment of a fine, many of those who had been justly condemned contrived by unfair means to be placed on inquisitions and juries, so as to be avenged on the accusers by means of false accusations. Two years before the Black Death, Parliament advised the king that the peace would be better preserved by Guardians duly selected in each county, than by Justices acting under a Commission of Trailbaston, and strangers to the neighbourhood. The suggestion did not have the immediate effect of abolishing special commissions, but the popular feeling which it indicated led, at a later period, to an increase in the number of these Guardians, to the acquisition by them of the name of Justice, and at length to the transfer into their hands of some powers previously held by the hated Justices of Trailbaston.

The transition of Justices of Trailbaston into mere

Justices of the Peace is well illustrated by the form of the commissions to both. One of the chief offences into which those who acted under spe- cial commissions were to enquire was that of carrying arms in time of peace—at fairs and markets, and in the presence of the king's ministers. The Statute of North- ampton, passed in the second year of the reign of Edward III., was specially designed to meet this evil, and was usually mentioned in the special commissions. As soon, however, as the Justices of the Peace were regularly appointed according to a definite system, they were commissioned to enforce the observance of the Statute of Northampton, as well as that of Winchester, and, in later times, of others made for the same purpose. Our modern Justices of the Peace, therefore, whose office is now practically little more than honorary, are the sur- viving monuments of a time when England was in a state of brigandage, which the people at large were not very anxious to suppress.

Origin of Justices of the Peace.

It may perhaps seem strange that, when kings and their advisers were striving, generation after generation, to prevent infractions of the peace, there was no well-understood definition of the crime of treason before the passing of the Statute of Treasons, in the reign of Edward III. There were previously, no doubt, some vague maxims on the subject, to which the statute gave fixity and precision ; but, when the position both of the king and of the national assembly was ill-defined, it was impossible that crimes against the governing powers could be classified with accuracy. Much has been written by lawyers and by historians to show, on the one hand, that strict hereditary succession to the crown has been the law from time immemorial, and, on the other hand,

The Law of Treason.

that the council of the nation, by whatever name known, always had the right of electing and deposing kings. To those who have considered the manner in which our forefathers actually passed their lives it will appear idle to speak either of an original right of succession, in the abstract, or of an original right of election. In accordance with the regard paid to the family tie, even among the most barbarous tribes, the custom arose that the son might, if he could, hold what his father had held before him. It was a custom which was naturally applied to the throne, as well as to a house or land. But men who have no knowledge of letters are not governed by abstract ideas, and deal with each matter according to the means at their disposal and the impulse of the moment. The king who showed signs of weakness was an object of attack ; and if he was dethroned, it was not by virtue of any fundamental principle in the old English constitution, but simply because the party of his enemies happened to be stronger than his own.

The absence of definite legal maxims, and the attempt to give the proceedings of a strong party a colour of legality, are both conspicuous in the treatment of Piers Gavaston, the favourite of Edward II. He was not accused of treason, or of Lése Majesté, which was the earlier name for High Treason of a particular kind, but he was sentenced by Parliament to perpetual exile as an open enemy of king and people. The offences which were, in the aggregate, construed as overt hostility, were not individually treasons according to the later statute. Gavaston, as alleged by the stronger faction opposed to him, had given evil counsel to the king, whom he had enticed to do wrong ; had collected all the king's treasure, and removed it out of the kingdom ; had

Illustration from the case of Piers Gavaston.

assumed to himself the royal power and dignity, by taking oaths from men that they would live and die with himself against all others ; had estranged the heart of the king from his lieges ; had put away good ministers, and substituted men of his own party ; had caused grants of crown lands to be improperly made ; had maintained robbers and murderers, for whom he had obtained the king's pardon ; had led the king to the seat of war without the consent of the baronage ; and had procured blank charters under the great seal, in deceit of the king and to the damage of the crown.

The charges brought against the Despensers, father and son, were substantially the same as those brought against Gavaston. When Gavaston returned to England and fell into the hands of his enemies, he was simply beheaded. The fate of both Despensers was, however, that of traitors, though they did not suffer according to due process of law. Both were drawn and hanged, and the body of the son was beheaded and quartered. The true character of these executions is best illustrated by the events which followed them. The victorious barons conducted themselves simply as victors in a private war. They not only imprisoned the adherents of the Despensers, but carried fire and sword into the lands of their enemies. They acted there precisely as a victorious but uncivilised king would have acted in a hostile country through which he was marching.

Illustration from the cases of the Despensers.

The deaths, however, of the Despensers are remarkable because they were brought to pass at a time at which the punishment for High Treason, afterwards fully established by law, first comes prominently into notice. In all the cases of Treason during the reign of Edward II.

of which the records have been preserved, the first object of all concerned—except the accused—was to give
horror to the sentence, the last to give fairness
to the trial.   The proceedings against Andrew
Harcla, Earl of Carlisle, are thoroughly characteristic of the age.   He was thrown into prison,
and the accusation against him was heard in his absence.
He had no opportunity of making any answer, and was
brought before his judges only to hear their judgment,
which the Court, sitting under a special commission,
delivered at some length.   The concluding sentences are
worthy of notice, as they show the grounds upon which a
portion of the horrible penalty for treason was justified.
' The award of the Court is, that for your treason you be
drawn, and hanged, and beheaded; that your heart, and
bowels, and entrails, *whence came your traitorous thoughts*,
be torn out, and burnt to ashes, and that the ashes be
scattered to the winds ; that your body be cut into four
quarters, and that one of them be hanged upon the Tower
of Carlisle, another upon the Tower of Newcastle, a third
upon the Bridge of York, and the fourth at Shrewsbury ;
and that your head be set upon London Bridge, for
an example to others that they may never presume to
be guilty of such treasons as yours against their liege
Lord.'

In those rude times men had of course not arrived at that refinement of doctrine according to which
only the sovereign's advisers are responsible for
the misgovernment of the sovereign.   It followed, therefore, without any abstract theories
of constitutional right, that when a king persisted in a
course of action which was injurious to the realm, or
which a party sufficiently strong chose to declare injurious,

he could be represented as a criminal, and subject to punishment. Parliament, or rather a powerful section of Parliament, in this manner gave a sanction to the deposition of Edward II., when it had been already accomplished in fact by force of arms. The transference of the crown to Edward III. was, indeed, no more and no less constitutional than the execution of Harcla was legal. It came to pass because it was the wish of those who had the might to bring it about. If Parliament decreed that Edward II. should cease to reign, Parliament also decreed that Roger Mortimer should be drawn and hanged as a traitor before he had been heard in his own defence. A later Parliament declared that the latter sentence was illegal, and there is, in fact, no better evidence of legality in the one case than in the other. A long list of charges was drawn up against Roger Mortimer, a long list of charges against Edward II.; but force, not law, was brought to bear against both. If any difference is to be detected in the mode in which the two sets of articles of accusation were compiled, it is, that so far as Mortimer was concerned, they were precise, so far as the King was concerned they were vague. Edward, said the Parliament, had shown himself unable to govern, and had been governed by others who advised him ill, had neglected the affairs of the realm, had lost the kingdom of Scotland and other dominions, had injured Holy Church, had violated his Coronation Oath, and had manifested no disposition to amend his conduct. It may have been true that he had erred in all these points, and there may have been a gain to England when he lost his throne; but he was a prisoner, unable to speak for himself, when his enemies denounced him in Parliament at the instigation of his adulterous wife and her paramour, and it is difficult to regard the end of his reign with more satisfaction than the hideous murder which put an end to his life.

When a sovereign has been declared unfit to rule, and a successor has been appointed by a dominant faction, the partisans of the old king and of the new alike feel themselves entitled to pronounce their enemies traitors. In the fourteenth century there was hardly so much as an attempt to conceal the motive by which the actors on either side were commonly impelled. To succeed was to gain possession of the lands forfeited by unsuccessful opponents. All the executions for treason at the end of the reign of Edward II. and the beginning of the reign of Edward III. were followed by a redistribution of property.

Accusations of treason from corrupt motives.

Mortimer, who was the chief agent in deposing Edward II., the husband of his paramour, the queen, basely deceived the Earl of Kent, whom he assured that the deposed king was still alive and a prisoner. The object was to gain what the Earl would lose by attainder following upon rebellion. The Earl, who was brother of King Edward II., and uncle of King Edward III., resolved to strike a blow for the release of the supposed captive. Before finally committing himself, however, to so desperate an undertaking, he attempted to ascertain whether Mortimer's statement was true or false. The superstition of the age suggested to him an infallible test. A certain friar was believed to have the power of summoning spirits, who would answer truly any question put to them. The Earl was made to believe that a demon had appeared, and had announced that Edward II. was still alive. It is not certain whether the friar was in collusion with Mortimer or simply gave the answer which he thought would be most agreeable to

Illustration : the Earl, the Friar, and the Spirit.

the Earl. The result, however, was, that an insurrection was planned, and that the Earl was condemned and executed as a traitor. The story of the Spirit and the Friar, as related by the Earl himself, was thought worthy of special mention in a letter written by Edward III., in which the Pope was earnestly requested not to accept as true any other versions of the affair.

At a time when men hoped to rise by treason and by false accusations of treason, it will be readily believed that the other paths by which wealth was sought were not commonly the paths of honour. Commissions to enquire concerning the wrongs done *Spread of corruption: attempts to stay it.* by government officials, abundant during many centuries, are specially abundant during the long and comparatively tranquil reign of Edward III. Under him greater efforts were made than had ever been made before to improve not so much the laws as the manner in which the laws were administered. Various expedients were tried, but the most comprehensive scheme was put into execution in the fourteenth year of his reign. Commissioners were appointed to investigate all manner of oppressions, wrongs, damages, and grievances charged against all persons holding office, or their subordinates. Not even the Justices of either Bench, nor the Barons of the Exchequer, were exempt from the enquiry, which applied to justices of every description. Escheators, sheriffs, coroners, admirals of fleets, constables of castles, foresters, gaolers, arrayers of the forces, archdeacons, deans, the heads of various departments of the Exchequer, and numbers of inferior officials were mentioned in the commission, the scope of which was to ascertain what hardships, and of what character, had been inflicted upon the people throughout England.

This gigantic project may be compared with one of
the labours of Hercules. It was an attempt, by no means

The Ordi-
nance and
Oath of the
Justices. successful, to cleanse away a foulness greater
than mythology has attributed to the Augean
stables. Yet one important result appears to
have followed it. The corruption of the judges was no
longer, if indeed it had been previously, a matter of
doubt ; and a serious effort was made soon afterwards to
check it by means of the famous Ordinance and Oath
of the Justices. By the Ordinance it was provided that
the justices should thenceforth administer equal law and
execution of right to all the king's subjects, rich and poor,
without respect of persons, and without regard to letters
or instructions from the king, or from any one. They
were to make oath that they would act in accordance with
the terms of the Ordinance, and that they would not
take, either directly or indirectly, either in private or in
public, from any one having plea or process pending
before them, any gift or reward of gold, or of silver,
or of anything whatsoever, except meat and drink and
those of little value, and that they would not accept
robe or fee from any one but the king so long as they
should hold the office of justice. In order to recompense
them for the sacrifice thus demanded of them, it was further ordained by the King and Council that their fees
should be increased to such a degree as ought reasonably
to be held sufficient by them.

This Ordinance was the last of any importance made
in the period embraced by the present chapter. Its provisions reveal to some extent the partialities of which the
Justices had previously been guilty, and, from the manner
in which reference is made to the future, have the effect
of condoning all that had been done in the past. Three

years after this most wholesome attempt to reform the administration of the law, society was thrown into utter confusion by the horrors of the Black Death.   But meanwhile there was a sufficient opportunity of testing the new system; and the year before the Plague is consequently a time at which the real character of the age may be seen in its most favourable aspect.   To show from copious and unimpeachable evidence, and in full detail, what kind of life our forefathers were then passing, is the object of the following chapter.

CHAPTER IV.

ENGLAND IN THE YEAR BEFORE THE BLACK DEATH.

A FOREIGNER visiting England in the year 1348 would have landed most probably at Dover, where men of many nations and of all ranks were continually meeting. There he would have seen ecclesiastics

Scene at Dover.
concealing in their convenient robes forbidden missives from Rome ; traders returning from the Low Countries with profits in base money, out of which they hoped to make profits still greater ; captains bragging loudly of their deeds at Calais, which the English had just taken ; adventurers intending to settle in the town from which the French had been expelled ; widows bound on a pilgrimage to the Holy Land, and attended each by a chaplain and two stout yeomen.

One of the first objects, however, which would have met the traveller's eye, when he set foot on English soil,

Sanctuary-men.
would have been a group of murderers and robbers, who were to be set loose somewhere on the continent of Europe, there to gain their living as best they could. Criminals who had taken sanctuary were permitted to leave it, unmolested, upon making oath before the coroner that they would quit the realm on a given day. Dover was the port most commonly assigned to them, and if they failed to reach it at the appointed time, they forfeited all the privileges of

abjuration. Unless, therefore, they joined some band of
brigands or were murdered on the way, they, no doubt,
presented themselves for embarkation, in strict accordance with the coroner's order. Thus the stranger might,
if he pleased, and if he spoke English, have heard from
these desperate wayfarers much that he might have desired
to know about the condition of the roads in every part of
the country. He might have found among them not
only some who had travelled from Surrey or Middlesex
in three days or four, but some who had travelled from
Yorkshire in nine.

Before he quitted Dover he might, if he had been so
fortunate as to escape an attack from pirates in his
passage across the Channel, have learned some- The Seamen
thing new concerning the manners and customs Ports.
of the sea-faring population. He would have found
there a race of sailors who were too hardy to fear death
in any form, and in whom courage took the place of every
other virtue. He might have listened to stories in which
the peril that had been encountered and survived gave the
point to every sentence, and in which the sons were exhorted to dare what their sires and grandsires had dared
before them. He would have discovered that the winds and
the waves were not the great excitements of life for men
who had battled with them from childhood, and that the
hand-to-hand struggle with other men was, on sea as on
shore, considered to be man's true vocation. He would
have been told of great deeds done by the seamen of
the Cinque Ports, and especially by the seamen of Dover
—how they were a terror to the French and the Flemings—how they were always ready to put off when there
was booty to be seized or revenge to be exacted—how
they constituted themselves the sole judges in all mari-

time affairs which affected their district, and sank the ships of their enemies, whether the king had declared war or not. Had he expressed his admiration of the English character as illustrated by them, they would have declared that they were not as other Englishmen, and cared nothing for the lubbers of the other coasts. He ought to know that any one of the Cinque Ports was more than a match for any other port in England. The Yarmouth men, indeed, thought much of themselves, though Yarmouth itself was no better than a dependency of the Cinque Ports, and had once brought a craft of out-landish look, and painted like a Flemish strumpet, to the South Coast, as a present for the king's son; but the Cinque Port men had soon shown that they and their ships were made of stouter stuff than Yarmouth busses or Yarmouth crews, and had smashed the pretty toy to splinters. They would do the like to-morrow, in spite of the admiral, if they had the chance; and if the traveller wished to know what spirits there were in Dover, he had but to watch when the tide was flowing, and he might see a prize brought into harbour.

Foreigners, except perhaps those who had been reared in the Italian cities, were not in the fourteenth century more accustomed to luxuries than Englishmen. Carriages and post-horses had been forgotten since the days of the Romans. The traveller from France, from Germany, or from the Low Countries would therefore have been unconscious of hardship when informed that his journey inland must be performed on horseback. If, by any chance, he had . demanded some better mode of transit for his luggage, he would have been told with truth that the Records of the High Court of Chancery were moved from place to place

Journey from Dover to London.

on a pack-horse, and that his goods could not be more securely carried than the most precious documents in the realm. As he rode onwards he would have become aware that there was an extreme dearth of provisions, that the whole of Kent had been exhausted in furnishing supplies to the force besieging Calais, and that, although the requisitions had ceased, the prices still betokened a famine. When he came to Rochester or any other walled town in the evening, after sunset, he would have found a watch at the gate, which would have regarded him with suspicion, and possibly have deprived him of his liberty till the morning. If, when he perceived that the gates were closed, he sought a lodging in the suburbs, he would have found but a surly landlord, belonging to a class which the lawyers believed to be in league with brigands. If he was not rejected by an inn-keeper who doubted his character, he would have been entertained by a host whose intentions he would have had good reason to fear. If he retired to rest without the walls, and escaped murder, he would probably have been disturbed by the hue and cry raised in pursuit of some robbers. If he slept in the house of a burgher, within the walls, he would, not less probably, have been roused by some nocturnal affray in the streets.

The journey from Dover to London, with pack-horses in attendance, could hardly have been completed in less than four days. If the traveller had escaped all the dangers of the road, he would, in somewhat less than a week, have found himself in sight of the greatest city of England, which he must have entered by London Bridge. He would have passed through the suburb of Southwark, already notorious for its sanctuaries and its stews. As his horse

picked its way slowly over the uneven ground near the
Surrey side of the river, he would, if he chanced to be a
Fleming, have been accosted in his own tongue by the
ribald women who had left Flanders for England to traffic
in vice.   If he had reached the foot of the bridge, crossed
it in safety, and been permitted to enter the city, he
would have perceived that at the end of every street and
alley there were stout chains and barriers either obstructing the passage or made ready to obstruct it when occasion should arise.   This, he would have learned, was a
device to impede the flight of burglars, thieves, and
other offenders who, when pursued, commonly ran
towards the river, in the hope of escaping to Southwark.
When he rode up to an inn and asked for a bed, he
would have had many questions put to him, and many
cautions impressed upon him.   If he stayed longer than
a day and a night, his host would have become responsible for him, as in the lawless days before the Conquest,
and would have been anxious that he should not bring
the house into ill-repute.   He would have been warned
that even citizens of good fame were not permitted to go
out after sunset, either with arms or without a lantern,
and that, if he had any prudence, he would not go out at
all till the morrow.   If he disregarded these hints, he
would have been likely to pass the night in the Tun on
Cornhill, or in one of the City Counters ; for if he fell
into the hands of the watch, though unarmed and bearing
a light, he would have been regarded as a stranger, wandering about the streets with the object of breaking the
king's peace.

    In the morning, no matter where he might have
lodged, he would not have had far to walk to visit any of
the markets.   From the eastern counties corn was brought

to Graschirche, or Gracechurch; from the western counties to Newgate; and in the open space near either he
would have seen troops of pack-horses with Scenes in the
panniers of grain or malt, and here and there markets.
a country cart. From the mode of conveyance he might
have inferred the condition of the roads which were
nearest to the city; but his attention would soon have
been diverted by a dispute between a peasant and a
corn-dealer or baker. It was the common lot of the
rustics to discover that they had mistaken a thief for a
purchaser, that the townsman insisted on keeping their
wares, and steadily refused to pay the price, and that it
was difficult to obtain redress when a citizen of London
chose to be dishonest, and his victim came from Upland.

Turn where he might, the traveller could hardly fail
to light upon some group which would tell him the character of the people he had come to see. Here, Public
perhaps, a baker with a loaf hung round his punishments.
neck, was being jeered and pelted in the pillory, because
he had given short weight, or because, when men had
asked him for bread, he had given them, not a stone, but
a lump of iron enclosed by a crust. There, perhaps, an
oven was being pulled down, because a baker had been
detected in a third offence, and had been compelled to
abjure trade in the city for ever. If there were no bakers
to be punished on any particular day, the pillories could
never have been all without occupants. They were used
to punish the sellers of bad meat, poultry, and fish, of
false jewellery, of oats good at the top of the sack and
bad below, the beggars who pretended to collect money
for a hospital and kept it for themselves, the gamblers
who played with loaded dice, the fortune-tellers who
promised to recover stolen goods, the suborners of false

accusations, the cut-purses, and the petty pilferers of every kind. It not unfrequently happened, too, that a passer-by might see some greater offenders exposed to the scoffs of the city rabble. Among them were forgers of charters, deeds, bonds, or letters, counterfeiters of the seals belonging to the Pope or to English nobles, bedels of wards who had wrongfully set the alderman's mark upon defective measures, personators of holy hermits, of the king's or the sheriff's officers, of summoners in the Ecclesiastical Courts, of purveyors. In another place might have been found a woman on the cucking-stool, to which she had been sentenced as a common scold. In some of the principal streets there would probably have been an opportunity of watching the process by which all kinds of sham wares—sham girdles, sham gloves, sham pouches, sham caps, and sham measures were publicly destroyed in a bonfire.

Should the stranger have grown weary of what he saw in the city of London, and strolled, in search of the

The highway from London to Westminster.

law courts, to the city of Westminster, a ghastly spectacle would have been presented to his eyes. All the lepers of London, and others from the villages of Middlesex, flocked to the most frequented road in England, and seated themselves upon it, or near the paths across the fields which led into it. The chief nobles of the realm, the clergy of the two cities, the judges, the pleaders, and the officers of the courts were continually passing to and fro, and, as each came near, the lepers would raise themselves from the ground, show their hideous sores, and beg for alms in the name of God. The foreigner who visited London in the year 1348, might have been told that an order was about to issue for the clearance of the highway, and that the lepers would be warned to betake themselves into the country, and to remain at a safe distance from all places of public resort, so that the business of the state might be conducted without danger of contagion.   Had he waited to hear the royal proclamation read, he might have been struck by the extreme feebleness of the attempt to preserve the health of the people, and to provide for the poor wretches who were the objects of terror. .The ordinary frequenters of the line of traffic were to be examined by competent persons, and, if pronounced leprous, were to be removed by the sheriffs.   It was the king's wish that, though they were to be cut off from intercourse with the magnates of the land, they should not suffer from the loss of alms ; and the sheriffs were instructed to stimulate almsgiving for their relief at every fitting opportunity.   But in the anxiety to banish them from one place, no care was taken to assign them another.   They were to be put away anywhere from public view ; they were not to show themselves even in quest of food ; but if they could find any messenger free from their disease, who would carry necessaries to them from the inhabited districts, they might be permitted to accept what was brought.   In those days there were hospitals for the Knights of St. John of Jerusalem, and for many a religious body ; hospitals for the sick existed apparently only in name ; of charity there was little, though of almsgiving there was abundance.

After inspecting the law courts, the foreign visitor would probably have entered Westminster Abbey.   As he mentally compared it with similar buildings Westminster on the Continent, an attendant might have in- Abbey ; its law-suits. formed him that business of great interest was about to be transacted close at hand.   The king had just directed an order to his treasurer and chamberlain to defray the expenses necessary for the due care of his grandfather's body. The corpse of Edward I., whose memory was always held in great reverence, had been carried to the Abbey, and there preserved in wax, which was renewed from time to time, and which it became necessary to renew in 1348. A bribe to a garrulous official was not less efficacious in those days than in the present, and the foreigner might not only have been present at the waxing of an English king's remains, but might, also, had he pleased, have acquired some knowledge of the tone of thought which prevailed among the abbot and monks. He would have learned that the chief grievance of the moment was the quashing of a jury-panel in a cause which would probably have been decided in favour of the monastery. The Court of King's Bench had held that as some of the jurors were the abbot's tenants, they could not be impartial. The matter in dispute was the liability of the abbot to repair the highway between Tothill and the 'Almorigate,' in Westminster, which had become a common nuisance, and was impassable alike to the king and his lieges. Had the traveller felt any surprise, at the moment, that so powerful a monarch as Edward III. had been compelled to turn aside from the main road because it had fallen into decay within a stone-throw of his own palace, he would have learned, after no long time spent in England, to hear far worse tidings without the least emotion.

If the landlord of an inn had been asked at this time in what direction a stranger about to leave London might State of the most conveniently travel, he would have replied roads. ' by the road to Hertford.' The king hawked this year on the banks of the Lea : he had commanded the

sheriffs of Essex and Hertfordshire to make due preparation for him, and to enforce the repair of all bridges by
distraint upon the persons who were liable for their maintenance. If the roads were good anywhere they would
be good in that country ; but if innkeeper or friend told
truth, they would have added that the roads were good
nowhere, and that it would be folly to expect better
travelling up-land than could be found near Westminster.
The burden of road-making, hateful to all land-holders,
was especially hateful to the clergy, who were continually
asserting that their land was free from it, and acting upon
their own assertions until the law courts settled the doubt.
The wayfarer, therefore, could not ride far without coming
to a spot in dispute, where there was no good Samaritan
to help him on his journey, and where he might probably
lame his horse, or break his own neck, through the neglect
of some neighbouring lord or abbot.

The whole aspect of the country was different from
that of the England with which we are familiar in the
nineteenth century. In many places the roads Difficulties of
were driven through tracts of wood-land, which travelling :
aspect of the
should have been, and perhaps were, cleared country.
according to law, for the space of two hundred feet on
either side. Enough corn was grown on the average to
support the population, but little, if any, more ; and the
greater part of the open land consisted of pastures, from
which was drawn England's chief export and source of
wealth—her famous wool and wool-fells. A far greater
portion of the soil, however, was under water than at present. There was many a bourne or beck which, like the
Holebourne in London, is now dried up ; many a river
which, like the Fleet, was once navigable, but is now barely
remembered by name. Pools and meres abounded in

every county. Every land-holder who owned a close had
his lakes and fish-ponds, which supplied him with much
of his food during many months of the year, and which
commonly proved themselves an irresistible temptation to
all the lawless spirits of the time. Through this abundance of wood and water, and the carelessness or wilful
neglect of those who should have repaired the roads, a
horseman was impeded by so many obstacles, on his
journey, that the ordinary Latin word used as an equivalent for our 'travel' was 'labour,' and members of Parliament were chosen with special reference to their powers
of labouring in this special meaning of the term. Nor
was the expression ill applied to those who had to
make their way in spite of broken bridges, of swollen
streams, of roads ill-repaired, and of morasses presenting
the appearance of firm and elastic turf.

Sloughs and pit-falls, however, were not the greatest
dangers by which the roads were beset. Though it
Dens of   might be notorious in the neighbourhood that
robbers.   there was a den of robbers near the highway,
there might still be no one to warn the traveller ; and
after he had been murdered, it was improbable that any
one would be found to say who had done the deed.

Such an incident as this, however, was altogether
insignificant when compared with the organised brigand-
Organised   age which prevailed in every part of the country.
brigandage. Houses were set on fire day after day ; men
and women were captured ; ransom was exacted on pain
of death to those who refused it, and even those who
paid it might think themselves fortunate if they escaped
some horrible mutilation. The ordinary powers of the
law were, as stated in many commissions of enquiry,
quite insufficient to repress the evil ; the clear space on

either side of the highway, even where the Statute of Winchester was not set at nought, had no effect in deterring bodies of armed men from attacks on weaker parties of travellers; the gangs which lived by rapine had no care to conceal themselves for their own protection, and lay in ambush only in order that their intended victims might not escape them.

The time at which it might have been hoped that merchants travelling together would have been most secure, was the time at which the brigands Attacks at reaped their richest harvest. Nothing was so fairs and markets. attractive to the robbers as a fair or a market. They commonly stationed themselves at a short distance from an entrance to the town at which one of these great gatherings was to be held, and did almost as they pleased with the wares, the money, and the persons of all who came to buy, to sell, or to make merry. Sometimes warning was given to traders on their way, and they prudently turned back; this was considered a great grievance by the abbot of Abingdon, who lost the tolls and profits which he expected to gain by Abingdon fair, and who complained that his monks were beaten, and the timber of his park was cut down and carried away.

Sometimes the leaders of the bands would change their tactics, and secure their prey by a still bolder and more comprehensive plan. They would wait Bristol in the until the fair was at its height, and the towns- hands of brigands. people and strangers supposed themselves to be free from danger. They would then make a sudden onslaught, with all the fury of an invading army, would destroy the temporary booths, lay waste the town itself with fire and sword, take the plunder that most pleased their fancy, and, harpy-like, mangle all that they could not

move.   In the year before the Black Death, Bristol had
been for some time in the hands of an armed force, of
which the leader seems to have possessed more than
ordinary audacity and skill.   His men regarded him not
only as their captain, but as their king.   He issued
proclamations in the royal style, commanding one thing,
prohibiting another.   He took military possession of the
port, seized the ships in it with their cargoes, and did not
even spare those which were about to sail with provisions
for the king's lieges in Gascony.   In a commission dated
some months later than the first attack, it is recited that
his followers, in no small number, were roaming about
the town with arms, setting the king's officers at defiance,
threatening, robbing, mutilating, and killing.   The document concludes, as in innumerable similar cases, with a
statement, gravely made, that such doings are contrary to
the form of the Statute of Northampton, and that the malefactors are to be lodged in gaol when found and captured.

Burghers and merchants were by no means the only
persons who suffered at the hands of the brigands.
Plunder taken alike from the King and his Subjects. Wherever there was booty of any kind to be
taken, it was almost certain that an attempt
would be made to take it—no matter whether
it was money, or a cask of wine, or a prisoner of war—no
matter whether it belonged to a chapman, or to a knight,
or to the king himself.   Two knights were conducting to
London a Scottish prisoner—one of the Stuarts—who had
been captured in the battle near Durham.   On the road
a gang of malefactors made an attack with such success
that they secured the prize and carried it back to Scotland, where they accepted a ransom of fifty pounds—the
real value of the prisoner being estimated at not less
than a thousand.   The king's envoy returned from Spain

in a Spanish ship, which put into Plymouth harbour.
Before she could be unladen, a band of armed men
forced their way on board, overpowered the crew, and
were not deterred from seizing anything they found by
the information that it was the property of the king or
his ministers. At Thame the servants of the Black
Prince went out to fetch supplies for his house and
provender for his stables ; they returned, beaten and
bruised, and without even so much as the carts and
horses which they had taken with them. A trader in
the employ of Queen Philippa was entrusted by her
with some of her jewels. He lived in a neighbourhood
where, it seems, one Adam the Leper had command of a
gang. As soon as it was known that booty was to be
had, a nocturnal assault was made upon his dwelling.
He resisted, and was besieged within his own walls.
When all other means failed, the house was set on fire,
and the merchant was compelled to give up the royal
treasure. At Wighton, also, Philippa sustained a loss of
five hundred pounds—a sum equal to many thousand
pounds of modern money; her collector of rents was
attacked and robbed on his way home ; and yet so feeble
was the law, or so faint the sense of justice in the abstract,
that there is appended to the very commission in which
the story is told a note which annuls it, and stays all
further proceedings—because the offenders had made
restitution !

So small was the respect for authority of any kind,
that even the king's most trusted messengers were in
peril of their lives after they were housed for Murder of the
the night. A serjeant-at-arms, despatched King's Ser-
jeant-at-
upon important business of State, halted, on his Arms.
journey northwards, at a Yorkshire village. The house

in which he stayed was broken open, and set on fire; and the child of his hostess, a widow, was burnt to death. The serjeant himself was dragged off to a neighbouring forest, and there deliberately butchered.

If it could be said with justice that one part of England was at this time more notorious for crime than another, the Marches towards Scotland might claim the pre-eminence. From Newcastle north-wards the whole country had recently been devastated by the Scottish invaders. The tenants of the king's demesnes had lost everything, even to their houses. They were wandering homeless, hither and thither, and many of them, no doubt, joined the outlaws, and resolved to inflict on others the sufferings which they had endured themselves. The warlike spirit which had been handed down from the barbarous ages was still pre-dominant in England, and naturally existed in greatest force near the seat of war. Centuries afterwards the border-land towards Scotland was famous for its crimes, and not the least of the benefits conferred by the Union was the annihilation of the Marches. It is, therefore, no matter for wonder that in early times the northern forests were the scenes of the greatest atrocities.

State of the Marches to-wards Scot-land.

The distinction, however, between the criminal popu-lation and the better classes was by no means well marked in the fourteenth century. If the townsmen suffered sometimes at the hands of the outlaws, there was a class of men in some of the towns which had no little sympathy with the brigands outside, and acted in a manner precisely similar. It is difficult to conceive that Bristol could have been taken and held by a hostile party of Englishmen, who had no friends within the walls. And, whatever doubt there

Crime and the right of pri-vate war.

may be upon that subject, it is at least certain that Yarmouth could send forth more than three hundred men, with ensign displayed, to harry the surrounding country, to burn, to rob, to hold to ransom, and to slay.   Nor is it less certain that the whole band and their leader were pardoned, in consideration of the good service rendered by him and by the men of Yarmouth to the king.   In such incidents is to be discerned the vitality of the ancient right of private war, of which brigandage was only one development.   Some of the Bristol men most probably had a grudge to satisfy against ship-owners of their own or another port ; the Yarmouth men may have had some quarrel with a neighbouring town or landowner ; but the criminal tendencies of modern times seem in many cases to have been handed down from a period when that which is now considered crime was thought very nearly akin to virtue.

The knights, or, in other words, the class corresponding to our modern country gentry, were commonly engaged in exploits which it is extremely difficult to distinguish from brigandage; and the clergy—from the abbots down to the chaplains —followed the example set them by the knights.   The Countess of Lincoln had a free warren and chace at Kingston Lacy.   A band, more than fifty in number, entered, killed the game, and deliberately cut down the timber, to the value of two thousand pounds of ancient currency, and carried it off.   Among the accused were the Abbot of Sherborne, the Abbot of Middleton, and the Prior of Horton.   Three knights, and a force more than sixty strong, with many chaplains in its ranks, broke a close belonging to the Archbishop of Canterbury, drove off his cattle, cut down his trees, reaped his corn,

Acts resembling brigandage committed by Knights and by the Clergy.

and marched quietly away with the plunder. A gang of more than seventy, among whom were no less than five parsons of churches, committed a similar offence at Carlton. Two parsons of churches were among those accused of breaking a park owned by the Earl of Northampton, and stealing his cattle in one place, a vicar of doing the like in another place, and two knights of breaking a house at Colne. The Prior of Bollington was charged with a robbery of horses, cattle, sheep, and pigs. A knight and a chaplain aided in taking goods and putting the owner under restraint. Three clergymen, who were either parsons or vicars of churches, and two others, who had attained some clerical dignity, were concerned with a knight and about thirty inferiors in damaging a park of the Bishop of Durham, at Howden, to the extent of a thousand pounds. A knight, a parson, and at least two others of the clergy, broke the close and house of a Prebendary of York. The Sheriff of Devonshire and his followers, not acting by virtue of a writ, made an attack upon one Richard de Stapleton, and deprived him of property worth a hundred pounds. It would be tedious to enumerate at greater length the deeds of violence recorded on one Roll of a single year; let it suffice to state that the Roll is only one out of many sources of information; that it consists of three parts; that each part consists of more than forty skins of parchment; and that among those skins there are few which do not contain one reference or many to some act of lawlessness committed by clerks or by knights.

In many cases there may be reason to suspect that the actors in these strange scenes believed their leader to have some title to the land on which the outrages were committed. The subsequent statutes against

forcible entry on land in dispute in some measure confirm this explanation. Possession by the strong arm had
for so many centuries constituted the best title
to land that the best legal claim to it was
almost valueless until practically asserted by
setting foot on the soil. These gallant knights
*They are il-
lustrated by
the subse-
quent Sta-
tutes against
forcible entry.*
and abbots, therefore, who were continually taking peaceful occupants by surprise, may in some cases have acted in
the name of justice ; but, unless it be assumed that the
title of ' chivaler ' necessarily confers the virtues collectively known as chivalry, it must be obvious that the
right to enter must have been a most convenient excuse
for any adventurer who coveted his neighbour's flocks
and herds, or timber, or crops, or horses, or even money.
It is a most significant fact that in many instances in
which the house was attacked, as well as the park or the
chace, the robbers succeeded in carrying off the title-
deeds as well as the timber.

A few examples may suffice to show how closely
connected was the mere forcible entry with open brigandage, and how close is the connection of
both with the primitive seizure of land and
other property by barbarians, and with those
acts which, when committed at the present day,
we denominate crimes. A tenant in chief of
a manor in Worcestershire died ; the escheator
*Close con-
nection of the
first barba-
rous taking
of land by
force, the
forcible entry
in assertion of
a right, and
open bri-
gandage.*
entered, in the king's name, according to the usual
custom ; and the legal course would have been for the
next heir, if there was one living, to await the finding of
the inquisition, which it was the escheator's duty to hold.
But one Guy Breton, probably with the object of asserting that the lands were not held as alleged by the king's
minister, and that the latter had no right to take them

into the king's hand, summoned his followers to his aid, expelled the men holding in the king's name, and took the rents and profits for himself. This may be regarded as a comparatively innocent case of forcible entry. That which follows may have been a mere forcible entry in design, but assumed a very different character in execution. The Bishop of Exeter complained that a great multitude of men, one of whom, mentioned by name, was a chaplain, banded themselves together and marched in military array to one of his manors. They demolished fences, gates, and doors, broke into the buildings, and carried off two hundred bullocks, a hundred cows, a thousand sheep, and various other goods and chattels. The whole neighbourhood was thrown into a panic at the sight of the armed men, who were in such numbers that it was at first supposed a foreign enemy had landed, and was collecting supplies for his army.

The temptation which forcible entry presented for the commission of deeds still worse is illustrated by an attack which was made upon a manor in Wiltshire, within the verge of the household of the king's son Lionel, who was Guardian of England during the king's absence abroad. The attacking force marched in military array to the scene of action, and began the attack by night. They soon forced their way into the dwelling-house, and killed as many of the inmates as they pleased. They ravished the widow of Michael de la Beche, and frightened her chaplain to death. They made a considerable number of prisoners, whom they forced to march with their own body in quest of new adventures. They set all law at defiance, and their actions were described as traitorous in the Letters Patent, in which the story is told. Among those accused

Crimes committed by Knights and Priors at the head of a military force.

of the outrage were a ' chivaler,' the Prior of Bristol, and the Prior of Holand. But even such deeds as these were by no means rare, and seem to have been a common ending of an attempt to enforce a real or pretended title to land by entry. A knight named Ercedecne, accompanied by a priest from Haccombe, the parson of the Church of Botus-Fleming, another clerk, and a numerous band, at one time seizes horses and other goods at Penpol-by-Saltash ; at another time he makes an attack, with the same associates, at Haccombe, and drives off cattle of no small value. At last it appears that he is living the life of an outlaw, marching from county to county at the head of his men, and doing habitually from inclination that which, perhaps, he did at first with no other object but to assert a right.

Side by side with the custom of entering upon disputed land by force still survived, though contrary to law, the kindred and no less ancient custom of gratifying personal animosity by private war. A knight was on the march with a band of armed retainers, and with some men-at-arms in the king's service. With him were the under-sheriff of Cambridgeshire and some inferior officers. It might have been supposed that so powerful a body would have been in no danger of attack, or at least that they would have been in no danger when near a county town. Yet Cambridge was the scene of a furious onslaught prompted, to use the words of the commission, by hatred and malice. The assailants were, as usual, in military array, gained a complete victory, killed the leader opposed to them, and seized everything of value which the escort had attempted to guard. The under-sheriff lost a great sum of money—a portion of the royal revenue. The king's writs also fell into the hands of the marauders, and the king's business was delayed because the sheriff was deprived of his instructions. The unpopularity of the under-sheriff may, indeed, have been incurred in the execution of his duties, and one of the motives of the exploit may have been dislike of the office as well as a grudge against the officer or his companions. But, whatever the causes may have been, the deed shows clearly enough that violence was still superior to law, and that war was still waged by private persons, even against the ministers of the king.

When a particular jurisdiction was impugned, it was maintained in precisely the same manner as a private feud or a claim to land, and with as little regard to decency as to law. A man was killed in the cemetery of Worcester Cathedral, in which the bishop asserted that the coroners of the township or city had no authority. The towns-people, however were of a different opinion, declined to await the coming of the county coroner, and proceeded to assert their claim by force. The two bailiffs (at that time the chief personages of the town) marched with the populace to the cemetery, in irresistible force, and carried off the body. They caused an inquest to be held on it by their own coroners, and afterwards had it buried within their own bounds. But a great number of them were resolved on vengeance as well as that which they considered justice. In warlike fashion they invaded the lands of the Priory, and laid them waste. They drove the retainers of the house before them to the Priory-walls. The Prior asserted that his men defended themselves as well as they could, without breaking the peace—an expression which probably means no more than that they were worsted in the encounter. The building was then

The township of Worcester asserts a jurisdiction against the Prior by force of arms.

besieged, and arrows were shot at the defenders whenever there was an opportunity. At last the townsmen
seem to have grown weary of their sport, and, after
attempting in vain to burn the Priory and Cathedral, left
the monks in peace. The commission of enquiry concerning the outrage ends with a curious anti-climax, and
dilates upon the loss sustained by the Prior—in hares
and rabbits !

When it is remembered that all these deeds appear,
among others like them, upon the rolls of a single year,
it may perhaps be thought that enough has already been
told to show how slowly innate barbarism was affected by
improved legislation. But before the age can be seen as
it actually was, there are many other matters to be
brought to light.

In the special commissions to hear and determine
accusations of those offences which may be described
under the general name of brigandage, it was Simple murders dis-
usual to insert the names of a number of sus- tinguished
from greater
pected persons, and to add that others unknown offences.
were also concerned. In other commissions, to enquire
who were the perpetrators of ill deeds, it is sometimes
stated that the offenders had acted in no small numbers,
sometimes that they were associated in conventicles, not
seldom that they were roaming about in vast multitudes.
It is impossible to extract from such vague expressions
any figures sufficiently precise to be compared with modern
statistics. Where the names of seventy are mentioned,
there is no method of ascertaining that they are not
a very small portion of a very large gang ; where only
ten are mentioned, there is no certainty that the ' others '
are not simply part of a legal form, and that the ten are
not all who were even believed to have been implicated.

A vast multitude may be five thousand or more, or fifty or less, according to the tone of mind of the describer or the elasticity of legal language. Apart, however, from these crimes of extraordinary magnitude, there were ordinary murders of single individuals, which came under the notice of the coroners, as in our own times. The rolls are unfortunately not complete for the whole of England; but for one county, and that the largest, they are, if not complete, at least sufficiently full of information to show how great a stride we have made towards giving security to life. In Yorkshire there were, in the year before the Black Death, at least eighty-eight cases of felonious homicide brought to the notice of the coroners in the ordinary course. In the whole of England and Wales, the average of verdicts of wilful murder returned by coroners' juries (including cases of infanticide) has, during the decade from 1860 to 1869, not exceeded two hundred and fifty. Yorkshire includes about one-tenth of the whole area of England and Wales; and eighty-eight murders in Yorkshire may therefore be taken to represent eight hundred and eighty in England and Wales. But Yorkshire was not, in the fourteenth cen-

Comparison of past and present totals.

tury, the most populous part of England; and the whole population of England and Wales did not, a few years after the Black Death, exceed two millions and a half. The population of England and Wales now exceeds twenty-two millions; and if it be conceded that the Black Death and succeeding pestilences swept away two millions out of four millions and a half, there was not, in the early part of the reign of Edward III., more than a fifth part of the number of inhabitants at present in England. In order, therefore, to compare the murders of the nineteenth century with the murders of the fourteenth, it is necessary to multiply eight hundred and eighty by five. The result is that, if it were possible to conceive society in the same state now as then, there would be four thousand four hundred simple murders per annum, in addition to all the horrors of brigandage and private war. In other words, the security of life is now at least eighteen times as great as it was in the age of chivalry.

Should it be asked what was the character of the women when such was the life of the men, the answer would be that women were, except in the very highest rank, almost as brutal as their husbands or their paramours. Women in England had burned women to death in the tenth century ; they had been set on the stool of filth, to be mocked as brewers of bad ale in the eleventh ; on the stool of filth they had been jeered as common scolds from time immemorial ; they were legally beaten by their husbands down to a comparatively recent period. They were in the fourteenth century such as the circumstances in which they had lived had made them—strong in muscle but hard of heart—more fit to be the mothers of brigands than to rear gentle daughters or honest sons. In the towns, some of them found employment in weaving, brewing, and baking ; but it would be difficult to define their exact position when thus occupied. The websters, brewsters, and baxters were at one time, no doubt, female slaves, who wove cloth or linen fabrics, brewed ale, and baked bread, for their lords. Afterwards some of them pursued their crafts for their own profit, until at last the feminine designation was applied alike to craftsman and to craftswoman. In the reign of Edward III. webster was no longer a word distinctive of sex ; nor in all probability were brewster and baxter. There

(marginal note:) The women hardly less brutal than the men.

is, however, the evidence of the statute book that women
still worked in brewhouses, still earned their living by
the laborious occupation of making bread for their fellow
townspeople, if not in London, at any rate in other towns.
To women were still applied those punishments which
had been introduced by the men whose practice it was to
buy their wives and sell their daughters. It is, therefore,
not surprising that women sometimes appear as the actors
in crimes which must have required masculine strength
and an absence of all the qualities now considered
feminine.

A bakehouse seems to have been the favourite receptacle for a dead body after a murder had been committed ; and the heroine of the following story did only
what others had done before her. At Middleton, in
Derbyshire, there lived a man whose wife bore a name
well known to the readers of mediæval romances—Isolda
or Isoult. As he lay one night asleep in his bed, this
female Othello took him by the neck and strangled him.
As soon as he was dead, she carried the body to an oven
which adjoined their chamber, and piled up a fire to
destroy the traces of her guilt. But though she had so
far shown the energy and power of a man, her courage
seems to have failed her at the last moment. She took
to flight, and her crime was ·discovered. She was not,
however, by any means an exceptional woman for the
period in which she lived. Not only do women appear
continually as the receivers of felons and stolen goods,
but they are frequently mentioned in the lists of names
given in the special commissions which relate to brigandage and the greater deeds of violence.

When such was the character of the men and the
women, there is, perhaps, not much reason to wonder at

the undisguised conflict of offenders with the ministers of justice. In many of the commissions of enquiry, to which reference has already been made, it ap- Conflicts with the ministers pears that the armed bands which infested the of Justice: bloodshed in country were in the habit of obstructing the Court. judges by force. This, to use the language of the records, they had done openly and notoriously on many occasions. Nor were brawls, and riots, and bloodshed by any means uncommon within the walls of the law-courts and in the presence of the Bench itself. At Cambridge, when the justices were sitting, a man drew a long knife and made an attack upon the Mayor. At York a number of men—no common outlaws, but the mercers, saddlers, bakers, skinners, spurriers, and tailors of the place—entered the castle, fell upon the sheriff's retainers and made them the prisoners instead of the prisoners taken according to the form of the law. At Somerton, where the justices of assise were hearing causes, one Robert Mansel made a furious onslaught upon Robert Brente in the justice-hall. Mansel had friends in court who drew their swords and knives when he set them the example, pursued Brente to the bar, and would have killed their enemy there in sight of the judges, the jury, and all the spectators, had not assistance been found. Yet so ordinary an event was this, so little was it regarded as an unpardonable offence, that the ringleader, after a few appearances at Westminster, was dismissed upon payment of a fine.

In these scenes it is not difficult to discern once more the old partisan spirit of the days before the Conquest. All who said or did anything offensive to any Partisanship: Intimidation man able to command a few followers were at of prosecutors and suitors. his mercy unless they could themselves com- mand a greater number. And when even the courts of

law were not sacred from violence the intimidation practised outside them may be easily conjectured. Nor are
we left to conjecture alone upon this subject. Not only
is it lamented in the Statutes of Winchester and Westminster the First that true verdicts could not be obtained
from juries, but the rolls show precisely what might have
been expected from the surrounding circumstances. At
Dalton, near Furness Abbey, an indictment was found, at
the sheriff's turn, against a notorious robber. His friends
were at no great distance, and in sufficient number to
overpower all who left the court. They distributed blows
and threats in profusion, and with such good effect that
no further action was taken in the matter until there was
a commission to enquire into the circumstances. In
Cambridgeshire some members of one of the bands of
brigands were appealed and indicted for maihem and
murder. The gang lay in wait for the appellors and the
finders of the indictments, punished them for what they had
done, and menaced them with loss of limb or life if they
continued the prosecution. The power of the banditti
could not be set at defiance, for all knew that the threats
would be carried into execution upon the least provocation;
and even one of the appellors who had lost his brother
did not dare to prosecute his appeal.

Intimidation, such as this, was not practised solely
towards jurors and parties to suits, nor solely by brigands,
Armed resist- nor solely against private individuals. It was a
ance to the
Collectors of service of no small difficulty and danger to col-
Taxes. lect the sums voted by Parliament to the king.
All who had to pay seem to have felt themselves aggrieved ; and the rolls teem with commissions to enquire,
county by county, concerning resistance to the officials
authorised to receive fifteenths, and tenths, and subsidies.

In innumerable instances it became necessary to distrain, and distraint was commonly the signal for a riot. The unfortunate collector had only too often to complain that the cattle which he had seized had been taken from him by force, that the king's writ had been torn to shreds before his eyes, that he had himself been compelled to fly, that he had been pursued from village to village, and that he had barely escaped with his life in the end.

The qualities of the knight errant and the gentleman have often been attributed to the highwayman and the brigand. Nor can it indeed be disputed that the highwayman and the brigand have much in common with the knight errant. It has often been supposed also that in an age when men ordinarily resort to force for the attainment of their ends, there is an absence of the fraud and cunning and chicane which are said to disgrace periods of greater refinement. Poets and romancers have taught that an open countenance could best have been found under a knight's helmet, a great heart under a knight's coat of mail, a hand incapable of forgery under a knight's gauntlet. If the outlaw has committed acts of brutal violence, they have been attributed partly to a wild love of freedom, partly to a hatred of the meanness which he discovers in those who respect the rights of others. A life of adventure, with the forest for a home, and the haunts of men for a hunting-ground, is a repetition, with a slight change, of the life led by the noble savage. And is it not noble to take that which others cannot keep, to gratify a wish as soon as it arises, to assert superiority over the rest of mankind by depriving them of their goods, their daughters, their wives, and their lives ? In such elements of nobility the peasants, and even the knights of the fourteenth century

Knights errant, brigands, and 'noble savages' are not incapable of the meaner crimes.

S 2

were only a little inferior to the Teutonic hordes who overran the Roman Empire, and those hordes only a little inferior to their remote ancestors who had gained a living by the chase.

The notion, indeed, of the savage, that civilisation is an unholy institution which deprives him of the world as a free hunting-ground, was by no means extinct in the reign of Edward III. In all those cases of forcible entry which have been already mentioned, the game found in the wood-lands was carried off as spoil by the attacking force, and innumerable instances might be given of exploits which had no other issue. These have in our own time degenerated into poaching affrays, of which the most formidable would have been altogether unworthy of notice five hundred years ago. It is, therefore, most important to enquire whether, when the savage loses his savageness he loses nobility at the same time; whether deceit and trickery become the substitutes for threats and blows; whether, as the intellect becomes more highly developed, the moral character becomes more contemptible. If it should appear that baseness and cruelty went hand in hand in the days of barbarism long passed away, it will be evident that the progressive diminution of cruelty is at least a clear advantage without any counterpoise on the other side.

There are some crimes which lie on the border-land between those which veneration for the past ranges in the class of the chivalrously venial and those which in modern times are considered unchivalrously mean. A bold lover, for instance, breaks into the house of the woman he desires to wed. She has no wish to place her fortune or person at his disposal, but he has a mind to secure one or both. He gives her

Crimes on the border-land between the 'chivalrously' venial and the unchivalrously mean.

a simple alternative—either to be ravished on the spot or to be married on the following Saturday. It is Wednesday, and to gain time she consents to the marriage. He is not content with her word, but exacts an oath ; he doubts her intention to keep her promise even after she has sworn ; he therefore watches her house, waylays her when she comes out, and repeats more forcibly in the open air the arguments which he had applied within walls. Such are the details of a case which appears among the records of criminal proceedings in the year before the Black Death, and which throws some light upon the treatment of heiresses who were frequently carried off by violence, and who were not protected by statute before the reign of Henry VII.

If it is possible for Romance to represent the abduction of heiresses and the marriage of women by compulsion as gallantries rather than as crimes, it is at least out of her power to represent embezzlement as an act of virtue. But the highest officials were, in the fourteenth century, not less ready to embezzle than to strike. The Master of the Horse North of Trent is no sooner dead than it is discovered that he has appropriated a thousand pounds of the king's money. His subordinates had, during his tenure of office, been following his example ; some of the animals entrusted to their care they had sold, others they had taken for their own private use, and the rest they had permitted to die of hunger. Commissions to enquire concerning the misdeeds of officers employed in every branch of the king's service appear on the rolls at the very earliest time at which enrolments begin to be made, appear at the time now under consideration, and seem to be almost characteristic of the age of chivalry. The

Dishonesty characteristic of the 'Age of Chivalry.'

knight who becomes owner of a ship—perhaps with the chivalrous intention of leading the life of a pirate—is not ashamed to take a cargo of wool and defraud the king by escaping out of port without paying duty. He despises the merchant, the burgher, the trader of every kind, and shows his superiority by accepting their money for the performance of certain services, and by omitting to keep his word after he has received his price. The custom of fixing the Staple of exported English wool on the continent gives him ample opportunities for the display of his skill in the art of cheating a townsman ; and in the year before the Black Death there was a complaint that many English merchants had been killed, and that their wool, to the value of twenty thousand pounds, had fallen into the hands of the French, because the men who had agreed to provide a sufficient convoy had refused to fulfil the engagement, after levying a toll upon every sack to be exported.

It need be no matter for wonder that in an age in which the traditions of barbarism retained much of their vitality, the first rude efforts at commerce were not, in all cases, remarkable for self-denial and good faith. The experience of many generations had proved that the shortest way to obtain possession of land was to take it; when property of another kind began to increase, similar modes of acquisition at once suggested themselves, and were very commonly adopted. It has already been shown that the citizens of London were burglars a century after the Conquest; it has been shown that in the reign of Edward III. the knights carried into trade and into their dealings with heiresses practices very similar to those by which a claim to a manor was ordinarily asserted either rightfully or

Commerce infected by Fraud at its birth.

wrongfully. Neither class had as yet any regard for honesty; and their simple idea of life was that they should gain whatever they wanted in any manner which seemed to promise the most rapid success. Commerce, for many a century in danger of being strangled by force, was thus also necessarily infected by fraud at its very birth. Where there was one individual who perceived that it was best both for himself and for the community to accumulate wealth by industry, there were a hundred round him to whom it seemed much easier to snatch the fruits of his labour away from him, or to deprive him of them by a trick. In such a state of society not only is violence naturally met by violence, but deceit is apt to be anticipated by deceit. It is most difficult for a man to be honest who doubts the honesty of all about him; and when the townsman developes a trade among neighbours who recognise only the rule of the strongest, he uses all the weapons with which nature has endowed him to thwart the designs of his adversaries, and only too probably disgraces his calling by some disreputable act of imposture.

Such considerations as these might naturally lead us to expect that fraud will be found more prevalent in proportion to commerce when commerce is weak *Intimate connection of Force and Fraud.* and the warlike spirit is strong, and that it will be less prevalent when the warlike spirit grows weaker—when commerce developes, and is developed by, intellectual improvement. Fraud and force are so nearly akin in the perpetration of crime that the diminution of the latter can hardly fail to be accompanied by the diminution of the former. It is but a natural correlation of social existence that when the country gentleman is no better than a brigand, the merchant is no better than a smuggler, and the tradesman no better than a cheat. It is no less a correlation of national growth that, when the land-holder has become more refined through the arts and the culture which have their birth-place in the towns, the townsmen themselves are gainers in an equal degree, and give up dishonesty to as great an extent as the land-holders abandon brute force. No class has yet been able to enjoy a monopoly of honesty, nor has any nation yet been able to dispense with punishments for fraud. Complaints have been made in every generation that it is more depraved than its predecessors. But we need only consult our Public Records to assure ourselves beyond doubt, not only that crimes of violence have greatly decreased, but that the very meannesses, deceptions, and crimes against property, which we are apt to lament, are our inheritance from a less civilised age, and have decreased with the growth of wealth and of knowledge.

Reference has already been made to the petty thefts and rogueries, to the false weights, false measures, and various arts by which the London tradesmen of the fourteenth century defrauded their patrons or the rustics who brought goods to market; and it is unnecessary to dilate further on the small details of such a subject. But the class corresponding to our modern merchants resorted to practices which can no more be justified than those of the little mediæval shop-keeper.

Treachery of merchants and knights.

True patriotism was not to be found in an age when 'the country' meant no more than the neighbourhood in which a man lived, and in which the guilty had good reason to hope that they would be declared innocent by jurors of their guild. It is, therefore, not surprising that English merchants were in the habit

of supplying nations at war against England with provisions bought at English fairs, and weapons wrought by
English hands.   When England was at war with France,
La Rochelle was supplied with food by English traitors ;
when England was at war with Scotland, the Scottish
camp was fed from English markets, and English soldiers
fell by English arrows shot from English bows by Scottish arms.   The knight was little behind the trader in
treachery, and a 'chivaler' who held the office of the
King's Arrayer of Archers levied a sum in excess of
that which was required for the due execution of his
office, and appropriated the whole to his own use.

The first thought of the exporter was how he could
escape payment of the duty; the first thought of the
importer how he could introduce base money   Evasion of
from abroad, and put it into circulation in Eng-   duties.
land.   Upon the rolls may be seen commission after commission to enquire concerning merchants who had fraudulently laden their ships and sailed without either paying the
sum claimed on behalf of the king, or rendering any account.
The offence, as is commonly added in the records, was
one of daily occurrence.   It was perpetrated in various
ways — sometimes, perhaps, by a well-laid scheme for
eluding the vigilance of the officers, sometimes by a false
declaration that the goods were to be conveyed from one
English port to another—most frequently, in all probability, by collusion with the collectors of the customs.

The importation of false coin was also one of the
commonest branches of the merchant's trade, and commissions were sent into the various counties for   Importation
the purpose of discovering who were the offen-   of false coin.
ders. The exportation of sterling English coin was contrary
to law ; but the practice of the mediæval traders was to

exchange it with foreign dealers for money which was either of light weight, or of base metal, and to take the difference of value as their profit. The consequence was a general want of confidence in the currency. But for this the king and his advisers were not less responsible than the dishonest merchants. It had long been a common expedient, when the crown was in want of funds, to debase the coinage of the authorised mints, and so to reap a temporary advantage at the expense of the public. The only excuse was that finance had never been made a study, and was but little understood. The great lesson to be learnt from these proceedings, when compared with the practice and principles of modern times, is that enlightenment, even if acting in no other way, has the effect of diminishing crime, both by adding to the facility with which it can be detected, and by showing that an ill example set by the governing powers fails to attain the desired object—except, perhaps, for a moment—and greatly retards the progress of civilisation.

It may seem strange to those who associate the meanest crimes with periods of the greatest refinement, English manufacturers of false coin. but it is nevertheless true, that in this age of barbarism there were native manufacturers of false coin who competed successfully with the importers from abroad. At Aylesbury, according to the record of a single Gaol Delivery, one person accused of false coining died in prison, and another was brought to trial for the same offence, and for having the instruments of a coiner in his possession. At Scarborough a man and his wife, with an assistant, had a factory on no mean scale, and made not only false money, but false plate. The metals which they used were copper, brass, and quicksilver. With these they counterfeited both silver and gold, and apparently supplied other coiners with the materials for deception. In London a coiner was sent to the Tower to await his trial for an offence which in those days was held to be treason; and there are numerous other instances in which persons were accused of having false coin in their possession, though not of having imported it.

The great quantity of base coin in circulation not only inflicted great hardships on those who incurred loss by accepting it in payment, but inevitably caused false accusations to be brought against many who had become innocently possessed of it. False charges connected with the coinage. The king's officers were always ready to make a charge when they had not received a bribe, and, no doubt, equally ready to conceal a crime when they were sufficiently paid. At Kingston-on-Hull the Examiner of the port caused two men to be apprehended for having some of the base money known as Lushboroughs. One of the prisoners alleged that he had borrowed fifteen shillings from the other, had added them to forty-five shillings of his own, and trafficked in Hull with the whole —a sum equal perhaps to sixty pounds of modern currency. Upon examination it was proved that the coins were Lushboroughs to the extent of a twelfth part. The Lushborough money was sent into the Court of King's Bench for inspection, and the Hull examiner retained the good coin in his own hands. The borrower pleaded, with perhaps unconscious sarcasm, that he was a layman, ignorant of letters, that he had never crossed the sea in his life, and that he did not import the base money. His fellow-prisoner admitted the loan, and declared that he received the coin as the price of some wool, and that he also had not imported it. The jury acquitted both, and the terms of the verdict showed plainly the motive of the

accusation. It was found that the examiner had appropriated all the good money—more than eleven-twelfths
of the whole sum seized. He was proclaimed in the
usual course, failed to appear, and was in the end declared
an outlaw.

This is no exceptional case, but simply an illustration
of the causes which produced the universal dissatisfaction
with 'the king's ministers.' There was no pub-

Dishonesty at
the Mints.
lic department of which the officers were not
hated ; but all those who were in any way connected
with the mints, having perhaps exceptional temptations,
had from time immemorial been notoriously depraved.
In the reigns before the Conquest the moneyers were in
the habit of making base coin for their own benefit ; and
they had continued the same practice afterwards. When
not employed by the crown, they probably carried the
traditions of their craft into private life, and were, no
doubt, the instructors of false coiners, as well as false
coiners themselves. In the year before the Black Death,
the records do not furnish one instance of detected falsification in any of the authorised mints, but the tone of
morals which still prevailed there is sufficiently illustrated
by a complaint of some Lombard merchants. They had
delivered to a master of a mint a considerable quantity
of silver, which he was bound, in accordance with a recognised custom, to coin and re-deliver to them in the
form of English money. They soon discovered, however, that it was no easy matter to obtain their due from
a government official. Their silver was gone, but they
applied in vain for coin or for satisfaction of any kind ;
and the last that appears of the matter is a commission to
enquire into the circumstances. The jury was to consist
partly of foreigners and partly of citizens of London—a

favour granted by the king; and it may be reasonably believed that the verdict was in accordance with the influence and wealth of the parties.

Closely connected with crimes against the Mint was the very common offence of counterfeiting seals, which was usually accompanied by that of forging letters or official documents. At Bedford, a man, was accused of habitually imitating the letters and seals of the good men of the neighbourhood for the purpose of obtaining money by false pretences. At Aylesbury one was accused of fabricating writings which represented that he was employed in the management of the studs of the king and queen, and could make certain demands in their names. In the commissions, only too frequent, to enquire concerning oppressions, extortions, and felonies committed in purveyance for the households of the king, queen, royal family, and magnates, the false personation of purveyors is the subject of a special clause, and was, beyond all doubt, a very common practice. It may be illustrated by the following case. One Adam Plummer presented himself on Whit-Sunday at Cranford. His dress was rich with silk and fur, and he displayed a trencher-knife with silvered handle. By his appearance and credentials he succeeded for a time in persuading the people of the village that he was William le Moyne, Constable of Rochester Castle, and a kinsman of the Lord Chancellor, who had a right to purveyance. He began to make purchases at purveyors' price, hired stabling for eight horses, and some meadow land near the town—all, as he said, under the Chancellor's authority— and paid only the God's penny, which in those days was supposed to make a contract binding. His movements, however, excited suspicion, and a messenger was sent to

Forgery: counterfeit seals: false pretences.

the Chancellor, who at once denounced the self-styled purveyor as an impostor and directed a writ to the Sheriff of Middlesex for his arrest. The usual scene of violence followed. The pretender resisted the attempts to take him and maintained a running fight with the villagers who pursued him with bows and arrows. At last he was wounded in the side, captured, and brought to trial; but, with the common good fortune which·attended criminals in his time, he escaped punishment by means of a technical flaw in his arraignment, and was dismissed upon finding sureties for his good behaviour.

Forgery and imposture of a similar kind aided in bringing every branch of the administration into disre-
Forged writs and returns in Courts of Law. pute. The Bishop of Exeter complained that he was the victim of a system of fraud by which other inhabitants of Devonshire had also suffered great damage. A trespass real or imaginary was made the subject of a writ forged with some skill and used with more audacity. Counterfeit seals were attached to the counterfeit writs, which some of the gang of conspirators had sufficient address to present to the Justices of either Bench as being returned into court by the sheriff with his endorsement. The persons against whom these sham legal proceedings were instituted, had no notice, and, as a matter of course, made no appearance. The false returns produced before the judges were evidence that the defendants had been summoned to appear and had failed; judgment went by default, and a real writ to carry it into execution issued to the real sheriff of the county. The sufferer by the scheme was therefore first made aware of it by the sheriff's officers coming to take possession of his lands and goods on behalf of the schemers.

Here, as elsewhere, it is difficult to distinguish between a knightly desire to appropriate land and the brigand's war against society in general. Those gangs whose exploits are told in song, with praises of their audacity and generosity, resorted to all, and more than all, the mean arts which are practised in more civilised times. A band of robbers in Suffolk seems to have been equally skilful in the use of brute force and threats, in smuggling wool out of port after it had been stolen, in importing bad money, in forging documents, and in counterfeiting seals. Sometimes they would present themselves at a house and assure the owner that unless he at once paid a certain sum he would be indicted on several counts at the next visitation of the justices. Sometimes they would adopt the shorter method of beating the householder until he paid as much money as they demanded. Sometimes they would appear in church on Sunday, make a sudden attack, and exact a heavy ransom as the price of life; and what they did on Sunday in church, they did on week-days in the market-place. One day a chaplain, who was a member of their body, disguises himself at the instigation of the others, as a merchant of Ghent, who was commonly employed by Philippa, the king's consort. He exhibits what appears to be her seal, but is in fact a counterfeit, and demands a large sum of money from her bailiff. The first attempt is unsuccessful as the seal is not thought a sufficient warrant. The chaplain returns soon afterwards with a forged letter in which the queen apparently asks for a still larger sum. This device also fails, and the chaplain again retires. After a sufficient interval of time, another brigand appears as a sheriff's officer, and produces a writ directed to the Sheriff of Suffolk under the King's Secret Seal to distrain the goods and chattels of

Forgery used as an aid to brigandage.

the bailiff for the required sum on behalf of the merchant
of Ghent.   He also shows a receipt for the money,
signed by the queen, which is of course, like the writ and
the seal, the work of a confederate.   The bailiff hesi-
tates ; the brigand, in his capacity of sheriff's officer,
tenders his advice, and again calls attention to the receipt.
In the end the bailiff satisfies the demand, and receives
the forged receipt in exchange for his coin.

Conviction in such a case as this, did not always lead
to punishment, even though the king might refuse his
pardon.   The man who would forge the queen's
receipt, would not hesitate to forge a transcript
of the King's Letters Patent.   A case appears on one
of the rolls of the year 1348 in which common report
attributed to one William Rydout, the practice of counterfeiting various royal letters.   He was apprehended, and
on him was found what purported to be a copy of a general
pardon of homicides and felonies granted to him by the
king.   The seal, however, had been torn off, and it seems
to have been held that the forgery was incomplete unless
it could be shown that the seal had been counterfeited.
Neither counterfeit seals nor instruments for making them
were discovered in the possession of the prisoner.   The
finding of the jury was, therefore, that the offence of
forging letters patent had not been proved.   The accused
was allowed to go at large on finding sureties for
his future behaviour, but his goods and chattels were
attached until his character could be cleared.   Such
looseness in the administration of justice, which has yet
to be further considered, was, no doubt, at once a cause
and an effect of the prevailing depravity.

The extent, however, to which forgery prevailed, at a
time when there were but few educated persons in the

Forged Par-
dons.

kingdom, cannot be estimated from the comparatively unimportant instances which have already been detailed. In the same year in which the rolls tell of those cases, there appears a commission to the Lord Treasurer, the Lord Chancellor, the Seneschal or Steward of the Chamber, and others, to enquire concerning a wholesale system of fraud by which, to use the words of the document, grave damage had been caused to the Exchequer, and manifest suffering and impoverishment to the people. Numerous payments and allowances, all of large sums, had been made on the faith of bonds to which had been attached counterfeits of the Great Seal, on the faith of forged bills, and sometimes even without the semblance of a warrant in any form whatever. The whole department was evidently in a state of the greatest corruption—rotten within, and the subject of predatory attacks from without. Other records of the period throw more light upon the matter, and show how powerless were the constituted authorities to apply a sufficient remedy, even if a remedy was honestly desired. Certain merchants had bound themselves to return into the Exchequer on a fixed day a number of bills which had issued from the Office of the Wardrobe, so that the king might be freed from the burden of debts of long standing. They had of course received, or were to receive, an equivalent in one form or other for the responsibility which they had thus incurred. But when the time came round they prayed for delay on the ground that forgery had been detected in many bills, and that they were afraid of presenting false instead of·real documents. The request was not considered unreasonable, and a writ was sent to the Treasurer and Barons of the Exchequer, instructing them that a respite had been granted to the merchants

Forgery of Exchequer Bills.

for three years—though of course the favour was not
accorded until arrangements had been made to pay for it.

The manner in which the forged bills were used, and
the magnitude of the evil are illustrated by the following

Mode of raising money upon forged Exchequer Bills. case, which was brought before the King in
Council. Nicholas Boylyel complained that
Walter Yarmouth, one of the king's ministers
(or, as we should now say, an officer of one of the public
departments), brought him a bill purporting to be sealed
with the seal of the King's Wardrober, and showing that
the king owed 312*l.* to a certain lord, named John Beau-
mond. Upon this security Yarmouth borrowed ten
pounds, leaving the document in pledge. Another day,
he produced three similar bills, similarly sealed, by which
it appeared that Godekyn De la Rule, a merchant, was
the king's creditor for more than 1000*l.*, and upon these
he obtained an advance of 31*l.* He returned time after
time, each time with bills for a larger amount, and succeeded every time in effecting a loan. His last exploit
was to raise fifty-two pounds upon three bills representing
2,400*l.* owed by the king to De la Rule. After this the
forgery was confessed by Yarmouth, whose sentence was
imprisonment for life. It is worthy of remark that the
rolls are full of instances in which hanging was the
punishment awarded to thefts of small amount, that the
bills forged by this government official amounted to no
less than six thousand and eighteen pounds of the money
of the period, and that according to some estimates the
sum must have been equivalent to more than a hundred
thousand pounds of modern currency.

An account of the forgeries for which the dark ages
were most remarkable would be incomplete without
some reference to those forgeries by members of reli-

gious houses, which have caused innumerable spurious charters or deeds of grant to be handed down to posterity. Though the crime was very common, both be-

Forgeries of Charters in Religious Houses.

fore the Conquest and after, it is not easy to discover many instances of conviction. Abbots and bishops had usually sufficient interest to keep accusations out of court, or, like the famous William of Wykeham, Bishop of Winchester, to obtain a general pardon, expressly framed in such terms as to cover all 'rasings of records.' A case, however, brought to light a little after the time now under consideration, shows one of the methods by which authority was given to false documents. A dispute arose between the abbot of Bruerne and the abbot of Cirencester, respecting the right to certain land. There was in existence a charter, by which Richard I. granted to a former abbot of Bruerne and his monks, various lands and liberties in various parts of England, but by which it was not possible to establish the claim against the rival house at Cirencester. It occurred to some one at Bruerne that if the name of an unimportant place could be erased, and the name of the coveted territory could be inserted instead, the charter would appear conclusive evidence in favour of his monastery. The device was carried into execution ; 'Fish-hide' disappeared, and 'East-leach' was substituted. It was not, however, thought prudent to exhibit in a court of law a document which had been thus ingeniously manipulated. The charter was presented for 'confirmation,' which was, perhaps, granted as a matter of routine, upon payment of a fee, but more probably by collusion between the monks and a clerk of the chancery. The official 'confirmation,' with which it was not necessary to tamper, was on the day of trial placed before the

judges in the Court of King's Bench ; it was a genuine
document and on the face of it sufficient to decide the
case.   The fraud was, however, detected—possibly
because the other parties to the suit were not unfamiliar
with the contrivance—and the Abbot of Bruerne was
summoned before the King and Council.   He appeared,
and declared that a monk of his house had made the
erasure, and taken the charter for confirmation entirely
without his knowledge, but admitted that he could show
no cause why the document and all confirmations of it
should not be annulled.   He was required to produce them
on a certain day, when he again appeared and made the
astounding statement that he had never seen the charter
which had been falsified, that it had been taken away
from the house by the monk whom he had named, who
could not be found, and who had it in his possession, if
indeed it had ever existed.   With this the Court seems
to have been satisfied, though, of course, the final confirmation of the charter was cancelled.

Attempts to deceive the unlettered by those who were
able to read and write seem, however, to have been the
natural growth of an age in which a little education made almost as great a difference between
Englishman and Englishman as now exists betwen savage and citizen.   Forgery, trickery, and corruption in
every form are the offspring of a period in which ignorance
rendered detection difficult, and in which violence was
their most ready ally.   Not only was it a common offence
to counterfeit a pardon, but frauds were perpetrated by
government officials for the purpose of saving an offender
from trial.   An unfortunate widow instituted a prosecution against the murderers of her husband.   In accordance with the forms of those days, the Clerk of the

Forgeries
committed
by Sheriffs.

Crown directed a writ to the Sheriff of Norfolk, in which county the crime was perpetrated, and instructed him to apprehend the accused, who were eight in number. One of them was named Brode; no attempt was made to capture him, and when the writ was returned his name was not to be found there. Upon inspection it was ascertained that while the writ was in the Sheriff's possession an erasure had been made, and 'Brode' had been converted into 'Crode'—so that there was in effect no warrant for the arrest of the person who was at the head of the list of the appealed.

A very similar case occurred in the same year in Hampshire. In this there was no question of forgery, but it illustrates the difficulty of obtaining justice for any wrong—a difficulty which we happily cannot realise to our modern imaginations without taking into consideration some very remarkable details. Another widow adopted the usual course of proceeding by appeal against the murderers of her husband. One of them was taken, but when the time for his trial came round, the Sheriff certified that he was in ill health, and could not travel without danger of dying on the road. Another day was fixed, and again the prisoner was not produced and the same excuse was made. The Court, however, decided that the Sheriff was not justified in his conduct, that his return was insufficient, and that he had acted with the object of showing favour to the accused. Like the Sheriff of Norfolk, he suffered no greater punishment than a fine, which in those days of corruption he could, no doubt, easily make good.

The conduct of the Sheriffs in the administration of justice was at that time neither worse nor better than that of their subordinates, or even of the superior judges.

[Marginal note: Partiality and general corruption of Sheriffs and other Officers.]

The Sheriff of Hampshire was implicated in another affair in which the Royal authority was quietly set at defiance. A trespass had been committed ; the offender had been sentenced in the Court of King's Bench to pay a certain sum, and the Sheriff had been instructed to execute judgment. Upon receipt of the writ, he deliberately refused to act. The Coroners of the county were then commanded to bring him into Court to answer for his contempt. Their reply was that the Sheriff was residing within the liberty of Queen Philippa, and that the duty of taking him devolved upon the bailiff of the liberty, to whom they had given the necessary instructions, but who had returned no answer. The Court held that this statement was insufficient, that the coroners were screening the Sheriff, as the Sheriff had screened the trespasser, and that they must be held responsible. In the mean time, however, the plaintiff in the original suit remained as completely without redress as though no verdict had been obtained.

A device commonly adopted by the Sheriffs, for the purpose of aiding the guilty or injuring the innocent, was
Juries packed by Sheriffs
to empanel a jury of which the members were known by him to favour the side favoured by himself. The writ in which he was instructed to summon the jurors contained also a caution that they should not be in any way connected with parties interested in the case. But he had power to name whom he pleased, and his partiality could rarely be detected unless his nomination included persons obviously disqualified from serving according to law. Sometimes, if he could not attain his object otherwise, he would openly disregard the law, and trust to his influence to save him from punishment. But his misdeeds in this respect were not unfrequently brought

to light. It was necessary, at this time, that jurors should be chosen in the district in which a crime was committed or in which a dispute arose; and it must be remembered that they were still practically witnesses of the facts, if not the only witnesses, though they gave a verdict. In spite of this, the Sheriff of Sussex took upon himself to return a panel of jurors, to try a case of homicide, not one of whom was qualified by his place of abode to sit. The defect was discovered, and the panel quashed. The Sheriff of Suffolk effected the same purpose in a manner, if possible, still more unjustifiable. He placed a number of outlaws upon a jury, which convicted an Ipswich man of trespass and other offences. The sufferer endured a long imprisonment in the Marshalsea Prison before he could obtain so much redress as an enquiry into the circumstances. In the end, however, the illegality of the proceedings was made manifest, and they were annulled.

Sometimes it is expressly stated that an accused person is too powerful for a trial in his own county to be impartial, and provision is made accordingly for a trial in London. But pressure could as readily be brought to bear upon the Judges and their officers in London as elsewhere. The Chief Clerk of the King's Bench had some connection with the Monastery of St. Paul's. He was one day within the walls of that religious house, when a Lancashire gentleman, accompanied by a servant, presented himself in great wrath. According to this gentleman's statement, the Chief Clerk had received a bribe, or a promise, of four marks, to delay proceedings in a pending action. This the complainant alleged to be to the advantage of his adversary, and, placing his hand on his knife, gave the Clerk a significant warning not to repeat the offence. His example was

Corruption in the Court of King's Bench.

followed by his servant, and the two retired with threatening gestures. This mode of dealing with an official was
of course a contempt of court, and was punished by a
fine ; but it does not appear that the charge brought
against the Chief Clerk was unfounded. There was,
indeed, a commission about the same time to hold an
enquiry concerning various deceptions and falsifications
for which the King's. Bench had become notorious, and
which had caused no small scandal at Westminster and
' damage to the people.'

Nothing, however, can better illustrate the manner in
which justice was sought, and the estimation in which

Forgery by
Counsel :
taking fees
from both
parties to a
suit.

courts of justice were held, than the audacity
with which money was taken from both sides in
a suit between the Abbot of Pershore and the
Abbot of Westminster. The matter in dispute
was the burden of repairing and maintaining Pershore
Bridge. One Geoffrey Aston declared himself ' of the
counsel' of the Abbot of Pershore, and received from
Adam le Clerk, on the part of the Abbot, a fee to obtain
a Commission of Enquiry, and further to act against the
Abbot of Westminster until the house at Pershore was
exonerated. After some preliminary investigations, the
cause was brought into the Court of King's Bench, to
which the Sheriff of Worcestershire returned a panel of
jurors. The return, however, was, either through collusion
or in accordance with the ordinary laxity of proceeding,
directed to Aston, to be delivered by him in the presence
of the Chief Justice and other Judges of the Court.
Adam le Clerk had come up to Westminster to act as
might seem best for the Abbot of Pershore ; and it was
agreed between him and Aston that it would be best to
destroy the panel furnished by the sheriff, and to sub-

stitute one of their own making. The sheriff's seal was
accordingly taken off, the despatch opened, the names of
suborned jurors put in the place of those named in the
genuine panel, and a counterfeit seal attached to the
forged document, which was then delivered into court.
No sooner was this done than Aston pretended to betray
his former clients, went to the Abbot of Westminster,
and offered himself as counsel against the Abbot of
Pershore. He was accepted, and bound himself by oath
to strive in every way for the success of his new client.
He received a larger fee than had been given on the
other side, and a still greater sum on the day of trial.
But when the cause was called, he took the part of the
Abbot of Pershore, which he had good reason to know
would be favoured by the jury. In the end, he was himself brought to trial for having been 'ambidexterous,'
and convicted, but incurred no greater punishment than
a fine. His accomplice in the forgery suffered no heavier
penalty, and both remained at large to exercise their
ingenuity still further.

The ecclesiastical courts appear to have been the
scenes of similar iniquities. A grand jury found that
three men in Holy Orders entered into a con- Deceptions
spiracy against one John Exeter, who was practised in
                                              the Eccle-
residing in Northamptonshire. They persuaded Courts.
a man to assist them by going in their company into the
City of London, personating John Exeter, and accepting
in his name a summons from the Summoning Officer of
the Court of the Archdeacon. The officer thus became
a witness of due service, and process was continued
against Exeter, who, being in complete ignorance, made
no appearance, and was consequently excommunicated.
A day was fixed for the trial of the conspirators, who

seem to have possessed considerable influence, or the wealth which could be converted into influence. When the time came for hearing, the Justices simply ordered proceedings to be stayed.

If the judges were not guilty of corruption in this particular case, there is at least no doubt that corruption

Bribery among the Judges : the Chief Justice of England convicted.

was as general among them as among the counsel from whom they were selected, and among the subordinate officials of the courts. Not only had extortion been the theme of innumerable documents enrolled on the public records for generations ; not only had the judges been dismissed in a body for their misdeeds ; not only were the bribes which they were in the habit of receiving from both parties to a suit the subject of popular songs, but at the very time now under consideration the Chief Justice of England was William Thorpe, who was convicted two years later of receiving gifts from parties appearing before him. According to the Ordinance for the Justices, framed two years earlier, every judge was, upon his appointment, compelled to make oath that he would not take either robe or fee, for the execution of his office, from any one but the king ; and an infringement of this solemn promise, placed his lands, and goods, and life at the king's mercy. Five separate instances in which money had been accepted were adduced against Thorpe, and in none of them did he deny the fact. The sentence pronounced against him was that he should be hanged, and forfeit all his lands and goods. The king, however, stayed execution, commanded that Thorpe should be imprisoned in the Tower, and, after a delay of no more than a twelve-month, granted a pardon, and restored a portion, if not all, of the forfeited possessions.

It is but too evident, from this and many other similar cases, that the offence which the Chief Justice confessed was not regarded as a very great crime. An oath had been broken in which the king had a special interest, and this seems to have been thought of far more importance than the character of the Bench or the welfare of the nation. A pardon, in those days, apparently cleansed a man from the stain of every mean action, and rendered him fit for the society of the most noble among barons or the most chivalrous among knights. It is necessary to bear these facts well in mind in attempting to estimate the culpability of such a Chancellor as Bacon, and the blessings which we enjoy in the present administration of the law.

Enough has now been said to show how wide-spread was the corruption of the period, and to explain the violence and lawlessness which appear at first Ill effects of sight irreconcileable with any firmly-established these bad examples. legal system. It has been sufficiently proved that the age of chivalry was an age of chicane, and fraud, and trickery, which were not least conspicuous among the knightly classes. It has been demonstrated that in town and country alike all the officers of the law, from the highest to the lowest, were open to bribery. It is not, therefore, difficult to understand how a legal organisation from which our own has been developed was wholly without respect, and utterly powerless to cope with offenders. It ceases to be wonderful that the barbarism of the past was able to assert itself in private wars and forcible seizures of land at a time when the Courts of King's Bench, Common Pleas, and Exchequer were all in existence, when the judges went their circuits as in our own time, and when legal cases involving difficult points were reported year by year for the use of the legal profession. The men appointed to carry out an improving judicial system were infected by the ancient traditions, and brought the laws into the disrepute which was justly incurred by themselves. Criminals of every kind not unnaturally believed that they would be protected in the perpetration of crime, or that they would at least secure impunity after the deed. It must have been for this reason that they undertook adventures which could not be brought to an end in a day, and which would have been perfectly impossible had the local authorities acted with vigour or even acted at all.

Not once nor twice, but time after time it is recited, in the commissions of enquiry, that after a close had been broken and a house attacked, the timber was cut down, the grass mown and made into hay, the corn reaped, and the whole spoil carried off. The knights and clerks who were implicated in these deeds mustered, perhaps, sometimes a force too powerful to be successfully opposed by any legal authority ; but at other times, when the attacking party was less numerous, it is not difficult to perceive the connivance of a sheriff or his subordinates. It is no injustice to the man who would pack a jury or rase a writ to suppose that he would shut his eyes and close his ears when a knight, who happened to be his friend, was robbing a knight who happened to be his enemy.

One of the greatest encouragements to criminals was thus the great probability that they would escape all Reluctance of punishment. Apart from the corruption or jurors to convict. partiality of officials which delayed a trial or rendered it impossible, a jury, even when not fraudulently empanelled, was usually inclined to take the part of persons accused. The lament in the Statute of Winchester that jurors could not be induced to find true verdicts against robbers or any breakers of the peace is fully justified by the rolls of a later date. Except when the culprits were 'clerks,' who were at this time extremely unpopular, acquittal was the rule and conviction the exception. A man of influence could exert his influence to save himself; a man of no influence had the sympathy of men who, if not concerned in the offence which they were summoned to try, could hardly have been guiltless of some similar act of lawlessness. If a man was taken with property in his possession of which he could not give a satisfactory account, it was usual to defer his trial, after he had been brought into court, until his fate could be decided by an Inquest of Fame. The meaning of this was that the general character of the accused, as found by a jury, was accepted as an indication of the guilt or innocence of the prisoner. The ancient practice of compurgation may, perhaps, have suggested this method of determining the issue, and the result was hardly more satisfactory than the result of the ancient practice. The 'country' which would not convict on a particular charge, would not, as a rule, declare a thief to be of ill repute, and the ordinary verdict was that the accused was of good fame.

Among other facilities for escape was the ease with which a law breaker could find shelter for himself and storage for his spoil. The Common Receiver is by no means a creation of our great modern cities, but has descended to us from the days when Europe was in a state of brigandage, and when the guilds assisted an accused brother to obtain an acquittal. Men and women are thus described in numerous cases recorded in the rolls, and were the fitting associates of the

Common Receivers of felons and goods.

classes described as common breakers of the peace, common thieves or robbers, and common malefactors.   There
is now a wider separation between those who live by
crime and those who live by honest means.   But the
difference has been caused not so much by the addition of
crime to the list of skilled professions as by the increase in
the number of industrial callings.   New outlets are thus
provided for the energy and ingenuity of those who
would, in former times, have joined the gang of a robber-
knight, earned a livelihood by forging writs and charters,
or been content with stealing a sheep and carrying it
home to be hidden by a wife or a mistress.

It happened by no means unfrequently that members
of a band of depredators betrayed their accomplices after

*Approvers :
their usual
fate : the rea-
sons for it.*

they had been apprehended.   This might naturally have been expected in an age in which
counsel sometimes accepted fees from both parties to a suit, and the judges were notoriously corrupt.
There was, however, little danger to any criminal from
this source.   The spirit of partisanship, if it was not strong
enough to prevent a thief from becoming an approver, was
at least strong enough to render his death almost a certainty
after he had made his accusation.   The great number of
these approvers and their almost invariable fate present a
curious illustration of the age.   If jurors were always
reluctant to convict, they were doubly reluctant when, as
the legal phrase ran, an approver offered himself.   The
charges brought by these men were, no doubt, very often
false and prompted by malice.   There was many an
Oates before Titus, though their opportunities may not
have been as great, or their schemes may not have been
as well made known to us as his.   But jurors would, in
those days, care little whether an approver spoke truth

or falsehood.   If any virtue was cultivated, any duty considered sacred, it was that of fidelity to a kinsman, a leader, or a comrade.   Thus much of good, though little more, there was in the old family-tie, the old land-tie and the old guild-tie.   To be untrue to an associate was, therefore, a crime of far deeper dye than robbery or murder ; and the jury, apart from all other considerations, had no eyes for the lesser offence in presence of the greater.   Any one who was appealed by an approver, was, for these reasons, as nearly as possible certain of an acquittal ; the approver himself, if he failed, as he nearly always did fail, to obtain a verdict, was sentenced to be hanged.

Jurors, too, had probably some suspicion of the manner in which men were induced to turn approvers after they had been captured and lodged in gaol.   Not many years had elapsed since some of the deeds perpetrated by gaolers in London had been brought to light, and it may be assumed that in such an age gaolers elsewhere were not more humane.   A whisper had gone abroad of the horrors of Newgate, which had at length become the subject of a commission of enquiry. There persons accused of minor offences had been thrown into the deepest dungeons with notorious robbers and murderers.   All had been threatened and tortured until they consented to do as the keeper of the gaol had bidden them.   Sometimes his object was no other than that of the brigands outside his walls—to make his victims pay for mercy ; but not less often it was to force the most atrocious criminals to implicate the innocent in the offences which they had committed.   The appeal by an approver was, therefore, on many grounds regarded with abhorrence.   It might, indeed, have been supposed that, as

Prisoners forced by torture to become approvers.

an inquest was held upon the body of everyone who died in gaol, to decide whether the death had been in the ordinary course of nature or had been caused by duress, there would have been some restraint upon the cruelty of gaolers.   But though there is ample evidence that the law upon this point was enforced there is not less ample evidence that death in prison was a remarkably common event.   Among all the prisoners none died so frequently as the approvers, who seem, indeed, to have sometimes at least resisted their tormentors until their strength failed them and to have lived only long enough to make their charge. Instances in which ' dead ' is set against the name of an approver are suspiciously common ; and one roll of the year before the Black Death shows that no less than fifty had died in the gaol of York Castle alone.

With the alternative before him of being executed according to law or killed by prison discipline, it may appear strange that anyone should be found to seek safety in a false accusation or in treachery to a friend—especially in an age in which such treachery was regarded as the most unpardonable of sins.   The only explanation seems to lie in the fact that, when communication was difficult and news travelled slowly, the fate of informers was not generally known, and in the fact that, although every man was ready to punish as a common enemy one who had shown himself a traitor, few had any real sense of honour, any chivalrous sentiment, which would deter them from attempting to save themselves at the expense of others.

When, however, the approver had once made his accusation, he seems to have been oppressed by the magni-

Conduct of approvers after making their accusations.

tude of his offence against the recognised code of morals, or to have been utterly broken in spirit by the tortures which he had endured. In those days mere physical courage must have been the most common of virtues, and could not have been wanting in the habitual criminals whose lives were passed in rapine and bloodshed. Yet the approvers appear but rarely as the actors in the trial by duel which afforded them their best chance of success ; and, when it was demanded against them, they seem to have lost all confidence in themselves. The following instance, by no means exceptional, may be mentioned in illustration. A man taken on suspicion of having stolen a number of sheep became an approver, and alleged that he had committed the offence with others, of whom he mentioned one by name. The accused declared his innocence, and offered to prove it by his body. The court allowed the wager of battle. It was accepted by the approver who was sent back to prison. But, before the appointed day the approver returned into court, and withdrew the charge. His fate might easily have been predicted. He was at once sentenced to death by hanging.

Charges made by approvers were by no means the only kind of accusation discouraged by popular opinion. An attempt had been made, since the Conquest, *Prosecution* to provide a legal substitute for the ancient *by appeal ; impunity of* blood-feud. Lawyers of the French and Italian *criminals.* schools had no sympathy with the barbarous doctrine that the next of kin had a right to blood or money for a slain relative. But they introduced into the class of prosecutions by them designated appeals a form of procedure according to which a widow could prosecute the slayers of her husband, or an heir male the slayers of his ancestor. In the event of a conviction, the king had no power to pardon ; and to this extent the family rights of past ages were respected and the injury done was regarded

as a private wrong. There was usually in such cases a con-
current indictment in which the offence was regarded as a
public wrong—done, in technical language, against the
king's peace. Damages for murder were thus abolished,
though damages were still awarded to those who were successful in an appeal of maihem (or maiming), and restitution
of stolen property was obtained by a successful appeal of
robbery or larceny. But it was hardly more difficult to secure conviction in an appeal instituted by an approver than
in an appeal instituted by a bereaved widow. The lawlessness for which the ancient wer-gild was but a cloak was
still dearly cherished ; and it was, no doubt, considered a
great hardship that an Englishman should not have the
privilege of killing a neighbour when he was prepared
to make a suitable compensation. In the age of chivalry
there was little sympathy for the fatherless and the widow,
who learned by bitter experience that to institute a
prosecution was only to add new trouble to their bereavement.

The happiest issue of which there was any reasonable
hope in any kind of appeal was that the accused would
escape capture and be outlawed for non-appearance. This was what most frequently happened ; and it could have afforded but little satisfaction to the prosecutors. Only a little less often it was
found that on the day of trial the accusers did not dare to
present themselves. It is, indeed, probable enough that
in some appeals of rape and robbery accusations had been
falsely made, and that a guilty conscience had a deterrent
effect. But this explanation will not apply to the numerous instances in which appeals of murder were abandoned by widows who had lost their husbands. The
penalty for this default would not have been lightly

Hardships suffered by injured accusers.

incurred, for it was that which in the case of a woman corresponded to outlawry in the case of a man. She was waived; she became, that is to say, a waif—a thing of as little consideration in the eye of the law as a stolen chattel thrown away by a thief in his flight. She had legally no dwelling-place save within the walls of a prison. Yet this was commonly the sentence upon a widow who had been imprudent enough to accuse her husband's murderers in the first excitement of her grief. Either the offenders employed such threats that she feared their violence more than the law's cruelty, or the neighbours were so much opposed to the proceeding by appeal that she knew it would be useless to ask for their verdict as jurors. In either case the remedy provided by law was practically useless.

If a resolute woman determined to run every risk, and appear in court, a dexterous counsel raised technical objections, by which her patience and resources were exhausted—sometimes even before the jurors were asked to speak. Walter Eye, for instance, a clerk, had to answer Mazeline le Long for the murder of her husband in one appeal, and others had to answer her in another appeal for having committed the crime with the consent and at the instigation of the clerk. Eye was tried first, and acquitted on the charge of murder. The widow was committed, and compelled to pay a fine for her release. The appeal against one of the others was then heard, and it was pleaded on his behalf that, as his principal had been acquitted, the accusation against him as an accessary necessarily fell to the ground. The court ruled that this was good law, and the widow was again committed, and again had to pay a fine. Two others failed to appear and were outlawed; but one of them afterwards came into court, and gave as a reason for his non-appearance that he had been in the army before Calais. He was bailed, and in the end received a pardon. The widow, after all her losses, had no satisfaction, and was burdened with the reflection that all her enemies, except one who died in prison, had both the will and the power to take their revenge for her attempt to punish them.

In the corruption which prevailed everywhere, and from which, as has been seen, gaolers were by no means Facilities for exempt, the criminal who could afford to pay the escape of criminals. might reasonably hope to escape from prison either before trial or after sentence. Gaol-breaking, as it is termed, is frequently mentioned in the records. The commission to enquire into the state of Newgate naturally suggests a suspicion that gaols were not very frequently broken without the connivance of some one who had authority within them. In the year before the Black Death there was a writ to apprehend the Keeper of the Marshalsea for having fraudulently permitted the escape of a number of prisoners who were in his custody, and who had been convicted of various trespasses. There is reason also to believe that the sheriffs played into the hands of the gaolers—sometimes for the purpose of detaining an innocent person in prison untried, and sometimes for the purpose of giving a favoured prisoner more time to make arrangements for his escape. Again and again it is recorded that a person brought into court for trial was sent back to prison 'for defect of country'—as it is expressed in the rolls, or, in other words, because there was no jury. It was the duty of the sheriff to summon a sufficient number of jurors, and, though they may sometimes have neglected to obey the summons, it is quite consistent with the facts already narrated to suppose that the sheriff was willing to incur a fine for the sake of damaging an enemy or gaining time for a friend.

Had the administration of justice been less corrupt than it was, criminals would still have had a great advantage in the difficulty which presented itself when any attempt was made to describe them in a legal document. Below the class of knights, surnames had not as yet become fixed ; and it would, perhaps, be hardly correct to say that they were everywhere fixed even in that rank. If a man is known as William Litster of Gateshead, William, his servant, is known as William Williamservant Litster of Gateshead. If a man is known as Robert of the Woghes, Nicholas, his servant, is known as Nicholas Robertservant of the Woghes. It is evident that in such cases as these the trade or the place of abode is made to serve the purpose of one designation, but that each is so loosely attached as to be moveable at pleasure, and to be applicable to the purposes of another designation. The consequences of such an imperfect nomenclature are, as might have been expected, most conspicuous in the records which relate to criminal matters. The judges, from this cause, looked upon any alleged pardon with the greatest suspicion ; and there, no doubt, existed a practice of rendering a pardon granted to one person useful to many. Juries, therefore, were continually summoned to decide the identity both of persons accused and of persons pardoned. A man who was put on his trial for homicide, as John Parker, alleged that he had received a pardon under the name of John, son of Richard Smyth of Watton ; another, accused with him, as Walter of Lyndeseye, alleged that he had received a pardon under the name of Walter Cosyn of Toynton, in Lyndeseye ; and

Advantages to criminals from the imperfect adoption of surnames.

in both cases the pardons were allowed. A question arose whether a prisoner described as Robert Stete Tournour of Tenterden had been outlawed or not; it was found that the person outlawed was Robert, son of Alexander Turnour of Thurleigh, and that the prisoner was Robert, son of William Flour of Tenterden. When there was so great an uncertainty as appears in these and very many other cases, it is obvious that there were almost insuperable obstacles to the apprehension of offenders not taken in the act, as it was nearly impossible to describe them correctly in a writ, even though their persons were known. So great, indeed, did the inconvenience become that in the reign of Henry V. it was thought necessary to provide a remedy by a Statute, in which it was enacted that the condition in life or occupation and the place of abode should be necessary to a complete description of a person in a legal document. Even this, however, was not effectual, and the Writ of Identity of name, which was commonly demanded in the reign of Edward III., was again the subject of a statute in the Reign of Henry VI.

Though pardons were regarded with suspicion when produced in answer to a criminal charge, there is no

Readiness with which pardons were granted.

doubt that they were granted with the utmost facility in an age when peace was never of long duration. As soon as war was declared, it was the custom to issue a proclamation, in which a general pardon of all homicides and felonies was granted to everyone who would serve for a year at his own cost. The terms were readily accepted, and the king increased his force by a number of men who would perhaps be inferior to none in courage, though they might not improve the discipline of the army. The rolls accordingly

abound with instances in which a pardon was alleged for
military service, and allowed without dispute.   Nor was
this the only advantage which a criminal derived from
foreign wars.   Even when he remained in England, in
pursuit of his ordinary occupations, he had only to secure
the good offices of some one who had influence with the
king.   An entry would then appear upon the rolls to the
effect that, at the special request of some nobleman
named, or of divers magnates and others serving with
the king in parts beyond the seas, who testified to the
innocence of the accused, a pardon had been granted to
him.   In such words impunity was granted to one of the
actors in the outrage in Wiltshire, in which a small army
sacked a manor-house, and in which two priors were said
to have been among those who committed rape and
murder.   It is hardly necessary to remark that the representations by which these pardons were obtained were
not always strictly accurate.   A curious case of deception,
which, from the self-denial and devotion involved, was
more venial than many others, was brought to light in
the year 1348.   One Walter Mast was indicted for murder,
and lodged in Scarborough Gaol.   His brother John
then joined the king's army, fought at Crécy, and during
the whole campaign passed by the name of Walter.   This
heroic liar then asked for a pardon in the name of Walter
Mast, and obtained it in the ordinary course.   But as the
homicide had been in gaol at the time of the battle, the
fraud was too transparent, and John had to confess the
deception of which he had been guilty.   He threw
himself upon the king's mercy, and was released, on
finding sureties for his future good conduct and paying
a fine.

To so great an extent, however, was carried the

practice of obtaining pardons on various pretexts that, even in such an age as has been described, it was felt to be a national reproach, and became the subject of many petitions in parliament. There was no check upon it except the power of individuals to institute an appeal against the wrong-doer, and the law by which the accused, when captured, was detained for a year and a day in prison to await the private action before he was brought to trial upon the indictment. This state of the law some-times had undoubtedly the effect of inflicting a year's imprisonment upon a criminal, or not less probably upon an innocent person ; but in other respects the appeal, as has already been shown, rendered little or no assistance to the cause of justice.

Among the crimes for which a pardon was granted in the year 1348, was one which shows how little respect Pardon for a there was for the services of the Church. It fraudulent burial. was convenient to one of the inhabitants of Great Yarmouth, or to his wife, that a report of his death should be spread abroad and believed. The wife devised a scheme, and employed a number of men to carry it into execution. In those days it was not very difficult to find a dead body, nor, when one was required, would there have been much hesitation in hastening the death of the living. A body was found, and represented by the wife to be that of her husband. She had removed to Lynn, where the deception could be more easily effected, and where neither the coroner nor the neighbours would attempt to identify the features of the corpse. No sus-picion was excited at the time, and the body was solemnly buried as that of her husband. The fraud, however, was afterwards detected, and one of the offenders was brought into court for trial. As frequently happened, there was no sufficient jury, and the accused was sent back to prison. Before the hearing of the case he obtained his charter of pardon, and it does not appear that his accomplices were ever apprehended.

The most probable motive for this false burial was the desire to stop pursuit of the person represented to be dead, and to make an end of all accusations brought against him. The device opened one more avenue of escape, in addition to the many which criminals already enjoyed. It leads, however, to a question which will have occurred to the mind of every one who has read the preceding description of the state of England—What influence was exerted by the Church in the midst of this wide-spread depravity?

One of the most common incidents in the courts of criminal jurisdiction was the claim of the accused to have Benefit of Clergy. It must have been notorious Benefit of everywhere that anyone who was entitled to Clergy. this privilege was practically exempt from the ordinary punishment for most of the greater crimes. The effect can hardly have been very edifying to the uneducated laity, who, however great their superstition may have been, had not the slightest respect for the ministers of religion. It was as likely as not that a priest could be made an accomplice in a fraudulent burial; and if he could not, there would have been no hesitation in deceiving him. Benefit of Clergy was not only one of the advantages enjoyed by a particular class of criminals, and an inducement to break the law, but was also a cause of hatred between one class and another.

The comparative impunity of clerical offenders, the lawlessness of the whole clerical body, and the unpopularity both of monks and of parish priests, are so inextricably interwoven, that it is necessary to bear each in mind in the consideration of the rest.   The subject, too, regarded as a whole, has an importance of a far wider

Light thrown by the Criminal Records upon the great religious movements of the fourteenth, fifteenth, and sixteenth centuries.

range than could have been suspected without the light thrown upon it by the records of criminal proceedings.   It is only through the inner national life which is there revealed that the great religious movements of the fourteenth fifteenth, and sixteenth centuries can be traced to their sources in the far-off past.   It is only there that some of the sentiments which animated the followers of Cranmer can be identified with those which were common throughout the whole country in the days of Wycliffe. It is only there that the need of reform in the Church presents itself at so early a period as a wide-spread conviction, apart from the tenets of particular preachers—as a conviction expressed in every county, not by elaborate treatises, but by short and significant verdicts, and by deeds not less significant.

When Benefit of Clergy was successfully claimed, the accused was handed over to the Ordinary, or, in other

Proceedings upon the claim of Privilege of Clergy.

words, to the safe keeping of the Bishop of the diocese, who usually sent a deputy to watch the proceedings in court, with power to receive clerks from the secular arm.   Sometimes the clerk was given up before trial, for purgation according to the direction of the ordinary ; sometimes a jury was empanelled to decide a matter of fact which affected the claim ; but most commonly the trial proceeded as in the case of an uneducated layman, and the accused obtained the protection of the Church only as a clerk convict. The judges, indeed, seem to have had the power of ordering a lay jury to give a verdict, even though the prisoner might assert his clergy immediately after he was brought into court. Thus in one case in which a clerk had committed various offences, had robbed his father's house, and had claimed the privilege of his letters, the order of the court was that he should be delivered to the ordinary, but that an inquisition should first be held by the country to determine the truth of the charges, and under what description the ordinary was to receive him. He then became a clerk convict; and the royal authority was so far maintained above that of the Church as to follow him to the Bishop's prison, where, as appears upon the record, he was to be lodged. After this stage of the proceedings the criminal was, according to the canon law, still able to exculpate himself before the Bishop by the ancient method of compurgation. He had but to make oath of his innocence, and to find others who would swear, as a matter of form, that they believed him, and he became again a free man, wholly purged from the taint of crime. This, it may well be believed, was not desired by the judges when they drew a distinction between cases which might be tried in the first instance before the ordinary, and cases in which a verdict must first be pronounced by a jury. But this, there is no doubt, was the final issue, even when a verdict of guilty had been pronounced; and against such a miscarriage of justice an attempt was made to provide a remedy by the introduction of a clause into the form of delivery, according to which the convict delivered was expressly deprived of purgation. The instances, however, are rare in which this precaution was adopted; and thus privilege of clergy was practically, for one class, an escape (secured by means of an oath and a fee) from every punishment for almost every felony. The clerk convict, indeed, was in a far better condition than the ordinary layman who had been acquitted ; for, by a Statute of the twenty-fifth year of Edward III., which, in this respect, probably declared the previous state of the law, he could not be afterwards arraigned for any felony committed before his conviction. When purged of the offences of which he had been found guilty, he was in the condition of a new man—blameless in the eyes of Justice, of good character from his infancy upwards.

At this early period, however, as afterwards, the definition of a clerk must have been a matter of some uncertainty. It was held by one judge as late as the year 1352 that the tonsure was necessary for a successful assertion of the claim to clergy, even though no objection to the claim was raised by the ordinary. But on the other hand, it is evident that this was not the common interpretation of the law, and that the qualification of being able to read must, in the usual practice, have been held sufficient. If not already, it was very soon afterwards a part of the duty of the judges to enquire whether gaolers had aided prisoners to gain a knowledge of letters, and to punish them when detected in the offence. Even at the beginning of the reign of Edward I., when men in orders could not legally marry, a statute was passed by which felons were deprived of their clergy if they had committed bigamy in addition to their other offences. Bigamy, in the clerical sense, meant marriage with a widow, or with two maidens in succession—with one after the death of the other. The act could not apply to matrimony committed after orders had been taken, and could hardly have been intended to meet cases so exceptional as those of married men who had forsaken their wives for the

The class to which the privilege was allowed.

sake of religion. The privilege had even in those days, there is reason to believe, been somewhat extended.

The truth seems to be that the Ordinary, if he pleased, claimed as 'clerks' all who had advanced so far in the preparation for orders as to learn the art of reading. Many tenants of the church lands, no doubt, availed themselves of the opportunity to learn letters at the nearest monastery, or, if they were in favour with the superior, were taught to read in prison and claimed at the trial. It was not until a later period that the ordinary could be compelled by the judges to accept a knowledge of letters as a proof of clerk-hood. After this change was effected in the law, the classes arrayed against each other were the educated with privilege against the un-educated without privilege ; before it, the unprivileged laymen were arrayed against the privileged clergy who practically extended their protection as far as they wished and no farther.

The doctrine, that a man who had been married might have privilege of clergy if he could read, and if the ordinary pleased, not only preserved a clerk convict from punishment in his own person, but secured for him the restitution of his goods *The advantages secured by the privilege.* after purgation, and operated to the benefit of his heir, who in the case of an ordinary lay conviction would have been disinherited. There is a curious case on record which shows, that though the tenant of lands died in the Bishop's prison after having been convicted of felony, and even before purgation, his son was still allowed to be capable of inheriting. One John de Valoignes held a manor and various other lands. He was accused of having broken into a mill and carried off a mill-stone, and a quarter and a half of corn, and was found guilty. He

claimed his clergy and was delivered to the ordinary after
having been convicted, to use the language of the record,
as far as the conviction of a clerk was possible. A cer-
tificate from the bishop in whose prison he had been
confined showed that he had died there without purgation. The escheator, in the ordinary course, took his
lands into the king's hand; the inquisition, usual after the
death of a landholder, was held, in the ordinary course,
to determine what were his lands, and how held, and who
was his heir; the jury found, according to the ordinary
course, that his heir was his son. Everything, in short,
was done which would have been done had Valoignes
never been convicted. But had he not successfully
claimed benefit of clergy the issue would have been entirely
different. The lands (unless, indeed, it could have been
proved that they were entailed, which, in this case, was
not even alleged) would have remained in the king's
hand a year and a day after the conviction of Valoignes,
and would then have escheated to the lords of whom he
held. The finding of an heir by inquisition would have
been of no avail to the son, for felony corrupted the
blood and extinguished all rights of inheritance.

It may easily be imagined how great was the jealousy
excited by such privileges in a society in which partisanship was regarded as a virtue. We have seen
how commonly laymen were acquitted; but if
it was probable before trial that a layman would
be found not guilty, if it was still more probable that an
approver would die or be hanged, it was almost certain
that any one who could claim benefit of clergy would be
convicted. In the whole of a series of rolls for the year
1348, there is hardly an instance in which a clerk who

Jealousies ex-
cited by it :
clerks always
convicted
when tried.

was tried was acquitted; and yet the number of instances in which clerks were tried is lamentably great. Stealers of cattle, burglars, habitual robbers, homicides, men guilty of sacrilege, and of habitually receiving felons or stolen goods are all protected as clerks after having been convicted of felony. Many even of the approvers, who as laymen would have been hanged, are as clerks delivered to the ordinary, and so contribute not a little to the ill feeling excited among the unprivileged. The lay jurors consequently displayed their party spirit with a consistency which shows that the facts of each case must have been entirely disregarded; for a clerk they gave always a verdict of guilty, for a fellow layman a verdict of not guilty as often as they dared.

The antipathy to the privileged class displayed itself also in more active measures than mere verdicts of guilty. No offence appears more frequently on the rolls, or is more surely followed by an acquittal, than burglary at the house of a parson. The Unpopularity of the Clergy. rectors of those days were among the very few rich men who possessed as many as half a dozen silver spoons. They did not live in castles, and their houses were easily broken. If the poor had little love for them as a class, the powerful cared little to protect them; and those among them who did not act as receivers on behalf of criminal relatives, were thus for many reasons the most common objects of attack.

The right, claimed by the Pope, of presenting or collating to bishoprics or livings which fell vacant in England, was by no means in accordance with national sentiments, as the Statutes of Provisors and Premunire conclusively prove. The extent to which the evil prevailed, and the resolute determination of King and Council to suppress it, are indicated also in various records. Innumerable warrants issued for the apprehension of persons bearing papal bulls or other prejudicial instruments, and the impugners of the king's laws, as those among the clergy were called who appealed to Rome against presentations made in England in opposition to papal inhibitions. Even the Archbishop elect of Canterbury was compelled to take an oath renouncing all expressions in papal bulls which might be prejudicial to the king in respect of the temporalities of the see.

The laity were not less eager to uphold their rights than the clergy, and the manner in which rights were up-
Forcible entries into churches: scandalous scenes. held in these times has already been illustrated in the earlier part of this chapter. Both sides, according to custom, asserted their claims by force. While the parsonage was the object of attack by one class because it was known to contain some plate, it was the object of attack by another because the possession of it was, for a time at least, a practical settlement of an ecclesiastical dispute. Forcible entry was as good a proof of the right to present, or to hold after presentation, as of the title to a manor ; and forcible entries into churches and rectories became, as a natural consequence, the subject of many a commission, and many a pardon. The actual holders were driven out ; the place of worship and the dwelling-house were both held by an armed band. The parishioners had the edifying spectacle before their eyes for weeks and for months ; the tithes, when due, or before, were collected and carried off with as much violence as might be necessary ; and the whole parish was the scene of a private ecclesiastical war.

Each party of course fought with all the weapons at its command, and in some cases the spiritual armoury was brought to bear upon the king's officers. A suit arose upon one of these disputed presentations, and the Court of King's Bench made an order against the Bishop of Exeter for a considerable sum of money. The sheriff of Devonshire received the king's writ, in which he was directed to enforce execution upon the bishop's goods and chattels. He entrusted the task to the under-sheriff, who seized many head of cattle upon one of the bishop's manors, and drove them to Exeter Castle. When the tidings were brought to the prelate, he fulminated sentence of major excommunication not only against the under-sheriff but against all the men who had acted under the sheriff's orders; and the excommunication was proclaimed in due form, at Barnstaple, by two priors and the parson of a Devonshire church. The bishop and his subordinates were summoned to answer for this act of contempt, and did in the end so far obey the law as to appear by attorney in the King's Bench. But in the meantime the whole county was thrown into a commotion, greater even than ordinary, by the scandal of open warfare between the secular and the ecclesiastical authorities.

Open warfare between the secular and ecclesiastical authorities.

In addition to these causes of unpopularity, there was yet another which took from the clergy the love of the indigent and the sick, who had at one time, perhaps, looked up to the Church as their only protector. Religious houses which had been founded expressly for the relief of the lepers and the poor had assumed, in some cases at least, a wholly different character. Their revenues were squandered by friars and nuns; their very lands were alienated at the caprice

Misapplication of revenues attached to religious houses.

of the principals, and contrary to the wish of the founders. These abuses are mentioned, even in the official documents of the time, as reasons for the failing devotion of the people. Complaints against Alien Priories—the 'cells' or branches of foreign religious houses, which enjoyed lands in England—had been heard even in Parliament, and were prompted by a not unnatural disinclination to see foreigners absorb revenues which might have supported more deserving English. In short, there was a prevailing impression, fostered still further by the reluctance of the wealthy abbots to do so much as repair the roads which passed through their lands, that the clergy uniformly attempted to evade the performance of duties comparatively light, while the laity were overweighted with the burdens of military service and heavy taxation.

Like the lawless deeds of the knights, the lawless deeds of the clergy were frequently done in asserting a real or supposed right, but like them also frequently assumed a form to which not even casuistry could give any other name than crime. So many exploits of a criminal nature, in which both knights and clerks were engaged, have already been narrated, so many offences of which clerks were convicted have been incidentally mentioned, that it would be invidious to devote a very much greater space to misdeeds purely clerical. But the subject has so important a bearing upon general history, and aids so much towards a true comprehension of the times, that it would be false delicacy to omit altogether some details which illustrate the writings of Chaucer and Wycliffe, and show whence came the bitterness remarkable in the Vision of Piers Plowman.

Bloodshed was as familiar to the clergy as to any other class—not only to those who were vaguely described as clerks, but to chaplains and parsons of churches. It must be borne in mind that the materials for the present chapter are, almost exclusively, the Public Records of a single year. To those who search them conscientiously they tell a tale of which it is impossible to miss the meaning. They present the state of society as it actually was ; and the following incidents, selected almost at random, give a better idea of the age than volumes of praise or vituperation. The parson of Stockton Church was appealed by a widow for having killed her husband ; he could not be found, and was outlawed. Another parson was appealed by another widow for having been one of four who killed her husband ; two of them could not be found, and of those two the parson was one. A parson was one of three accused of another murder by a widow. A clerk convict was delivered to the ordinary after having been found guilty of killing a man on one occasion, and robbing a widow on another. The prior of St. Sepulchre's, Warwick, and one of his brother monks were also accused of homicide. The parson of Trent Church, less lawless than some of his brethren, committed a few offences then regarded as mere trespasses, for which a fine was ample punishment. A verdict had been found, with respect to a certain chantry, by a jury summoned to act under the escheator. The parson disapproved of their finding ; and, as the escheator was his friend, he had no difficulty in possessing himself of the record. He broke the seal, tore the document to pieces, and threw the fragments into the fire. He used to amuse himself by hunting without the king's licence, and by breaking his neighbours' parks when sport invited him. The Court of King's Bench condemned him to make certain payments for his plea-

Familiarity of the Clergy with violence and bloodshed.

X 2

sures, but it does not appear that destroying a legal document was in this instance regarded as a more serious offence than poaching.

If the ordinary conduct of the clergy was not of a character to command the respect of the laity, the respect of the clergy for members of their own body was by no means exalted. Monks of various orders were in the habit of throwing off the religious habit when they pleased, and of wandering about the country in disguise. In the warrants for their arrest they are further described as ' apostates, whose insolence must be repressed, who are bringing ruin upon their own souls and scandal upon the brethren of their order.' Instances in which attacks are made by clerks upon clerks are by no means uncommon ; but perhaps the best example of demoralisation in a religious house is presented by Ramsey Abbey. There, on the first Sunday after Easter, the refectory was broken open, and the silver cups and salt-cellars, the mazers, and the rest of the plate belonging to the house were carried off. When the loss was discovered, it was discovered also that three of the monks were missing, but it was never known precisely how many were implicated. Of these three only two were captured ; one died in prison, the other was found guilty of burglary and robbery, and handed over to the ordinary as a clerk convict ; the third, no doubt, joined one of the gangs of brigands which infested the country, and in which he found his true vocation and congenial society.

Want of respect among the Clergy for members of their own body.

It was in such deeds as these, and in deeds of a similar character, that the lay robbers found encouragement and inspiration to perpetrate acts of sacrilege which could not otherwise have occurred in an age

Sacrilege a common offence.

remarkable for superstition.   Nothing, however, was held
sacred by the thief, who perceived that men called holy
did not hesitate to steal.   Church-breaking is an offence
which is by no means uncommon on the rolls of the
criminal courts.   At Scarborough, the chapel of the
Blessed Virgin Mary was broken, the rings of gold and
silver with which her image was decked were torn from
its fingers, the clasps from its dress, and every ornament
from its body.   The very cross which was deposited in
the chapel was carried off, and found in the house of a
receiver.   It is somewhat strange that such a crime was
not regarded with any of the fanaticism which was displayed a few years later towards those unfortunate heretics
whose only offence was a mere religious opinion somewhat different from that of their persecutors.   In this
case of chapel-breaking the ordinary course of the common law was followed ; the chief offender happened to
die before he was brought to trial ; the accessaries after
the fact—or receivers—urged, as usual, that they could
not be convicted as accomplices until the principal was
convicted on the main charge, and they were, as usual,
dismissed on finding sureties for future good behaviour.

Such were the relations between clergy and laity as
disclosed by the records of the year before the The circumstances which
Black Death.   At this time Wycliffe, as well as moulded the
minds of
the author of Piers Plowman's Vision, and, per- Wycliffe,
Chaucer, and
haps Chaucer, were young men, and at the age the author of
Piers Plow-
at which impressions are most easily made. man's Vision.
They saw with their own eyes those wild and lawless
scenes, the faint reflection of which in contemporaneous
documents may excite the wonder of modern lawyers
and modern moralists.   They knew how commonly
forgery was practised by all who could write, how readily

verdicts in opposition to facts could be obtained from
packed juries, how easily judges could be bribed, how
thoroughly corruption was diffused through every class.
In the Vision, and in the writings of Wycliffe, it is possible also to discern the mental effects of the most terrible
pestilence which ever devastated Europe. The horrors
of the time seem to have given men new intensity of
feeling and greater depth of thought, and to have left a
shadow behind them which could not be wholly dissi-
pated. Chaucer, as courtier, and perhaps because he
was a younger man, took the humours of the time more
gaily. But in the works of the three authors may be
found all that is necessary to explain what the rolls leave
unexplained, and to complete the historical picture of the
age so far as history can render any picture complete. In
them we have, as it were, a bridge connecting an old
state of society with a new, and enabling us to pass freely
over the gulf which at first sight appears to separate a
period of religious stagnation from a period of great religious activity. There is indeed nothing remarkable in
the teaching that a national affliction is a punishment for
the sins of a nation; there have before and since been subtle
satires like those of Chaucer, as well as bitter complaints
like those of the Vision. But the period selected as the
subject of the present chapter is the earliest period in the
history of the world at which it is possible to see in
copious and authentic records the surrounding circumstances moulding the minds of great writers.

As there were apostates from some of the religious
orders, it is by no means impossible that Lollardism had
begun to show itself even before the Black Death had
given a more serious turn to all human thoughts. The
friar, according to the poets, was always welcome in the

layman's house when the layman himself was absent;
and for the man who was licentious the religious garb
served as a most useful introduction. As, Their works,
therefore, renegades had little to gain by a mere with the Public Records,
act of apostasy—unless, like the monks of complete the
picture of the
Ramsey, they carried away the plate—there is age.
good reason to suspect that a necessity for reform was
already perceived by some of the more conscientious
members of the religious orders. The abbot and fellow-
monks who lodged within the walls of the monastery,
and the 'limitour,' or monk who held a licence to beg
within a limited district, alike found that the habit of their
order would, if discreetly managed, ensure for the wearer
more ample fare by day, and a softer couch at night, than
could be obtained without it. The courtier and the rustic
have precisely the same facts to tell, though they employ
somewhat different language. When Chaucer says—

> " A frere there was, a wanton and a merry,
> A limitour, a full solemné man,"

and when he adds,

> " Somewhat he lispéd for his wantonness,
> To make his English sweet upon his tongue,"

the words call up the image of the libertine monk as
effectually as all the coarser invective of the Plowman.
The Plowman, however, is most successful in conveying
the notion that the clergy, who ' were loth to swink,' or
work, swarmed all over the land—

> " Hermits in a heap
> With hooked staves
> Wenten to Walsingham
> And their wenches after;"

and, continues he,

> " I found there freres,
> All the four orders,
> Preaching the people
> For profit of themselves."

It is impossible, also, to avoid the suspicion that Chaucer is quietly satirising the nuns in his description of Madame Eglantine, the Prioress. She is represented as a kindly woman, and—for the fourteenth century—most charming; but it is not without a motive that the poet adorns her with a brooch, and that on the brooch there is a Latin inscription which is, when translated into English, ' Love overcomes all things.'

In Chaucer's writings, too, as in the corruptions of which the Records show that the courtiers were guilty, The Court: may be perceived the tone of the Court under the state of education. Edward III. A century and a half had wrought but little external change. Such as the courtiers were at the end of the twelfth century they appeared to be even towards the end of the fourteenth. There was, however, this difference—that in the fourteenth century the Court possessed a Chaucer, and in the twelfth it had none. There had now been for more than two hundred years a class, small indeed, but ambitious, in which the males were compelled by their vocation to have a sufficient knowledge of at least two languages. The pleadings in court had been in French since the time of the Conquest; the reports of leading cases, or year-books as they were called, beginning with the reign of Edward I., were also in French; but most of the treatises on law, the official writs, and the greater part of the Public Records, were in Latin. The Rolls of Parliament were partly in Latin, partly in French. It was, therefore, absolutely necessary that every one who was a candidate for any legal appointment, or aspired to be a pleader, should be conversant with both Latin and French. During the first few reigns after the Conquest, a lawyer might perhaps have required no more intimate acquaintance with English than a familiarity with the technical terms of law and finance which had been in use before the time of the Conqueror. But the very adoption of those terms into the legal vocabulary aided in keeping alive a certain interest in the tongue of the subject population. The contempt implied in the exclusion of English from all the higher functions of a language was not, indeed, mitigated by a statute that it should be spoken in courts of law till Edward III. had been thirty-six years on the throne, when the distinction between Englishmen and Frenchmen, implied in the presentment of Englishry, had been abolished only two and twenty years. Before this time, however, the native speech had been so far recognised as to be thought worthy of a place upon a roll of Letters Patent, in the reign of Henry III., where a translation appears in English of a solitary document enrolled elsewhere in French. It must then have made its way steadily upwards as the development of parliamentary government brought the different classes into closer contact; and Chaucer would not have written in English had it not in his days been commonly spoken at Court.

So much of education and of mental culture, therefore, as is implied in the acquisition of three different languages was possessed by a knot of courtiers in the time of Edward III. The native heads of religious houses could speak English, and such French as Chaucer ridiculed under the name of French of the school of Stratford-at-Bow. Those of the clergy who performed religious services could patter a prayer in Latin if they could not understand it. A few monks had sufficient knowledge to translate the Latin charters of their monasteries—a few legal officials sufficient to draw out a writ, and enrol the proceedings of the courts. There must also have been some Englishmen who, from the necessities of their callings, had acquired a superficial knowledge of French, such as a Swiss courier or a German waiter now possesses of English. The mass of the people, however, was in the densest ignorance ; and in a complaint made in Parliament, concerning foreign ecclesiastics who held benefices in England, there· is the clearest evidence that English was the only language generally known. It is there expressly stated that these intruders from abroad could not understand the language of the common people, and that the· common people could not understand theirs. Traders of the higher class, who passed to and fro between France, the Netherlands, and England, had some education, and must have been able to speak French as well as to read the inscription on a coin. But the lower class of retail dealers, who had never been beyond sea, had no knowledge of letters, as may be inferred from the defence already mentioned of two of them, when accused of having base money in their possession. Nor, indeed, could such a privilege as Benefit of Clergy have been made to depend upon ability to read, as it was long after this time, had reading been an accomplishment possessed by any but a very small class outside the ranks of the clergy themselves.

Education, having thus for many generations been the exclusive property of a few, but having been, for those few, of a very high order, had caused a most remarkable contrast. It had developed a Black Prince who knew how to be generous to a fallen foe in the midst of almost incredible cruelties. It had developed a Chaucer, and a minute section of society which could appreciate him, in the midst of a people which was only beginning to be civilised even

Effects of the adoption of the English language by the Court.

in the principal towns. But there was no small gain when the courtier began to write in English. The ring of Chaucer's verse could not fail to be heard by Englishmen outside the court. Though it was not like the ring of the Plowman's ruder metal, it could be understood by the Plowman and his listeners, and the sounds raised by the Plowman could be understood at the court. Thus the adoption of the English language in the higher ranks was the first step towards the diffusion of that mental cultivation which had previously been restricted to a class. Thus at last, and thus only, a truly national life became possible. The Pope and the clergy had been satirised in song in the reign of Henry II., but the songs had been written in a language to which the people were strangers ; if the villein hated the abbot at whom the courtier laughed, there was all the antipathy between courtier and villein which exists between men of different races speaking different languages. But when the courtier imitated the speech of the villein, and each discovered that they had, in some respects, common wants and common aims, there was already the beginning of a new state of society. Courtiers could lead villeins and townsmen against other courtiers for higher aims than the possession of manors, or even of thrones. Common speech was leading the way to free speech, common grievances to common action. Though the Canterbury Tales may seem to be wholly unconnected with the heretics of St. Giles's Fields, the circumstances which moulded Chaucer's thoughts into English were the circumstances which placed Oldcastle at the head of the Lollards. Many a generation, indeed, was yet to pass away, and many a trouble to be endured by England, before a brutal and superstitious populace could be even partially imbued with a spirit of Christian charity. Many a quarrel was to arise, many a battle to be fought, many a human being to be burnt, before the printing-press, when invented, could be brought to the aid of humanity and scatter even a few crumbs from the tables of thinkers among the ignorant and thoughtless. But national unity became possible when there was a national language spoken by prince and peasant. The bitterness engendered by conquest was softened when the conquerors learned the tongue of the conquered, and when the townsman began to feel that there was no longer a foreign master at his gates, who might any day revoke the charters granted with reluctance to English burghers. Men engaged in commerce began to be a little more confident; with confidence came an extension of trade. Some ingenious speculator abroad, perceiving the increased demand for parchment, on which alone it was the custom to write, manufactured paper as a substitute, and thus prepared a foundation, without which printing would have been useless. Such were the small beginnings of those mighty changes which the world has seen since the reign of Edward III., and which acquire new force with every movement. Before the Black Death they had gone no further than a recognition of the English language as becoming to the lips of men in every grade, an increase of wealth following upon the development of the wool trade, and a corresponding growth of town influence and strengthening of town corporations.

The reasons for the selection of the year before the Black Death to be the theme of so long a chapter as the present may be summed up in a sentence. It is a year in every way representative. By a sytematic examina-

tion of its records, the state of society during a long
period can be more favourably studied than by a perusal
of all the chronicles from the time of Henry II. The Year
downwards. A mere narration of a few political before the
Black Death
events, a description of a struggle between a representative year: the
opposite parties, and a catalogue of the laws age of Chivalry at its
which have been passed, though aids to a com- best.
prehension of the life led by our forefathers, are not
sufficient to bring the actual conditions of that life clearly
before us. The meagre stories of mediæval annalists,
and the dry details of the Statute Book, are but the
skeleton of history; the flesh and blood can be seen only
in the every-day doings which appear upon the records,
and which only there appear' in their true proportions.
As these documents were drawn up year by year, the
information which they convey reproduces all those
phases of human existence which came within the ken of
the law courts at any given time, and is free from the
distortion or exaggeration which are inevitable in the
pages of the chronicler, or in any mere series of extracts.
The year before the Black Death, too, closes one well-
marked division in the History of England. All that
the legislation of Henry II. and of Edward I. could
effect had already been effected ; the parliamentary form
of government was established beyond all danger of
overthrow, and there was nothing in the relations of
England with other countries which could cause her internal condition to appear otherwise than to the greatest
advantage. There were, as there had been for centuries,
wars and rumours of wars, but the arms of England were
almost uniformly successful, and peace was not in those
days regarded as a possible blessing, nor indeed as a
blessing at all.

This, in short, was the age of chivalry at its best;
neither statesmen nor lawyers could further improve
the habits of the people so long as that age was to
continue, because it was the highest possible development of those institutions (if institutions they can be
called) which had been introduced by the destroyers of
the Roman empire. Later history shows in every century the gradual decay of barbarism. Though barons
were long afterwards strong enough to be king-makers,
the national sentiment soon began to declare itself against
the sovereign powers claimed by private individuals.
The towns taught peasants the value of their labours,
and attracted them from the ranks of a baron's army to
the greater independence promised in the exercise of
some city craft. Statutes against liveries, or in other
words, against the uniforms worn by soldiers serving
under petty princes, followed each other in a rapid succession, which showed, not less clearly than the Wars of
the Roses, how feeble was a mere enactment against
customs handed down from generation to generation.
But the stronger the townsmen became, the more were
all their interests opposed to knightly brigandage and
lordly independence; and when striving for their own interests, they were striving for the interests of the nation.
The merchant of the fourteenth century desired peace no
less than the merchant of the nineteenth; but most of all
he desired, what seemed to be least within his reach,
peace and harmony within the realm of England itself.
His efforts would have been hopeless had he not secured
representation in the national parliament; and long as it
was before they bore fruit, it might have been still longer
had not the Black Death come to his aid at a time when
he enjoyed more prosperity than had been possible for

him since the days of the Romans, and when feudalism
was already falling into decay.   The year 1348 is thus
one of the great land-marks of the past as well as the
year in which the old society appears to greatest advantage.   It is only when we have thoroughly realised to
ourselves what that society was that we can know how
different is the state of society in which we live ; it is
only by measuring our distance from that far-off land-
mark that we can know how much we have advanced.

It is with difficulty that a terrible pestilence can be
calmly regarded as a benefit to mankind.   Yet, when
mankind lived as they were living in England   Scenes to be
before the Black Death, any event which, even   witnessed by
                                                the survivors
indirectly, tended towards a favourable change   of the Plague.
in the conditions of life must be considered a gain to
posterity.   For our ancestors we can only feel the deepest
commiseration when we remember what they have
suffered in order that we may enjoy.   In those days not
only were ignorance and crime in close alliance, but both
were strong in their union, and were always closely attended by superstition and disease.   There was no knowledge of the laws of health to give courage in meeting
the plague, no sincere religion to give comfort in death
or bereavement.   Those who were to survive the coming
pestilence were to survive horrors such as, perhaps, the
world has never seen, either before or since.   In the
midst of bloodshed, fraud, and debauchery, and with a
grovelling dread of the Unknown, they were to hear first
a whisper from the East of a new malady creeping,
but not slowly, ever nearer to England.   If one traveller
brought the news that it was in India, another was following with the tidings that it was already in Europe.   The
next could tell a more appalling tale with new circumstances

of mystery; for he had heard that even the dull earth trembled at the approach of the Death—that sometimes it opened to swallow up whole cities, as though to anticipate or complete the ravages of a new master. The gossiping friars could soon excite the pity of their female admirers by accounts of the fate which had befallen their brethren in France—for at Montpellier, it was said, there were but seven Friars Preachers left out of a hundred and forty, and at Marseilles not one out of a hundred and sixty. Before the autumn of 1348 was ended, a rumour spread that the shores of England were already attacked by an enemy more deadly than Scot or Frenchman. If any one asked where the blow had fallen first, he received more answers than one; for the evil spread too rapidly to be traced to a single source. Here, as elsewhere, the Plague followed the course of the sun, from east to west. Where it struck it slew—not only surely, but swiftly. Many died in a few hours; few survived the third day. Ere many weeks had passed, all public and private business ceased. The judges no longer went their usual circuits, no longer sat in the courts at Westminster. Men of all ranks seemed to lose even the desire to get wealth or to keep it.

No rank and no occupation gave exemption from the Black Death. The clergy perished in numbers so great that the churches were commonly left without a priest to perform any of the services. The Archbishop of Canterbury, newly consecrated by the Pope, returned to England only to die within a few days after he reached London. So terrible was the mortality in the country, during the following year, that none could be found to tend the sheep and cattle, which wandered as they pleased among the corn—itself left standing for want of reapers. The plague among men was soon accompanied by a murrain among beasts, caused, perhaps, in part by inevitable neglect; and this tells more plainly than the baseless conjectures of mediæval chroniclers, how great was the loss from the plague itself. Although heaps of carcases lay rotting in the pastures, the immediate effect upon prices was the reverse of that which it would have been had the population suffered no diminution ; and live stock could be bought for less than one-half of that which had been its market value before the outbreak of the pestilence. However great, therefore, may have been the decrease in the supply of cattle, the decrease in the number of human beings who created the demand must have been proportionately far greater. But other causes, as will be shown in the next chapter, not only raised the price of all provisions in a few months to its former level, but called forth an Act of Parliament limiting the sums to be charged by dealers in provisions.

A strange variety of scenes, indeed, was witnessed by those who carried the recollection of the year before the Black Death into the stormy times which Object of the followed it. The disorganisation of a society Chapter. present most imperfectly organised, and the growth of a new system out of the decay of the old, are subjects which must be reserved for treatment elsewhere. The object of the present chapter has been attained, if it shows with sufficient clearness what was the actual condition of our forefathers in the year 1348, how insecure were their lives and their property, and how vast is the difference between them and us in manners, in sentiments, and in knowledge.

CHAPTER V.

FROM THE BLACK DEATH TO THE ACCESSION OF HENRY VII.

ONE of the invariable effects of a Great Plague is to loosen the bonds by which men have previously been held together. This was observed alike by Thucydides during the Great Plague in Athens, and by Defoe during the Great Plague in London. On the one hand is developed a recklessness which sets at nought all the conventional restraints of society, and all the natural ties of affection, and on the other hand a depth of feeling which carries religion to fanaticism. And though there was neither a Thucydides nor a Defoe to describe the Black Death, we may be certain that the operation of similar causes upon human beings was not very different in the fifteenth century from that which it was in the seventeenth, nor from that which it had been in the time of the Peloponnesian war. Those who did not faint by the way became, according to their temperaments, either more callous or more earnest than they had been before the calamity. Much of the fabric of the mediæval constitution was thus destined to crumble away when its powers of cohesion, never very strong, were weakened from within, and when it was assailed by new forces from without.

The Black Death taught malcontents, both lay and

The social effects of every Great Plague.

ecclesiastical, their strength.   The labourer, whether
bond or free, learned the value of his labour ; the Effects of the
preacher who was dissatisfied with his bishop, in England.
or with the superiors of his order, learned how easy it
was to obtain an audience composed of men who had
other reasons for dissatisfaction.   Thus an impulse was
given to causes which were indeed already at work, and
which would have produced sooner or later their natural
effect, but the action of which might have been retarded
for many generations, had no pestilence set them in
motion.

The first sign of the changes which were to be
brought about, was the demand of all labourers, and
especially of those employed in agriculture, for The Statute
increased pay.   The mortality, everywhere ter- of Labourers.
rible, had been greatest among the labouring population.
When the supply of labour was diminished, its value of
course became higher.   Employers began to compete for
it, and to offer new terms.   Workmen, discovering their
own worth, raised more and more the price which they
asked for their services.   With labour all kinds of goods,
and especially provisions, became dearer ; and Parliament,
in alarm at what seemed a subversion of the ancient
order of society, passed the famous Statute of Labourers,
by which the employed were forbidden to receive, and
the employers to give, more than had been paid for labour
before the Plague, and dealers in provisions were restricted to prices which the lawgivers considered reasonable.

In this statute is the first legal recognition of the fact
that the feudal system could not include all the rural population in its grasp.   Two classes of labourers The bond
are mentioned—those who owed, and those who and the free.

did not owe obedience to a lord—the bond and the free ;
and as those who held by a free tenure and tilled land of
their own were not included in the provisions of the Act,
it is clear that there had grown up a class of men, nominally at least free, and yet without any definite means
of support. This is further made apparent by a very
stringent clause against giving alms to beggars able to
work.

The origin of the lowest grade of free-men has afforded
a subject for the dissertations of many historians, and is
Sketch of   necessarily obscure in proportion as our ear-
the history of
villenage.   lier history is incomplete. When Southern
Britain was conquered by invaders from beyond the
North Sea, most of the natives who were not slain,
or who did not find refuge in towns, must have submitted to be, under one name or another, the slaves
of their conquerors. At a somewhat later period, when
land became the property of individuals, and none
was common to a tribe, the dependence of the smaller
holders upon the greater reduced the weaker freemen
to a condition not very widely distant from slavery.
In an age so brutal as that before the Norman Conquest,
none could have enjoyed the lord's protection unless he
was content to do the lord's bidding, whatever it might
have been. A refusal could easily have been avenged by
an accusation involving a heavy pecuniary penalty, which
the accused would have been unable to pay, and which
would have reduced him to the condition of a slave. Once
made a slave, the refractory churl could be sold and
shipped off to Ireland, or to any other country in which
Christianity was professed.

When Domesday Book was compiled, a distinction
was observed between the slave and the villein—the one

probably representing the actual slave originally made in war, the other the churl, who held a plot of land, but who was compelled to perform services, either fixed or uncertain, for his lord. It has often been asserted that these two classes were sub- jected to a harsher rule after the Norman Con- quest than before, but there is not a tittle of contemporary evidence in support of that proposition. On the contrary, one of the most remarkable of the Conqueror's laws is that in which the exportation of slaves is prohibited ; and the exportation appears to have ceased from that time forwards. In the benefits of this law the churls or villeins participated as well as the slaves, because the prospect before them, should they have the misfortune to be re- duced to actual slavery, was by no means so dark as when they might have been carried off, like sheep, to a foreign country. Indeed, it is doubtful whether penal slavery was a recognised institution after the Conquest, and it is certain that the institution did not long survive.

Improvement in the condition of slaves after the Norman Conquest.

To close the market against the foreign purchaser was necessarily to diminish the value of the slave in England. Human beings born in slavery must have increased in number at a far more rapid rate than before ; they must have become at once more difficult to watch, and less worth the trouble of watching. Before the Conquest the runaway slave might fear to see a slave-dealer in every man he met ; after the Conquest it was not the interest of anyone, except of his owner, to pursue him. His greatest danger lay in the old laws concerning strangers, and in the duty imposed on the sheriff to send him back to the place whence he came. But it was possible for him to find employment in the towns ; and, at the worst, he might meet a welcome among

The slave becomes an inferior villein.

some of the bands of outlaws, who could not then export him. Thus at a very early period after the Norman Conquest the name of slave disappears, and the lowest ranks of men in the rural districts are called villeins. It is true that there was a legal difference between the villein in gross, whose bondage was to the person of the lord, and the villein regardant, whose bondage was to the land, and who could be sold only with the land which he held in villenage. In the deeds relating to the sale of villeins, it is declared sometimes that the land is conveyed with the villein who occupies it, sometimes that the villein is conveyed with his goods and chattels, and all his following or issue ; and in the latter case his value seldom exceeded four pounds of the money of those early times. But documents of either kind are rare ; the villein regardant passed with the manor when it was conveyed, and he was not necessarily mentioned in the conveyance ; the villein in gross was but very seldom sold by himself. The distinction between the two classes was necessarily very faint, because whenever, as must commonly have happened, the villein in gross was permitted to till a plot of land, and his children tilled it after him, their position was practically that of villeins regardant, and was little likely to be disturbed.

At the time at which the Statute of Labourers was passed, the descendants of the men who had, before the *The villeins not the only labourers.* Conquest, been slaves saleable in a foreign market belonged to one of three classes. Some of them were villeins rendering base services to a lord, and acquiring a prescriptive right to the land on which they were permitted to dwell ; some were townsmen prospering as members of a craft-guild, or earning a livelihood by one of the many occupations to be found in every

town ; some were, perhaps, in turn, brigands and agricultural labourers—now robbing a merchant on his way to
a fair, now receiving wages from steward or farmer, who
asked few questions when grass was to be mown, or corn
reaped, now begging on their way to the head-quarters
of their gang.

Among these three classes, the villeins felt the hardships of their lot more keenly than the others, and the
Statute of Labourers added to their discontent. Discontent
Their lords had, according to the act, the first among the
villeins : its
claim to their services ; but where there was a causes.
dearth of labour they were to serve other masters as soon
as their lord's work was done.   They were to be paid
apparently at the rate fixed by the statute ; but according
to the strict letter of the law, their earnings were not
their own but their lord's.   In many cases, no doubt, and
perhaps in the majority, they were, as a favour, permitted
to retain the money which they were able to make after
the lord's dues had been rendered ; but the lord's power
of seizure was none the less a reality and must have been
a subject of bitter reflection to the villein and to all his
household.

The spectacle, too, of freemen working in the same
field and secure from the claim of every lord after they
had received the reward of honest industry, Growth of a
class of free
must have added a new sting to the sense of labourers.
injury which is never absent from the bondsman.   Not
only was there a roving class among whom the first title
to freedom was the flight of some ancestor to a town, or
his reception into a gang of robbers, but there were men
who had in their own persons, or in those of their forefathers, been freed from villenage in due form of law,
and whose origin was neither higher nor lower than that

of the men still condemned to bondage.   Even before the Conquest freedom was sometimes granted to a slave; and in the year 1338 Edward III. empowered commissioners to liberate the villeins of the crown manors upon receipt from them of a certain sum of money.   There is an appearance of liberality in this permission to the villeins to redeem themselves, when the amount of their ransom belonged already to the king as their lord.   But coin is easily concealed, and a sudden demand upon all the royal villeins for all they possessed would have been a dangerous exercise of cruelty and power even in the fourteenth century.   When, therefore, the king's necessities compelled him to take the money of his bondsmen, the most prudent course was to give them their liberty in return.   Other lords did likewise, and thus the class of inferior freemen was continually growing, and by its presence aggravating the discontent of men who were not yet free.

The Black Death, and the Statute of Labourers which followed it, though they did not immediately cause a rebellion, yet rendered a rebellion inevitable whenever a favourable opportunity should present itself; and a rebellion was in those days certain to be accompanied by most atrocious crimes. Even the strong arm of Edward III. barely sufficed to keep back the coming tumult.   A re-enactment of the statute, and commissions to enforce it, were of little avail against an increasing competition for labour to which a new impulse was given by a recurrence of the pestilence in the year 1361.   Edward, who from his success in war commanded the respect of all classes, and who was not wanting in the arts which win popularity, ended his reign in comparative tranquillity.   Neither he nor his advisers

The coming changes accelerated by the Plague.

knew that in attempting to limit prices by law they were committing themselves to an impossible task. To them it seemed a part of good government to maintain all the old land-marks of society, and they perhaps deluded themselves into the belief that they were succeeding in their aim. But when the sceptre dropped from the hand of a vigorous man into that of a weak boy, everything was ripe for an outbreak ; and it was not long before the outbreak came.

Beneath the already ruffled surface of villenage there had been a subtle influence at work which rendered the storm doubly formidable. Discontent with the existing religious institutions was not confined to the laity, but showed itself openly among those monks whom the law termed apostates, as well as among some of the secular clergy. With perfect good faith, no doubt, but with a zeal which the times rendered dangerous, these religious reformers preached against the existing state of society, and deduced from the Scriptures the doctrine that all men are equal. Nor did they restrict themselves to the maintenance of this principle in the abstract. They possessed what was denied to most of the villeins—the arts of reading and writing ; and they could translate with more or less accuracy a Latin record into English. Transcripts of Domesday Book were procured for the villeins, whose advisers assured them that in these documents they had proof of the freedom enjoyed by their forefathers at the time of the Norman Conquest, and that freedom was their birthright, not only according to the laws of God and of reason, but also according to the law of the land.

In the very first year of the reign of Richard II., the villeins in all parts of the country, acting apparently on a

They were accelerated also by religious discontent.

preconcerted plan, refused to do the bidding of their lords. When threatened with punishment they exhibited their transcripts of Domesday, declared themselves free, and banded themselves together in threatening array. Parliament immediately passed an act declaring that the interpretation put upon the passages in Domesday by the villeins was false, and that the transcripts should be of no avail to any one who produced them in evidence. All refractory villeins were to be committed to prison without bail if their lords should so desire. Thus the semblance of a legal claim was met by the semblance of a legal enactment; but a statute denying the right of a subject to justify himself by reference to the most venerable legal document in the realm was in itself so unjustifiable and raised so great an outcry that it was repealed in the next year. The question of law remained undecided, but the lords and their bondsmen prepared, after the manner of the time, to settle the dispute by force.

Claim of the villeins to be free.

An attempt to show from Domesday Book that the lower ranks generally were in an inferior condition, at the accession of Richard II., to that which they had enjoyed at the time of the Conquest, was necessarily foredoomed to failure. At the earlier period there were slaves in the land liable to exportation until the Conqueror forbade the practice; at the later period even a villein in gross was seldom or never removed from one part of England to another. It might, however, have been quite possible to prove that a particular plot of land, held nominally by a freeman when the Great Register was compiled, was held in villenage under Edward III. But such a fact, even if demonstrated, was not of itself sufficient evidence that the tenant had suffered

Legal aspect of their case.

any wrong in the eye of the law. Penal slavery had become extinct, but it was still possible for a freeman to become a bondsman according to due legal process ; and even as late as the reign of Henry VI., a collector who had been appointed by the Bishop of Durham, and whose payments had fallen in arrear, entered into a recognisance to become a bondsman unless he made good the deficiency before a given day. To adduce a single document as a bar to the claim of the lord was therefore as useless as it would now be to assert a claim to land on the ground that it had been held by a remote ancestor, and to disregard all intermediate conveyances. The true title of the villein to be called a freeman lay not in ancient writings nor in legal quibbles, but in his value to the state and in the changed circumstances of the times. To seek for precedents in remote antiquity is, if the search is indefinitely continued, to bring back as models for civilised men all the customs of savages. The hopes of mankind lie not behind them but before, not in prescription but in progress.

At the very time when the sense of political wrong was inflamed by discontent with ecclesiastical institutions, the primacy was united with the chancellorship The passions of the lower in the person of Archbishop Sudbury. It classes inflamed by the was believed, rightly or wrongly, that a poll-tax Poll-Tax. on all persons of the age of fifteen years was imposed by Parliament at his suggestion. Taxes were usually farmed out, and collected, with all the roughness and ruthlessness which marked the times, by the farmers or their agents. False claims and every form of corruption had been the subject of complaint and enquiry from the earliest reigns of which any records have remained. But when a proof of age was required for the girls of every household, the collectors, who, like their betters, were filthy-minded and brutal, received, as it were, a legal authority to offer the coarsest of insults to the most innocent of maidens. They took care to avail themselves of the privilege, and in some instances, when the father of the family happened to be present, paid the penalty of their pruriency with their lives. The whole of the population below the rank of freeholder or burgher received the provocation which was hardly even needed to force them into revolt. One cry resounded throughout the whole of England : Down with the tax—death to the Archbishop !

The grievance of the tax, when added to the grievance of bondage, was sufficient to convert a number of local riots into a general rebellion. The men of Kent were soon on the march ; the men of Essex marched too, in a separate column, on the opposite side of the Thames ; and the commonalty of the neighbouring counties on either hand hastened to join the rebels. At Maidstone, the Archbishop's gaol was attacked, and John Ball, a preacher of the new school, who had been imprisoned for teaching false doctrine, was released, and appointed chaplain to the insurgents. The leading spirits were Thomas Baker, Wat Tyler, Jack Straw, and a few others whose names betokened their callings. On the Kentish side of the river, however, the chief actor was Wat Tyler, by whose name the rebellion is generally known. He led his men to Blackheath, their numbers increasing every hour, and swollen at last by the London apprentices, who were as pleased as the villeins with the preaching of John Ball, and who believed that no satisfactory answer could be given to the question—

Wat Tyler's rebellion.

> When Adam delved and Eve span,
> Who was then the gentleman ?

There was no force near London strong enough to meet the rioters, who were for a time able to dictate their own terms. Their objects, apart from the ex- Aims of the tinction of villenage, which was the chief article rebels. insisted on, are vaguely stated by the contemporary chroniclers, who seem to have had but little sympathy for them. The abolition, however, of some monopolies with respect to buying and selling, enjoyed by town corporations, the right of every man to rent land at fourpence an acre, and to take fish and game wherever he could find it, and the reform of ecclesiastical abuses, seem to have been the chief points at which those who knew their own minds were aiming. But, even in more civilised times, the original cause of a rebellion is forgotten in the heat of tumult, and an indiscriminate thirst for blood takes the place of a desire for redress ; in an age of ignorance and brutality the horrors of mob-rule are almost indescribable. It was the ignorance of the age which had made Wat Tyler master of London, which was yet to prompt a petition of the landholders that no villein should be taught to read, which was to be modified only in the long course of years, and which is not annihilated even in the nineteenth century.

From specific complaints the rioters advanced to the general proposition that all laws were unjust, and that all lawyers ought to be killed. It followed, of London in the hands of course, that no man could be justly imprisoned. the mob : slaughter of The Marshalsea prison was soon broken open ; the lawyers. the inmates of that, and, no doubt, of the other gaols also became recruits in the ranks of the mob. So bitter was the feeling against all who were in any way connected with the law, that they were beheaded whenever they were met ; and, when their houses were stormed,

it was said even the oldest men among the rebels showed
the agility of rats and the endurance of men possessed.
The Temple, as being the head-quarters of the enemy,
was burned, with all the priceless manuscripts it contained.

Fire and sword were carried from one end of London
to the other. With a not ill-founded suspicion that all
Destruction   legal documents were on the side of the old-
of docu
ments and   established order of society, Wat Tyler and his
treasures.   men broke open the buildings in which it was
known that muniments were stored, and gave them to
the flames. At Clerkenwell, where stood the Priory of
St. John of Jerusalem, the work was so well done, that
little remained but the bare walls of the church. The
prior, Robert Hales, who was also Treasurer of England,
possessed at Highbury a manor which he had converted,
according to the notions of those days, into a second
Paradise. Where they had found a paradise, the mob
left only desolation and ruins. The most magnificent
dwelling-house in England was that of the Duke of
Lancaster—the Savoy Palace. It had but recently been
built and stored with every known kind of treasure—
with jewels and plate, with books and charters, and with
apparel which could not be surpassed in the palace of
any king in Europe. Against the Duke the insurgents
at this time bore a special grudge—bred of disappoint-
ment. He had, to a certain extent, supported Wycliffe ;
they had been deluded, by some recruits from the north,
into the belief that he had freed all his villeins, and, in
the enthusiasm of the moment, they had declared that
he should be their king, just as they had declared that
John Ball should be their primate. Before they reached

London, however, they were undeceived; and, in the bitterness of their wrath, they declared that they would have no king bearing the Duke's name—John, they marched to the Savoy, battered down its walls, and burned all its precious contents. A gang of them entered the cellars and remained there, drinking and making merry till the falling masonry had blocked up every outlet. The cries of these self-made prisoners were, it is said, heard for seven days, but neither their enemies nor their comrades made any effort to rescue them.

Not only in the Savoy did drink flow freely. Where it was to be had it was taken—with the consent of the owner or without. The men who were al- Brutal orgies ready brutal enough became still more brutal of the mob. as they drank. Private vengeance was gratified as well within the ranks of the rioters as without, and rioter slaughtered rioter as he lay helplessly drunk or insensible. The apprentices, who seem to have regarded all masters as enemies, beheaded them whenever an opportunity presented itself. Wealth was regarded as a cause of offence; the more wealthy a trader was, the greater was the danger to his life; to be rich, and to have advanced money on the security of any tax, was certain death. One of the most prominent merchants in London was one Richard Lyons, who had been a farmer of subsidies and customs, and had been accused in parliament of bargaining with Edward III. in a manner disadvantageous to the country, but profitable to himself. He had been thrown into prison, and his property had been seized ; but the sentence had been reversed, partly, as was commonly believed, through the influence of Alice Perers, the mistress of Edward. Upon this unfortunate man, who does not appear to have been guilty of any more heinous offence than that of engaging in the ordinary mercantile transactions of the time, the mob fell with more than their ordinary fury. They visited upon him the sins of the collectors, tore him from his house, dragged him through the streets into the open country, and murdered him at last in a hedge.

A common remark at the time was that the rebels always cut off the heads of their victims. It is a com-

Imitation of public executions : fate of the Archbishop of Canterbury. mon remark in our own days that great crimes always produce imitators. The beheading and quartering of traitors had, no doubt, produced its effect upon the imagination of all classes. To imitate the public executions with which they had grown familiar by report, if not through their own eyesight, was one of the first impulses of the victorious mob. They were in power, and they regarded their enemies as traitors. They had vowed vengeance against Sudbury, the Primate and Chancellor ; and their vengeance could not be satisfied except by such punishment as kings considered meet for rebellious subjects. He had taken refuge in the Tower of London, together with Sir Robert Hales, the Treasurer, who, like himself, held a lay and an ecclesiastical office, and with some subordinates whom the mob hated for the part they had taken in the collection of the poll-tax. The rioters besieged the Tower, and it was observed, alike by the chroniclers and the songwriters of the day, that the gentlemen appeared to have lost heart, and did not fight as became them. Through lack of courage or of management, the Archbishop, the Treasurer, and five others, fell into the hands of the besiegers, and were dragged to the block on Tower Hill. There they met the fate which others had undergone and were yet to undergo, with only a little more pretence of legality, at the hands of the executioner. As the heads fell, after the blows of the axe, they were fixed upon pikes and poles, raised aloft, so that the features might be recognised, and carried in triumph before the yelling victors. The procession was one with which the neighbourhood was already, and was yet to be, only too familiar. It ended at London Bridge, where the bleeding heads were set on high for all the world to see.

The rebellion, which had hardly been less formidable in other parts of the country than in the home counties, was at length suppressed, but only after pro- Immediate mises had been made by the young king, which effects of the rebellion. parliament afterwards refused to ratify. The villeins dispersed, supposing themselves to be free-men ; they returned home only to find themselves villeins as before. Many of them were punished by the very death which they had themselves inflicted on others. Tresillian, the Chief Justice, who tried them, is said to have shown as little mercy to them as they had shown to the lawyers ; and all who were accused before him were executed with the severity which by law was due to the crime of high treason. Villenage was destined to die out rapidly through the increased value of labour and the demand for labour in the towns ; but the immediate effect of Wat Tyler's insurrection was to increase the exasperation of class against class. The rioters had shown what men persistently kept in ignorance can do in a brutal age when driven to desperation. The young king, though he had behaved with great courage, had shown that even kings may, under pressure of circumstances, promise that which they have no legal power to perform.

With a rankling sense of injury, the oppressed classes

seem to have looked for consolation in the new religious

tenets, which had already made progress among them. Wycliffe, in translating the Bible, had, as his adversaries maintained, thrown pearls before swine. The few who had acquired the art of reading and could procure a copy, were thus, to a certain extent, enabled to expound the words of Scripture to their fellows, and could, no doubt, draw a very effective contrast between the state of society actually existing and that which ought to exist according to the law of God.

Had the higher ranks of the clergy taken a less prominent part, at this time, in political affairs, it is pos-

sible that what was called heresy would have been more easily suppressed, and the eccle- siastical organisation would have been in higher favour. But whenever there was any great political scandal it was more probable than not that a bishop's name would be mentioned in connection with it. An instance, by no means singular, of the charges which were rife against the great dignitaries of the Church, may be found not in the words of a prejudiced Lollard, nor in the vague sentences of a pompous chronicler, but in the more trustworthy records of the Parliament and the Chancery. William of Wykeham, bishop of Winchester, who is best known to posterity as the munificent founder of the great Public School at Winchester, and of New College at Oxford, held a number of high offices under Edward III. He was Clerk of the Privy Seal, Chief of the Secret Council, Governor of the Great Council, and, at one time, Chancellor. For eight years he was entrusted with the administration of the whole of the revenues of the kingdom, and received on behalf of the king the ransoms of the King of Scotland and the King of France. More than eleven hundred thousand pounds passed through his hands during this time, and it was alleged that nearly the whole of this vast sum, besides French coin, had been diverted by him from its proper receptacle—the royal Treasury. It was said that he had, against the express instructions of the Black Prince, released a number of distinguished French hostages, in order to make a profit for himself. Accusations of a more precise nature were made against him of having remitted fines due to the king from certain persons and for certain offences ; but the most disgraceful of all was that he had, for a bribe, tampered with the Chancery Records, and so defrauded the king of half the dues upon a licence of alienation, of which also the particulars were given. Judgment was given against him by members of the Great Council ; and the temporalities of his bishopric were seized into the king's hands. Then followed a transaction discreditable alike to king and to subject. The bishop undertook to supply the king with three ships, to send fifty men-at-arms and fifty archers on board each ship, and to pay them, according to the king's scale of pay, for a quarter of a year. For this service he recovered the temporalities of his see, and afterwards, in the revolution of the political wheel, he obtained a full pardon and exoneration from the services which he had undertaken to render to the state.

Whether William of Wykeham was guilty of forgery and peculation, whether the Bishop of Norwich was rightly condemned in parliament for having traitorously received money from the French, whether the charges which were brought against almost all public men by their adversaries were true or false, can never be known with certainty. The men who were convicted or acquitted upon insufficient evidence in the fourteenth century cannot be tried upon sufficient evidence in the nineteenth. But it matters little to those who would form a true estimate of the times whether all men in power were dishonest, or all political parties were in the habit of making false accusations against their opponents. The general tone of morality is the same in either case ; those who would be base enough to ruin an enemy, by pronouncing him guilty of a crime which had never been committed, would be base enough to commit that very crime when they had the opportunity.   It was in an atmosphere of unscrupulous intrigue, of restless ambition, of pitiless hatred, of treachery, of dishonesty, and even of murder, that the leaders of the day drew the breath of life. The commons grew familiar with proclamations in which every well known name was brought before them as the name of a criminal ; and among the best known names were the names of the bishops.   Only a few months before the temporalities were restored to William of Wykeham, Edward III. entered upon the fiftieth or jubilee year of his reign.   The event was celebrated by a general pardon of felonies committed before the beginning of the year. But the one person whose offences were at that time declared to be unpardonable was William of Wykeham ; and it was expressly provided that he should 'nothing enjoy of the said graces.'   As soon as the old king was dead and a minor was on the throne, the bishop's deeds were no longer unpardonable, but pardoned.   What a theme for the discourse of a Lollard preacher !

The part taken by the clergy in political affairs, together with certain other practices, was also leading political discontent still more directly towards an alliance with religious discontent, and preparing the way for the execution of heretics. The religious corporations were in the habit of acquiring to themselves the revenues of parish churches by a process which was happily termed Appropriation. An advowson could then as now be bought ; the owners of advowsons could then more easily than now be persuaded to part with their property in exchange for masses or other spiritual benefits. No sooner had a monastery, a prebend, a bishopric, or a half religious half military order attached a benefice to itself, than it became perpetual parson of the church, with a right to the tithes and the glebe. It appointed a vicar to perform the religious services, paid him as it pleased, and retained the surplus in its own hands. The consequence was that the vicars grew dissatisfied, because they had not a sufficient allowance for their support, the secular clergy felt aggrieved when they saw a monk in a pulpit which they regarded as their own, and the poor complained loudly that they were deprived of what was legally their due. It had been the law in England, as elsewhere, long before the Conquest, that a fourth and afterwards a third of the tithes should be devoted to the poor ; and in this ancient maxim may perhaps be found the germ of parish relief. But the ancient constitution of society was such that the old rule could never have had much practical value, except so far as the poor were members of the ecclesiastical body. The Statute of Labourers, however, with its stringent provisions against beggars, and still more a Statute passed in the year 1388 for the suppression of mendicancy and vagrancy, with the increase in the number of free-men who had no settled occupation, naturally led men to enquire how those who were starving ought to be fed. The ill-paid vicars and the apostate monks, no doubt,

Appropriations : the clergy, the tithes, and the poor.

knew well enough the letter of the old law ; if they wished
for sympathy, they and all the teachers of the new doctrines, had but to point towards the stateliest building at
hand, and to tell their hearers that an Abbot or a Prior
within—an alien, too, perhaps—was growing fat on the
goods which belonged to the commons, while the commons themselves were dying of hunger.

Songs, more vigorous than delicate, were composed
and sung from village to village, and their themes were,
Agitation like that of Piers Plowman's Vision, the vices
against the and rapacity of the clergy. The luxury of the
clergy : popu-
lar songs. prelates, who rode out with escorts such as were
the escorts of kings, the greediness of friars, who became
dealers in wool, and dishonest in their dealings, the in-
continence both of monks and of the secular clergy, who
squandered their gains in decking their mistresses, the
absurdity of image-worship, and the good deed done by
some Wycliffites, who beheaded the image of St. James,
were the common topics of the songsters and rhymers.
The practice of kidnapping the children of wealthy
parents, in order that their inheritance might become the
property of a religious order, was the subject not only of
a political poem, but of a complaint in Parliament. Even
the courtiers, and those who had no sympathy with the
Lollards, denounced, like John Gower, the corruptions of
the Church ; and when the king asked for money the
Commons suggested that it should be taken from the
religious houses of aliens.

Against this formidable agitation the clergy could
bring most powerful engines to bear. They said little
in defence of the ecclesiastical system, which it was their
interest to uphold, but much of the speculative doctrines
which were an essential part of the teaching of the

agitators. Superstition was as yet but little weakened ; and it was not difficult to impress those minds which had given no attention to the new belief with the notion that a doubt concerning the Real Presence, or the efficacy of penance, pilgrimages, and image-worship, was a crime fraught with the most terrible consequences, both spiritual and temporal. The Church, too, was still a great power in the state, and when Richard II., a weak sovereign, was succeeded by Henry IV., a sovereign whose title was disputed, the king could not, without great danger, have appeared positively hostile to the clergy. While, therefore, the repeated protests of the Commons in Parliament against ecclesiastical abuses could not be set at nought by the House of Lancaster, which had gained some popularity through affecting a desire for reform, the wishes of staunch churchmen were not without their weight. Hard pressed on either hand, Henry IV. discovered a middle course by which, perhaps, the throne was saved for him and his son. He gave to both sides a portion of what was asked. On the one hand he assented to a re-enactment and extension of the statutes against accepting papal provisions, and to the petition of the commons that in cases of appropriation one of the secular clergy should be appointed vicar. On the other hand, he permitted the clergy to do their worst against all whose doctrine was erroneous, and aided them by giving a sanction to a new statute, which rendered the burning of heretics easier. Henry V. adopted the same policy; and the first year of his reign was remarkable for two most dissimilar events —the suppression of Alien Priories and the accusation of Sir John Oldcastle.

The clergy denounce the crime of heresy: policy of Henry IV. and Henry V.

It has been held by lawyers that the writ for ' the burning of a heretic ' existed at the common law before this time, but issued only by special warrant from the king. The punishment of burning, in its worst form, was certainly inflicted long before the Conquest, and *The writ for* it may possibly have been applied to heretics *the burning of a heretic.* before the reign of Henry IV. But heresy rarely appeared in England before the fourteenth century, and, except in the case of the Paterines (who, though not burnt to death were not less cruelly punished), it is difficult to find an instance even of a contumacious heretic. It is still more difficult to find an instance of a relapsed heretic, to whom the stake was considered specially appropriate. Nor would it be profitable to discuss, as many historians have done, the questions whether Sautre perished by a writ which Henry IV. had no legal power to sign, and whether the statute which required sheriffs by virtue of their office to commit heretics to the flames, upon the command of the diocesan, was invalid through want of assent from the Commons. To those who have followed this history up to the present point, it will appear idle to look for a nice consideration of technical details at a time when the papacy was trembling, and a dynasty was in danger. All we know, and all we need know (whatever may be the legal aspect of the matter to a modern constitutional or ecclesiastical lawyer) is that the ecclesiastical party triumphed when victorious in doctrine, just as one political party triumphed in turn over another, and executed its adversaries—sometimes, perhaps, according to law, sometimes certainly in spite of it.

The first to suffer for the crime of heresy in this new persecution was William Sautre. He is described, *Execution of* in the writ for his execution, as 'sometime *Sautre.* chaplain.' According to the same document, he had fallen into a 'most damnable' heresy, had abjured

it, and had afterwards relapsed. Sentence was, therefore, passed by the Convocation of the Province of Canterbury, that he should be degraded from all ecclesiastical
rank, and that he should be left to the secular power—
Holy Mother Church having no further concern in the
matter. The king, being zealous for justice, and true to
the Catholic faith, wishing to defend Holy Church, to
root out all heresies, and to visit with condign punishment
all convicted heretics, directs his commands to the mayor
and sheriffs of London. He informs them that, according
to law, and the canonical institutions, such heretics ought
to be burnt with fire. He requires them, therefore, to
cause William Sautre, who is in their custody, to be
carried to some public place within the liberties of their
city, to be put into the fire, and there burnt to death, as
a manifest example, to excite the horror of Christians.
Sautre died, as too many were yet to die, a martyr in
the literal sense of the word—a witness to the hideous
barbarism of the age in which he lived.

Other burnings followed, and the English populace
seemed for a time in danger of becoming as familiar
with the shrieks of burning heretics as with   Arrest of
the bleeding heads and quarters of beheaded   Lollards
                                                throughout
traitors. Writs for the arrest of Lollards were the kingdom.
sent into every county, and many, whose names are unknown in history, no doubt perished, if not in prison or
at the stake as heretics, upon the gallows as traitors.

With such questions as have agitated controversial
writers upon religion, this history has no concern—with
questions whether this heretic recanted, and the other
asked for mercy, whether the execution of one was a little
more or a little less legal than the execution of another.
The one important fact must always remain, that the

clergy desired the death of heretics by fire, and that there was not sufficient humanity in the kingdom to raise an outcry against such cruelty.   The only protest which was made, or was said to have been made, was that which was natural to the age—an attempt on the part of the persecuted to escape from their persecutors by force.

The most distinguished member of the heretical, Lollard, or puritan party, was Sir John Oldcastle, one

Sir John Oldcastle.

of the very few men in the position of landholders who went even so far as to adopt openly the opinions of Wycliffe.   He was pronounced a heretic in an ecclesiastical court, and he was afterwards sentenced to death by Parliament, not only as a heretic but as a traitor.   The proceedings were of an unusual character, and it has been suspected that Oldcastle suffered through a forged record of indictment and process of outlawry

A charge which, if proved, might implicate a number of the chief personages in the land in a conspiracy to

Oldcastle's indictment as enrolled in the King's Bench—the erasures.

crush by fraud one whom there could have been little difficulty in crushing by force seems, at first sight, hardly to demand investigation.   But as it is one of the rare cases in which the evidence can be brought before those who live in the nineteenth century as clearly as before those who lived in the fifteenth, there is some temptation to put so important a matter to the proof.   An indictment, in which Oldcastle's name is mentioned, is enrolled on the judgment roll of the Court of King's Bench.   In the same indictment appear also Walter Blake of Bristol, chaplain, and Roger Acton, of Shrewsbury, knight.   Oldcastle's name stands first, and there is not the slightest doubt that it has been written upon an erasure.   The parchment has for a space of more than two lines been scraped, it shows the roughness which always follows abrasion, and when held up to the light, it is seen to be obviously thinner in the suspected part than elsewhere. The two lines are written in a hand which, though strictly contemporaneous, is different from that which precedes and follows, and with ink which is considerably lighter. Nor is this all. In another part of the document, in which Oldcastle's name occurs incidentally in the original hand, the word 'said' has been prefixed by interlineation in the hand in which the two doubtful lines are written. This is an indication, to all who are familiar with records or legal documents, that, whatever else may have been written where there is now an erasure, the name of Oldcastle was wanting. In these instruments, whenever a person has been once mentioned, he is described at every subsequent mention as 'the said.' So far then it is beyond all question established that the indictment of Oldcastle as enrolled in the King's Bench is not, word for word, the document which might at one time have been read in the same place.

The indictment bears date the first year of the reign of Henry V. The subsequent proceedings in Parliament were not instituted immediately, but four years His outafterwards. In the meantime Oldcastle, who lawry. failed to appear to the indictment (if there ever was one against him), was outlawed.

According to law, a person who had been indicted for treason, who did not appear, and who had been outlawed, might, if afterwards captured, be sentenced to The sentence death as a traitor, and executed without further upon him. trial. It was Oldcastle's misfortune to be taken three or four years after his outlawry. The Commons desired that the proceedings relating to Oldcastle in the King's Bench should be produced in the House. Certain documents were brought in and read in the presence of Oldcastle himself, against whom judgment was given 'by authority of Parliament, and by virtue of the aforesaid outlawry.' The sentence was that he should be drawn through London to the new gallows in Giles's, and there hanged, and burned hanging.

In the Rolls of Parliament a reference is made, not vaguely, to the records of the King's Bench, but to the *Enrolment of the proceedings on the Rolls of Parliament : the discrepancies.* term and to the very membrane on which the indictment is to be found ; and the reference agrees with the place in which the indictment already described appears. Two copies of the instrument accompany the record of the proceedings in Parliament, but neither of them agrees precisely with the original document in the King's Bench. Neither of them contains the names of the two persons accused with Oldcastle ; and all matter relating to them alone is excluded. In a substantive part of the indictment, too, where the names of Blake and Acton occur in the King's Bench record, without any mention of Oldcastle, the name of Oldcastle alone has been substituted in the Parliamentary transcripts. Thus a document which, as it stands on the King's Bench Roll, affords evidence that the name of Oldcastle was at one time not included among those of the persons indicted becomes in the Parliamentary transcript a record of the indictment of Oldcastle alone.

In spite, however, of the grave suspicion suggested by these facts, and in spite of the frequency with which the *Forgery or carelessness?* 'rasing of records' is mentioned during these troubled times, it would be unjust to assert that any person in Parliament was a party to a forgery. There is a memorandum appended to the King's Bench Roll, by which it appears that the Chief Justice himself produced in full Parliament *so much of the document as referred to Oldcastle.* From this it may be inferred that the imperfect transcript in the Rolls of Parliament had at least the official authority of the Court of King's Bench. Nor is there reason to suppose that any alteration except that which gave the whole indictment the appearance of referring to Oldcastle alone—was made after Parliament had asked for the proceedings in the King's Bench. There is ample evidence on another membrane of the roll that Oldcastle, with a number of persons accused of being implicated in the conspiracy, was outlawed in the second year of the reign of Henry V.—three years before sentence was passed in Parliament. If therefore forgery is to be imputed, the forger must have been some official connected with the King's Bench, and he must have introduced Oldcastle's name almost immediately after the indictment against Blake and Acton was presented to the court. In almost all rolls, too, it happens sometimes that the marks of erasure are visible in places in which it is impossible that the eraser can have had any dishonest intention, and there remains, therefore, the bare possibility that in this case a careless clerk may have made a mistake, and that a knife may have been used to save labour and parchment. The judge had power to direct such alteration, if necessary. But, on the other hand, the erasure is of unusual extent, and the rest of the document does not support the theory of a corrected mistake. There has been given in the fourth chapter of this history sufficient evidence to show that it would have been no very difficult task to corrupt an officer of the court ; and when a record of the highest importance bears such marks as the indict-

ment of Oldcastle, even though we might in charity pronounce that forgery is ' not proven,' we should still have to
pronounce that there has been carelessness and concealment
of carelessness hardly less culpable than forgery itself.

At this early period all proceedings in cases of treason
were tainted with prejudice, and, according to our modern
notions, were violent and unjust. If Oldcastle
suffered through a forged indictment, others
before and after have suffered in a manner which
hardly less deserves reprobation. Nothing could be more
unjust than to import the *odium theologicum* into Oldcastle's case, and to represent that he was, so far as the
accusation of treason was concerned, an instance of a man
condemned by the clerical party contrary to the usages of
the time. Parliament, it is true, added the punishment of
burning to the punishment of hanging, because Oldcastle
had been pronounced guilty of heresy as well as of
treason. But when the party in power was convinced
that Oldcastle was dangerous to it, his death, in one way
or other, was certain, and would have been certain had
there been not a single Bishop in the realm. What we
have most to regard in this case is not so much the individual as the times. In the preceding chapter it has
been shown what moral tone was pervading all classes ;
Oldcastle's death was only one out of many illustrations
which might be selected. It is our good fortune to live
in an age when all classes, clergy and laity alike, have
participated in a great improvement. To mark out a
particular class as the one scape-goat of the past, would
be to show ignorance alike of the causes which made that
past what it was, and of the causes which have made this
present what it is.

It appears by the King's Bench document to which

(marginal note:) Oldcastle's death not to be attributed to the clergy alone.

reference has been made that Walter Blake and Sir Roger Acton were found guilty of treason by jury, according to the ordinary course, and were sentenced to be drawn through London and hanged, where Oldcastle afterwards suffered, at the new gallows in St. Giles's. This spot was selected for the scene of the executions because, according to the accusation, it was in St. Giles's Fields that the conspirators were to have met, and that their forces were to have assembled. Their scheme, according to the indictment, (which seems to be genuine so far as Blake and Acton are concerned,) was to put the king and his brothers to death, and to abolish the royal dignity, to set Oldcastle at the head of affairs with the title of Regent, (which would have been equivalent to President or Protector) to proclaim that there were to be no bishops, and no orders of monks in the land, to force all who had been members of those orders into secular occupations, to destroy all relics in churches or religious houses, and to establish a form of government in accordance with their own opinions. Those who consider how completely this was an anticipation of what was actually accomplished in the time of Cromwell, and how well it accords with the similar, but less precise demands of Wat Tyler and his fellows, will have little difficulty in believing that there may really have been a conspiracy, even though Oldcastle may not have given his consent.

Aims of Oldcastle, Blake, and Acton.

The double punishment of hanging and burning, inflicted on Oldcastle, is the best illustration in action of the alliance which the clergy had now succeeded in effecting with the upper classes of the laity. Both parties believed that they had a common interest in crushing a common enemy. The one resorted

Alliance of the clergy with the upper classes of the laity.

to its usual weapon—a charge of treason—the other to a weapon which it had not hitherto had many occasions of using in England—a charge of heresy. The effect, however, of this alliance was, for a time at least, to place two weapons instead of one in the hands of either party. A charge of treason could be rendered more formidable by the addition of a charge of heresy—a charge of heresy by the addition of a charge of treason. Heresy was by no means strictly defined in any law, and the diocesan appears to have had the power of deciding whether any particular doctrine was heresy or not. There was also an offence falling within ecclesiastical jurisdiction, which, if not strictly heresy, was of so heretical a character that according to some lawyers a writ 'for burning a heretic' might issue, at common law, against persons who had been found guilty of it. This was the offence in which the belief, descending from time immemorial, was noticed in the first chapter of the present history, and which is specially prominent from the beginning of the fifteenth to the end of the seventeenth centuries—the offence of witchcraft.

Every one is familiar with stories, which were current in generations not long since passed away, of men and of women who had read more than their neigh-bours, who acquired the reputation of students, and who, if they incurred the least unpopularity were set down as witches or wizards. In the earlier part of the fifteenth century, when letters were but just reviving, a lay-man or a lay-woman who showed any strong appetite for learning was infinitely more likely to be an object of suspicion than at the end of the eight-teenth. The orthodox clergy, of course, maintained that the most suspicious form of study which lay people could

Charges of Witchcraft: study pro- nounced dis- graceful to lay people.

undertake was that of divinity. The consequence was that the clerical party enlisted as far as they could every knightly prejudice on their side, and represented a thirst for knowledge as essentially unchivalrous. It was easy, too, to foster a belief that no one could know, or even wish to know, more than his neighbours, except through the influence of the Devil. Oldcastle was one of the very few laymen of the day who had a spirit above this popular prejudice ; and a contemporary song against the Lollards contains an allusion to him which well expresses the dominant sentiment of the age :—

> I trow there be no knight alive
> That would have done so open shame
> For that craft to study or strive ;
> It is no gentlemanne's game.

When the jealousy and dread of superior knowledge were prevalent, it was impossible that the hunt for Lollards should not suggest a hunt for sorcerers. The pestilences, too, which had overrun Europe must have stimulated the sale of charms, and given a new power to quacks of every kind, and to superstition in every form. The reign of Henry IV., remarkable for the burning of Sautre, and writs to arrest heretics, is remarkable also for an attempt to suppress witchcraft. The king had been informed that many sorcerers, magicians, enchanters, necromancers, diviners, and soothsayers, were practising every day their horrible and detestable arts, and causing others to be perverted and brought into ill repute. It was feared that even greater evils might follow unless some· remedy were shortly provided. A bishop was therefore required to search for sorcerers within his diocese, and to commit them to prison after conviction, or, *should it*

Connexion between charges of heresy and charges of witchcraft.

seem expedient, before, to be kept there until repentance
or further orders.

The most terrible and the most disgraceful of all executions for witchcraft, though Englishmen had too great
a share in it, was. not brought to pass on English soil.
The Maid of The story of the Maid of Orleans is so well
Orleans.   known and so painful that it is unnecessary to
do more than recapitulate its leading incidents.   She was
a simple country girl, the monotony of whose life was
relieved only by rare converse with a traveller halting at
the remote inn where she served.   The great subject of
the day was the misery of France overrun by the English.
She could talk of little else when any rough wayfarer
condescended to give her a word ; she could think of
nothing else when left to brood by herself.   With a
nature full of affection and energy, she had neither child
nor husband to love, nor any object in life for which she
could work.   The whole strength of her character was
forced into two channels—imagination and devotion.   To
wish France free and Charles on the throne was to see it
all with her mind's eye ; to kneel down in prayer was to
pray for the realisation of the picture.   Before long this
mental exaltation found a relief in action.   The possible
future, ever present to her mind, needed only a passionate
faith in religion to appear an inspiration.   The dreaming
waitress and stable-girl became a prophetess and a heroine.
Her belief gave her strength to wear a man's armour and
do more than a man's deeds of arms.   She showed to all
posterity a proof that a firm purpose, supported by an
undoubting trust in the future, is of almost unlimited
power.   Strong warriors fell before her as though they
had been babes ; the appearance of her banner was the
signal for a rout ; and ere many weeks had passed she saw

her dreams converted into facts by the coronation of Charles, as king of France, at Rheims. It was her misfortune afterwards to be captured by a Burgundian force. She was sold to the English—for prisoners of war were not uncommonly regarded as articles of commerce in the days of chivalry—and, while in their hands, she was tried for heresy and witchcraft. An ecclesiastical tribunal, composed chiefly of Frenchmen, was brought together, and pronounced that her victorious standard had gained some magical force through her incantations, and that her inspiration was from the Devil. She was thrown into prison, and afterwards, on pretence that she had recanted and again fallen into her evil ways, she was burnt alive in the market-place of Rouen.

A few months after the execution of Joan of Arc, in France, when the young Henry VI. was in the tenth year of his reign, his Council was devoting considerable attention to witchcraft in England. A writ issued for the arrest of Thomas Northfeld, a member of the order of Preachers in Worcester, and a Professor of Divinity, who was to be brought before the King's Council, together with all suspected matter belonging to him, and especially his books which treated of sorcery. In the same year, one Margery Jourdemayn, together with a clerk and a friar, were brought before the Council, which decreed that the two latter might be released from prison on finding sufficient bail for their future good behaviour, and Margery also, provided her husband would be her surety. There is also every reason to believe that, although the extreme penalty may have been rarely exacted, there was for many years a species of crusade against persons suspected of practising the forbidden arts, who no doubt had but an ill time among their neighbours,

Search for sorcerers in England.

even if they were not brought into a secular or ecclesiastical court. Ten years after the accusation against Margery Jourdemayn, it appears that the king gave a warrant to the Treasurer for the distribution of rewards among those doctors, notaries, and clerks who were exerting themselves for the destruction of 'the superstitious sect of necromancers, enchanters, and sorcerers.'

At this time, too, just before the Wars of the Roses, the charge of witchcraft became, like the charge of heresy, a political engine. One of the most distinguished sufferers was the Duchess of Gloucester, whose husband had been appointed one of the guardians of the realm upon the accession of the child-king, Henry VI. After the death of the joint guardian, the Duke of Bedford, the Duke of Gloucester occupied the highest position in the kingdom next to that of the imbecile youth who occupied the throne. The chief competitor for power, in opposition to the Duke, was Cardinal Beaufort, bishop of Winchester, to whom the person and education of the young king had been entrusted at the beginning of the reign. The clerical party, of which the Cardinal was the head, resolved to strike a blow at their enemy through his wife. The Duchess was seized at Leeds and thrown into prison ; and she was afterwards brought up to London to take her trial for witchcraft.

The charge of witchcraft as a political engine : the Duchess of Gloucester.

The prelates who were to conduct the examination sat in St. Stephen's Chapel at Westminster. They were Cardinal Beaufort, Cardinal Kempe, five bishops, and other clerical dignitaries ; and the king himself was present. The Duchess was led into the chapel, and formally accused of having consorted with that Margery Jourdemayn whose name has already been

Her Trial.

mentioned (and who was known as the Witch of Eye), as well as with other sorcerers. By their aid, it was said, a waxen image of the king had been made, which the Duchess had set before a fire, so that it might gradually melt away. Incantations had been used for the purpose of connecting the melting image with the living king—so that as the one slowly lost its form and likeness to humanity, the other might sink slowly into the grave. The sense of humour must have been strangely wanting in the august assembly which sat to investigate this charge. Not one of the whole number seems to have been struck with the incongruity of a king and the most powerful of his spiritual advisers sitting solemnly in a consecrated building, of which the name was famous, to ascertain whether a great lady and a silly woman had or had not —melted a piece of wax.

It need hardly be said that the Duchess was found guilty. Her husband's political opponents would have had her executed after the manner of heretics, Her condemnation and penance. but the young king, now arrived at manhood, had sufficient good feeling to save her life. She was induced to confess, and condemned to a penance which could hardly have inflicted less torture on her than burning itself, and was no doubt devised chiefly for the humiliation of her husband. It seems to have made a profound impression upon the populace ; and in one of the songs of the period she is made to bewail her fall, and to tell the whole story of her punishment :—

> Thorough London in many a street
>   Of them that were most principal,
> I went barefoot upon my feet
>   That some time wont to ride royal.
> Father of Heaven, and Lord of all,
>   As thou wilt so must it be ;
> The syn of pride will have a fall ;
>   All women may be ware by me.

After walking through the streets to be jeered by such
a mob as was the mob of London in the fifteenth century,
she was carried off to the Isle of Man, there to pass the
rest of her days in prison.   The Witch of Eye was
burnt in Smithfield, and a male sorcerer was hanged at
Tyburn.

Charges of witchcraft, once having taken their place
among the engines of political warfare, did not, during

The Duchess
of Bedford
and her
daughter
Queen
Elizabeth
suspected of
witchcraft. the Wars of the Roses, stop short of the royal
household, or even of kings.   Edward of York
having, by the aid of that Earl of Warwick
who was afterwards known as the king-maker,
driven Henry VI. from the throne and seated
himself upon it, by the title of Edward IV., was betrayed
into an act of great imprudence.   At the very time when
his chief supporter was negotiating for him a marriage
with a princess of Savoy, a sister of the Queen of France,
he hastily married a lady who, though of gentle blood,
was in no sense a fitting mate for the King of England.
She was the daughter of a small landowner or knight,
named Woodville, and she had married another small
landowner or knight, named Gray, who had fought on
the side of the Lancastrians against Edward, had been
killed in battle, and had left her a widow with a family
of young children.   Her mother, however, had more pretensions to princely rank, but had descended from it in
marrying Woodville.   Jacquette of Luxembourg had
married that Duke of Bedford who had been joint
Guardian of the Realm with Gloucester upon the accession of Henry VI.   After the death of her first husband,
she appears to have preferred love to position, and thus
became the mother of one queen, the grandmother of
another, and the great grandmother of Henry VIII., the
second king of the Tudor line.

In modern times the marriage of Edward IV.—a notorious libertine—to Elizabeth Gray would have been attributed to infatuation ; in the fifteenth century men went farther, and attributed infatuation to witchcraft. The king, who had many enemies before, made enemies of his best friends in taking John Gray's widow to wife. Rumours were soon spread by them that, whatever the queen might be, her mother at least must be a witch. As the silly story passed from mouth to mouth, it caused the Duchess of Bedford an alarm which—with the fate of the Duchess of Gloucester in her recollection—was by no means groundless. She took a course which, however ludicrous it may appear in our time, was perhaps, in those days that which wisdom would pronounce the safest. She ascertained the names of some of the persons who had been maligning her, and prayed that they might be called to answer before the Great Council. She complained that three images of lead, of the length of a man's finger, had been shown from hand to hand as the instruments of her sorcery. One of them, it was said, was in the likeness of the king, another of the queen ; and it was no doubt insinuated that the influence which the queen retained over him, after his passion might have been expected to die out, was due to magical arts. The first act of the men required to exculpate themselves before the Council was to deny that they had ever said a word to incriminate the Duchess. An image, it was admitted, had been handed about, but the Duchess's name had not been mentioned in connection with it ; and one man went so far as to add that he had 'never heard no witchcraft of my Lady of Bedford.' Upon this, the Council pronounced that she was cleared of suspicion. On her petition it was commanded that the proceedings

should be ' enacted of record,' so that the decision might
be of use at any future time. Yet had she known
past history or her own age, she might have foreseen that
all her precautions would be of no avail, should she
ever be without a powerful protector. When Edward IV.
was dead, and the Lords and Commons offered the
throne to the ' Most High and Mighty Prince, Richard,
Duke of Gloucester,' they gave not a thought to what
had gone before. They declared that the pretended
marriage between King Edward and Elizabeth Gray was
' made by means of sorcery and witchcraft, committed by
Elizabeth and her mother, Jacquette, Duchess of Bedford,
as the common opinion of the people and the public voice
and fame is through all this land.'

Towards the end of the reign of Edward IV. and
immediately after his death, accusations and counter-
accusations of witchcraft, or of similar mal-
practices, were the common weapons both of
the court and of its adversaries. It has commonly been represented that Thomas Burdett suffered
as a traitor because, when he heard that a favourite
white buck of his was killed, while the king was hunting
in his park, he had petulantly expressed a wish that the
buck had been in the king's belly—horns and all. In
the indictment which remains of record there is no mention of the buck or of its horns, nor of anything which
can refer to this story, except, perhaps, the charge that
Burdett disseminated seditious rhymes and ballads, composed with the intention of drawing away from the king
the love of his subjects. A deer-hunt was, probably
enough, the theme of many a song which may have
given offence at court. But the charge actually made
against Burdett in the King's Bench was, that he trea-

Charge of witchcraft against Thomas Burdett.

sonably imagined and compassed the death of the king, with the assistance of one John Stacey and one Thomas Blake. These two men, it was alleged, in order to carry the traitorous intention into effect, worked and calculated by art magic, necromancy, and astronomy, the final destruction of the King and Prince of Wales. They treasonably revealed to other persons the result of their calculations and devices, which was that both the king and the Prince must shortly die. It is further stated in the indictment that, according to the determination of Holy Church, and the opinions of divers doctors, it is forbidden to any liege-man thus to meddle concerning kings and princes, by calculating their nativities without their permission. The three were found guilty. Blake obtained a pardon through the intercession of the Bishop of Norwich; but the other two underwent the hideous sentence passed in those days upon traitors.

Closely connected with the charges against Burdett were the charges soon afterwards made against George, Duke of Clarence. In the attainder passed against him, it is alleged that he had accused the king of injustice in bringing a false accusation against Burdett, and in securing a conviction by bribing servants and others to divulge pretended conversations of a treasonable nature. But the most remarkable part of the bill is that in which he is accused of having imputed necromancy to the king. Not only, according to this document, had Clarence said that Edward removed by poison those whom he could not destroy by law, but that he reached by witchcraft those whom he could not reach by poison, and caused the Duke himself to waste away as a candle is consumed in burning. There is a well-known story

The duke of Clarence charged with having imputed witch-craft to Edward IV. himself.

in the chroniclers that Clarence was permitted by the king to select his own mode of death, and that he was drowned in a butt of malmsey.

Whatever may have been the end of Clarence, there seems to be no doubt that, unlike that of most so-called traitors, it was not by public execution — a remarkable exception in an age when the publicity of an execution was secured by distributing pieces of the traitor's body throughout the kingdom, and when every punishment consisted, in part at least, of exposure to the insults of a brutal crowd. It was no doubt through some remains of interest at court, or through the king's sense of the dignity of the blood-royal, that the Duke obtained the favour. After the death of Edward, not even his mistress could save herself from the ignominy of being jeered by the mob. Jane Shore was the last of the principal actors in the series of trials connected with witchcraft, which are a conspicuous feature of the disputes between the Houses of York and Lancaster, and of the quarrels between the members of either House. This unfortunate woman, who seems to have committed no crime, except obedience to the will of a licentious and tyrannical king, was summoned, at the instance of Richard III., to answer the accusation of sorcery. For some reasons, which it is unnecessary to investigate, the proceedings were not carried out to the usual conclusion, and Jane was tried in an ecclesiastical court for adultery and lewd behaviour, which it was easy enough to prove against her. She was pronounced guilty, and condemned to do public penance— walking through the streets barefoot, and carrying a lighted taper. We can, perhaps, imagine what would be the sufferings of any city dame condemned to be the

Accusation of witchcraft against Jane Shore.

laughing-stock of a London crowd in our time.   But this would be nothing to the treatment which would, in the fifteenth century, have befallen a royal paramour set up as a show at St. Paul's, even when she attracted, as it seems Jane Shore did, the sympathy of some spectators.

Of all the strange coincidences and apparent contradictions which present themselves in history, none seem, at the first glance, so strange as the coincidence that the belief in Witchcraft comes into the most marked prominence at the very time which is remarkable also for the introduction of Printing.   While contemplating the effects of a delusion which evinces the darkest ignorance, we are suddenly dazzled by the appearance of an art which we are in the habit of associating with the greatest enlightenment.   How can such a contrast have been brought to pass ?   Is learning powerless to eradicate superstition ?   Are human affairs a medley in which everything is to be attributed to chance and nothing to law, and of which the component elements change their nature and re-distribute themselves by caprice ?

A strange coincidence: introduction of printing at a time when accusations of witchcraft became most prominent.

To such questions as these there is a sufficient answer in the surrounding circumstances of the period under consideration, and in the very means by which the art of printing was invented and set in use.   The forces which had been at work for centuries had for centuries been opposed to one another.   On the one hand the spirit of private war had been arming baron against baron—one body of retainers against another ; on the other hand the spirit of commerce and the spirit of invention had been slowly acquiring strength in the towns, though checked by the barbarism which continued to exist both within and with-

Attempt to explain the contrast: the towns and the country.

out the walls. Edward IV., made king by the aid of a baron king-maker, accused and accusing others of witch-craft, and yet becoming the patron of Caxton, was but the head of a nation which as yet hardly deserved the name, and in which widely different interests produced contrasts even greater than those which are produced by a more complex civilisation.

In order, however, to estimate correctly the progress indicated by the invention of the art of printing, which, from its after effects, is apt to excite unbounded admiration, an attempt must be made to understand the condition of certain other arts at the time when the inventor or inventors lived. We shall then perceive that the amount of ingenuity required is by no means in proportion to the value of the results by which the introduction of the new art was followed. In almost all essential points, printing is identical with an invention of which the origin is lost in remote antiquity. No nation which was in any way brought into contact with the ancient Roman civilisation could long be ignorant of the construction and use of the seal. A seal is neither more nor less than stereotype used for the purpose of printing on wax. Such an instrument was in the possession of every land-holder and of every corporation in England, centuries before the adaptation of an old device to a new material and for a new purpose. Nor is the connecting link between the ancient seal and the type, consisting of moveable letters, like some of the connecting links for which naturalists have sought in vain, a mere matter of inference. The earliest attempt to print was made by means of a block, or, in other words, of a page of type in which the individual letters could not be moved. This was simply a large seal, from which an

Degree of progress indicated by the invention of printing.

impression was taken by means of ink, instead of by in-
dentation upon a soft material like wax. The blocks,
though clumsy, might long have sufficed for such printing
as was required, when there was little desire to read any
books, except now and then a romance, or a controversial
treatise on divinity, and when the expense of parchment
was an effectual check upon the multiplication of copies,
had not paper of a fine texture ceased to be a too expen-
sive substitute for skins.

At the end of the fourteenth century there was, in
Europe, sufficient commercial enterprise and sufficient
mechanical skill to produce a linen-paper, of Improvement
which even a modern printer might avail him- in the manu-
                                             facture of
self.   There seems to be no doubt that in the paper.
earlier part of the same century paper was sometimes made
from cotton, that there was then made the first rude attempt
to manufacture it from linen rags, and that a few years
sufficed to render the new art of practical value.   As
commerce increased, and deeds grew more numerous,
and records multiplied, the demand for parchment became
far stronger than it had been in earlier times ; and, as the
supply was limited, the price necessarily rose.   The inconvenience must have been very great, and have given
a strong impulse to the inventive powers of the townsmen who had been the chief causes of it.   The activity
of the towns and many features of their internal condition are most opportunely brought into prominence by
writs sent out, in conformity with an order of Parliament,
in the year 1388, and by the returns in which the various
guilds set forth their ordinances.   The dearness of skins
prepared for writing (which the ancient palimpsests show
to have been not altogether a recent annoyance) and the
slowly growing competition of paper, find more than one

curious illustration in these documents.   The ordinances of the Guild of Saddlers and Spurriers at Norwich are written on a piece of vellum which has once served as two leaves of a book.   Lines had been ruled on each side of each page, and the holes made for the thread, in binding, tell, like the lines, the past history of the skin.   When the clerk of the guild had to prepare the return, he flattened out the fold which made the division between the two leaves, disregarded the damage done by the binder, and wrote across the ruled lines, just as though they had had no existence, and he had been dealing with a new skin.   When such parsimony as this is apparent on the face of a parliamentary return, it is not surprising to discover that the regulations of another guild had been, a few years earlier, written on paper.   But, perhaps, the most striking evidence of the attention now excited by the want of materials for writing exists in the original writs sent to the guilds after the order had been made in Parliament.   Many of them, though seeming at first sight to be written on parchment, are pronounced by experts to be written on linen-paper, with the wire marks plainly visible upon close inspection.   It is by no means impossible that some fraudulent dealer in parchment may have deceived the clerks of the Chancery with spurious wares ; but, whatever the true explanation may be, the use of paper with the apparent sanction of legal officials is a matter of some importance.

Step by step with the advance of commerce and of business in the law courts, the art of writing made progress among the higher classes.   If we did not know what was the state of society in the middle of the fourteenth century, we might have some difficulty in understanding how it

Paper a substitute for parchment: increase of correspondence.

came to pass that no king of the French line, before Richard II., is known to have written so much as his own name. It is possible, indeed, that some of his predecessors were not absolutely unable· to form a letter, and that ancient custom alone forbade the sovereign to make a signature in the modern sense of the term. Still there could hardly be a better sign of the times than the abandonment of this ancient prejudice and the substitution of a name for a cross. The influence of the royal example was widely felt, and families of position began to perceive that.correspondence between their members would not be degrading, even though each correspondent might have to use the pen with his own hand. Letters written soon after this time are still extant, and suggest yet another cause for the increasing dearness of parchment and the increasing demand for paper.

Not the least curious among the curious movements which followed the Black Death, within a century and a half, is the interchange of uses between writing and sealing, stamping, or printing. On the one hand penmanship was beginning to show that it would, sooner or later, take the place of the seal in various transactions between man and man ; on the other hand the seal was, so to speak, taken to pieces, and each piece, consisting of a single letter, was used in endless combinations to make an impression with ink upon paper, and so to multiply the books which could previously be multiplied only by the scribe. The impression of the seal upon wax, long afterwards a necessary appendage to all documents which were to be produced in a court of law, was at first equivalent to a modern signing of the name ; it was supposed to be a proof that the owner of the seal had set his hand to a deed or writing in token of approval.

Interchange of uses between the pen and the seal.

So far was this doctrine carried that the ancient felony which corresponds to our forgery could not be committed with the pen, nor, in any way, without a counterfeit seal. There are numerous records which show that even to fabricate writs was no felony unless the seal was counterfeited. To heat a knife in the fire, cut through a seal (made of beeswax), substitute a false writ for the true one, and attach the real seal to the false writ was a very common practice ; but the offence was held to be no more than a trespass. In the reign of Henry IV. a man was accused of having counterfeited the Great Seal. This was High Treason. The jury, however, found that the Seal had not been counterfeited, but that the impression, which had belonged to a genuine document, had been removed and made to serve for a document which was spurious. The magnitude of the crime rendered the judges anxious to award the criminal a fitting punishment, and, after some delay, they declared that Treason had been committed, and passed the usual sentence. But the lawyers of a later time have not been satisfied with this judgment, for which there is no warrant in the Statute of Treasons ; and there can be little doubt that, according to the strict letter of the law, the offence which had been committed was not capital. There was thus a great want of precision in the definition of a crime which was one of the most prevalent in that age. The subsequent improvement in manners, and the spread of education to which printing has greatly contributed, have had the effect not, as might have been feared, of increasing the number of forgers with the number of persons able to write, but of checking forgery by rendering detection easy, and sharpening the wits of lawgivers and judges.

Writing, printing, sealing, and forgery.

The introduction of paper no doubt helped to extend the art of writing, just as the art of writing helped to extend the demand for paper ; and thus, when some skill had been attained in paper-making, there existed the only two incentives required for the development of the art of printing—a nascent love of letters, and a material on which books could be printed more cheaply than on parchment. The coincidences of time are very striking. Good paper was first made during the reign of the first English king who signed his own name, and from that time only half a century was required for the ancient seal, which had been unchanged for ages, to be developed into the printing-block, and the printing-block into moveable types. The honour of this adaptation, like that of most adaptations, is claimed by rival nations. It does not, however, like that of most mechanical inventions, belong to England ; but the new art was introduced into England by Caxton during the reign of Edward IV.

A plain statement of preceding events greatly diminishes the wonder at first excited by the appearance of Caxton during the Wars of the Roses, and when the belief in Witchcraft was at its height. The invention of printing was not very marvellous at the time, and its possible effects were not manifest for many a generation afterwards. Real changes in the manners of mankind are rarely effected at one stroke, either by a new law or by a new invention ; and had not the same causes which brought the first printed book into existence gained new strength with every generation, it is possible that even the art of printing might have languished for want of support, and that the printing-press might long have remained a mere curiosity, like the balloon or the electrical engine. It

The improvement of paper, and the invention of printing due to the spirit of commerce.

was the commercial spirit which had rendered printing possible. It was the commercial spirit which introduced printing into England; for Caxton was early in life a member of the Mercers' Company in London, and was afterwards, from his knowledge of mercantile affairs, commissioned by Edward IV. to negotiate a treaty with the Duke of Burgundy. The commercial spirit, also, by fostering all the other arts, fostered the tastes and the culture upon which the art of printing depended, or, in other words, which created the demand for printed books. Bishops and barons had for centuries been opposed to any innovation—the one class content with its own superior but limited knowledge, the other with its own rude courage and dense ignorance ; and so the barons and the bishops might have gone on for centuries more, had they not had new stores of learning forced upon them by the burghers.

The first use of the printing-press in England may be taken to mark the time at which the commercial spirit

The commercial spirit and the spirit of private war.

had so far gained upon its old enemy that it could contend on equal terms with the military spirit of the worst kind—the spirit of private war. The contempt—even now by no means extinct—which the land-holders had always felt for the towns-men, was somewhat mitigated—as contempt always is—by the success of the persons despised. King Edward IV. not only patronised Caxton and gave his countenance to traders, but, as was whispered, condescended to increase his revenue by commercial ventures of his own. The burgher might hope that he would one day be able to hold up his head and claim equality with the descendants of the men who had perhaps owned his forefathers as slaves. One of the most powerful families

in England, indeed, had already been founded by that
Michael de la Pole who had been created Earl of Suffolk, had held the office of Chancellor under Richard II.,
and had been but the son of a rich merchant—lender
of money to Edward III.

Prejudice in the country against the towns, and prejudice in the towns against the country (beginning,
perhaps, in the remote past, when some bar- Country
barian horde had starved a city into submission, robbers, and
town
and had treated with contumely the citizens thieves.
whom they had robbed), had been perpetuated by diver-
sity of interests and habits. The burgher, with some
justice, regarded the knight as a brigand; the knight, not
altogether without reason, regarded the burgher as a
cheat. Had the knight possessed a monopoly of honesty,
he might with a better grace have denounced the burgher
as a contemptible seeker after the filthiest of lucre.
Had he had no beam in his own eye, his opinion upon
the mote in the eye of the burgher might have been
a little more worthy of attention. But those among the
burghers who had some of the instincts of thieves were
loth to acknowledge the truth of reproaches from gentlemen who had some of the instincts of robbers.

It must be confessed, however, that the dishonesty
which showed itself every day during the growth of
English commerce might justly have been termed The knight's
shameful by any one but a brigand. The knight complaints
against the
or the lord sent to the markets at Bristol or townsman.
Gloucester for cloth to make the uniforms of his little
army of retainers. The outside appeared to be all that
was needed, but as soon as the piece was unrolled the
greater part of it was found to be made of inferior wool,
to be deficient in breadth, or even to be of different

colours. He bought rings and beads for his mistress, a pommel for his sword, cups with covers to set on his table, and candlesticks to adorn his hall, believing them to be made of gold or of silver ; but that which he thought was gold was gilded copper, and that which he thought was silver was silvered latten or brass. He laid down in his cellar what a merchant had said was a tun of wine, but he was defrauded in the measure, of many a gallon. He stocked his larder with salted herrings, salted salmon, and salted eels to last through the winter ; and when the barrels were opened they were seen to contain a few good fish at the top and a number of broken and inferior fish below. He went abroad as ambassador to a foreign court and had to hear complaint after complaint that his fellow-countrymen had exported wool of less weight and of worse quality than the purchaser had contracted to receive, and that no man knew what he was buying when he bought the worsted of Norfolk. When the envoy returned, it was only to hear that smugglers were every day evading the export duties on wools and woolfells, and the import duties upon such luxuries as cloth of silver or gold, velvet, silk, and damask. The very money due to him he could not safely accept until he had complied with a statute which declared the ill-repute of the current coin by the provision that all payments in gold must be made by weight. It is not surprising that he should then have retired to his country-seat and waited among his flocks, and his herds, and his game, until he could find employment for his lance and his charger.

Thus the sins of individuals were attributed to a class, and townsman remained an epithet of contempt or ridicule long after townsmen had become free and rich. The burgher turned gentleman was destined to be one of the fittest subjects for a comedy as soon as comedy revived, and is even now a subject from which it is easy to raise a laugh! Yet in the days when The social Rome was mistress of the world, town life was pretensions of town and believed to make the gentleman, and the rustic country. was commonly represented as a boor, so stupid that he would watch on the banks of the river in the hope of seeing all the water flow away and of walking across the bed left dry. Never was joke more grimly thrown back against the joker than when robber hordes dismembered the Roman Empire, possessed themselves of the towns, and declared themselves to be the most noble and honourable persons on the earth. In the present day gentlemen do not, as they did in the fifteenth century, think it beneath their dignity to dwell in a city; but even in the present day it is not difficult to trace many social distinctions to the ancient feud between citizen and knight. We have, however, the good fortune to live in an age when men of leisure are no longer brigands, and when, instead of seizing the wares and the coin of traders, they appropriate only the greatest share of that polish which town-life gives, and of which but little falls to the lot of the busy trader who created it.

To one who asks how the successor of the brutal marauder became an accomplished gentleman, there is but one answer. Save in one point—that dignity All mental culture traced of bearing which has been remarked even among to the towns. savages who have been accustomed to command— it is the townsman who has made the gentleman what he is. If the gentleman has a taste for architecture, the architecture is itself the product of town-life. The towns directly or indirectly found the wealth to bring the materials together; the architect himself was commonly a townsman—the offspring of a villein who had run away from his lord.   If the gentleman has a taste for painting, his taste comes from the same source as his taste for architecture.   The very demand, created by the Church, for architects and painters, during the Middle Ages, was but a reminiscence of the old Roman culture, which had to some extent affected the professors of the Christian religion, and which had grown out of the love of the Romans for the life of the town.   In the monasteries, where some monks were taught Latin and writing, the knowledge which was cultivated was but a slender relic of the knowledge once cultivated in the Imperial City. Scarcely an art can be mentioned which has not had its origin in town-life, which has not come to us immediately from towns comparatively modern, or through the Church from the towns of antiquity.   All that trains the eye to appreciate new combinations of form and colour, all that gives the intellect strength, all that gives urbanity to manners, can be traced through one channel or another to the association of men in towns.   The very wealth which constitutes one of the distinctions between the civilised and the barbarous is the growth of the towns, and not least the growth of the towns when it takes the form of an increase in the value of land.   A plentiful harvest is garnered not less by the wits of the townsman than by the hands of the ploughman, the sower, and the reaper ; and the farmer has to confess, year by year, new obligations to the mechanic.

While, therefore, it is not difficult to sympathise with the knight who, looking at the townsman in only one aspect, proclaimed him to be a cheat, it is impossible not to sympathise with the townsman who broke through the barriers of caste, and civilised the knight in spite of him-

self. We have seen how fraud and force went hand in
hand in the early days of commerce, how commerce had
to struggle against the lawless spirit of the brigand, how
dishonesty within the walls was but the counterpart of
robbery without. Yet the very existence of laws and
bye-laws for the suppression of roguery and violence
shows that there were at a very early period some knights
who were not at heart highwaymen and some traders who
were not at heart thieves. In every age there are some
men who are a little better than their fellows ; and their
excellence, when circumstances are favourable, is but the
mediocrity of a later time, the beginning of a series of
steps towards improvement. As Oldcastle was a gentleman who did not despise learning, so we may believe
there were merchants who did not despise honesty.
There is nothing, indeed, of which we may be more
certain ; for, had deception been the one essential feature of
trade, it would have been impossible to create that confidence between man and man upon which trade depends
for its existence. But though we of the nineteenth century are better able to judge what has been done for the
world by towns, and manufactures, and inventions, we
may, perhaps, spare a little compassion for some rude
old knight, of the fifteenth, whose lot it was to hear, time
after time, that the useful son of his hereditary slave had
had the spirit to wander away in search of freedom, and
afterwards that the runaway was growing rich in a chartered town. He believed, no doubt, that the world was
coming to an end, that virtue in every shape was dying
out, and that when a landowner could not retain possession
of his own ' natives ' there was an end to all the laws of
property. Who cannot imagine the spleen with which he
would denounce the changes going on around him, and

the strong epithets he would apply to the fugitives and
to the men who sheltered them ?   He has, indeed, made
the English language bear testimony to his indignation,
for when he most wished to describe the townsman as
capable of everything base and of everything underhand
—as a liar after the fashion of all slaves, as a thief by the
very act which stole a human body from its lawful master,
and converted it into a citizen—he could think of no
more comprehensive term than—villain.

If it be asked how the towns could have gained
power, and how commerce could have grown during
such a lawless period as that in which the Wars
of the Roses were fought out, an obvious
answer presents itself. The Wars of the Roses,
though brought into greater prominence by historians,
could hardly have been more injurious to the country
than those civil wars on a smaller scale, which knight
had for centuries been waging against knight, and baron
against baron.   It matters little whether peace is disturbed in order to raise one king and overthrow another,
or in order to settle the claim to a manor or an honour.
The service and the sentiments of the retainer were the
same in each case.   He fought for the lands of his lord
or of his lord's enemy, because his lord commanded him ;
and, because his lord commanded him, he fought for
Henry of Lancaster or Edward of York.   During these
greater civil wars, however, the disorganisation which followed the Black Death was slowly but continuously
giving aid to the towns.   Many villeins, no doubt, sought
their fortunes within the walls immediately after the pestilence, many after the tumults of which Wat Tyler's
rebellion is the best known example, still more, perhaps,
as single fugitives year by year when opportunity offered

The towns and the fugitive villeins.

and highly coloured accounts were brought to the bondsmen of the freedom which the towns were offering as a gift.

For generations the towns had been, to all the discontented rustics, what the Cave of Adullam and the strongholds of En-gedi were to David and those men in distress who appointed him their captain. It is no wonder that when youthful deserters from the manor and its bondage came, full of energy, to the towns, the towns grew stronger in population and in enterprise ; still less is it a wonder that when the older inhabitants were continually admitting men who began life as outcasts, the outcasts did not become all at once the most honest of mankind. The marvel is that the townsmen were able to hold together as a class, that their very existence was not ended by the mutinous spirit of the new-comers, and that under such disadvantages they succeeded at last in giving us the splendid civilisation which we now enjoy.

Towards this result it may well be believed that the guilds contributed not a little in their day. As a recruit soon learns to be proud of his regiment, a runaway villein soon learned to be proud of his guild, or to have a fellow feeling with his fellow workmen. This sentiment was strengthened by his inherited animosity against the landholder ; and he was, no doubt, soon taught to be as good a citizen as his older neighbour. In very early times, if Glanville is to be trusted, a runaway from the country might hope to be admitted within that highest of all guilds, which appears to be closely connected, if not absolutely identical, with the guild merchant, and was in fact the corporation or governing body of the town. Somewhat later he might, if he failed in this, hope at least to be enrolled in

The Trade-Guilds : position of a guilds-man.

some craft-guild, as a goldsmith, a spurrier, a tailor, a saddler, or a workman in one of the other trades which were growing in number and in importance. As a guilds-man of the latter kind, he would apparently have been in a position somewhat like that of a modern workman who works not for a master but for his own profit, and who might be fairly called a small tradesman. The object of the craft-guild was to protect such workers against the competition of persons who were not members, just as one object of the guild recognised in the earliest charters was to secure collectively as great a monopoly as possible for the particular town in which it was established. It was not founded, like modern trades-unions, to assert the rights of labour against capital, but to keep the market for the goods supplied by its members to those members exclusively. As, however, capital gradually increased, a new phase of society presented itself. The craft-guild became powerless and even meaningless, so far as the mere workman was concerned, and useful only to his employer. The City companies, famous for the banners which they exhibit on the 9th of November, and for their hospitality at other seasons, are the nearest modern equivalents of the ancient craft-guilds. They have, it is almost needless to remark, little in common with those combinations of craftsmen which have become prominent in the nineteenth century.

In the time of Edward IV., one branch of industry at least had advanced so far that a new comer could not

Employers and employed : their early relations. hope to participate at once in the privileges of the guild, and must have been content to work for the wages offered by an employer of labour. Three hundred years earlier, the guilds of weavers in the various towns were composed, it may be believed, of men who worked with their own hands, sold what they had made for their own benefit, and met together on equal terms. But before the Wars of the Roses were ended capital had asserted its power in a manner which must have been more irritating to the unmoneyed workman than its mode of operation in the present day. The present mode of paying wages was that which the workman then regarded as a possible improvement in his condition. Partly, perhaps, because coin was scarce and of uncertain value, and partly because old customs are but slowly changed, the earlier capitalists paid their men half in coin and half in the produce of the men's labour. This practice was considered a great hardship ; and if the employer set on his goods a price higher than they would command in the market, the employed must necessarily have been sufferers. Whenever there is a grievance, it is supposed to be of recent origin by the persons aggrieved, who picture to themselves a happy time when such things were not permitted, and see in the past more than all they hope to gain in the future. So the working men of the fifteenth century believed that their forefathers lived in an age when employment and money were to be had for the asking, just as the villeins believed Domesday Book would show that their ancestors had all been free. Yet it is not difficult to perceive that a guilds-man who had saved a few pounds would be glad to employ some less fortunate weaver, who would be content to work for the privilege of selling a portion of the cloth he helped to make. This is the beginning of the distinction between employer and employed. It is, of course, capable of any extension ; and a guilds-man would naturally assume the power of giving work to a subordinate who was not a member of a guild. Thus the provident guilds-man

was developed into the manufacturer, his poorer or less
thrifty brother into the mere ' hand' ; but the latter passed
through an intermediate stage when he was half working-
man and half retail dealer.   Of his own free will he
elected to be wholly working-man, and there can be little
doubt that when he made the choice he was the best
judge of what would be to his own interest.

The time at which printing was introduced into
England, remarkable for other coincidences, is remarkable also as the time at which classes began

New group-
ing of classes. to be grouped anew, and to show, as a whole,
some indication of the shape which they were to take
in later times.   While villenage was being extinguished,
partly through the action of the villeins themselves,
partly through the preaching of the Lollards, and partly
through the assistance of the towns, there began to be a
new relation established between man and man.   In
previous times, when wealth had been amassed in trade,
it had been amassed by the ship-owner and the money-
lender ; it now began to be amassed by the employer of
labour in new and extended fields of industry.   Not only
the master cloth-weavers but the owners of mines were
becoming sufficiently prosperous to find that there were
difficulties in dealing with large bodies of workmen who
demanded payment in coin alone.   In other branches of
commerce Englishmen began to feel that they need not
be wholly dependent on imports for a supply, and their
native genius began so far to display itself that they even
succeeded in establishing an export trade in guns.

Not the least curious feature in the history of our
towns during this period is the persistence of the guild
social or religious in its old form and in full vitality,
while the craft-guild, though still existing, was losing its

original character and showing signs of old age.   Reference has already been made to the ordinances of various
guilds returned to Parliament in the year 1388. The religious
Later records show not only that the social or or social
guilds; their
religious guilds continued to be an important relation to
earlier and
element in town life, but that they were suffi- later times.
ciently popular to obtain new endowments and a new
constitution as late as the latter half of the fifteenth
century.   Though there was much in their traditions
which was evil, there was much in their practice which
was good.   They are a connecting link between that spirit
of partisanship, with all the attendant lawlessness, which
prevailed before the Conquest and those associations for
mutual aid and charity which are the pride of the nineteenth century.   Of the ill which they did enough has
already been said ; it is but fair to say a little of the
benefits which they conferred, at any rate, in later
times.

A guild which was not instituted for trading purposes
of any kind was connected with a church in some town
or city; and the same church might have more than
one such guild attached to it.   Thus of two guilds, in
the parish church of Houghton, one was described as
the guild, brotherhood, or fraternity of the Holy
Trinity, another as the guild of the Blessed Virgin
Mary.   Some of the members, in almost every case, were,
according to the terms of the ordinances, to be men and
some women.   On stated days the brothers and sisters
assembled at the church to which they belonged.   They
were all clad in the uniform of the guild, and bore lights
as part of the religious ceremony which was to be celebrated.   After prayers they marched to their guild-hall,
where the board was spread, and where ale flowed as

freely as was becoming.   In a large town the streets
were almost continually enlivened by processions of these
numerous guilds, with their music, their lights, their
wreaths of leaves and of flowers.

It was not, however, by what they did to justify our
forefathers in describing the mother country as Merrie
England that the social guilds best deserve to be remembered.   They were to the fourteenth and fifteenth
centuries what the Burial Club, the Friendly Society, and
the Insurance Office are to the nineteenth ; and they
even rendered assistance to a brother or sister in misfortunes which could now be lightened only by an appeal
to private friendship or to public sympathy.   Not only
did they aid to bury the dead, to nurse the sick, to feed
the aged and the orphans, to succour those whom a fire
had left homeless ; they sent a friendly messenger to a
brother or sister cast into prison, they made a purse for
those whom robbers had brought to destitution, they even
found a portion for guild-maidens whose fathers had not
sufficient wealth.   In spite of all their disbursements on
behalf of their own members, their connexion with the
Church caused them, like the Church itself, to grow rich ;
and out of their endowments they sometimes assisted a
casual wayfarer or pilgrim, relieved some of the poor of
the town in which they were established, and even built
alms-houses for the permanent support of the impotent.
That their social meetings led to some irregularities is by
no means improbable, if the character of the age is borne
in mind ; and some unfriendly reports of free living may
have caused at last the dissolution of the religious guilds
at the same time as the dissolution of the monasteries.
It would be idle to regret that they perished when their
time had come, for they would have been ill-suited to

towns in which the population is numbered by millions, and they would have perpetuated that narrowness of mind which refused charity to all but the orthodox, and which prompted a brother who was a juryman to swear hard in favour of a brother who was a criminal. But the brighter side of these associations reflects not a little light upon the good work which the towns were doing, and enables us to discern how the liberality of modern times has grown out of the restricted sympathies of the past, as they in turn grew out of the still more slender sympathies which had preceded them.

We have now seen what were the chief movements which, during a century and a half after the Black Death, were preparing the future of England. We *Recapitula-* have seen the bondsmen chafing under their *tion : Pro-gress made in* bondage and ready to make common cause with *the 15th century.* any one—gentleman or outcast, Royal Duke or Lollard preacher—who would aid them to gain their freedom. We have seen heresy burnt out for a time at the stake, only, like the Phœnix, to rise again from its own ashes. We have seen Wycliffe giving the Scriptures to the people in the vulgar tongue, and accused by the opposers of progress of throwing pearls before swine. We have seen printing come to the aid of a growing thirst for knowledge. We have seen the towns not only increasing in wealth and strength, but able to extend a helping hand to the villeins, to threaten the extinction of villenage, and to transfer labour not only from place to place, but from the position of a lord's due to that of the labourer's property with a market-value of its own.

In all this we see the infancy of modern society, but the obstructions to its growth without the town gates had been little if at all diminished since the days

of the Black Death. The study of the Roman Civil
Law, which had expanded the views of lawyers in
the thirteenth century, and the earlier part of

Obstructions
to progress :
evasions of
the feudal
Mortmain law
by the clergy.

the fourteenth, was afterwards made to serve
the party spirit of a class. The clergy—and
especially the monastic houses—always anxious
to extend their possessions, had always shown much ingenuity in evading the law.   It was necessary for them to
obtain the king's licence before they could legally acquire and hold lands in mortmain.   But by various
subterfuges they continued to increase their wealth and
to get the better alike of the common law and of various
statutes made to assist it.   Towards the end of the reign
of Edward III., and perhaps earlier, it became an ordinary
practice to grant land in such a manner that the fee was
conveyed nominally to certain persons, who held only for
the benefit of a religious house.   By this device the
religious house escaped all penalties, and yet took all
the profits of the land conveyed.   A statute was passed
in the reign of Richard II. which must at least have
checked, if it did not put an end to, the practice, by declaring
conveyances of land to the use of religious corporations as
much subject to the law of mortmain as a direct conveyance of land to religious corporations themselves.   But
the introduction of uses, fraudulent as it was in intent, had
a permanent effect upon English law.

It is not a little remarkable that the incongruous
union of Roman with feudal doctrines, designed to further
the wishes of individuals in opposition to the

Incongruous
union of the
Roman Law
with the
feudal land-
laws.

commands of king and parliament, received in
the end a legal sanction, and produced an offspring in which the modern conveyancer has
the most implicit trust.   During the Wars of the Roses

the conveyance to uses, like the entail, was commonly employed to secure lands against forfeiture for treason. At the time, it served the purpose for which it was intended, so far as any legal subtlety could serve that purpose in an age when might was stronger than right. But by a curious retribution the very scheme which was devised to increase the wealth of the Church, and used to preserve the power of the barons, became in later days the instrument which rendered the transfer of land comparatively easy, and aided to change the relative position of classes. It has been shown how commerce was almost of necessity polluted by fraud in its early existence in England ; fraud, too, was the almost inevitable accompaniment of the purchase and sale of land, when land in England began to be bought and sold with more freedom than the old feudal system had permitted. The difficulties which lawyers of our own time perceive in any attempt to pass land more easily from hand to hand are difficulties which can be traced back to the first applicacation of uses. The principles to which it has given rise have been simplified as far as simplification seems possible ; and our alternative is to accept a cumbrous machinery, which enables purchases and settlements to be made with tolerable security, or to sweep away every vestige of antiquity, and to open between the past and the future a great gulf, which might, perhaps, cause a landholder to tremble for the fate of his grandchildren. This is the penalty we pay for the disingenuous arts by which our forefathers strove to make themselves stronger than the laws of England.

In other respects the mere forms of the law underwent little change during this period, and that little was without immediate effect upon the manners of the people.

The names of criminal proceedings had long been very nearly what they are now; there had been nominally

Absence of improvement in legal pro- cedure: the jurors still witnesses; perjuries.
the same Courts, the same Judges, the same Justices of the Peace, the same Trial by Jury. Yet all was as different from the present ad- ministration of justice as that is from the rude legal devices of any half-civilised people. In civil cases, indeed, the trial was more like that of modern times than the criminal ; a jury was empanelled, documents were produced, and witnesses were examined in court. But even in civil causes the jurors were chosen from the neighbourhood in which the suit arose, and were expected to give a verdict not simply upon the evidence laid before them, but also upon their own knowledge of the facts. If they pronounced in favour of the weaker party, they always had before them the danger of an attaint—which was equivalent to a prosecution for perjury. When they were convicted, their goods were seized, their meadows were ploughed up, their woods were felled, their houses were demolished, and they were themselves committed to gaol, and declared to be ever after infamous and incapable of taking an oath in a Court of Record. A wholesome warning to perjurers, no doubt, and one which a Chief Justice of England who lived in the reign of Henry VI. considered sufficient to check the crime of perjury! But in Fortescue's ' Praises of the Laws of England,' it is easier to detect the hand of the panegyrist and the courtier than to discover the true condition of the country. A statute of that very reign, like innu- merable preceding and succeeding documents, bears tes- timony to the almost incurable habit of forswearing themselves, which jurors and compurgators had con- tracted in the long course of centuries. This could never

be amended until, on the one hand, partisanship lost some of its power through the weakening of the barons, and, on the other hand, a clear distinction was drawn between jurors with unbiassed minds and witnesses who laid the facts before them.

In criminal trials it does not appear that during Fortescue's term of office the law had advanced so far as to permit the examination of witnesses in court. The indictment, indeed, was a record of the finding of the Grand Jury, themselves at once the witnesses and the accusers. This, or the depositions of approvers extorted in gaol by threats or by torture, or the criminal's own confession on the rack, or in answer to a judge's examination, must have been the evidence upon which men were hanged and women were burnt.

It has, indeed, been denied that the use of torture was known to the English law. That it was known, however, is certain, though it was not legally permitted, except by licence from the King or Council. In one form, too, it could be applied by order of a judge, not indeed to extract evidence, but to make a mute prisoner plead, or to punish him for not pleading. Before the infliction of this ' peine forte et dure,' the accused was warned three times of the penalty which would attend obstinate silence, and allowed a few hours for consideration. If the prisoner, whether man or woman, still persisted, there was pronounced the Judgment of Penance : —That you be taken back to the prison whence you came, to a low dungeon into which no light can enter ; that you be laid on your back on the bare floor, with a cloth round your loins, but elsewhere naked ; that there be set upon your body a weight of iron as great as you can bear—and greater ; that you have no sustenance,

Treatment of the accused: the ' peine forte et dure.'

save, on the first day, three morsels of the coarsest bread, on the second day three draughts of stagnant water from the pool nearest to the prison door, on the third day again three morsels of bread as before, and such bread and such water alternately from day to day until you die.

A person accused of felony, however innocent, had no protection except the right of challenging jurors, no means of preserving the legal descent of his lands to his heir, when he feared a just or unjust conviction, except silence and the resolution to endure the press—for in felonies, short of Treason, standing mute was not equivalent to a conviction. No one could be certain that he would not some day be at the mercy of any scoundrel whom malice or the duress of prison incited to mention his name—unless he happened to possess the good-will of his neighbours ; and the good-will of neighbours was, in those days, not to be purchased for so small a price as mere innocence. Chief Justice Fortescue, who praises in one work the laws of England as the best that had ever been known, praises, in another, the English character for qualities which will hardly command admiration in modern times. He preferred theft with violence to theft without ; and he has bequeathed his sentiments to posterity in a few words which tell more of the tone of society than many a bulky volume. More men, he says, were hanged in England in one year for robbery or manslaughter than in France in seven, because the English had better hearts ; the Scotchmen, also did not dare to rob, but only committed larcenies.

These words bring before us the greatest impediment to the towns in their struggle against that spirit of lawlessness which had been introduced after the fall

Continued lawlessness : remarkable sentiment of Chief Justice Fortescue.

of the Roman Empire, which Englishmen of the rural districts were prone to regard as an inherited virtue, and with which the country infected, to a less extent, even the towns themselves. Those Better Hearts, for which the Chief Justice of England had a tender regard, were the great support of tra- ditional institutions, or, to use more accurate language, of traditional disorder. But as excellence of any kind is deserving of respect, and as the days of chivalry were now drawing to a close, there may be some advantage in glancing at the deeds of knighthood without the walls, as well as at the humbler, but more fruitful efforts of the burghers within. There is no doubt that the knights of those days had great hearts in the old sense of the term, and it would be unjust to depreciate the value of physical courage in moments of national danger. Fortunately, the industry and care of a great lawyer have secured to us a view of chivalry in its best aspect; and though regret can hardly be caused by the extinction of those knightly instincts which prompted men to incessant deeds of arms, unmixed blame can hardly be awarded to men who strove to render victory an art and the concealment of pain a science.

The 'Great Hearts' of the English: Chivalry in its best aspect.

A treatise which was copied for the use of Sir Matthew Hale tells us how the best among those better hearts which were the glory of old England prepared themselves for the Trial by Battle in cases of Treason. It has thus a direct bearing upon the History of Crime, and illustrates incidentally the customs and the sentiments of the period. It was com- piled early in the reign of Henry VI. by John Hill, who describes himself as Armourer and Sergeant in the Office of Armoury with King Henry IV. and King Henry V.

The 'Battle of Treason' described by a Royal Ar- mourer.

' The first honour in arms,' he says, ' is that a gentleman
fight and win the field, either as appellant or as defendant,
in his Sovereign Lord's quarrel, in a battle of treason
sworn within lists, before the Sovereign Lord himself.'

As in a court of law, the appellant had a counsel who
was assigned to him before the Constable and the Marshal,
and who was bound to teach him ' all manner of fightings
and subtleties of arms that belong to a battle sworn.'
Not the least responsible duty of this counsel was to take
care that the appellant was properly clad and armed.
The minute details which the armourer gives are of value
only to the antiquary ; but the object which was to be
kept in view in all the preparations is of far higher interest.   The perfection of the armour and arms was,
of course, a subject of anxious forethought ; but it was
considered even less important to protect the champion
and give him the best weapons of offence than to conceal
the wounds he might receive from his adversary.   To
this intent he was provided with shoes made of red
leather, and with red hose to draw over his leg-harness
or greaves ' because his adversary shall not lightly espy
his blood, for in all other colours blood will lightly be
seen.'   Such deliberate valour as is indicated in these
precautions deserves, beyond doubt, to be called noble ;
and it is because knights were as brave and as calm in
battle as in their own chambers that their contemporaries
and the men who lived after them acquired the habit of
summing up all the virtues in the one word—Chivalry.

It was also a part of the counsel's duty to engage
three priests, each of whom was to sing a mass on the
day of battle—one the Mass of the Trinity, one the Mass
of the Holy Ghost, and one the Mass of Our Lady, or
of any saint or saints to whom the knight had sworn

devotion. Throughout the night before the encounter a light was kept burning in the champion's room and his counsel watched him and observed how he slept. In the morning he went to church. His harness was laid out at the north end of the altar and covered with a cloth ; the Gospel was read over it, the three masses were sung, and at the end of the third a priest gave a blessing. He then repaired to the field fully armed and ready for the conflict ; he sent his counsel to the King with a request that he might have free entry when he came to the barriers, and that a chair or tent might be set up for his use. The request was, of course, granted, and he approached with his confessor, counsel, armourer, and servants. His counsel bore before him a long sword, a short sword, and a dagger. At the barrier he was met by the Constable and Marshal, who said, ' What art thou ? ' He told his name and the cause of his coming, and was then admitted with his followers.

As he entered ' he blessed himself soberly, and so twice,' ere he approached his Sovereign Lord. And twice he and his counsel did their obeisance before they came to the steps of the king's seat. They knelt, and, as they rose again, again made obeisance. They then went back to the tent, but, before entering it, turned round once more, and once more made obeisance to the king.

When the defendant appeared on the field the appellant again left his tent, and stood fully armed, ' taking heed of his adversary's coming in, and of his countenance, that he might take comfort of it.' The weapons of both parties were then brought before the King and examined in his presence by the Constable and Marshal. If there was no fault in the arms the appellant was immediately afterwards summoned to the First Oath.

When the appellant had sworn to the truth of his accusation before the king, he returned, with the same formalities as before, to his tent. His counsel, who had carefully noted the terms of his oath, remained in the king's presence to hear what was sworn by the defendant. Unless the defendant swore that 'every word and every syllable of every word' sworn by the appellant was false, the appellant's counsel might ask judgment without further ceremony. But if the defendant swore as required, the counsel returned again to the appellant's chair to await the summons for taking the Second Oath. The Second Oath was followed by the Third Oath, and if the appellant persisted in making his accusation every time in the same terms, and the defendant every time denied it without equivocation, evasion, or cavil, the tents were removed and the lists prepared for the actual battle. Upon this the appellant's counsel asked for a place within the bar on the king's right hand. ' The cause is this— that such pity may be given to the king, of God, that none of them shall die that day.' The counsel remained in the place assigned till the king had given his judgment. But should the king not see fit to stay the trial, the order was given to cry ' Laissez Aller,' and the champions fought to the death.

There is a ground on which, perhaps, this mode of trial might be justified ; it was the most merciful to the

Single combat and the spirit of private war.

person accused of treason, as there was no other hope for one whom a dominant party had resolved to destroy. Yet what must we think of an age in which it was common for knight to be matched against knight in a deadly conflict—not as gladiator was matched against gladiator in the Roman arena, for a show, but with a solemn appeal to religion, and with a mockery of the forms of law ? It was only the persistence of the petty spirit of private war which could have kept such an institution in existence in a country in which there was already a growing love of commerce and even of letters.

One purpose, indeed, it might have been made to serve, and might be made to serve even now, could the supreme commanders of mighty armies be per- suaded to disband their hosts, and to stake their hopes of conquest upon the issue of a single combat—emperor with emperor, king with king. Unfortunately, however, the experiment was tried without success in the days of chivalry—when, in spite of oaths and appeals to God, monarchs had a latent though more operative faith in favourable opportunities and in strong battalions. Richard II., in the ardour of youth, sent a challenge to the king of France to meet him in single combat, or in a combat in which only the two kings and the three uncles of each should take part, or in a battle to be fought with the whole forces of the two kingdoms on a day and at a place appointed beforehand. By the issue he wished the war begun in the reign of Edward III. to be decided, and all matters in dispute to be settled. The reason he gave is certainly much to his credit, but was in direct opposition to the martial spirit of his age, and was little likely to elevate him in the estimation of his contemporaries. He wished, he said, to stay the effusion of Christian blood, the desolation of the land, the deflowering of virgins, the violation of married women, and all those sufferings of innocent persons which were too numerous and too horrible to be described by the pen or even put into language. His captains, no doubt, laughed at this extraordinary out-

Single combat might have been useful in national disputes: challenge of Richard II. to the French king.

burst of humanity, and lost all respect for a sovereign who shuddered at the screams of a woman or a few drops of Frenchman's blood. Had Richard's challenge been accepted, and his opinions too, the battle of Azincour would never have been fought, and there would have been less glory for Englishmen. But the soil of France would not have been stained with English blood, the Maid of Orleans would not have been burnt at Rouen, and the English and French nations might in later times have been friends instead of enemies. The whole struggle of the English kings to gain possession of the French throne was neither better nor worse than the struggles of a feudal lord to gain possession of his neighbour's manor. The common people in both countries could only lose by war. The king of England might have succeeded in making Paris his capital and England itself a mere province, and thus might have gratified an utterly selfish ambition. For this object men had to die and women to weep, and when at length the conflict ceased, and the balance was struck, it appeared that England was the richer only in the possession of some rolls of parchment in which dead monarchs were proudly styled Kings of England and of France.

The generous sentiment which prompted Richard II. to spare human blood and suffering in war is, perhaps, to be detected in one of the earlier statutes of his reign, by which an attempt was made to stay the ancient and knightly practice of forcible entry. Richard, indeed, was only a boy when the Act was passed, but he was a boy who had shown self-reliance at the time of Wat Tyler's rebellion, and who differed from the nobles about him in being less resolutely brutal. The townsmen, it is possible, may have

Private war, and forcible entry: Statute against forcible entry.

begun to discern that private war, as well as war with foreign nations, was directly opposed to their interests, and the burgesses in parliament may have availed themselves of the opportunity presented by Richard's minority to place upon record a protest against the lawlessness of the kingdom. There can, however, be little doubt that the young king's sympathies were with them, and that any influence he might have possessed with his advisers was exerted in favour of order and against the prevailing love of bloodshed.

The Statute against Forcible Entries had for many generations little more effect than Richard's protest against the slaughter of subjects and the burn- The Statute ing of homes for the purpose of determining private juris- the territory over which a king should rule, or diction. the principles according to which a crown should descend. It will be shown in another volume that the old habit long seemed ineradicable, and was not sensibly checked until the powerful house of Tudor put in force a much abused but useful machinery to root the evil out. Richard II. was quite powerless against the barons ; and ten years after the passing of the Act against forcible entry he was persuaded or compelled to make a grant, such as might have been made in the days of Stephen or of Edward the Confessor. He gave to John Devereux, knight, the castle and manor of Leonhale, in Herefordshire, with all its liberties and franchises, among which he mentioned expressly the trial, judgment, and punishment, alike of Englishmen and Welshmen, for theft, robbery, murder, or any other crime perpetrated on the manor ; and he provided that disuse on the part of Devereux's predecessor should be no bar to the exercise by him of this private jurisdiction. It is true that the castle was on the Welsh Marches, which, with the Marches towards Scotland, were the most disturbed, and therefore the most lawless parts of the kingdom. But to create or to strengthen any private jurisdiction at all was to throw back indefinitely the prospect of a firm and settled government, which should be peaceably acknowledged throughout the realm. A sanction given to a baron or knight, in the independent exercise of an authority which, in a well-ordered government, belongs to the State or to its head, was an encouragement to the assertion of independence in every other form—to forcible entry, to private war, and even to general civil war itself.

The chief good effected by the Statute against forcible entry, and of the statutes against engaging retainers and giving them liveries enacted in the same reign, was in the way of suggestion to later sovereigns and later parliaments. In subsequent reigns attempts, long destined to be vain, were made at intervals to enforce the provisions of these Acts, and even to assimilate the course of procedure within liberties enjoying private jurisdiction to that of the realm at large. These early efforts, prompted in part by a desire to extend the royal authority, in part by the desire of the townsmen for a more settled government, were useful, if for no other purpose, at least to inform posterity what was the actual condition of the country. Thus Henry VI. and his Council in Parliament ordain, in accordance with the terms of a petition, that no lord shall knowingly receive, cherish, hold in household, or maintain brigands, robbers, oppressors of the people, manslayers, felons, outlaws, or ravishers of women. They forbid the giving of liveries or tokens, the bribing

Statutes against retainers and liveries also ineffectual.

of judges, and maintenance in every form, and they require all who have the privilege of excluding the king's officers from any liberties to summon suspected persons, and exact an oath for the observance of these provisions. The most important of the privileged districts were the Counties Palatine. But the very existence of the Counties Palatine and of similar little kingdoms within the kingdom of England was opposed to the whole spirit of the ordinance. The holders of these liberties acted as though they were bound to enforce obedience from their inferiors, but not to give obedience themselves. They had kingly powers, and thought themselves entitled to act as kings. Thus, in spite of statutes, ordinances, and commissions, we find the Bishop of Durham becoming party to a deed by which one Sir William Eure agrees to be his retainer against all men in peace and in war, upon condition of receiving twenty pounds a year; and the deed appears without concealment upon the rolls of the Bishop's Chancery.

The evils which can be traced back to the days when barbarous tribes and petty chieftains settled on the ruins of Roman civilisation were, it seems, but little The force of ancient cus- abated after the lapse of a thousand years. tom and the force of ma- They were evils which had existed before terial pro- gress evenly Rome became great, and which are character- balanced. istic of uncivilised or half-civilised peoples. They had disappeared, or nearly disappeared, with the growth of wealth and the increase of culture in the Roman towns; and like causes were destined once again to produce like effects, though the time was not yet come. During the Wars of the Roses, and immediately afterwards, two forces were almost evenly balanced—the force of ancient custom, which was in fact lawlessness, in the rural dis-

tricts, and the force of material progress, which was preparing the establishment of order, in the towns.   A
remarkable form in which the opposition of these two
forces to each other displayed itself was the charge of
' Scandalum Magnatum.'

As early as the reign of Edward I., when the towns
had just succeeded in obtaining their charters, a statute

Charges of 'Scandalum Magnatum' associated with the growth of a new class.

was passed which made it a grave offence to
devise or tell any false news of prelates, dukes,
earls, barons, or nobles of the realm.   Others,
too, were enumerated as being within the meaning of the act—the Chancellor, the Justices of either
Bench, and all the great officers of state; but they were
named after the territorial magnates, and the majesty of
the law was set beneath the dignity of rank.   The reasons
both for the passing of the statute and for the terms in
which it was passed are easily enough to be traced in the
manners of the times.   When the great landholder arro-
gated to himself the privileges of a little king, he naturally
regarded evil speech against his kingship as a crime
closely akin to Treason, and very different from evil
speech directed by one petty trader against another.
'Scandalum Magnatum,' however, could hardly be committed until there had grown up a somewhat powerful
class, distinct from that of the magnate, his retainers, and
villeins.   The evil which he saw in the rise of this new
class was far less formidable under Edward I. than it had
become under Richard II., when, however, the land-
holders had no difficulty in re-enacting the ancient statute
and adding more stringent provisions.

It is about the time when we may believe the disorganisation following the Black Death and the insurrection
of the villeins had begun to strengthen, relatively at least,

the population of the towns that the offence of slandering
great personages comes into notice, not only in the statute-
book, but through definite accusations. One Case of Sibille and the Earl
Walter Sibille, a citizen of London, is accused in of Oxford.
Parliament of having uttered slanderous words concerning Robert Vere, Earl of Oxford. The chief point in
the alleged slander was that Sibille had attributed to the
Earl a practice which was notoriously common among all
the great landholders—the practice of maintenance, or in
other words, of supporting with his influence and wealth,
both in law courts and out of them, those retainers who
had sworn to serve him, right or wrong, in peace or in war,
against all other men. Sibille was condemned to pay
five hundred marks, and was committed to prison until
payment should be made. There he probably remained
during the remainder of his life, unless he was a man of
extraordinary wealth.

A case which shows still more clearly how deadly a
weapon the charge of 'Scandalum Magnatum' could be
made in the hands of a powerful noble is that Case of Cavendish and Michael de la Pole, the Chancellor.
of John Cavendish, a fishmonger of London.
He accused in Parliament Michael de la Pole,
then Chancellor, of partiality and bribery.
After the charge and the answer had been heard, the
matter was referred to the King's Justices, who assumed
that the Chancellor was innocent, committed his accuser to
prison, and imposed a fine of a thousand marks for the
slander. Pole happened, at that time, to be stronger than
the party opposed to him, and to have the power of crushing an adversary. But only three years later he was again
accused of corruption, and of that kind of corruption
alleged against him by Cavendish—of letting records be
rased, and judgments sold with impunity, and of procuring

pardon for murderers and traitors in order to fill his own coffers. Whether the Chancellor was innocent or guilty it is now impossible to ascertain ; but it is quite certain that a swift retribution was in store for all who ventured, even in the ordinary course of law, to accuse any man of rank of having done wrong, unless the accuser was supported by a stronger party than the accused.

In some instances there can be little doubt that a scandalous and unfounded charge was the instrument

Fabrication of false charges : case of Ferriers and the Beggar. employed to destroy an enemy, and that the persons who fabricated it were most justly punished. A Sir Ralph, or Lord, Ferriers was accused of having entered into treasonable correspondence with the French, of having suggested an invasion of England, and of having named a favourable day for an advance upon London. The evidence against him was a packet of letters written apparently by him, and with his seal attached, and addressed to the French Admiral and other French nobles. He declared in Parliament that he was innocent, and requested that he might have counsel to defend him. This, as in cases of far later date, was refused, and he was remanded to prison. His friends, however, made strenuous exertions to save him, and, upon a second hearing, some facts were brought to light which certainly ought to have been known and examined before he was placed under restraint. The letters had been found by a beggar in a field in the suburbs of London : so at least the beggar had told the Lord Mayor. But a mere glance at them was sufficient to expose a most clumsy imposture. There were in the same packet letters purporting to be written by Ferriers to Frenchmen, and letters purporting to be written by Frenchmen to Ferriers, and all written in the same hand.

The seal too, though in other respects well imitated, was found to be of a different size from that used by Ferriers; and it was held to be beyond a doubt that some of his enemies had attempted to ruin him by conspiracy and forgery. He was acquitted, and the beggar was sent to prison under suspicion.

In his anxiety to prove his innocence, Ferriers used an argument which is an unpleasant commentary upon knightly deeds and knightly sentiments. He had had command of the English garrison at Calais; and he alleged that, had he wished to play the traitor, he might again and again have received a heavy bribe from the French to deliver up the place to them, just as other English commanders had delivered up other fortresses for money. This charge of treason in its most degrading form—the treason which would betray national interests to a foreign enemy for gain —was rife throughout the period included in the present chapter. At the beginning of the reign of Richard II., the Rolls of Parliament teem with accusations against officers who had, as alleged, accepted French gold for the surrender of strongholds in the hands of English troops. Now a Weston, now a Cressingham, now an Elingham, a Trivett, a Ferriers, and a Farndon in the same accusation, have their names inscribed on the records of the National Assembly as traitors who have sold their own and the national honour for a paltry fee from a hostile commander. We cannot know with certainty whether these men were guilty or not. But we can at least perceive that to make terms, rather than fight to the death or starve, suggested, not without good reason, a suspicion of foul play in an age when true knights donned red

[margin note: Charges against English knights of surrendering fortresses for bribes.]

buskins over their armour, so that none might know how much blood was flowing from their wounds.

Whether Englishmen were betrayed or not, it was an evil sign for England that they were continually crying The cry of 'We are betrayed!' 'We are betrayed!' Either there was a party in Parliament whose trade it was to make these foul accusations, regardless of truth, or the men who were accused were guilty of the offence. Sometimes it happens that the sum received is mentioned in the record—as, for instance, the sum of twenty thousand francs in the joint charge against Elingham and his associates. Sometimes, too, a very feeble answer was made by the accused, who ended by submitting themselves to the King's mercy. And if, in some cases, there is reason to suspect that an unfortunate soldier was ruined by the personal animosity of an adversary, the suspicion is little creditable to our forefathers, and cannot wholly remove a foul blot from our national archives.

These charges disappear for a time, while the English arms are successful in France, but are renewed Charges of corruption against William de la Pole. as soon as misfortune again lends them some sort of colour. William de la Pole, Duke of Suffolk, was accused of an intrigue to establish his own son on the throne of England, through a royal marriage and the aid of the French king. He had lent his influence, it was said, in favour of releasing the Duke of Orleans, who had been taken prisoner at the battle of Azincour, in order that the French might the more easily recover their lost provinces from the English, and might thus be disposed to favour his pretensions. He had, it was said, disclosed the king's counsel to the Bastard of Orleans and others of the French nation, and informed them of the strength of the English ordnance and ammunition in France. He had, it was said, delayed the shipping of English arms for use against the French, and had actually delivered up a portion of the English conquests in France without any authority.

Could it be said that regularity was known in trials for treason as early as the reign of Henry VI., the manner of dealing with the charge against Suffolk would deserve to be called extremely irregular. The king alone gave a decision, and expressed *His fate.* an opinion not indeed that Suffolk was innocent but that the grave charges against him had not been proven. On the other hand, the king pronounced that the Earl had been guilty of such trivial offences as were commonly imputed to men who had had any opportunity of committing them—of inciting sheriffs to tamper with writs for the hindrance of justice, of procuring the king's pardon for the sheriffs who had been guilty of maintaining wrong doers, of staying processes of outlawry—in fact of abusing power in every way short of treason. Henry's sentence upon him for these venial errors of judgment was banishment for five years. His enemies, however, according to the custom of the time, resolved that their work should not be half done. It was not very difficult to find a sea-captain, hardened by many years of piratical adventure, who would name his price for committing a murder. Soon after the ship, which was to carry Suffolk into exile, had sailed from Dover, it was boarded by some ruffians who were on the watch for him. His head was struck off and his body thrown into the sea.

In reading of those crimes which were the most conspicuous part of public life, it would be difficult to fix upon any one point in which the non-trading classes were better in the reign of Richard III. than they had been in the reign of Edward II. The events which occur under Edward II., occur with little variation, except in the names of the actors, under Richard II. ; they repeat themselves again and again during the Wars of the Roses, and have changed their form but little when Edward V. and his

brother are murdered in the Tower. That tenacity of purpose (unrestrained by any consideration of right or wrong) which marks the age of chivalry, displays itself, with a sickening sameness, in deeds of blood which no lord or knight hesitated to do when he wished to preserve what he had gained or take to himself what belonged to another. In those days men supped, indeed, full of horrors; and we who live in a happier age cannot know our own good fortune, except by contemplating, for a little while at least, that bygone time in its true aspect. We cannot realise to ourselves the persistence of the same spirit through many generations, except by abandoning the antiquated method of the annalist who made a catalogue of facts for each year, and omitted to show the likeness of one year to another.

One of the many atrocious crimes committed in the reign of Richard II. was the murder of the Duke of Gloucester. It was such a deed as would be a private execution, without any preceding trial, of a Liberal or Conservative leader by opposing Conservative or Liberal ministers, with the alleged cognisance of the sovereign—the sovereign being the nephew of the victim. The Duke was arrested and shipped off to Calais. An accusation of treason was then prepared against him and other nobles. But when a warrant was sent to the Earl Marshal, then Governor of Calais, to bring him to England for trial, the answer returned was that he had already died of apoplexy. His real fate was probably told by one John Hall, a servant of the Duke of Norfolk, in subsequent proceedings in Parliament. Hall confessed that he met at Calais three of Norfolk's esquires, and some members of Norfolk's household, a valet or yeoman of the chamber to the Duke of Albemarle, and William Searle, a valet or yeoman of the chamber to King Richard. They were acting under Norfolk's orders, and, with a strange appeal to religion, they were all 'sworn upon the Body of Christ, before a certain chaplain of St. George in the Church of Our Lady of Calais, that they would not disclose' the murder which they were about to perpetrate.

After this ceremony they went towards a house called The Prince's Inn, and the Duke of Norfolk with them. Norfolk bade them enter, and left them to their task. Soon afterwards Gloucester was brought to the house. When he saw the valets of the king and of Albemarle, he said, with deliberate irony, 'Now I see I shall do well.' He was then conducted to a chamber, where he was told it was the king's will that he should die. He answered, 'If it so be, welcome Death.' The two valets requested him to see a chaplain and make his last confession. To this he assented, and the preparations for the solemn murder were complete.

Gloucester was then made to lie down, a feather-bed was thrown over him, and, while some of the other murderers held its sides, the two valets lay upon the top, throwing their weight upon the Duke's mouth. The pious ruffians who took no active part in the crime fell on their knees around the bed, and wept, and prayed for Gloucester's soul, while Hall, the informer, kept the door.

Hall gained nothing by betraying his accomplices.

It seemed to the Lords, as it is expressed on the Roll of Parliament, that he had deserved as grievous a death as could be adjudged to him, 'because the Duke of Gloucester was so exalted a personage.' The sentence passed upon him was like the sentence in cases of treason—that he should be drawn from Tower Hill to Tyburn gallows, and disembowelled; that his bowels should be burned before him; that his body should be hanged, and afterwards beheaded and quartered; that his head should be sent to Calais, where the deed was done, and there set up; and that his quarters should be at the king's pleasure. 'And execution was done the same day.'

It was an event so thoroughly in accordance with the lack of justice commonly shown in high places as *Attainder after death.* hardly to deserve notice, that Gloucester was declared guilty of treason after his death. His case differs from many others not because he was condemned unheard, but because he was made a traitor by the retraction of a previous pardon. The power, now and long afterwards exercised by Parliament, of proceeding by Bill of Attainder, was simply a power of effecting that which could not, with certainty, be effected by the ordinary legal processes.

By no mere coincidence it happened that another Duke of Gloucester, in the reign of Henry VI., half a *Similar fate of another Duke of Gloucester.* century later, was also suddenly accused of treason, was also found dead in a bed, and was also generally believed to have been murdered, like many another noble, and like the two kings, Edward II., and Richard II. Murder was not then, as it is now, considered a crime of terrible heinousness: it was simply one of the most ordinary means of gaining any important end.

We have seen how Richard II., when little more than a boy, showed some generous instincts, without any lack of courage. The times in which he lived transformed him, before he reached his prime, into a man without the resolute will of less scrupulous man-slayers, and without the consistent virtue which commands the respect of posterity. He could not reign except by the aid of crime ; and the crimes which were as nothing to his ministers made him ashamed. He ended by being more contemptible than those who had begun by being more criminal. Like Edward II., he was accused of misdeeds which, when committed by a subject, are treason ; and, like Edward II., and many subjects who have been called traitors, he was removed from public gaze in a manner which leaves little doubt that he was murdered.

Effect of surrounding circumstances upon the character : Richard II. an illustration.

It is difficult to feel sympathy for any of the actors in these mediæval tragedies. If it were possible to regard the Richard who was dethroned as the Richard who faced the mob of insurgent villeins in London, and wished to fight the French king single-handed, in order to spare the blood of his subjects, there would be few characters in history more deserving of compassion. But the Richard who prompted the murder of his uncle, or consented to it, the Richard who was accused of causing the Rolls of Parliament and other records of the realm to be destroyed, erased, blotted, and re-written, is quite another man. The Richard who said, ' I do confess that I am utterly insufficient and useless for the government of the kingdom, and that, for my notorious misrule, I deserve to be deposed,' is no longer to be recognised as the self-reliant youth who would have given his own life for the good of his people. Nor was this the lowest

depth to which he fell. When he abandoned his royal
estate, he was reduced to such abject servility that he
said he trusted his cousin Henry, who was to succeed
him, would be a good lord to him. From one who had
never done an evil deed, and who was abdicating of his
own free will, such words might have had some grace
and dignity ; but it is hard to conceive any expressions
more unkingly and more unmanly from a king who had
enervated himself by debauchery, and attempted to save
his throne by homicide.

Richard II., when he had abandoned his royal rank,
disappeared. The uniform process by which the secret

Effects of secret crimes: personators of murdered kings. crimes of this period brought forth a brood of
open misdoers is well worthy of remark. That
which happened after the murder of Edward II.
happened in a very similar form after the murder of
Richard II., and again after the murder of Edward V.
and his brother. In our own time morbid brooding over
a deed of bloodshed frequently impels the innocent to
self-accusation. In the fourteenth and fifteenth centuries
the effect of such a deed, when a whisper of it went
abroad, was to suggest some practical means of turning
it to profit. False personation, or a false report that the
king still lived, followed the death or disappearance of
each of the three murdered sovereigns. We have already seen how it followed the death of Edward II. ;
we have yet to see how it followed the death of Edward
V. ; and. in the meantime, this is the most appropriate
place to show that it followed the disappearance of
Richard II.

A general belief seems to have spread through almost
all parts of the kingdom, but especially through Cheshire,
Cumberland, and Westmoreland, that Richard had made

his escape into Scotland, and was there living in retirement. This opinion was of course most dangerous to the new occupant of the throne, and warrants were issued for the arrest of all who had spread it. When Henry IV. was in the fifth year of his reign, he granted a general pardon to all offenders, except William Searle, Richard's valet (who, after having been concerned in the murder of Gloucester, had pretended to carry letters from his dead master), and Thomas Warde, of Trumpington, who had taken the name of the dead king. Warde was the natural successor of the imaginary Edward II., who caused an earl of Kent to fall, the natural predecessor of Lambert Simnel and Perkin Warbeck. Crimes which are alike in their character, are alike in their consequences.

The period included in the present chapter begins at a time when the murder of Edward II. was still within the recollection of men in the prime of life ; it ends Richard III. with the death of a man who caused his two 'chivalry.' and nephews to be killed, and who did not scruple to call his mother a harlot in order that he might himself be called a king. But such was the age of chivalry—so far at least as the ' chivalers ' were concerned—and all the minor events of life were consistent with the great deeds of usurpers and of chivalrous assassins.

That respect for women which is of modern growth, and which is commonly supposed to be chivalrous, is sought in vain among the records and chronicles 'Chivalry' of the Middle Ages, and appears only in modern and the condition of romances, the authors of which have not truly women. realised the character of the times of which they have written. The wild romances of an earlier date, to which an Eastern tinge was given by the Crusades, abound, it is true, with instances of apparent devotion shown by a knight to his mistress. Yet, even here, it will be found that all the knight promises or does is to maintain against all comers the superior beauty of his lady gay as compared with the lady gay of any other knight. This was, no doubt, gratifying to the vanity of the woman, but did not preserve her either from insults or from hard knocks. We have seen how common was the practice of exposing women, whatever their rank, to the ignominy and indecency of a public penance in the streets of London. Their condition in other respects was in perfect harmony with such exhibitions—hardly less so in the days of Jane Shore than in the days of Alice Perers.

Alice Perers, like Jane Shore, was a king's mistress. She soothed the last hours of Edward III., over whom she acquired such influence that she sat at his bed's head when all the Council stood waiting outside his bed-chamber door. When men could not obtain what they wished by any other means, they commonly made what interest they might with her to gain the good-will of the king, and rarely if ever in vain. Her power, like all other power in those times, excited the envy of the less powerful; but it hardly appears that the openness with which her position was acknowledged was thought a great public scandal. So long as the old king lived she was probably in a happier condition than any woman in England. As soon as he died the Parliament saw no loss of dignity in declaring all her lands and goods forfeited, and in banishing her from the realm, on pretence that she had been guilty of maintenance—an offence of which few landholders had not been guilty in at least an equal degree. Alice,

The Mistresses of Kings: Alice Perers.

however, seems to have been very skilful in managing her own affairs, for she married not long afterwards one William Windsor, who obtained restitution of her lands. It is to be feared that the man who would knowingly marry a royal mistress would not prove a better husband than the average knights of his time.

Among the landholders, an unmarried but virtuous girl seems to have led a far less pleasant life than a royal mistress. Affectionate confidence between parents and children was very rare, if it existed at all; and that ancient spirit which had caused *Mothers and daughters : chastisement of a young lady.* the sale of brides, and made a woman a chattel, was hardly even yet extinct. It was customary for the relatives to seek a husband suitable in wealth and rank, and to arrange a marriage as a matter of business. Until the maiden was wedded she was kept strictly under control; and the kind of discipline which was enforced is well illustrated by a letter written late in the reign of Henry VI. The writer was the widow of a landholder, and she was corresponding with the brother of the young lady whose case she describes and whom she is anxious to serve by finding a husband. This young lady was under the care of her mother, and the following was her condition :— She might not speak with any man, not even with her mother's servants; 'and she had since Easter, the most part, been beaten once in the week or twice, and sometimes thrice in a day, and her head was broken in two or three places.'

The only indication of any real improvement in the condition of women since the days of the Black Death was, as might have been expected, in the towns. Not only were the more laborious oc- *The only improvement in the condition of women was in the towns.* cupations, at which women had been compelled to work, now falling to the lot of men, but an increase of wealth and luxury was providing for women occupations more befitting their sex. We hear less of female bakers and more of female weavers; and in the reign of Henry VI. we find a complaint made by the female silk-workers in London that Lombards and other foreigners were invading their handicraft, which was one requiring art and skill. The silk-women gained their point, and the Lombards were excluded under a penalty of twenty pounds.

Town-life, however, had as yet effected but little perceptible diminution in crimes of violence even within the

The towns were affected by the lawlessness of the country.

towns themselves; and while the 'peine forte et dure' was applied in gaol, riots and affrays were common enough in the law-courts—hardly less common in the reign of Henry VI. than they had been in the reign of Edward III.

The principal Courts sat commonly in 'the Great Hall of Pleas within the King's Palace at Westminster.' One

A brawl in Westminster Hall.

morning the Judges were sitting in the Court of Chancery, in the Court of King's Bench, and in the Court of Common Pleas; and at the same time the Lords Spiritual and Temporal of the King's Council were assembled in another part of the Hall. Court was but imperfectly separated from Court, and the Courts from the Council. The origin of all these bodies from the one ancient Court or Council of the king was still called to mind by the meeting of all under the same roof—and that the roof of the Royal Palace—and by the easy communication from one to another. In the part of the Hall assigned to the Court of King's Bench there suddenly arose a great commotion. The Deputy-Marshal of England was reading a document relating to the Marshal's Office when one Ralph Garneys sprang forward with clenched fist and struck him in the face. In the struggle which ensued the whole of the Courts were thrown into confusion. All the Judges had to leave the Bench, the Council was broken up, and tranquillity was restored only when the Hall was cleared of officers as well as of rioters.

A scene not less characteristic of the age was enacted during the same reign in the Star-Chamber. This appears to have been then the meeting-place of the House of Lords rather than of the Committee which was afterwards known as the Star-Chamber Court. On one occasion Henry VI. was present with the Lords sitting in Parliament. An esquire named William Talbois had some grievance against Ralph, Lord Cromwell. A number of armed followers appeared with him in the Chamber and made a sudden attack upon Cromwell, who was sitting in his place in Parliament, and whom they nearly succeeded in killing before they were interrupted. Talbois, it is true, was afterwards committed to the Tower, but his enterprise was none the less illustrative of the times; and he lived to be included in a Bill of Attainder passed against Lancastrians in the following reign.

The influence which the example of the townsmen was feebly beginning to exercise upon the landholders was counterbalanced by the influence which the ancient habits of the landholders still exercised upon the townsmen. In spite of statutes and proclamations, the great lords not only engaged retainers, but rode with them armed into the towns. It was only consistent with the old traditions and the crimes perpetrated on every side that attempts should be made to intimidate judges as well as to bribe them. Thus, in the year 1451, when the sessions of Oyer and Terminer

were being held at Walsingham, four hundred armed
horsemen appeared to support a popular defendant, and
effectually over-awed the plaintiffs and their party.
No legal forms, however excellent, are of any avail when
the whole constitution of society is tainted with hereditary
lawlessness.

An effort was made, in the reign of Henry IV., to stay
the savage practice of maiming an enemy, which had been
Mutilation introduced, after the Romans left Britain, by the
still a
common Teutonic invaders, which was, as the Roman
offence. Emperor and the laws drawn up in England
before the Conquest tell us, a common punishment among
barbarians, and which sensibly affected the manners of
the nation as late as the reign of George I. Henry
assented to a statute which, for the first time, declared that
it was a felony to cut out the tongues or put out the eyes
of the king's subjects, of malice aforethought. It was
not for many a generation afterwards a felony to slit the
nose, to cut off the nose or lip, to cut off or disable any
of the limbs. The progress indicated even by the law
passed under Henry IV. may be judged from the fact
that the offences against which it provides are said, in the
preamble, to be daily practised.

That modern sentiment, indeed, which jealously pro-
tects human life and human blood was still almost
General want unknown. The affection which has often been
of tender-
ness. attributed to the servants of a great feudal lord
exhibited itself, at his death, in a furious riot within his
house. They could agree in nothing except that the
master's goods should be distributed among themselves ;
and each took and gave hard blows to secure a greater
share than his fellows.

Military discipline, when the military spirit was at its

height, was also unknown according to our present ideas of it. The English soldiers, who could not hold France for England, and were to return defeated, if not disgraced, began their campaign by harrying their own country in their march to the port from which they were to sail. There was made in Parliament, in the reign of Henry VI., a piteous complaint from the inhabitants of Dorsetshire, Hampshire, Sussex, Kent, and other counties lying on the sea-coast. Their kinsmen, they said, had been murdered, their wives and daughters ravished, their cattle and goods stolen, by the king's soldiers who had passed that way, and they prayed that some remedy might be provided for the future. These practices, no doubt, were forbidden, but forbidden in vain. In the reign of Edward IV. there was also an expedition to France, and when the soldiers returned they behaved no better than the soldiers of Henry VI. Their crimes were so numerous and excited such bitter outcries that the king in person went with the judges on circuit to try the offenders. It is related, as a remarkable fact, that he allowed even his own domestics to be hanged if they had been caught in the act of robbery or theft.

Brutal conduct of soldiers bound for foreign service.

If soldiers marching to do battle against a foreign enemy committed brutalities in England, which they could hardly surpass in France, it is not difficult to imagine what must have been the sufferings of the country people when English king was fighting English king on English soil. The loss of the French possessions added new bitterness to English quarrels; and the general belief that English garrisons had lost fortresses through treachery was expressed by Jack Cade when he made a charge of such treachery against Sir John Fastolf. It is to this popular belief that we are, in all

Horrors of the Civil Wars.

probability, indebted for Shakspeare's description of Falstaff's ragged regiment, and for many points in Falstaff's character. But neither Jack Cade, whose rebellion may be considered the beginning of the Wars of the Roses, nor the leaders on the side either of York or of Lancaster regarded the misdeeds of their adversaries as food for a comedy. Men were terribly in earnest in those days, even when they played the traitor ; and their jokes were, for the most part, grim and practical. It mattered, perhaps, little that housewives thought as much of long-bows and arrows, of cross-bows and bolts, of pole-axes and armour for the defence of their homes, as of furniture for their bedchambers or fittings for their malthouses. It mattered little that a letter could be sent from one part of England to another only by a trusty special messenger, or by the uncertain hands of a pilgrim or a chapman travelling to a fair. It mattered little that money could not be safely carried in any way from any country town to London, because the roads or paths were infested by thieves. All this was but the ordinary condition of England in time of peace, as that time was called when there were no greater deeds of arms than riots, routs, and affrays, forcible entries, and murders by great gangs of robbers. It mattered not very much that pestilence infected the towns, as pestilence always infects them during wars, for they were so ill-drained and ill-built that they were rarely free from some kind of plague. But worse evils even than these befel the English people during the Wars of the Roses, if we may believe the Petition of the Lords and Commons to Richard, Duke of Gloucester, immediately before he became Richard III., King of England. As usual, a contrast was drawn between the great ' prosperity, honour, and tranquillity' of a past time not definitely fixed and the miseries still fresh in the memory of living men. After that bygone period of happiness, always seen as in a mirage, the rulers of the land, it was declared in Parliament, delighted in adulation, were led astray by sensuality and concupiscence, and followed the counsel of persons who were insolent, vicious, and inordinately avaricious. Felicity was turned into wretchedness, prosperity into adversity; order and the law of God and of man were confounded. The kingdom was ruled by terror, justice was put away and despised, and murder, extortion, and oppression took its place. 'No man was sure of his life, his land, or his livelihood, of his wife, of his daughter, or of his servant; every good maiden and woman standing in dread to be ravished and defouled.'

At the accession of Henry VII., which is usually regarded as the time when the dark ages came to an end, and when our modern civilisation began, nearly eleven hundred years had passed since the Romans had left Britain to her own intestine quarrels and to the inroads of pagan pirates, whose chieftains could not write and despised the effeminacy of men who could. From the time when marauders, crossing the German Ocean, had established their supremacy and given the name of England to the south-eastern portion of the island, there had been many customs and many habits of thought which the long centuries had been unable to soften, or even to change. And thus when the first Tudor ascended the throne there was less security for life and property, less love of art and of letters, less of all that culture without which civilisation cannot exist, than there had been when the last legion embarked for Rome.

Less security and less civilisation at the accession of Henry VII. than before the Romans departed.

There was one force at work, however, which was destined to raise England higher among nations than But there was hope of a higher civilisation through free labour. Rome herself had ever risen.   England was becoming almost imperceptibly what she had never before been—the land of the free.   While the towns, whatever their origin, were sending representatives to a national parliament, the institution of slavery, in its last form of villenage, was gradually dying out even in the country.   The towns, whatever their grandeur, had never in the days of the Romans become grand by the aid of free labour.   Nor, perhaps, would England have advanced as she did, had not religious discontent formed a bond of union between country and town.   There were two kinds of freedom which had long been coveted—freedom of the person from the ownership of a lord, and freedom of the mind from the dictation of a priest whose morals did not command respect.   Neither had yet been attained ; but some progress had been made towards the attainment of one, and a great, though long a vain, struggle was about to be made for the other. There was a natural sympathy between the fugitive villein and the enterprising townsman, whose opposition to the landowner in all political matters was hereditary. There were, no doubt, many bad passions excited by the change implied in the emancipation of those villeins who became not copyholders but working manufacturers. Yet to this emancipation the greatness of England is to be traced.   The labourer who is not free has little interest in his work, and is little likely to become an inventor.   It is to the inventive power of her sons that England owes her wealth and all that her wealth has gained for her. She had many benefactors unknown to fame before Arkwright made her richer by the spinning-jenny, or Watt by the practical application of the steam-engine, or Stephenson by an adaptation which for the first time gave us better communications than the Romans had left us. All the intellectual energies of the race, which slavery had buried too deep for movement, burst into activity when the weight was removed. Thus it has come to pass that England's capital is at once the largest, the richest, the healthiest, the most secure, and the most accessible of all the great capitals which have ever existed in the world.

Under the Tudors, too, England was to enjoy a government which, if not settled and regular, according to modern ideas, was infinitely more settled than any which had preceded ; and a settled govern- ment is the greatest blessing which a nation can enjoy— even though it may not be in the best form which a philosopher could conceive. The Barons had thoroughly exhausted themselves in the Wars of the Roses, and had less strength than at any previous time for making or un-making kings. The causes which gave strength to the Crown gave strength also to the Commons. Commerce began to flourish, towns to increase, and London to extend itself so far that many proclamations were made with the object of stopping its growth. In one sense, therefore, it may fairly be said that modern civilisation began with the reign of Henry VII.

Prospect of a more settled government.

It yet remains, however, to be shown how stubbornly the ancient ignorance and brutality fought against new ideas and strove to maintain their own place in the world. It yet remains to be shown how recent are our greatest improvements in the administration of justice which may, perhaps, be one day still further improved. Many a

The resistance of ignorance and brutality still to be stub-] born and long.

generation was to pass away before even trial by jury as
we now understand it could fully supplant that trial which
was known by the same name, but in which the witnesses
were the jurors and the jurors the witnesses. Many
a generation was to pass away before even persons
accused of treason could obtain a fair hearing at the bar of
the Lords—many before it ceased to be a crime to hold
religious opinions different from the opinions expressed in
an Act of Parliament. Men were long afterwards to be
burnt for heresy, and women for treason, and great lawyers
were yet to profess on the Bench their irrevocably fixed
belief in witchcraft.

If the introduction of printing, the prospect of an
undisputed succession to the crown, the diminution of
villenage, and the attention which was now
being directed to commerce and maritime enterprise be excepted, there was little to distinguish
the end of the fifteenth century from the middle
of the fourteenth. These, indeed, are great exceptions.
But corruption still went hand in hand with violence.
There was as yet no confidence in any judge or in any
officer. Peculation by a chancellor and peculation by a
sheriff alike excited complaints, but neither excited surprise. Education by means of printed books was little
given and little coveted ; the education which is given by
public acts of bloodshed was brought home alike to man
and to woman, to the aged and the infant. A hasty word
was commonly punished by the dagger ; a claim, rightful
or wrongful, was commonly enforced by a troop of armed
men. The gibbet, with a robber hanging in chains, was
one of the objects most frequently presented to the eye.
A petty thief in the pillory, a scold on the cucking-stool,
a murderer drawn to the gallows on a hurdle, were spec-

General sketch of society at the end of the Middle Ages.

tacles as familiar when Henry VII. ascended the throne, as a messenger from the telegraph office is to ourselves. London Bridge, which is now thronged with travellers peaceably making their way to a railway terminus, was then a narrow thoroughfare, with unglazed shops on either side, with the obstructions of a drawbridge half way across, and perhaps chains at either end. Its chief adornments were the heads of traitors, fixed on poles, as a warning to all who might lack the skill to be on the right side in any future commotions. The fatherless and the widow, if claiming kinship with the king, might sometimes gain possession of the mutilated remains of father or husband, after a few days' exposure to the jeers of the mob. Those who were less fortunate suffered, in addition to their bereavement, the pangs of reflecting that the features which were most dear to them were to be impaled, as an exhibition, during the king's pleasure, which was, in fact, the pleasure of sunshine and storm and natural decay. Nor was London the only city to which was given this impressive caution. The head of a traitor was often sent to the neighbourhood in which the treason had been committed; and there was no town so little favoured as not to receive ever and anon the ghastly present of a quarter, wherewithal to decorate its walls or its gates.

Such, even in their last years, were those middle ages which some teachers would have us believe richer than our own in graces and in virtues. Admiration and loathing are matters of taste; but the facts which have been adduced are, it may be hoped, sufficient to prove that the questions asked in the first page find an answer in the slow march of history. Crime, in its worst forms, is, beyond doubt,

The transition into the modern state of society remains to be treated.

an inheritance from past ages; many, if not all, of the criminals of to-day are the offspring or the imitators, under somewhat different conditions, of more numerous and more brutal criminals who lived in days gone by. The transition of the mediæval state of society into the state of society in which we live will be the subject of another volume.

APPENDIX.

———o·o·o·o·o———

REFERENCES AND NOTES.

A FEW words, in addition to what has been said in the Preface, are, perhaps, needed in explanation not so much of the references and notes themselves as of certain omissions.

It would be a wearisome task to give reasons, which have been given elsewhere, for disregarding the melancholy ravings of a General 'Gildas,' the inventions ascribed to an 'Ingulph,' the innume-Remarks. rable silly stories told even by more trustworthy mediæval chroniclers. It is unnecessary to inflict upon the public all the labours of authorship— to write a catalogue of all the evidence which has been rejected, with the reasons for the rejection. It is, as I am only too painfully aware, an act of great pretension to write the word 'History' upon a title-page. But the greater includes the less, and the capacity to form an independent judgment upon the value of different authorities is claimed as soon as the book has received its name. Criticisms upon all the possible sources of a history would occupy a far greater space than the text of the present work. Suffice it to state that no information has been wittingly put aside, except for two reasons—either because the information seemed to be of little importance to the History of Crime after the plan had been drawn out, or because it seemed to be untrustworthy.

As the history is founded throughout upon contemporary evidence, the opinions of modern authors, even upon minor points, have been, as a rule, excluded. There is a great temptation to quote the words of men whose reputation is established beyond cavil, and whom it is impossible not to respect and even to venerate. But, on the other hand, references to books in which materials have been used, as well as to materials themselves, have the great disadvantage of blurring that broad line which ought always to be drawn between first-hand and second-hand information. Nor, indeed, could the mention of great names be of service to the present work, for, so far as I have been able to learn, there is no other history of similar scope. Preceding writers have, therefore, been mentioned only for one of two reasons—either because they have published collections of original materials, or because they have representative names associated with doctrines neither impugned nor accepted in the present history. They have never been cited to prove any point which has been put forward in the text as proved.

The application of the Appendix to the text, it is hoped, will be free from difficulty. For every chapter of the history there is a corresponding chapter of references and explanations. In the side-notes of the Appendix the corresponding pages of the text are indicated. Thus the whole of the sources of each chapter are brought together, and those digressions which it has previously been the custom to throw into an Appendix find their natural place in the Appendix still, but are no longer entirely isolated.

CHAPTER I.

THE short description of prominent criminals in the second paragraph
is founded on visits to the dockyard at Portsmouth and to Pp. 2–3.
Evidence for
description of
the appearance
of various
criminals.
various prisons, as well as on observations made in courts of
law. The 'furtive' look of the professional thief will also be
found among other characteristics mentioned by an ob-
server of more experience in 'Female Life in Prison, by a Prison
Matron.' Vol. i. p. 177.

The passage in which the Gallic or British sacrifice of criminals is
described is founded chiefly on Cæsar 'De Bell. Gall.,' lib. vi. c. 16.
Cæsar, however, does not there attribute the custom to the Pp. 10–12.
Evidence of
ancient British
customs;
estimate of its
value.
British priests, but to the Druids of Gaul; and for that reason
the subject is introduced into the text with considerable
diffidence. The assertion that human sacrifices of some
kind were common in Britain is confirmed by Tacitus ('Annal.' lib. xiv.
c. 30). The identity of the customs established by the Druids in
Britain and in Gaul is assumed by the Roman writers on the subject—
by Cæsar, by Tacitus, and apparently also by Pliny ('Hist. Nat.' xxx. 4).
Unless, therefore, all matters preceding the Roman occupation, and
during the early part of it, are to be ignored, it is necessary to mention
them in the spirit in which they are mentioned by the best authorities.
It would, however, have shown excessive credulity to sketch the alleged
Druidical form of punishment by fire without a warning that the sketch
is warranted only by historical testimony which is not of the highest kind.
The Roman writers, though contemporaries, were, perhaps, all dependent
on others for their information, and were, in that case, as much narrators
at second-hand as though they had lived in the next generation.   Still
they had, like men who relate events which they have heard from their
parents, opportunities of ascertaining the truth second only to those enjoyed by eye-witnesses. To accept all their statements as correct in every
particular would be to assume for them an accuracy which they cannot
possess; to disbelieve them altogether would be to carry scepticism
into obstinate incredulity; to discriminate with precision between the
true and the false would be impossible, unless eighteen centuries could
be annihilated and the scenes of which the Romans had heard could be

re-enacted before our eyes. Nothing is left but to admit that the manners of these early times must always remain in some obscurity— that they can be regarded only through the eyes of the foreigner, and that belief and disbelief in any detail are equally dangerous.

The punishments in the amphitheatres have been rendered so familiar not only to classical scholars but to the readers of general history that it *P. 12.* is unnecessary to occupy space or time by reference to autho- *Note on Roman punishments in the arena.* rities in illustration of the subject. It is only necessary to remark that the persistence of these punishments during the whole period of the Roman occupation is proved by innumerable passages in the Theodosian Code, and that its existence in Britain is proved by the remains of the amphitheatres themselves.

For the description of the Roman criminal law in force during the Roman occupation of Britain, the 'Codex Theodosianus' has been *Pp. 13-25.* followed as the best guide. It was compiled just after the *Note on the use made of the Theodosian Code.* time at which the Romans probably abandoned the island. It could not, therefore, have been introduced into Britain in the form of a code; but it is a compilation founded on earlier imperial laws, many of which were only 'declaratory,' and it necessarily gives, down to the latest date, the general principles according to which Roman 'judices' were expected to administer justice in Britain (as in other provinces) on all points on which the Roman had superseded the native criminal law. The edition of the Code which has been used is that of 'Jacobus Gothofredus,' by J. D. Ritter, in the third volume of which is the ninth book of the Code—'De Criminibus, deque Processu Criminali.' It is to be understood that the 'Tituli' and chapters to which reference is made below are those of the ninth book except where it has been found necessary to mention others.

P. 14. The equality of all ranks in the eye of the law, when an *Law of Læsa Majestas, or High Treason.* accusation of treason was made, and in that case only, is asserted in Tit. 35, ' De Quæstionibus.'

That a slave who made an accusation against his master was to be *References concerning the use of the more cruel punishments by the Romans.* punished 'gladio' appears by Tit. 6, c. 3; that a slave who was a receiver of thieves was to be burnt, by Tit. 29, c. 2; and that one who committed adultery with a free woman was to be burnt, by Tit. 9; and the punishment of the coiner by Tit. 21, c. 5.

The remarkable punishment of the parricide is the subject of Tit. 15. It is well known that a monkey, as well as the serpent, was at one period *Pp. 15-16.* sown up in the sack with the offender. Cc. 1 and 2 of *Laws showing the gradation of punishments under the Empire.* Tit. 10, 'Ad Legem Juliam de Vi Publica et Privata,' show that forcible entry on land, Tit. 9 that adultery committed by a free woman with a slave, and Tit. 14, c. 1, that infanticide were capital offences. Sentence to the mines is awarded to violators of sepulchres in Tit. 17, as well as elsewhere to other offenders. 'Deportatio,' or transportation, appears as a penalty under the 'Lex Julia de Ambitu' in Tit. 26, c. 2, and elsewhere. The 'Pistrinum,' or hand-mill, as the 'pœna leviorum criminum,' occurs in Tit. 40, cc. 3, 6, 7, &c. The city of Rome is mentioned in these passages, but the punishment was in all likelihood put in practice elsewhere.

It is hardly necessary to give particular references for the use of torture by the Romans. Abundant instances will be found in Book IX. of the Theodosian Code. The assertion that kings of England could afterwards give a licence to torture is founded on the Pipe Roll, 34ª Henry II., Northamptonshire, Ro. 10, where occur the following words :—'Petrus Filius Ade reddit compotum de xxxv. marcis, quia cepit quandam mulierem et eam tormentavit *sine licentia Regis*.' This, and similar passages, show that the Orders in Council for the application of torture only succeed previous orders issuing from the king.

<small>P. 16, 17.
Evidence concerning the use of torture by Romans and English.</small>

The precautions taken by the Emperor Constantine against the punishment of the innocent, or premature punishment of the guilty, appear in the Cod. Theod. Lib. ix. Tit. 40, c. 1; the ordinance that witnesses must be sworn and that one witness is not sufficient in Lib. xi. Tit. 39, c. 3; the reference to the emperor in doubtful cases in Lib. xi. Tit. 36, c. 1.

<small>Merciful provisions in Roman laws.</small>

According to Lib. ix. Tit. 1, cc. 5, 8, 9, no one could be held 'reus' or put to the torture except after 'inscriptio,' or 'subscriptio,' by the accuser. The infliction of unnecessary hardship upon untried prisoners is forbidden in Tit. 3, c. 1; and the imprisonment of women in the same room with men in c. 3. Tit. 1, c. 7, is 'De audiendis reis intra mensem,' and the purport of c. 18 and of Tit. 3, c. 6, is similar. Tit. 36 gives the provisions 'ut intra annum criminalis actio terminetur.' Tit. 1, c. 19, contains the rule that judges are not to listen to approvers. The date of this is A.D. 423, but it appears in the form of an order for the observance of a law of old standing, and is, as we should now say, declaratory.

<small>P. 17.
Roman laws to secure liberty of the person.</small>

Constantine's letter, 'Ad universos Provinciales,' appears in Tit. 1, c. 4; the rule that even senators should be tried in the province where they were accused in c. 1. In Tit. 28, c. 1, it appears that 'hi judices qui peculatu provincias quassavissent' were guilty of a capital offence; they had, before the year 392, been punished by fine.

<small>P. 18.
Roman laws to protect the Provincials.</small>

The law of Valentinian, that the goods of the convict should go to his children, appears in Tit. 42, c. 6. This was not established without some vacillation (*see* cc. 1 and 4). There is a provision in the laws known as those of Edward the Confessor (xix.) for the benefit of a criminal's wife, who is to have a share of the husband's goods; and

P. 19.
Laws in favour
of the wives
and children of
criminals. this may be traced back as far as the Laws of Ine (57). *See* also the 'Laws of King Æthelstan' V. i. 1. There is little doubt that the clause was inserted by the influence of the clergy, who may have known something of the Roman law. That it was not in accordance with the feelings of landowners is evident from the Conqueror's Laws (i. 27), which show that the privilege was not enjoyed by the wives of persons subject to the innumerable private jurisdictions of the Pre-Norman times in England. It was in fact wholly inconsistent with the general tenour of the laws or dooms which were introduced when the Teutonic invaders came, and could hardly have been of any avail. (For the influence of the Church in improving the condition of women, *see* pp. 90–93 of the present volume.) At a later period the wife of a traitor saved her dower, but the first English statute which declares that the jury need no longer enquire what goods and chattels were possessed by a felon is 7 & 8 Geo. IV. c. 28, s. 5.

Branding on the forehead those condemned 'In Ludum vel in Metallum,' is prohibited in Cod. Theod. Lib. ix. Tit. 40, c. 2. Tit. 12 is

P. 20.
Roman Laws
concerning
slaves. the 'De emendatione Servorum' of Constantine. The 'sævitia immanium barbarorum,' to which he there refers, will be found without difficulty in the 'Ancient Laws and Institutes of England,' *passim*.

The class compared with the feudal villeins is that to which the names 'coloni' and 'tributarii' are given in the Codex Theodosianus.

P. 21.
Evidence of
the Theo-
dosian Code
concerning the
owners and
cultivators of
land. The term 'adscriptitii,' with which the readers of the earlier English law books are well acquainted, is also sometimes applied to these 'coloni.' Their condition, as described in the text, may be learned from Lib. v. Tit. 9, Tit. 10, and Tit. 11.

The landlords of these 'coloni' in the provinces were originally, it may be inferred, the 'decuriones.' It is in all probability no mere incidence that in the Roman army there were also 'decuriones,' who were cavalry officers of high rank. The ease with which land could be alienated, or a particular interest in it granted away, and the position of the 'emphyteuta,' who might be called a perpetual lessee, are subjects to which reference is made again and again in the Theodosian Code.

That the 'possessores,' as well as other persons of substance, had to contribute towards the repair of roads and walls is apparent from the

P. 22.
Laws concern-
ing the colonial
courts. Cod. Theod. Lib. xv. Tit. 1, c. 34, and Tit. 3, Lib. xi. Tit. 17, c. 4, and other passages. That they were compelled to serve in the 'Curia' as 'Decuriones,' is made thoroughly manifest in Lib. xii. Tit. 1, 'De Decurionibus,' the 192 chapters of which abound with information concerning these 'curiales.'

Curiously enough, too, a letter addressed by the Emperor Constantine 'ad Pacatianum Vicarium Britanniarum' (Lib. xi. Tit. 7, c. 2), not only serves to show that Britain was on the same footing as other parts of the empire, but assists in determining the functions of the 'decuriones' as revenue officers.

Proof that these courts existed in Britain.

The exemption of the 'decuriones,' 'omni corporalis contumeliæ timore,' appears in Lib. xii. Tit. 1, cc. 39, 47, and many other passages. The nomination of wealthy plebeians to fill the office of 'decurio' is enjoined in c. 53; of merchants, provided they were landowners, in c. 72; and of plebeians who were 'agro vel *pecunia idonei*,' in c. 133.

It is too well known that 'collegia' of certain craftsmen as well as religious 'collegia' existed from a very early period for any reference in proof of the fact to be necessary. The practice of joining a 'collegium' of 'fabri,' or of 'fabricenses,' to avoid service as a 'decurio,' is mentioned in Lib. xii. Tit. 1, cc. 62 and 81. The precise character of these 'collegia,' as of others mentioned in Lib. xiv. Tit. 8, it is not easy to ascertain; it is sufficient to know that they existed, and their existence in Britain is proved by an inscription found at Bath, in which is mentioned a 'Collegium Fabricensium' by two found at Middleby, in which are mentioned 'Collegia Signiferorum,' and by one found at Chichester, in which is mentioned a 'Collegium Fabrorum.' These inscriptions have been printed in the 'Monumenta Historica Britannica,' at pages cxii. cxviii. and cxix. respectively. The 'Collegia Signiferorum' were of a religious character, and may perhaps be identified with the 'Collegia Dendrophororum' mentioned in the Theodosian Code, Lib. xiv. Tit. 8, c. 1. Public works are the subject of Lib. xv. Tit. 1. In chapters 1 and 14 will be found the decrees against removing the ornaments from one city to another.

Pp. 23-25. Laws concerning Roman companies or guilds: proof that they existed in Britain.

The description of a journey in Roman Britain may be justified by the remains of Roman roads still existing, by the list of roads and of towns given in Antonine's 'Itinerary' ('Monumenta Historica Britannica') pp. xx.-xxii., and by the remains of Roman towns and Roman villas which have already been brought to light. It would be tedious to give a list of the Roman villas known to have existed in Britain; but, to show that they did exist in great numbers, reference may be made to descriptions of them in the 'Archæologia,' vol. viii. pp. 363-376; vol. ix. pp. 137-138, and 319-322; vol. xiv. pp. 62-68; and especially to vol. xviii. pp. 112-225 (description of villas in Gloucestershire, with plates of pavements and pillars); pp. 203-221 (description of villa at Bignor, with plates of pavements); vol. xix. pp. 177-178; (further account of villa at Bignor); and pp. 178-183 (villa at Great Witcombe remarkable for the perfection of its

Pp. 25-26. Evidence for the description of a journey in Roman Britain.

baths). The state of the arts in Roman Britain is still better shown by the plates in 'An Account of Roman Antiquities discovered at Woodchester, in the County of Gloucester,' by Samuel Lysons, F.R.S., &c., and by the plates in the 'Reliquiæ Britannico-Romanæ,' published by the same author.

It is hardly necessary to adduce proof that Romans travelled in carriages with post horses or mules from the days when Horace said, (Sat. i. v. 86) 'rapimur rhedis' downwards. That, however, the use of horses was, under the empire, permitted only to persons of certain rank is apparent from the Cod. Theod. lib. ix. Tit. 30; ' Quibus equorum usus concessus est aut denegatus.' The provisions were made for Italy, but it may be inferred that they applied *a fortiori* to remote provinces. The mention of a mint may be justified by the Roman coins, with marks indicating the British towns at which they were struck.

P. 25.

The approach to a Roman villa and its gardens are described from Pliny (Epist. ii. 17, and v. 6)—the villa itself from a comparison, of the remains found at Bignor, Woodchester, &c. (Lysons 'Woodchester,' and the paper in the 'Archæologia' already mentioned), with Pliny's account of his own villas, and with the more perfect remains discovered at Pompeii (*see* Sir William Gell's 'Pompeiana,' *passim*). The Bignor, Woodchester, and Witcombe villas alone, however, furnish so many of the details—the fragments of pillars and of pavements, the baths and the hypocausts—that it is unnecessary to travel beyond them, except for explanation. What has been spared in Britain is at least as magnificent as that which corresponds to it at Pompeii. When the pavement and the pillars are known, the frescoes and the gardens can easily be inferred.

Pp. 26–28. Evidence for the description of a villa in Britain.

An essay on the condition of free Roman women under the empire would be out of place in this work. It must suffice to state, in proof of what is advanced in the text, that their position was by no means unenviable (as compared with that of barbarian women) even in those earlier days when they were under 'Tutela' and that the ' Tutela mulierum' itself was no longer an existing institution when the Theodosian Code was compiled. The code shows great tenderness towards the wives even of criminals, and a laudable desire that innocent women should not be impoverished through the crimes of their husbands. The love of the Roman women for dress, and the use made by them of false hair, are well known from the writings of the satirists, and from the representations which remain.

P. 29. Note on the condition of women under the Empire.

The position of a Roman Governor in Britain, and his establishment, with the *cynægium* and every other evidence of the Roman organisation, are shown in the ' Notitia.' The part relating to Britain is printed in

the 'Monumenta Historica Britannica,' pp. xxiii.–xxiv. The words and thoughts attributed to Pacatian, 'Vicarius Britanniarum' (Vice-gerent under the Governor of Gaul) are, it is believed, in accord- P. 31.
ance with the events and the sentiments of his age (about Note on the position of the
A.D. 319). After the death of Constantine, the condition of Roman Governor in
Britain must have been less happy, and the incursions of Britain.
the barbarians became formidable. Before that time Britain, like the rest of the empire, was agitated by the rival claims of men ambitious of the purple; but it was not till a little later that the quarrels and the brigandage which always follow the disintegration of a military power began to prepare the way for Picts and Teutons.

The prediction, put into Pacatian's mouth, that an edict forbidding Romans to teach barbarians the art of ship-building would issue too late was verified in the year 419, when those were declared Note (with
guilty of a capital offence who 'conficiendi naves incognitam reference) on imperial edict
ante peritiam Barbaris tradiderunt' (Cod. Theod. Lib. ix. against teach-ing barbarians
Tit. 40, c. 24). This referred apparently to the Eastern to build ships.
empire. Some of the barbarian dwellers on the shores of the German Ocean seem to have been acquainted with the art of sailing as early as the time of Carausius (towards the end of the third century).

The belief of the Romans in witchcraft is, in its details, so marvellously like the belief of the English as late as the seventeenth century, that it might well form the subject of a narrow-minded essay Pp. 32–33.
on the descent of English from Roman customs. To those Note on the diffusion of
who have passed years in the study of races, and their origin, superstitions.
the similarity appears simply as a link in the chain of superstition which encircles the earth, and binds together the human beings of all countries. It would, of course, be just as great a proof of ignorance to assume that English superstitions have descended from Roman superstitions exclusively as to assume that every resemblance between an English institution and a Teutonic institution necessarily proves identity of race. The wider the range of investigation the more valueless are such arguments shown to be. To use the language of science, differentiation is in proportion to civilisation ; the more uncivilised tribes are, the more they resemble each other in their habits and manners. If an opinion be only ancient, it can be traced to half-a-dozen different sources with equal plausibility ; this one in particular is as probably Teutonic as Roman, as probably Roman as Teutonic, and not less probably common to all the earlier inhabitants of the island. But as Rome possessed a literature before Germany possessed a town, it is to Rome that we are indebted for the first minute account of the powers attributed to a witch by any of the more western nations.

Horace, besides many other mentions of her name, addressed two of his Epodes to Canidia (Epod. 5 and 17. *See* also Sat. i. 8).

The dread entertained by the Roman veterans of the supernatural

Pp. 33–34.
Evidence con-
cerning super-
stitions, from
Horace, Taci-
tus, Pliny, and
the Theodosian
Code.

power possessed by the Druids, and the omens which preceded the revolt of Boadicea, are mentioned by Tacitus ('Annal.' xiv. 32). Pliny ('Hist. Nat.' xxx. 4) speaks with horror of the extent to which magic was practised in Britain in his time; and there is no doubt that his words convey, if not the truth, at least the common belief in Rome. The punishment of sorcerers by fire, and by the other more cruel punishments, is the subject of Lib. ix. Tit. 16, of the Theodosian Code.

The superstitions of the pagan world, and their effect upon Christianity in the times of Tertullian, Origen, and Eusebius, are so con-

Pp. 35–38.
Evidence, from
the Early
Fathers, of the
superstitions
with which
Christianity
must have been
infected when
first introduced
into Britain.

spicuously brought to notice in the works of those authors, that a selection of particular passages for reference is hardly necessary. For the teaching, however, that the Roman spectacles had their origin in idolatry, which was equivalent to the worship of demons, it will suffice to refer to Tertullian, ' De Spectaculis,' iv. *et seq.* Origen's belief in charms for putting demons to flight is to be found ' Contra Celsum,' i. 22, iv. 33, 34, &c. His identification of demons with the heathen gods, and his doctrine that they hovered in the air above the earth, that they licked up the blood of sacrifice, and that they could be fettered by the devices of magic, will be found ' Contra Celsum,' v. 46, and vii. 5. In the same work, too (viii. 36), and in the ' De Oratione' (11), is the far more attractive description of Guardian Angels.

That Christianity, when first introduced into the British islands, contained a mixture of doctrines such as is to be found in the writings of these Early Fathers, may be inferred almost to demonstration. A ceaseless communication between all parts of the Roman empire was kept up by the military system. The British recruits went with their legions where necessity called them; and legions recruited from almost all parts of the known world were stationed in Britain. Every form of religion thus found its way to Britain as to Rome. There is, indeed, a silly fable in Bede's ' Ecclesiastical History ' to the effect that Pope Eleutherus sent a successful mission to convert an imaginary British King Lucius. It is but a clumsy plagiarism of the story of Augustine and the King of Kent. Its falseness may be shown by facts which also prove the composite character of the Christianity existing in the British islands before a pope seriously determined to attempt the conversion of our forefathers.

The difference between the Scottish and Roman methods of celebrating Easter, which was brought into prominent notice in the latter half of the seventh century, is described by Bede ('Hist. Eccl.' iii. 25.), who might easily have learnt the particulars. This would have been impossible had Britain accepted its Christianity from Rome in the second century. The pope Eleutherus, who has been named as the contemporary of Lucius, lived many years after the first Paschal controversy ; and Anicetus, one of his predecessors, had already argued with Polycarp against the celebration of the Christian festival simultaneously (as sometimes occurred in the Scottish Church) with the Jewish Passover. The observances which the Romish priests anathematised in Britain, centuries after the time of Eleutherus, could not have been derived from Rome; nor, on the other hand, can they be traced exclusively to converted Jews, to any of the Asiatic Churches, or to Alexandria. They appear to have differed in some respects from those of every other Church, and to have been dependent on no particular authority. The various passages in Greek and Latin writings, in which reference is made to Christianity in Britain, have been collected in 'Councils and Ecclesiastical Documents relating to Great Britain, &c.,' by Messrs. Haddan and Stubbs. They prove, however, only the bare fact that Christianity in some form was known in Roman Britain.

The intermixture of customs disclosed by the Easter controversy in Britain had, without doubt, its counterpart in a similar intermixture of superstitions such as was to be found throughout the Christian world in the third century.

The statement in the text, that we know little or nothing of the superstitions brought by the Teutonic invaders into Britain, may, perhaps, seem strange to the admirers of the Eddas. But this history is written on the principle that only contemporary evidence is to be accepted ; and a collection of Scandinavian myths made at the end of the eleventh century, cannot, in any historical sense, throw light on the Teutonic superstitions of the fifth. *Pp. 37–38. Note on the statement that it is uncertain what superstitions were introduced by the Teutonic invaders.* The poem of 'Beowulf' (edited by Kemble), it is true, supplies here and there a link, but not enough to construct a chain of any strength.

The principal evidence of the superstitions existing in England between the time of the conversion of our forefathers to Christianity and the Norman Conquest is to be found in the 'Ancient Laws and Institutes of England,' edited by Mr. Thorpe, and in the 'Saxon Leechdoms,' edited by Mr. Cock- *Pp. 38–41. Evidence of the superstitions in England after the mission of Augustine.* ayne for the series of Chronicles, &c., published by the Master of the Rolls.

In order to avoid the use of the pre-Norman letters in printing, and at the same time to attain precision, the spelling of proper names which appears in Mr. Thorpe's modern English headings to 'Ancient Laws' has been adopted in references made to that collection. It may seem inconsistent to mention 'Canute' in the text, and to refer else-

where to the laws of King 'Cnut.' But the reason for referring to the
Note on the laws of King 'Cnut' is the same as the reason for writing
orthography of
pre-Norman 'Canute' in the text—that every one may understand what is
names. meant. 'Canute' is, in the plain English of the nineteenth
century, the name of a Danish king who once ruled in England ; the technical description of a certain source of information, as printed in the
best edition, is the 'Laws of King Cnut.' A long dissertation on the orthography of the pre-Norman names which occur in the history of
England would be out of place, and the subject is of little importance.
It seems, however, sufficiently clear that 'Alfred' is to be preferred to
'Ælfred,' 'Edward' to 'Eadweard,' 'Canute' to 'Cnut.' 'Alfred,'
'Edward,' and 'Canute' are names familiar to every one, and are good
English, inasmuch as they appear, so written, in the works of classical
English historians. 'Ælfred,' 'Eadweard,' and 'Cnut' are forms to
be found in MSS. of early date, but the spelling in such MSS. is not
uniform. There is good MS. authority for 'Eadward,' as well as for
'Eadweard,' and for 'Eadwerd' as well as for 'Eadward.' Alfred,
indeed, was almost always written 'Ælfred' before the Conquest, but
before the Conquest 'ecclesia' was almost always written 'æcclesia.' It
is therefore as correct and as incorrect to write 'Ælfred' for Alfred as
to write 'æcclesiastical' for ecclesiastical. If we are justified in drawing any inference at all concerning the character æ as used in England
before the Conquest, we are justified only in drawing the inference that
it was equivalent to one value of the Latin *e*, which was equivalent to the
Greek ε. The character *æ*, as used in modern English type, ordinarily represents, not a short vowel like the Latin *e* and the Greek ε, but a diphthong
compounded of the two letters *a* and *e*. If, therefore, the commonly
received spelling of Alfred is to be altered, the name should become
rather Elfred than Ælfred. Accuracy even in trifles is commendable,
and scholarship is a handmaid useful to history ; but the substitution of
'Ælfred' for Alfred, of 'Eadweard' for Edward, and of 'Cnut' for
Canute is a change which scholars will not unanimously accept as an aid
to accurate writing.

Archbishop Theodore's Book of Penance, xxvii., in the 'Ancient
Laws, &c.,' shows the belief in the power of human beings to raise storms
Pp. 38–41. and commit other iniquities by the aid of demons or false
Evidence of
the supersti- pagan gods. This document (as explained in the Preface
tions in Eng-
land after the to 'Councils and Ecclesiastical Documents relating to Great
mission of
Augustine. Britain, &c.,' edited by Messrs. Haddan and Stubbs) is
(Continued.) probably of later origin than that assigned to it ; but if so,
it only shows more clearly the persistence of superstitions. An ordinance for the expulsion of 'heathendom,' at the end of the tenth or
beginning of the eleventh century, will be found in the 'Laws of King

Ethelred,' v. 1. Still later, 'heathenship' is defined, in the Secular 'Laws of King Cnut,' 5, as the worship of heathen gods such as the sun, moon, *wells, stones,* and *trees.* After the evidence from the early Christian Fathers, it is hardly necessary to adduce any further arguments in support of the proposition that these superstitions are in no way distinctively Teutonic. The passage in Tac. 'Germ.' 16, in which it is stated that the Germans live where a spring, or a grove, or pasture may invite them, refers obviously to the facilities for getting such necessaries as water, wood, and fire ; and there is nothing in the context to suggest any other interpretation. Had superstition been studied as a common affection of humanity, the words would never have been perverted (as they often have) to establish a theory that every custom and every institution can be traced exclusively to one particular race. A fair case might indeed be made out for the derivation of all later superstitions from those existing in Britain during the Roman period, but this would be a narrow and unphilosophical view. That they would all have existed, had there been no Low German invasion, is certain ; that many of them would have existed had no race preceded the Teutonic, is probable. Any argument from such materials in proof of descent must therefore be a waste both of time and of ingenuity.

To return, however, to the evidence of the superstitions existing in England before the Norman Conquest, the ' Liber Pœnitentialis Theodori ' and the 'Pœnitentiale Ecgberti' abound with illustrations none the less valuable if, as Messrs. Haddan and Stubbs maintain, the so-called 'Penitential' of Egbert is, like that attributed to Theodore, of later date than has been assigned to it. Penances for the practice of magic by priests are to be found in the 'Lib. Pœn. Theod.,' xxvii. 8, 10, and in the ' Pœnit. Ecgb.,' iv. 18. Witchcraft practised by women is mentioned in both those treatises, and in some of the secular laws ; but the belief in the power of witches to kill their victims appears most plainly in the 'Confessionale Ecgberti,' 29.

The belief that persons suffering from mental derangement were possessed by devils appears in numerous passages in the 'Saxon Leechdoms,' and especially in vol. ii. pp. 352, 354, 356, where charmed remedies for the expulsion of the intruders are carefully described. Christian charms for finding what has been lost, and other purposes, are to be found in the same collection, vol. i. p. 392, vol. iii. p. 288, &c. The use of the ' Pater Noster ' and 'Credo ' as charms, is distinctly recommended also in the ' Pœnitentiale Ecgberti,' ii. 23.

The custom of accepting cattle and sheep as a satisfaction for a human life is attributed to the ancient Germans by Tacitus ('Germania,' 21). There is not the slightest reason to doubt his statement, as it is confirmed by the subsequent laws of the Germans in all the provinces of

the Roman empire which they overran.   When they became acquainted
with money, they received it, instead of live stock, as com-

P. 41.
Evidence of
ancient Ger-
man manners
and customs. pensation, but in other respects the custom remained unchanged.   The practice could not, like many others, have
been adopted by them from the Romans, who had at least
advanced far beyond that stage of barbarism.

The other details of German manners (given at the same page) are
from the 'Germania,' cc. 5, 12, 22, carefully compared with the passage in
Cæsar, 'Bell. Gall.,' vi. 22–23, which seems to be founded on very
accurate information, and clearly indicates that the writer had know-
lédge of the Teutonic tribe within its Mark.

The assertion in the text that the family feud and the system of
composition for murder are common to various tribes, and in no way

Pp. 42–43.
Evidence that
the blood-feud
was common
to various
races. exclusively characteristic of the speakers of Teutonic or
even of Aryan languages, may be easily proved.   There are
numerous passages in the 'Iliad' and elsewhere which show
what was the practice in the Homeric age, and perhaps considerably later.   The scene delineated on the shield of Hephæstus is,
perhaps, as good an illustration of manners and customs as could be
desired, and occurs in 'Iliad,' xviii. 498.   Should further confirmation be
required, it is to be found in 'Iliad,' v. 266, xiii. 659, xiv. 483, &c.
In the Welsh Laws of Hoel Dda payments for murder are as fully recognised as even in the Teutonic laws.   *See* 'Ancient Laws and Institutes of Wales' (Record Com.) *passim*.   In them the Welsh word
'galanas' is seen to be exactly equivalent to 'murdrum,' *i.e.* to represent both the deed and the fine for it.   The claim of the kindred is also
everywhere recognised.   The 'Ancient Laws and Institutes of Ireland
—Senchus Mor' (published under the direction of the Commissioners
for publishing the 'Ancient Laws and Institutes of Ireland') show also
the existence in Ireland of the institution of the fine for murder, and the
liability of the kindred.   *See* vol. i. pp. 185, 189, 259, 273 ; and vol. ii.
p. 285.   The blood-feud among the Jews is mentioned in Numb. xxxv.
21, Deut. xix. 6, Josh. xx. 5, &c. ·The custom of setting a price upon
a human life is intimately connected with the recognition of slavery,
which, as is well known, is almost universal among barbarous and semi-
barbarous tribes.   According to Lady Mary Wortley Montagu, it survived in Turkey in the eighteenth century with some customs nearly
related to slavery, and, perhaps, survives there still.   'Murder,' she says,
'is never pursued by the king's officers, as with us.   'Tis the business of
the next relations to revenge the dead person; and if they like better
to compound the matter for money (as they generally do), there is no
more said of it.' ('Letters and Works of Lady M. W. Montagu,' edited
by Moy Thomas, vol. i. p. 363.)

The introduction of composition for murder by the Teutonic tribes in countries in which they adopted the Roman law, or permitted it to exist, is well illustrated by documents in Savigny's 'Geschichte des römischen Rechts im Mittelalter,' vol. ii. pp. 13–19 (Heidelberg edition). *Pp. 44–46. Evidence that it was continued by Teutonic Conquest.*

The existence of the custom in England before the Norman Conquest is so well known, and is established by such abundant evidence, that it is only necessary to refer to the 'Ancient Laws and Institutes of England' *passim.*

The statement in the text that Britain is lost or nearly lost to history from the end of the Roman period to the end of the seventh century, may excite surprise in those who have not criticised the writings of the intervening period which have been called historical. I have in another work given my reasons for distrusting the evidence to be found in any of them. *P. 46. Note on the first appearance of England in history.* The laws, some of which may be of the earlier part of the seventh century, are, of course, most valuable as far as they go.

The commutation of penances is illustrated in the 'Ecclesiastical Institutes,' which constitute the latter portion of the 'Ancient Laws and Institutes of England'—in the 'Liber Pœnitentialis' and in the 'Capitula' which are there attributed to Archbishop Theodore, and in the similar compilations of *Pp. 47–48. References concerning the commutation of penances.* later times. Further light is thrown on the subject in Cockayne's 'Saxon Leechdoms,' vol. iii. p. 166.

The distinction between the freeman and the slave in the enjoyment of facilities for religious observances appears in many of the 'Ancient Laws,' &c., but is most clearly shown in the 'Laws of King Alfred,' xliii., in which *Pp. 48–49. Laws showing the distinction between freemen and slaves in England.* are mentioned the holidays enjoyed by freemen, but denied to slaves.

In all the 'Ancient Laws,' &c., it is apparent that the punishment of mutilation was, as a rule, inflicted only on the churl and the slave. As might have been expected, the punishments vary somewhat in various reigns, but show no progress towards humanity. The most severe are to be found in the 'Laws of King Alfred,' the 'Laws of King Æthelstan,' the 'Laws of King Cnut,' and the 'Leges Regis Henrici Primi.' It *Pp. 49–51. Laws concerning the punishment of slaves and freemen in England.* is in the last collection that flaying ('excoriatio') is mentioned as a punishment (lxxv. 1), but there is some doubt about the reading. The exact date of these laws and their sources are uncertain, but it is probable that they were compiled after the reign of Henry I., certainly not before it ; and they exhibit all the ferocity of the earlier laws in existence before the Norman Conquest. By most of the laws compensation was permitted in the case of theft, but in the 'Laws of King Æthelstan'

death was the penalty both for freeman and for serf. In them (iii. 6)
are found the brutal punishment for free women, the stoning of the
male serf, and the burning of the female by other females. The summary
infliction of death on thieves detected in the act appears in the 'Laws
of King Wihtræd,' 25–26 ; in the 'Laws of King Æthelstan,' i. 1, &c.

The ordeals by water and hot iron are frequently mentioned in the
various 'Ancient Laws and Institutes.' The description, given in the
Pp. 52-55. text, of the mode of proceeding is from the 'Laws of King
Laws concern- Æthelstan,' iv. 7. The 'corsnæd,' by which the monks
ing the
Ordeal.   cleared themselves, appears in the 'Laws of King Ethelred,'
ix. 22, 24, and in the 'Laws of King Cnut,' Ecclesiastical, 5. The
origin of this test may, perhaps, be traced to the well-known effect of
fear, or other strong emotion in paralysing the salivary glands, and so
checking deglutition. In the last-named law is mentioned also the
purgation by simple oath on the 'housel.'

Compurgation, as applied to the clergy, is, to a certain extent,
explained in the same place, and, as applied to the laity, in the 'Laws
Pp. 55-57. of King Ethelred,' i. 1, and the 'Laws of King Cnut,'
References con- Secular, 30. The matter, however, is somewhat obscure.
cerning Com-
purgation and The form of oath is, in the 'Ancient Laws and Institutes,'
its relation to
trial by Jury. among the 'Oaths' of which the date is uncertain. First of
all the accused swears (5) 'By the Lord, I am guiltless, both in deed
and counsel, of the charge of which N. accuses me.' Then each
compurgator swears (6) 'By the Lord, the oath is clean and unperjured which N. has sworn.' In the latter case 'N.' stands, of course,
for the accused. The functions of the early jury, compared in the text
with those of the compurgators, are best ascertained from a study of the
'Rotuli Curiæ Regis,' which begin in the reign of Richard I., and of
which the earliest have been edited by Sir Francis Palgrave, and published by the Record Commission. The history of juries is, however,
further discussed in Chapter II., etc.

The view propounded in the text that the guild and the peace-union,
or peace-pledge, were but different developments of the same institution,
Pp. 57-58. is not, perhaps, precisely that of any other author. It
Laws concern-
ing the Guild seems, however, to be consistent with the evidence, and is
as a part of the
Police system. in harmony with contemporaneous and later events. The
guild is first mentioned by that name in the 'Laws of King Ine,' 16,
in which it might be supposed to be the social or voluntary guild, but
that the laws among which reference is made to it are of a public character. The original is not less obscure than the English translation which
follows :—' He who slays a thief must declare on oath that he slew him
offending ; not his guild-brethren.' It might even refer to the practice
of swearing together, which was not to be enforced when there was only

a question of killing a thief.   From this passage alone, however, which is so vaguely worded, it would be unsafe to infer much.   But the word 'gegildan,' correctly, perhaps, translated 'guild-brethren' in the instance in which it occurs in the 'Laws of King Ine,' has most undoubtedly that signification in the 'Laws of King Alfred,' 27, 28 :—'Of kinless men.— If a man, kinless on the paternal side, fight and slay a man, let the maternal relatives, if he have any, pay a third of the "wer," his guild-brethren a third, and for a third let him flee.   If he have no maternal relatives, let his guild-brethren pay half, and for half let him flee.   If a kinless man be slain, let half the "wer" be paid to the king, half to the guild-brethren.'

In these laws it is quite clear that the 'gegildan' have a responsibility similar to that of the tithing or hundred in later times, and that they also have a privilege of receiving compensation similar to the privilege of the family.   It is not difficult to perceive here the identity, in origin, of the social or voluntary with the political or compulsory guild.

Among the 'Laws of King Edgar' is an 'ordinance how the hundred shall be held,' in which the tithing is mentioned by name.   It is quite evident that the members of the tithing and the hundred mentioned in this instrument, have precisely the same responsibilities and advantages as the 'gegildan' mentioned in the earlier laws, and are, in fact, so far as the common-wealth is concerned, the same body under another name.

Pp. 58-60. References concerning the Guild, the Tithing, the Hundred, and the Manor.

In the same collection (ii.) it is ordained that every man shall have a 'borh' responsible for him.   The 'friðborh' (peace-pledge), however, can historically be identified with the frank-pledge of Norman times, which again can be identified with the 'decenna,' 'dozein,' or tithing.   It is therefore not too much to assert that the guild is the foundation of the whole system of police which prevailed before the Conquest.   This view seems, too, to be confirmed by the 'Laws of King Æthelstan,' v. —'Judicia Civitatis Lundoniæ.'

The remarks in the text upon the relations of the hundred and the manor to the tithing are founded upon the ordinance in the 'Laws of King Edgar' concerning the holding of the hundred, and upon the similar passage in the laws attributed to Henry I. (vii. and viii.), com-pared with the 'Rotuli Hundredorum,' and the 'Placita de Quo Warranto' (*passim*) as published by the Record Commission, and with innumerable unpublished records in which the 'visus franci plegii' is mentioned as belonging to a manor.   Nothing, perhaps, more clearly shows the practical identity of the Hundred Court with the Court of the Manor in some matters than a passage in the Inquest of Sheriffs, A.D. 1170 (printed in Stubbs' Select Charters from the MS. Bodl. Rawlinson, 641).   Mention is there made of those who hold the 'Hundreds of the

Barons.' The expression refers to Hundred-Courts, the profits of which are held by Barons from the king, either 'ad firmam,' or 'in custodia.' The Court of the Manor, in one of its aspects, was, as is well known, called ' Court Baron.'

The care with which the Danes were anxious to enforce the Law of Peace-Pledge appears in the ' Laws of King Cnut,' Secular, 20.

Instances of voluntary guilds existing before the Norman Conquest will be found in Hickes' 'Thesaurus Antiq.' Sept., vol. i., Dissertatio

Pp. 61–62.
Evidence concerning voluntary guilds.

Epistolaris. *See* also Kemble's ' Codex Diplomaticus,' No. 942. A translation of the rules of these pre-Norman guilds is given in Mr. Kemble's ' Saxons in England,' vol. i., Appendix D.

The Massacre of the Danes is recorded in the ' Anglo-Saxon

Pp. 62–64.
Evidence concerning assassination.

Chronicle,' *anno* 1002 ; and in the same year there is a good example of the assassination of magnate by magnate, and of the manner in which the deed was regarded.

The existence of guilds of burgesses in towns in England before the Norman Conquest is shown by Domesday Book (as photozincographed),

Pp. 64–65.
Evidence of Domesday concerning guilds of burgesses.

Kent, p. 1, ' In Dovere . . . erat Gihalla Burgensium,' and p. iii., ' In Civitate Cantuaria . . . burgenses habebant de rege xxxiii acras terre in gildam suam.' The remark in the text concerning gold-workers in England is founded not only on some passages in the Chronicles, but on the more trustworthy evidence in Domesday, where the mention of them is so frequent as hardly to require a particular reference.

The facts given in the text respecting the names of towns will not be disputed, and require but little further comment. The names prevailing

Pp. 66–73.
Note on the names and origin of towns and shires.

before the Conquest (the 'ceasters,' etc.) will be found in the ' Anglo-Saxon Chronicle,' or in the works of Bede, *passim.* Modern chesters (including the forms caster, caistor, etc.) to the number stated in the text, or beyond, may be found by a study of the Population Abstracts, or of any work which gives the names of places with some minuteness. The Roman ' colonia' of Lindum gave its name not only to Lincolnshire, but, perhaps, at an earlier time to Lindsey, as a portion of that county was once called. It is only necessary to add that the identification of ' York' with ' Eburacum,' which may seem rather forced, is not a conjecture, but can be established through successive stages. Eburacum becomes in the language of the Teutonic conquerors Eoforwic, both the *b* in one case and the *f* in the other being equivalent to our *v*. The *f*, as in Leofwine (Lewin), and innumerable other instances, is, in pronunciation, softened into *w*. Eoworic is then plainly enough no other than York. The most enthusiastic advocate for the continuance of the Roman towns is Mr. Coote, in his

'Neglected Fact' in English History ; the most enthusiastic on the other side is Mr. Kemble, in the chapter and appendix on towns in 'The Saxons in England.'

The remarks at p. 71 of the text do not require the support of authority in this place. The facts on which they are founded are obvious to every one ; and where a city has a tradition concerning its foundation, the robber or the soldier (whichever title may be preferred) always plays a part in it.

The derivation of the name of the shire from the name of the town, in the majority of instances requires no further proof than a reference to any map of England.

The ancient German mode of life in huts, but not in towns, is described by Tacitus ('Germania,' 12, 15, 16, 21, 22, etc.). No details have been introduced into the text for which there is not his authority.

P. 73.
Evidence of
the ancient
German mode
of life.

Ignorance of the use of coin among those Germans who were at a distance from the Roman frontier is shown in Tac. 'Germ.' 5. Though the amount of the 'wer' was commonly estimated in money in England, it is evident that the Teutonic conquerors brought the primitive custom of barter with them, for it is provided, even in the 'Laws of the Conqueror' (i. 9), that the 'wer' may, if preferred, be paid in the shape of horses or bulls.

Pp. 74–75.
Evidence con-
cerning the
early use of
coin.

It appears by the 'Laws of King Æthelstan,' i. 14, that there were in his time moneyers in all the chief towns—more or less according to the magnitude of the place.

The *trinoda necessitas* of the allodial tenure is so familiar to all students of history that there is no need to give authorities in proof of its existence in England or elsewhere.

P. 75.
Notes on the
use of roads
and walls by
the Teutonic
settlers.

The adoption of the Roman roads with the Roman term for a paved way, 'strata,' is known to every one who has heard of Watling Street, Ermin Street and Icknield Street, There is, perhaps, no greater testimony to the permanence of Roman influence throughout Europe than is to be found in the word 'Street,' appearing at every corner of every town in England, and in the word 'Strasse,' which has travelled with Roman arts to parts of Germany which were inacessible to Roman arms.

The pages upon the early tenure of land, and its modification by the position of the towns, were written after the con-sideration of a vast mass of evidence. The ancient German custom is established by Tac. 'Germ.' 26, which passage represents the Germans as being but little advanced beyond the point they had attained in the time of Cæsar. *See* 'Bell. Gall.' vi. 22.

Pp. 76–80.
Note and evi-
dence concern-
ing Teutonic
and primitive
land-tenure,
and the early
tenure of land
in England.

The partition of the Promised Land among the Israelites by tribes will be familiar to every one. The agrarian disputes and laws of the Roman Republic show the existence in Italy of land analogous to 'folc-land.' The illustration from modern Indian villages, in which Aryan dialects are spoken, is from Sir Henry Maine's 'Village Communities in the East and West.' The work contains information from the far East which is of great assistance in the investigation of the early tenure of land. *See* especially Lect. iv. It is after consideration of the information given in these books, of the dissertation upon the Teutonic Mark in Mr. Kemble's 'Saxons in England,' of the explanation of folc-land and boc-land in Mr. Allen's 'Inquiry into the Rise and Growth of the Royal Prerogative in England' (pp. 125–155, edition of 1849), and of certain facts which must be obvious to every one, that the statements in the text are put forward. The view taken is not precisely that of any one of the authors mentioned, but it may be hoped that it is not inconsistent with the evidence adduced by them or found elsewhere.

The word Mark (*mearc*), in the sense of land-mark or border, occurs frequently enough in the early laws and charters, and is familiar to every

P. 77.
Note and evidence concerning the 'Mark.'

one as the Marches and as Mercia. As the boundary not of kingdoms in the modern sense, but of smaller territories, it occurs in many of the documents printed in Mr. Kemble's 'Codex Diplomaticus,' in the 'Laws of Hlothhære and Eadric,' 15, and in the 'Laws of King Wihtræd,' 8. That its original meaning was simply a border may be inferred from the cognate Latin word 'margo.'

The private jurisdiction of the land-holder was commonly known, after the Norman Conquest, as 'sac, soc, tol, team, and infangentheof,'

P. 82.
Note on private jurisdictions in the country.

all of which may have belonged to the tribe within the Mark. The 'fossa' and 'furca' are commonly mentioned among the appurtenances of manors, and were obviously necessary adjuncts to 'infangentheof,' or the right of judging thieves caught on the manor. The fact that possession by a lord had superseded the more primitive mode of tenure long before the Conquest is abundantly evident in the early laws. It will suffice to mention the 'Laws of King Æthelstan,' i. 2, in which it is provided that any man who has no lord may be slain as a thief. The instances of private jurisdictions enjoyed by land-holders are so numerous in Domesday Book that to cite a few particular passages would be to weaken the proof.

The private jurisdictions in towns, before the Conquest, are almost

P. 83.
Evidence of Domesday, &c., concerning private jurisdictions in towns.

as conspicuous in Domesday as those which were enjoyed without the walls. The 'xii lagemanni' of Lincoln, however, some of whom were succeeded by their sons, in the interval between the death of Edward the Confessor and the compilation of the Great Survey, were, like those of

Stamford, on a somewhat different footing from some magnates who enjoyed ' sac ' and ' soc ' elsewhere. They resembled the twelve senior or superior thanes of the wapentake (whose functions, as will hereafter be seen, merged in those of the Grand Jury), and the ' xii judices ' of the city of Chester, who seem to have enjoyed their privileges as a body rather than as private individuals. *See* Domesday Book, as photozincographed (for Lincoln, and Stamford), ' Lincolnshire,' pp. i. and ii., and (for Chester), ' Cheshire and Lancashire,' p. i. But for the exercise of private jurisdictions in towns by individuals in their private capacity, *see* (with respect to Norwich) 'Norfolk,' p. xv., where it appears that Stigand had sac and soc over 50 burgesses, and Harold over 32 ; *see* (with respect to Canterbury) ' Kent,' p. iii., where are mentioned five private jurisdictions ; *see* (with respect to Huntingdon), ' Huntingdonshire,' p. i, where are mentioned four private jurisdictions; and *see* (with respect to Hereford), ' Herefordshire,' p. i., where it appears that the moneyers of the city had their own sac and soc. It must be understood that these cases are not cited as a catalogue, but merely as specimens. The manner in which these powers were exercised in the towns was probably not very different from that of their exercise elsewhere. The curious jurisdiction at one time attached to Baynard's Castle is described in the ' Liber Custumarum,' part i. 149–151, ed. Riley, as well as in the ' Memorials of London,' published by the Corporation under the same editorship. Its first origin must, of course, be matter of conjecture.

The extent of the jurisdiction possessed by towns in their municipal capacity is only a matter of inference. The ' burh-gemot ' was to meet three times a year according to the ' Laws of King Edgar,' Pp. 83–84. ii. 5, and the ' Laws of King Cnut,' Secular, 18, but the Note on municipal jurisdictions. manner of its meeting cannot be ascertained. In some tions. towns the reeve (' port-gerefa ') may have been in no higher position than that of the steward of a manor; and this condition may, perhaps, be described by the expression 'in dominio.' London, as is sufficiently apparent from the charter of the Conqueror confirming its privileges, was not ' in dominio '; of the other towns it appears from Domesday that some were and some were not ' in dominio.' The condition of towns, is, however, further discussed at the beginning of Chapter III. It may suffice, for the present, to suggest that in lawless times lords attempted to gain complete mastery over towns, and towns took advantage of such circumstances as might favour them to recover or increase their liberties. Sometimes, too, the king may have granted his real or supposed rights of jurisdiction to a lord, either lay or ecclesiastical, as a mark of favour or with the object of raising money.

The constitution of the various kinds of ' Gemot,' or court, before the Conquest, is very obscure. In the ' Laws of King Edgar,' ii. 5, and in the ' Laws of King Cnut,' Secular, 18, it is provided that the Shire-moot is to meet twice a year under the bishop and the ealdorman. The

Pp. 84-85.
Note on the
moots or courts
in existence
before the Con-
quest, and on
the proceed-
ings in them.
Hundred-moot, it appears by the ' Laws of King Edward,' 11, compared with the ' Laws of King Edgar,' concerning the Hundred, 1, met once in every four weeks under its reeve. It probably presented the more important cases to the superior shire-moot, and in this sense performed some of the functions of the grand jury. The existence of a supreme court—apparently only of appeal—over which the king presided, may be inferred from the ' Laws of King Æthelstan,' i. 3, the ' Laws of King Edgar,' ii. 2, and the ' Laws of King Cnut,' Secular, 17. On this subject there are many controverted points, but it is hardly worthy of discussion for the purposes of the present work.

What may have been the judicial preliminaries to compurgation and ordeal it is impossible to determine with precision, but the excessively rude, not to say ludicrous, character of the proceedings in disputes concerning land is illustrated by a document published in Hickes' ' Thesaurus Ant. Sept.,' vol. i., ' Dissertatio Epistolaris,' pp. 2–3 ; and mentioned by Mr. Kemble in the introduction to his ' Codex Diplomaticus,' p. cix. A son sued his mother for certain lands ; three thanes left the court and went five miles to enquire of her concerning the facts. She fell into a great passion, and declared that she had no lands belonging to her son, and that he should have none belonging to her. She then expressed a wish that after her death all her goods and lands should be given to a female friend of hers, and requested the thanes to make this known in the Shire-moot. So they rode back and told their story ; and the husband of the lady in whose favour this strange kind of will was made rode off to a church and had it entered in a book there.

The sketch of society previous to the Norman Conquest is founded on the various documents printed in the ' Ancient Laws and Institutes

Pp. 86-88.
Note on the
general charac-
ter of the pre-
Norman Laws,
&c.
of England.' It is there made clearly manifest that the same spirit of ferocity pervaded all the laws—down even to the time of that compilation from earlier sources which is attributed to Henry I., and which might be styled the ' Laws of Edward the Confessor' with as much or as little propriety as the laws commonly so called. The Laws of Edward the Confessor, for which a clamour was raised after the Conquest, were only the customs in use before the coming of the Conqueror—not a code of any particular date. This is one of many cases in which a reference to evidence taken as a whole, and in accordance with the general spirit, is better than a reference to a particular letter selected here and there. An allusion has been made to Asser, the biographer of Alfred, who may have been Alfred's friend and companion, and whose work may really have descended to us.

No one, however, who is conversant with the history of manuscripts would unhesitatingly accept the Life of Alfred attributed to Asser as an unquestionable authority. It is unfortunate that the only early MSS. of this biography which are said to have existed have perished or disappeared. The genuineness of the work is of no great importance to this history, and great labour would be required to settle the point. The general character of Alfred, so far as the statements in the text are concerned, is established by his Laws and by the ' Anglo-Saxon Chronicle.' The same Chronicle and the ' Laws of King Cnut' suggested the remarks upon Canute ; the same Chronicle and the contemporary Lives published in the ' M.R.' series, the remarks upon Edward the Confessor.

The description of life attributed by Bede to the pagan chieftain just before conversion is in the ' Hist. Eccl.' ii. 13. This must be accepted as a picture of rural manners at least as late as Bede's time ; and it seems fair to assume that if the laws did not become less brutal during the three following centuries the general mode of life could have been but little improved.

P. 87.
Note on the persistence of the same general conditions of life.

The monasteries, as they grew wealthier, no doubt made some progress in architecture ; new churches were built in the towns, and the successful merchant might possibly arrive at the rank of thane (*see* ' Ancient Laws, &c., of England,' Ranks, 6). But later history shows how little progress had been made before the Norman Conquest.

The position of the ' wite-þeow,' or insolvent criminal reduced to slavery, and therefore capable of stealing his own body, is described in the ' Laws of King Ine,' 24. *See* also the ' Laws of King Æthelstan,' Procemium. The custom of the ancient Germans to stake liberty at games of chance is described in Tac. ' Germ.' 24. The ' Ancient Laws and Institutes ' abound with

Pp. 89–90.
Note on slavery in England.

passages in which the sale of a Christian slave into a heathen country is forbidden ; but sale into a Christian country is not forbidden. William the Conqueror forbade sale into any foreign land (' Leg. Will. Conq.' iii. 15), and from this we may infer that the practice was still common in his time. William of Malmesbury indeed (' Anglia Sacra,' ii. 258) speaks of the export of great numbers of slaves, but though he lived not very long afterwards, he did not relate what was within his own knowledge. The evidence of the Laws is far more trustworthy, and is sufficient to establish the fact.

The practice of buying a bride with cattle or money is regulated in the ' Laws of King Æthelbirht,' 77–78, &c., and in the ' Laws of King Ine,' 31. In the event of the person sold becoming a widow, half the sum given for her seems to have been set apart for her support, provided the husband did not die without issue ; the other half seems to have become absolutely the property

Pp. 90–91.
Note and evidence concerning the practice of wife-buying.

of the seller. Marriage settlements and dower may have been developed out of these primitive arrangements, but it is impossible to explain them away as not being in themselves a process of bargain and sale. If there could be a doubt on the subject, the provision in the ' Laws of King Æthelbirht,' 31, would set it at rest. The obligation of the adulterer to buy a new wife and deliver her to the injured husband is the best commentary on the nature of the nuptial contract.

The incidental remarks upon the preaching and practice of the clergy are founded upon a comparison one with another of the instruments described as 'Monumenta Ecclesiastica,' in the 'Ancient Laws and Institutes of England.' No statement has been made for which there is not ample evidence; but the general correctness of the sketch given in the text can be estimated better by a study of the documents in general, than by verification of a few references to particular passages.

Pp. 92–94. Note on the character of the clergy.

The ward on the highways is described in the 'Laws of the Conqueror,' i. 28. It may have existed before the Conquest, but it is not mentioned in any of the earlier laws, and the point must, therefore, necessarily remain in doubt. The responsibility of a host for his guest after two or three days' sojourn is mentioned in the ' Laws of Hlothhære and Eadric,' 15 ; ' Cnut,' Sec. 28; 'Will. Conq.' i. 48, and ' Ed. Conf.' 23.

P. 94. Note on Watch and Ward, &c.

Lanfranc's abhorrence of the manners and customs of his flock will be found in ' Lanfranci Opera,' vol. i. pp. 19–21, Letter No. 3, ed. Giles. The conquered, too, hardly spoke more highly of themselves than the conquerors spoke of them. *See* the contemporary 'Life of Edward the Confessor,' edited by Mr. Luard for the M.R. series, p. 432.

Pp. 94–95. Reference to Lanfranc's description of England, with evidence in confirmation.

CHAPTER II.

The word ' Englishry ' has been used in the text at p. 96 and elsewhere to denote collectively the native subjects of the victorious Normans.   It is formed after the analogy of the ' Jewry,' the ' Irishry,' the 'chivalry,' the ' Jacquerie,' &c., and is appropriate as being French in form.   In the ' Presentment of Englishry,' the word is used in a different sense—meaning the condition of a person born of English parents.

P. 96.
Note on the
use of the word
'Englishry' in
the text.

The statement that God handed over the inhabitants of England to be exterminated by the conquering Normans will be found in ' Henr. Huntingd.' lib. vi. (Scriptores post Bedam, p. 367). It is a repetition (*mutatis mutandis*) of the statement in ' Gildas,' that the Britons were exterminated by the invaders from Northern Germany.

P. 96.
Reference to
Henry of
Huntingdon
concerning the
Norman Con-
quest.

The adoption of the principle which made the hundred responsible for the murders committed within its limits, and the restriction of the responsibility to cases of murder in which the English were not the sufferers, are shown not only by the Laws attributed to the Conqueror, i. 22, and the Laws of Henry I. i. cxi., but also by the Rotuli Curiæ Regis of a later date (Ric. I., &c.). The diminution in the number of acts of violence and robberies, under the rigorous rule of the Conqueror, is mentioned in the compilation commonly called the ' Anglo-Saxon Chronicle,' *anno* 1087.   It is there mentioned that a traveller might preserve his money on his journey, *if a man of sufficient courage and strength.*

P. 98.
Evidence con-
cerning the law
of Murder im-
mediately after
the Conquest.

The letter of Lanfranc, quoted in illustration of the actual condition of society at this time, is No. 32 in Giles's edition, p. 51.   The appointment of Robert de Limesey, to whom it is addressed, as Bishop of Chester, is mentioned in the ' Anglo-Saxon Chronicle,' and in 'Florence of Worcester,' *anno* 1085–1086 ; the removal by him of the see from Chester to Coventry, in ' Florence of Worcester,' *anno* 1102, and his death at Coventry, also in ' Florence of Worcester,' *anno* 1117.

Pp. 98–99.
References
concerning the
sack of a Mo-
nastery by a
Bishop.

The letter in which Gregory VII. mentions the custom of buying and selling wives ' in insula Anglorum,' is in Giles's edition of Lanfranc's Letters, vol. i. p. 59, Letter No. 40.

Pp. 99–100.
Reference to
Gregory VII.
on wife-selling.

The mutilation of criminals as a perpetual warning to the ill-disposed

P. 100.
Reference concerning mutilation under the Conqueror.

is recommended in the 'Leges. W. Conq.' iii. 17; the disapprobation of the synod held in London will be found in Giles's 'Op. Lanf.' i. 307, as well as in Wilkins' 'Concilia,' i. 363–364.

It has been suggested that the trial by combat was recognised in England before the Conquest because it was common to the Northern

P. 100.
Note on the introduction of trial by combat.

nations. Not only, however, is there the negative evidence of its absence from the laws which constitute our only sources of information, but there is the positive evidence of later charters, which clearly show that the native townsmen at least were not familiar with the practice, and considered it a privilege to be excused from the necessity of fighting to prove their innocence. See (*passim*) the Charters to towns in the 'Rotuli Chartarum.' This instance shows the extreme danger of inferring the existence of any customs in England solely from their existence among 'Teutonic' nations elsewhere.

The character of Lanfranc given in the text is founded generally upon the acts of his life and his writings. References to particular

Pp. 100–102.
Note on the character of Lanfranc.

passages apart from their context would in this, as in many other cases, be worse than useless. Lanfranc's horror of clerical marriages, and the story of the married Bishop of Lichfield, are to be found in Giles's edition of Lanfranc's works, vol. i. p. 22, Letter No. 4.

The alleged introduction of feudal principles into England at the time of the Conquest is very briefly touched in the text, because a long

Pp. 102–103.
Note on the introduction of feudalism into England.

disquisition upon the subject would obviously be out of harmony with the objects of the present work. Those elements in the tenure of land which had a tendency to produce crime have, it may be hoped, been sufficiently indicated in the first chapter; and the continuance of the same elements is made apparent in those portions of the history for which materials are more abundant, as, for instance, the portion relating to the reign of Edward III. It should, however, be mentioned that the general spirit of the laws collected in the 'Ancient Laws and Institutes of England' is to draw a clear distinction between the man who is a Hlaford or lord, and the man who has a lord over him. Military service was an incident of allodial no less than of feudal tenure; and the reliefs, aids, &c., which were considered the most oppressive parts of the Norman rule, were excrescences which should not be confounded with the feudal system itself. It is tolerably obvious, therefore, that the dispute concerning the first introduction of feudalism into England is a dispute about words rather than facts.

The encroachments of Gregory VII., and the manner in Pp. 104-105. which they were met by William, appear in Lanfranc's Letters, Reference concerning Gregory's encroachments. 10 and 11, Giles, vol. i. p. 31 *et seq.*

The separation of the ecclesiastical from the secular The law separating ecclesiastical from secular jurisdiction. jurisdiction is the subject of one of William's charters. 'Ancient Laws, &c., of England,' Leges Will. Con. iv.

Domesday Book may now be very conveniently studied in the photozincographs of it published, county by county, under the direction of the Master of the Rolls. They are fac-similes, and Pp. 106-109. to consult them is equivalent to consulting the Book itself. Note on Domesday For that reason reference has been made to them in this Book and the Great Rolls of work, rather than to the old edition. A 'Great Roll,' as the Exchequer. each of the great Exchequer rolls is usually styled in the document itself, is, perhaps, better known as a Pipe Roll, or Great Roll of the Pipe. The first of these most valuable records was published by the Record Commission, under the editorship of Mr. Joseph Hunter, who succeeded in fixing its date—the 31st year of Henry I.—by a very exhaustive process of reasoning. The later rolls, beginning with the second year of Henry II., follow in succession year by year with hardly an interruption until the abolition of the Pipe Office in the reign of William IV. They are preserved and may be consulted in the Public Record Office.

The punishment inflicted on the moneyers for coin- Pp. 110-111. ing false money in the reign of Henry I. is recorded in References concerning the Sim. Dunelm. ('Decem Scriptores') Col. 254. punishment of coiners.

There are notices of the punishment to be inflicted on the same class in the 'Laws of King Æthelstan,' the 'Laws of King Edgar,' the 'Laws of King Ethelred,' and the 'Laws of King Cnut,' in the 'Ancient Laws and Institutes of England.'

The passage relating to the reign of Stephen, for which there are but scanty materials, is founded on that portion of Roger Hoveden which relates to the period ; on the concluding passage in the Pp. 111-115. 'Anglo-Saxon Chronicle,' and on the 'Gesta Stephani Regis.' References concerning The terms of the Treaty of Peace are most fully given by events in Stephen's Matthew Paris, who, though not a contemporary, may, per- reign. haps, have had access to a contemporary document. It would be unsafe to accept his version alone, but there is no dispute respecting the general tenour of the agreement made at Wallingford be- Pp. 115-118. tween Stephen and his rival. References concerning the The somewhat contradictory contemporary versions of murder of Becket, and Becket's quarrel with Henry II. have been collected by the events which pre- Giles in the first two of his volumes of 'Becket's Life and ceded it. Letters.' The text, it is hoped, will not be found inconsistent with any of these accounts. The details of the murder are chiefly from the narrative of Edward Grim, an eye-witness, which, however, has been compared with the others. *See* Giles, vol. i. p. 76.

The Assise of Clarendon, a most important document, will be found in Palgrave's 'English Commonwealth,' vol. ii., pp. clxviii.–clxix., printed from 'Bib. Reg.' 14, C. 2. A somewhat different text is given by Mr. Stubbs, in his 'Select Charters,' &c., pp. 137–139, from Bodl. Rawlinson, C. 641. 'Villata' has been translated 'vill' instead of township in the text, because the vagueness of the original seems to be, in this way, better preserved. 'Villate' is hardly English. It should also be mentioned, in addition to the explanation of the words 'lawful men' (legales homines) given in the text, that the expression implied freedom from legal disability of every kind (outlawry, excommunication, minority, infamy incurred by perjury, recreancy, etc.).

Pp. 118–123. References to Public Records, Glanville, &c., concerning legislation under Henry II. : its relation to previous and subsequent laws, and to Trial by Jury.

The functions of the reeve and twelve elder thanes of the wapentake are briefly described in the 'Laws of King Ethelred,' iii. 3. It is not there stated before whom their accusation is to be laid.

The compurgation by twelve in the Hundred, is mentioned in the 'Laws of William the Conqueror,' i. 51, and there only. It is an important connecting link between the reeve and his twelve assessors, the twelve jurors of the Hundred, according to the Assise of Clarendon, and the compurgators according to the wager of law. The oath in every case resolves itself at best into an oath concerning general repute. The later jury system was an adaptation of the old customs to new ideas of evidence.

The predominance of the number 12 in the Danish laws rather than in the laws not of Danish origin is further illustrated in 'Alfred's and Guthrum's Peace,' 3. The twelve men in each county sworn, under the Conqueror, to reproduce the Laws of Edward the Confessor are mentioned in the preamble to the Laws so called.

The wager of law is recognised by Glanville i. 9, and may be traced through the law-books for many centuries (*see* Coke upon Littleton, 294–295). It seems to have been the general legal doctrine that no wager of law could be allowed where trespass or injury with force was alleged against the defendant. Blackstone accepts this view, iii. 22. The following passages, however, may perhaps indicate that the wager of law was in some places more generally adopted. They also show the preference for the number 12 in the North. They are from the Court Roll of Cotam-Mandeville among the Durham Records in the Public Record Office, and are of the early part of the reign of Henry VI. :—

Pp. 123–124. The Wager of Law.

Memb. 2 dors. 'Nicolaus Watson queritur versus Johannem Neuton

in placito transgressionis de eo quod interfecit unum porcum suum ad valenciam iii. *s.* cum uno baculo ad dampna Nicolai v. *s.*   Et predictus defendit vim et injuriam et dicit quod in nullo est culpabilis et defendit per legem, unde habet diem ad vadiandum legem se septima manu ad proximam curiam cum vicinis vel se duodecima manu cum extraneis.'
And,
Memb. 3 dors. 'Thomas Webster queritur de Henrico Elwyk et Johanna uxore de eo quod ipsa interfecit unam ovem et agnum et unam aucam matricem ad dampna ipsius Henrici iiij. *s.*   Et predicti Henricus et Johanna defendunt, etcetera; et dicunt quod non sunt inde culpabiles. Et inde profert facere legem, et unde habent diem de lege facienda se duodecima manu ad proximam curiam.'

The contemporaneous spelling and manner of extending contractions have been reproduced in the foregoing and other Latin records which have been printed for the first time in these Notes. Note on the spelling, &c., of Latin documents.

Glanville describes the Grand Assise (and contrasts it with the duel), in his treatise 'De Legibus Angliæ,' lib. ii. cc. 1–17, and the punishment for jurors who committed perjury on the Grand Assise, in lib. ii. c. 19. The analogous inquest on persons alleged to have died in the crime of usury is mentioned by him in lib. vii. c. 16. Pp. 124-128. The Grand Assise, &c.

The scheme for the selection of the jurors of the Hundred who were to make their presentments to the justices, at the beginning of the reign of Richard I., will be found in Rog. Hoveden, Ed. Stubbs, vol. iii. p. 262.

The Assise of Northampton (A.D. 1176) will be found in Bened. Abbas, i. 108, and the Inquest of Sheriffs is printed, from a MS. in the Bodleian Library, in Mr. Stubbs' 'Select Charters,' &c., where also the Assise of Northampton is reprinted.

It is possible to detect local influence still asserting itself on the Bench of itinerant justices even after the Inquest of Sheriffs. The names (which are given in the Pipe Rolls) show the need of the 21st article of the 'Capitula Placitorum Coronæ' of the reign of Richard I. It is there expressly provided that no sheriff shall be justice during his shrievalty, and that no one shall act as justice in any county of which he has been sheriff since the king's coronation (Rog. Hoved., Ed. Stubbs, vol. iii. p. 264). The remarks concerning the removal of sheriffs in the year 1170, or 16 Henry II., are founded on the list of sheriffs made by the author of the present work, from the Great Rolls of the Pipe, and printed in the 31st Report of the Deputy-Keeper of Public Records, pp. 262-366. The chroniclers, with their usual love of exaggeration, assert that 'nearly all' the sheriffs were displaced.

Savigny's 'Geschichte des römischen Rechts im Mittelalter' contains

documents affording ample proof that the Roman Law was not forgotten
on the Continent during the Middle Ages. The introduction of the
subject among the studies at Oxford in the year 1138 is
mentioned in Gervase ('Decem Scriptores') Col. 1665. Its
influence upon the lawyers of the time of Henry II. may
be inferred from the Prologue to Glanville's treatise, which
is imitated, or rather copied, with very little variation, from the
'Proœmium' to Justinian's Institutes.

P. 133.
Note on the
study of the
Roman Law
in England.

The actual operation of the legal system sketched out in the Assises
of Clarendon and Northampton becomes apparent in the series of
Pipe Rolls in the Public Record Office. Thus in the roll
of the year 22 Henry II., the 'Justicie errantes' are mentioned, and the pecuniary proceeds of their visits begin to
appear in the accounts ; but the eyre was not completed till
the 23rd year, in which appear the amercements of counties
which had escaped the visit of the justices in the 22nd year.

Pp. 135–137.
Note (with
references to
the Great Rolls
of the Exche-
quer, &c.) upon
the early ope-
ration of the
system of
eyres.

Some care is required to separate the accounts of one eyre from those
of another, as the sums due were not paid at once, but in instalments,
year after year, and the accounts of a new and an old eyre may appear
on the same roll, or the accounts of a previous eyre on the roll of
a year during which there was no eyre at all. The new accounts are
distinguished from the old by the heading ' Nova Placita, Nove Con-
ventiones.' But here again there is a possible source of error, as the
same heading is applied to the new pleas, &c., belonging to jurisdictions
other than those of the justices of the criminal eyre ; and the justices
in eyre are not usually designated by that name after 22 Henry II.
But here also it is only necessary to bear in mind the subject-matter of
which the justices in eyre had cognisance according to the Assise of
Northampton, and the intervals of the criminal eyres at once become
apparent. The result may be verified by an inspection of the names
of the justices, which always show that the Bench of the true criminal
eyre was composed in part, though not in every case wholly, of judges
who were not merely local magnates, and who were, no doubt, connected with the central King's Court. With these precautions a little
industry will suffice to detect that the eyre which followed that of 22
and 23 Henry II. was carried out in 24 and 25 Henry II., or, in other
words, that from the commencement of one to the commencement of
the other there was an interval of two years.

A comparison of the Pipe Rolls of the end of the reign of Henry II.
seems to show that the interval between eyre and eyre had become
already somewhat greater. The length of time occupied by an eyre,
and, perhaps, the dilatoriness of some Exchequer clerks, which have
rendered it necessary to describe a single eyre as belonging to two

years, are throughout a source of confusion. There was, however, an eyre of which nearly all the accounts appear in the thirty-first, and another of which nearly all the accounts appear in the thirty-fourth year of the reign of Henry II., and if the interval between the two was not quite three years it must certainly have been more than two years.

Though there were to be four judicial visitations, in the year for holding assises of Novel Disseisin, according to John's Magna Carta, the eyre proper seems to have languished after the death of Henry II. The periods of the criminal eyres, however, could be ascertained only by a very careful inspection of the whole of the Pipe Rolls, and the result would hardly be worth the labour.

The extension of the interval between the eyres in the reign of Henry III. to seven years seems to be established by a passage in the 'Monachi Wigorniensis Annales,' 'Anglia Sacra,' i. 425. It there appears that a resolve was taken to resist the entry of the justices in eyre into Worcestershire, because seven years had not elapsed since their last visitation.

The division of criminal jurisdiction in Glanville's time (reign of Henry II.) into that of the justices in eyre, for greater offences, such as homicide, and that of the sheriff for minor offences, such as larceny, will be found in the last sentence of Glanville's work. The 'gemot' of the shire under the presidency of the sheriff was probably held at the same times every year as before the Conquest. *See ante,* pp. 443–444. The defects—and, indeed, the worthlessness—of these county courts, easily to be conjectured from the general state of society, are brought prominently forward in the statutes relating to criminal matters passed in the reign of Edward I.

It has been supposed that the distinction between Norman, or Frenchman, and Englishman was at an end in the reign of Henry II., and that all marks of inferiority had then been removed from the English people. The authority of the 'Dialogus de Scaccario' does undoubtedly seem at first sight amply sufficient to establish this belief. The treatise is in manuscript both in the Red Book and in the Black Book of the Exchequer, and is printed at the end of the 'History of the Exchequer' by Madox, who attributes it, apparently on good grounds, to 'Ricardus Filius Nigelli.' The supposed writer was Bishop of London in the reign of Richard I., and had previously been Treasurer at the Exchequer.

Pp. 137–139 Note (with references to the Great Rolls of the Exchequer, the 'Dialogus de Scaccario,' Glanville, Bracton, the Statutes, &c. concerning the end of the distinction between Norman and Englishman.

There is no necessity to controvert the received opinion with respect to the authorship of the 'Dialogus' or the period at which it was compiled. But there is no doubt that, whatever its authorship, it is incorrect in this well-known passage:—'. . . ut centuriata . . . fisco condemnaretur, quædam scilicet in xxxvi, quædam in xliiii l. . . .'

' Sed jam cohabitantibus Anglicis et' Normannis et alterutrum uxores ducentibus vel nubentibus, sic permixtæ sunt nationes ut vix discerni possit hodie, de liberis loquor, quis Anglicus quis Normannus sit genere ; exceptis duntaxat adscriptitiis qui villani dicuntur quibus non est liberum, obstantibus dominis suis, a sui status conditione discedere. Ea propter pene quicunque sic hodie occisus reperitur, ut murdrum punitur, exceptis his quibus certa sunt, ut diximus, servilis conditionis indicia.'

In the first place the sum here alleged to have been paid by the Hundreds when a Frenchman had been slain is inconsistent with the passages relating to this subject in the Laws of the Conqueror and in the Laws attributed to Henry I. In the 'Dialogus' it is stated that the sum of forty-four pounds was in some cases paid for a single murder, whereas forty-seven or forty-six marks is the maximum according to the laws. The mark was two-thirds of the pound, and forty-four pounds would therefore be sixty-six marks. The Laws attributed to Henry I. are at any rate not of earlier date than his reign, and the fact that they agree so closely as they do with those of the Conqueror in the sum for which the Hundred was made liable renders it extremely improbable that there was any change in the interval between the compilation of the two sets of laws. It is also perfectly clear from the Pipe Roll of 31 Henry I. that the maximum did not exceed the sum mentioned in the Laws, and that, at this period at any rate, the maximum was rarely or never exacted. The Roll of Henry I. affords a most certain conclusion on this point, because, unlike some of later date, it contains the statement that each payment is for one murder, not as elsewhere ' pro murdŕ,' which might be one or many. The sums vary from a hundred shillings to fifteen marks ; in later Rolls the payments are not so large ; and there seems no alternative but to pronounce that the author of the ' Dialogus' was completely misinformed.

The Red Book has xxiiij. l. where the Black Book and Madox's text have xliiii. l.; but though the maximum is thus brought lower, it cannot be made to agree with the Laws or with the Rolls. The reading xxxvi. is common to both MSS. ; 36 l. would be 54 marks ; 24 l. would be 36 marks—the one sum too high, the other too low for the legal maximum, and both too high for the sum commonly exacted.

The statement that the distinction between Englishman and Frenchman had practically come to an end in these criminal matters is obviously of diminished authority when an important error has been detected in the context. It seems also to be sufficiently refuted by the considerations put forward in the text of the present work, which ought, however, perhaps to be confirmed by more specific references. In the Pipe Rolls of the latter part of the reign of Henry II., the ' false present-

ments,' which must, no doubt, be interpreted as false presentments of
Englishry, are very frequent, as are ' concealments ; ' and ' false presentments of Englishry' by name are to be found on the Pipe Roll 34
Henry II., under Berkshire, Somersetshire, &c. The presentment of
Englishry is an essential feature in the ' Rotuli Curiæ Regis,' of which
the earliest were published by the Record Commission, and edited by
Sir Francis Palgrave. The entries are very short, but suffice to show
the presentment in actual operation. One of the chief functions of the
justices at this time (temp. Ric. I.) seems to have been to decide
whether the presentment was duly made by the Hundred, and whether
a death came under the technical definition of murder or not. Death
by misadventure or starvation might be a ' murdrum ' if there was no
presentment of Englishry. Perhaps, however, the most convincing
proof that the distinction between victors and vanquished was continued
beyond this time is to be found in Bracton. He gives a definition of
murder, which agrees in the main with that of Glanville. Glanville says
(lib. xiv. c. 3) : ' Dicitur murdrum quod nullo vidente, nullo sciente
clam perpetratur, præter solum interfectorem et ejus complices, ita
quod mox non assequatur clamor popularis.' According to Bracton:
' Murdrum est occulta extraneorum et notorum hominum occisio, a
manu hominis nequiter perpetrata, et quæ, nullo sciente vel vidente,
facta est, præter solum interfectorem et suos coadjutores et fautores,
et ita quod non statim assequatur clamor popularis.' ' Bracton, who
lived in the reign of Henry III., is by no means a servile copier of
Glanville, who lived in the reign of Henry II., and the account which
he gives of the Hundred and of its murders is much fuller than that
of his predecessor. But what is most remarkable is that the form of
the ' presentment of Englishry,' which is wanting in Glanville, is given
at length in Bracton. It might almost be inferred that this form had
been finally matured in the period between the compilation of the two
treatises—especially as French and English are carefully distinguished
in charters of John's reign. Whether that is so or not, however, there
is at least no doubt that the custom of proving a murdered person to
be English, if possible, was in complete vitality in the time of Bracton,
who states that the fact had to be proved by the nearest relatives
(Bracton, pp. 134–135). This and the fact that the presentment of
Englishry was not formally abolished before the Stat. 14 Ed. III.,
St. i. c. 4, seem to establish beyond all reasonable doubt that Englishmen were not equal with their conquerors in the eye of the law for
some generations after the time at which it is commonly supposed that
the nation ceased to wear any badge of subjection.

The testimony of the next of kin concerning the parentage of the
dead deserves perhaps to be regarded as one of the links connecting

the old system of procedure with our modern custom of deciding matters upon evidence.

The references concerning the progress of the towns are given in the notes to the next chapter.

The story of Bucquinte and the other housebreakers who were merchants in London is from Benedict Abbas, Ed. Stubbs, i. 155. The

Pp. 141–142. Evidence of Crime in London and other towns in the 12th century. persistence of the old regulation which made innkeepers responsible for their guests, from the period before the Conquest to the period under consideration and afterwards, and the stringent rules against night-walking, show clearly enough the lawlessness of the towns—the least lawless parts of the kingdom.

The assertions concerning false weights and measures, and other devices for cheating, are founded on the Great Rolls of the period, *passim,* and on Neckam, 'De Naturis Rerum,' c. clxxix. M.R. Series, p. 315.

The general description of the Court is from Mapes, 'De Nugis Curialium,' and in particular from Dist. i. 1–5, and 10, from Peter of

Pp. 142–146. References concerning the Court of Henry II. Blois, especially Ep. xcv. (Editions of Migne or of Giles), from Neckam, 'De Nat. Rer.' cc. 40, 129, 158, etc., and from the tone of all the chroniclers and letter-writers.

The details of the treatment of women and the views entertained concerning matrimony are from Neckam, 'De N. R.' c. 155, from Peter of Blois, Ep. lxxix., and from John of Salisbury, 'Polycrat.' lib. iii. cc. 4 and 14, and lib. viii. c. 11. An account of the love of gaming and the loaded dice will be found in Neckam, 'De N. R.' c. 183.

Pp. 146–148. References concerning the character of the clergy. The appointment of the three Bishops as Chief Justices ('Archijusticiarios'), to check the iniquities of their subordinates, is mentioned in Rad. de Dic. ('Decem Scriptores'), An. 1179. Col. 605-6.

Richard I.'s lament over the depravity of his clergy is in Gervas. Chron. 1595.

Peter of Blois' description of a bishop of his time is among his Letters. Ep. xviii. (The numbering is the same in the editions both of Migne and of Giles.)

Pp. 148–149. References concerning the clerical brawl when the Primacy was in dispute. The account of the dispute between the Archbishops of Canterbury and York, and of the riot in the Councilchamber, is from Will. Newb. lib. iii. c. 1, from Rad. de Dic. ('Decem Scriptores') 588–589, and from Benedict Abbas, Ed. Stubbs (M.R. Series), vol. i. 112–113.

Pp. 149–151. References concerning the value and stealing of relics. The early pilgrimages to the shrine of Becket are recorded in Benedict Abbas, vol. i. pp. 72 and 91.

The stealing of St. Petroc's body from one religious house at the instigation of another is narrated in Benedict Abbas, vol. i. pp. 178-180, and in Rog. Hoved., Ed. Stubbs, vol. ii. p. 136.

The statements concerning the distribution of charities and the real fountain-head of mediæval alms are founded on a careful inspection of the original Great Rolls of the Exchequer (Pipe) from year to year. These most valuable documents may be easily consulted in the Public Record Office, and the information of which use has been made in the text will be found in them at the beginning of the entries for each county. *See* especially the Rolls from 2 Henry II. to 10 Richard I. The fact that the religious houses did receive and lodge poor travellers is not disputed, and might be easily established by one of the articles in the Assise of Clarendon. In that most important document, secs. 15 and 18, will also be found the regulations respecting wayfarers arriving at a town, and the registration of those who fled [from their lords] out of one county into another.

Pp. 151-153. Note and references to Records, &c., concerning the support of the sick and poor in the 12th century.

The rise, or reappearance, of various heresies in the South of France in the twelfth century is mentioned in Will. Newb. lib. i. c. 19, and in Chron. Gervas. ('Decem Scriptores') 1451. The appearance of the Paterines in England and their doctrines are described in Will. Newb. ii. 13, and in Mapes, 'De Nug. Cur.' Dist. i. c. 30; their sentence in Will. Newb. lib. ii. c. 13, confirmed by the Assise of Clarendon, sec. 21. The absence of all compassion for the condemned and starving heretics is most remarkable both in the account of William of Newburgh and in a letter of Peter of Blois, No. cxiii. Accounts of the Brabazons or heretical brigands will be found in the Chronicles already mentioned, and an indication of the manner in which their numbers were recruited, in Mapes, 'De Nug. Cur.' Distinct. i. c. 29.

Pp. 154-157. Note and references concerning the doctrines and treatment of the first heretics in England.

The paragraph in which is sketched the history of the Jews in England immediately after the Conquest is founded on the 'Carta Judæorum Angliæ,' printed in the 'Rotuli Chartarum,' p. 93, on the notices of the Jews on the Great Roll of the Pipe 31 Hen. I., on Benedict Abbas, Ed. Stubbs, i. 182, and on various entries on the Great or Pipe Rolls of the reign of Henry II. (in the Public Record Office).

Pp. 157-159. References concerning the Jews in England in the 12th century.

The coronation of Richard I., and the attack on the Jews by which it was followed, are described in Benedict Abbas, vol. ii. pp. 79-84, and the riot in Will. Newb. lib. iv. c. 1. There are accounts of the massacre of Jews at York in Will. Newb. lib. iv. cc. 9-10, and Bened. Ab. vol. ii. p. 107. The riots at Lynn, Stamford, and Lincoln, are mentioned in Will. Newb. iv. 7, 8, 9. It appears from Bened. Ab. vol. ii. p. 84, and from Will. Newb. lib. iv. c. 11, that a few of the culprits were hanged. The names of others and the amercements inflicted on them may be found on the

Pp. 159-163. References concerning the coronation of Richard I., and the subsequent massacres of the Jews.

Pipe Roll 3 Ric. I. Ro. 1 dors., and Ro. 6, and repeated on the Pipe Roll 4 Ric. I. (in the Public Record Office).

The·rapid sketch of the first two Crusades is from the ' Gesta Dei per Francos.' For the First Crusade see especially Willermus Tyriensis, lib. i. cc. 27–29, and Albertus Aquensis, lib. i. cc. 25–28. For the conduct of the Count of Tripoli see Will. Tyr. lib. 21. But the whole of the ' Gesta ' illustrate the morals of the period.

Pp. 164–166.
References
concerning the
first two Cru-
sades, and the
morals of the
Crusaders.

Richard's character is apparent enough in the contemporary Chronicles. For his various revolts against his father it may in this place suffice to refer to Bened. Abbas, Ed. Stubbs, i. 42, ii. 7, 9, 61, etc., and to Rog. Hoveden (Ed. Stubbs), vol. ii. pp. 47, 362, etc. The ordinances for the voyage to the Holy Land appear in Rog. Hoved. vol. iii. p. 36 (Ed. Stubbs). They have been printed from Hoveden in Rymer's Fœdera (Record Commission Edition), vol. i. part i. p. 52.

Pp. 166–169.
References
concerning the
character of
Richard I.,
and the Ordi-
nances for the
punishment of
Crusaders in
the third
Crusade.

CHAPTER III.

THE charter of William I. to London is printed (from the alleged original) in the 'Munimenta Gildhallæ Londoniensis'—'Liber Custumarum,' vol. ii. part ii. p. 504, edited by Mr. Riley for the M.R. Series, and the charter of Henry I., from an 'Inspeximus' on the Patent Roll, 2 Edward IV. part v., in Rymer's 'Fœdera,' vol. i. p. 11, Rec. Com. Edn. In the latter charter appear the exemption of the City from the 'murdrum,' the privilege of trial by compurgation, and the right of hunting. A charter of the reign of Henry II. to Lincoln ('Fœdera,' i. 40, Rec. Com. Edn., from the 'Cartæ Antiquæ,' formerly in the Tower) contains a general confirmation of ancient liberties and laws extending back to the time of Edward the Confessor ; but some doubt seems to have arisen in the interpretation of the passage, for by a later charter of the reign of Richard I. ('Fœdera,' i. 52, Rec. Com. Edn., from the same source) the 'quietantia murdri' is granted in express terms. Winchester receives, in the first year of Richard's reign, a charter ('Fœdera,' i. 50, Rec. Com. Edn., from the 'Cartæ Antiquæ'), in which the citizens have the privilege of clearing themselves in Pleas of the Crown 'secundum antiquam consuetudinem civitatis.' Gloucester acquires the same privilege by John's charter ('Rot. Chart.' p. 56).

Pp. 170–175. Charters showing the privileges acquired by the towns during the first two centuries after the Conquest ; freedom from the murder-fine, &c.

Among the towns which had, in the reign of John, acquired for their inhabitants the privilege of clearing themselves in Pleas of the Crown, in the same manner as the citizens of London, were Lincoln, Norwich, and Northampton. *See* the 'Rotuli Chartarum,' published by the Record Commission, pp. 5, 20, 45, 56 ; and for Lincoln *see* also the charter of Richard, to which reference has already been made.

Richard's charter to Colchester, with privilege of hunting, is printed in the form of an 'Inspeximus' of the reign of Edward IV. in Madox's 'Firma Burgi,' p. 28. An instance, by no means singular, of the grant of a borough to its inhabitants *honorifice*, in the terms in which land is commonly granted, occurs in the charter to Huntingdon ('Rotuli Chartarum,' p. 157).

The existence of a Guild Merchant at Lincoln, from the time of Edward the Confessor downwards, is asserted in the charter, already

mentioned, of the reign of Henry II. References have been given
(at p. 440) to Domesday concerning the pre-Norman guilds at Dover

Pp. 173-174.
Note and re-
ferences to
Charters,
Glanville, &c.,
concerning the
guilds or com-
munes of
towns at the
end of the 12th
century, and
beginning of
the 13th.
and Canterbury ; and, from the manner in which the ' Burgenses' of various other towns are mentioned collectively
in the book, there is good reason to suspect that guilds
existed where they have not been described under that
name. *See* especially Norfolk, p. 16, where twelve burgesses are said to have held a church. The 'xii. lagemanni '
of Lincoln itself may indeed have been a hereditary town-
corporation. The charter of John, in which the guild mer-

chant is described as already existing at Gloucester, will be found in the
' Rot. Chart.' pp. 56–57. Of the previous charters to Gloucester one is of
the reign of Henry II. (' Cartæ Antiquæ,' DD. 3), and one of the reign of
Richard I. (' Cartæ Antiquæ,' DD. 4). In both the 'Burgenses' are
mentioned, in neither the guild ; and it is by no means improbable that
wherever ' Burgenses' are mentioned as a body, a guild of burgesses or
a guild merchant is meant. The statement that the numerous charters
of John's reign in which towns are permitted to have their guild merchant and hanse or hanse-house, do not necessarily imply the creation of
a new institution, but may be simply intended to confirm an ancient
custom, is further justified by such passages as the following. In the
charter to Ipswich (' Rot. Chart.' p. 65) the words are 'Concessimus . . .
quod habeant gildam mercatoriam et hansam *suam*'—that they may
have *their* guild merchant and hanse. The words ' *suam* hanshus ' are
used in Archbishop Thurstan's charter to the men of Beverley in the
reign of Henry I. ; and ' sua hanshus ' is there mentioned as belonging to
the citizens of York (' Fœdera,' Rec. Com. Edn., i. 10, from the ' Cartæ
Antiquæ'). Henry II. confirms to the men of Southampton *their* guild as
they had it in the time of Henry I. (' Inspeximus' of the reign of
Edward III., printed in Madox's ' Firma Burgi,' p. 27). In many other
cases the words are simply ' concessimus eis gildam mercatoriam,' as in
the charters to Lynn and Yarmouth (' Rot. Chart.' pp. 138 and 175) ; but
even this form is quite consistent with the previous existence of a guild
merchant, which was now to be placed on a legal footing. Instances,
too, of various guilds or communes existing without warrant have been
collected from the Pipe Rolls of the reign of Henry II., by Madox
(' Firma Burgi,' pp. 26, 27). The establishment of a new guild in a
town which previously had no corporation of any kind seems to be
indicated by the form of the grant to Niort (' Rotuli Chartarum,' p. 59) :
—' concessimus quod burgenses de Niorto *faciant* et habeant communam in villa sua de Niorto.' A question might, of course, be raised
whether a ' communa' is precisely the same thing as a guild merchant
or town guild such as existed in England ; it seems to be sufficiently

answered by the words of Glanville : 'Item si quis nativus quiete per únum annum et unum diem in aliqua villa privilegiata manserit, ita quod in eorum communam, sicut gildam, tanquam civis receptus fuerit, eo ipso a villenagio liberabitur.' Lib. v. c. 5.   One edition has, instead of ' communam, sicut gildam,' the reading 'communem gildam ' (for which there appears to be no good MS. authority) ; another has 'communiam, scilicet gildam.'   Mr. Stubbs, the Regius Professor of Modern History at Oxford, informs me that of the two Bodleian MSS. of Glanville, one reads 'communiam s. gildam,' the other 'communam s. gildam.'   The MS. in the British Museum, Reg. 14. C. 2, to which I referred upon his recommendation, and which appears to be the best, reads 'communam sicut gildam.'   The Cottonian MS., Claud. D. 2, reads, 'communam scilicet gildam.'   All the MSS. seem, therefore, practically to imply that a guild is a kind of 'communa.'   Further confirmation is to be found in the fact that 'communa' is often used as an equivalent for a guild of any kind in those ordinances of guilds which are written in Latin.   *See* Toulmin Smith's ' English Gilds,' p. 201, and the text of the ordinances printed in that book.   The whole Jewry collectively is sometimes described as the ' communa' of the Jews of England.   The Jews had, too, a communa in each of the towns in which they were permitted to reside, and their communa paid the tallage very much as the ' commune concilium ' of a town, or its representatives paid dues claimed from the town as a whole.   It seems to follow that where there was no ' communa ' there was no .guild, and that wherever there was a guild there was *ipso facto* a communa, though there might have been a communa where, perhaps, there was not, according to technical language, a guild. *See* the Jews' Rolls, Pells (Exchequer of Receipt), *passim*.

The acquisition of freedom by a villein, through residence for a year and a day in a chartered town, is mentioned in the passage just quoted from Glanville ; it is also expressly confirmed in the charters to some of the towns, as for instance, in the charters of Henry II. to Lincoln and Nottingham (Rymer, ' Fœdera,' i. p. 41, Rec. Com. Edition, from the ' Cartæ Antiquæ '), and in the charter of John to Hereford (' Rot. Chart.' p. 22). The privilege was, no doubt, claimed, if not allowed, at a much earlier date.   It appears among the Customs of Newcastle-on-Tyne, said to have existed in the time of Henry I., drawn up in the reign of Henry II., and preserved in the Tower.   *See* the ' Acts of Parliament of Scotland,' vol. i., Preface, pp. 33–34. Note. (There is a short confirmation printed in Rymer.)   ' Burgagium ' is there mentioned as the condition of a free-townsman in opposition to that of a villein.   A free tenure existed before the Conquest in favour, if not of individual burgesses, at least of the burgesses of a city collectively.

Pp. 174–175.
References to Charters, &c., concerning freedom acquired by fugitive villeins after a year's sojourn in a charteredtown and concerning burgage-tenure.

Thus according to Domesday, Kent, p. 3, there were lands which the burgesses of Canterbury 'tenebant, *in alodia*, de Rege.'

It may be possible to trace the principle of representation in the jury of the Hundred and other judicial contrivances, but the towns seem to afford the first example of representation combined with a true election as distinguished from a mere nomination made directly or indirectly by the Sheriff. This is only the natural consequence of the charters, of which the most important rendered the towns independent of the Sheriffs. Instances in which the 'commune concilium' was to elect its representatives and send them to Westminster to treat with the Chief Justice, and render an account, will be found in the charters to Gloucester and Ipswich, in the reign of John ('Rotuli Chartarum,' pp. 57 and 65). Charters to other towns at the same period show that the same principle was coming into operation elsewhere, though not yet carried out in its integrity. *See* the charters to Shrewsbury and Derby ('Rotuli Chartarum,' pp. 142 and 138).

Pp. 176–178. Charters showing the growth of the representative principle in towns.

The statement that the chief commerce of England was the export of wool to Flanders, and the inference that the greater part of the land was grass-land, are founded upon a careful inspection of the original Pipe Rolls for a long series of years, extending as far as the beginning of the reign of Edward III. The notices of guilds of weavers in various towns in the twelfth century have been collected from the earliest of these Rolls by Madox in his 'History of the Exchequer,' c. 10, § 5. For the other illustrations of English trade at this period, *see* Hemingford *alias* Hemingburgh, iii. 27, the Patent Rolls 55 Henry III., mm. 6, 10, 15 ; 5 Edward II., part 2, m. 5 ; and 2 Edward III. m., 14.

Pp. 178–179. Records, &c., concerning early English commerce after the Conquest.

It was by the Statute of Merchants 13 Edward I. and by the Statute of Westminster the Second (c. 18), of the same year, that land became a security for debt. By the one was created that species of estate upon condition which was known as an estate held by Statute Merchant, by the other that which was known as an estate by *elegit*. In each case the land was held in pledge by the creditor until the debt was paid.

The roll upon the authority of which the proportion of town population to country population has been estimated in the text is the Vascon Roll, 18 Edward II., part i., written in the French of the period. It would be difficult to overrate the importance of the evidence which it furnishes when regarded as a whole. Its value was known to Sir Matthew Hale. In his MSS. in Lincoln's Inn Library, vol. lxxxvi. under the heading 'Musters and Souldiers' appears this note :—' De numero hominum ad militiam electorum separatim singulis locis et comitatibus Angliæ, quibus instructi armis, &c. (Vascon. Rot. 18 Ed. II.).' It is possible, indeed, that

Pp. 179–183. Roll showing the distribution of population in England under Edward II.

the scribe may have carelessly omitted one or two names (as, for instance, those of Colchester and Cambridge), or may have intended to insert them at another time, but there is no reason to doubt that the record gives a faithful account of England in the main, and may be fully trusted. It is strange that a document so rich in information should not have been printed in any of the editions of Rymer's ' Fœdera,' and still more strange that extracts should have been made from the second part of the Roll, which is not in any way of so remarkable a character. Such an extraordinary omission well justifies the remark thrown out by Sir T. D. Hardy in his Syllabus of the ' Fœdera,' that a ' Supplement' is urgently required.

The statement that Jews inhabiting their quarter of each large town were, like certain Christian inhabitants, styled a ' communa,' is founded on a Roll headed '4, incip. 5, Edward I.,' among the Jews' Rolls (Pells) in the Public Record Office. Elsewhere (Bundle 556, No. 8) it appears that there was a ' communa' of the whole of the Jews in England.

Pp. 184–188.
Records, &c.,
concerning the
position of the
Jews before
Pandulf be-
came Legate.

The regulations for the Jewry under Richard I. will be found in Rog. Hoved., vol. iii. pp. 266–67, Ed. Stubbs, and the substance of them in the ' Memorials of Richard I.,' vol. i. (Itin. Reg. Ric.), Ed. Stubbs, p. 449.

The story of the Jew of Bristol is from Matthew Paris, ' Historia Major,' *anno* 1210.

Tovey's ' Anglia Judaica' contains at p. 79 the order (printed from the Close Roll 2 Hen. III., Part 2, m. 10) for all Jews to wear a badge, and at p. 77 a document (from the same roll and membrane) which shows that the Jews were a common object of attack to the Crusaders in England. The attempt of Stephen Langton to apply the badge to Jewesses as well as Jews will be found in the ' Concil. Oxon.,' A.D. 1222, Wilkins, i. 591.

Pandulf's policy of expulsion and his complaint that the clergy, and especially the Abbot of Westminster, were oppressed by their Jewish creditors may be seen in the ' Royal Letters,' Henry III., No. 369, Public Record Office. (Printed M.R. Series, vol. i., pp. 35–36.)

Pp. 188–190.
Records show-
ing that the
Clergy were in
debt to the
Jews, and de-
sired their
expulsion.

The pledging of tithes by the parson of Morcott is mentioned in the ' Ancient Miscellanea, Exchequer, Queen's Remembrancer, Jews,' Bundle 556, No. 1, in the Public Record Office. It appears by the same Roll that the parsons of Luffenham and Whissendine, and the Prior and Canons of Brock were also in debt to the Jews— and this as early as the reign of Richard I. The interest charged varies from a penny to threepence per week per pound lent.

The cartoon, in which Isaac the Jew, of Norwich, is the principal figure, is drawn on the Jews' Roll (Pells), 17 Henry III., in the Public Record Office. His wealth and position, as one of the chief Jews, are made apparent by the Close Roll 9 Henry III., m. 1 (vol. ii. page 67 b. of the edition printed by Sir Thomas Hardy), and by the 'Royal Letters,'

Pp. 190–191. References in explanation of a caricature of Jews, A.D. 1233.

Henry III., No. 736 (page 18 of vol. i. in the 'Royal Letters' printed in the M.R. series). Mosse Mokke is mentioned as a Norwich Jew in the Fine Rolls (printed by the Record Commission), vol. i. p. 285, and as having been hanged—no doubt for some alleged offence against the coin—at p. 408.

Particulars concerning the appearance of the 'Caursini' 'Caturcenses,' or Pope's money-changers ('scambiatores' or 'mercatores') in England

P. 192. References concerning the 'Pope's money-changers.'

will be found in Matthew Paris, 'Historia Major,' annis 1235, 1253, &c., and in the 'Historia Minor,' M.R. series, vol. ii., pp. 382–384. The attempt of the clergy to deprive the Jews of food appears on the Close Roll of 7 Henry III., part 2, m. 29, đ., printed in 'Anglia Judaica,' p. 83.

That the offences of concealing property and bribing the justices

Pp. 192–193. References concerning bribery of Justices by Jews.

were commonly practised by the Jews is established by the Close Roll, 36 Henry III., m. 14, dors. (printed in 'Anglia Judaica,' p. 131), taken in connection with Matthew Paris, annis 1251 and 1252.

For particulars of a riot in which the Jewish quarter was the object of attack, *see* Patent Roll, 48 Henry III., m. 11 ('Anglia Judaica,'

Pp. 193–194. Records showing a change in the position of the Jews.

pp. 161–162). For losses sustained by the Jews through protections·given against them in favour of the Crusaders, *see* 'Royal Letters,' Henry III., No. 601 (vol. ii. p. 98). The pledging of the Jewry to the king's brother, the Earl of Cornwall, is mentioned in the Patent Roll, 39 Henry III., m. 13 (Rymer's 'Fœdera,' i. 315); its transfer to Edward, the king's son, in the Close Roll, 46 Henry III., m. 19 ('Anglia Judaica,' p. 157); and to the Caursines, in the Patent Roll, 47 Henry III., m. 9 ('Ang. Jud.,' pp. 158–159). The regulations by which it was rendered illegal for Jews to possess a freehold are given in 'Anglia Judaica,' pp. 188–191, from a MS. in the Bodleian (N. E. A. 19).

The Statute of the Jewry (temp. Ed. I.) is printed in the Statutes of the Realm, i. 221. A document which recites crimes committed

P. 194. Statute of the Jewry, &c.

by the Jews against the Catholic faith, and ends with a command that Jewesses should wear badges, is on the Close Roll, 7 Edward I., m. 6. đ. ('Anglia Jud.,' p. 208).

Particulars of the alleged crucifixion of a child by Jews at Lincoln, and of the subsequent trial, are given in Matthew Paris, 'Historia Major,'

Pp. 194–196. References concerning charges against the Jews, executions, &c.

anno 1255 (Wats. p. 785); in the 'Royal Letters,' Henry III., No. 193, printed M.R. series, vol. ii. p. 110; and in the Patent Roll, 40 Henry III. m. 17, đ. ('Angl. Jud.,' pp. 137–138). The insult to the Cross at Oxford, and punishment of Jews for the offence are detailed in the Close Roll, 53 Henry III. m. 12 ('Angl. Jud.' pp. 170–173). The hanging of 218 Jews in London alone, besides a great number in other cities, for offences against the coinage, is mentioned in the 'Chron. Dunst.' (Ed. Luard, M.R. series), p. 279, and in the ' Flor. Hist.' attributed to Matt. Westm., p. 409, etc. The practice of laying false informations against Jews after these executions is the subject of an instrument on the Close Roll, 7 Ed. I. m. 7 ('Angl. Jud.' pp. 211–213).

In London a Jews' synagogue had been given to the Friars Penitent according to Close Roll, 56 Henry III. m. 3 ('Ang. Jud.' pp. 192–193). It appears in a letter from Peckham, Archbishop of Canterbury, to the Bishop of London that Jews were afterwards forbidden to hold religious services in their own houses, on the ground that, according to law, no more than one synagogue in any town was permissible. *See* Wilkins, ' Concilia,' vol. ii. p. 88 (from Reg. Peckh. f. 16, a).

At p. 180 of the same volume appears sentence of exile passed on the Jews at a synod held in London. This document, however, is not well authenticated, and, much as the clergy might desire such a decree, they had not the power to enforce it. But the fact that the Jews were expelled by the secular power is proved by writs relating to the matter directed to the sheriffs of various counties in the 18th year of the reign of Edward I. *See* Close Roll, 18 Ed. I. m. 6 (' Anglia Jud.' p. 240), and Patent Roll, 18 Ed. I. m. 14 (' Anglia Judaica, p. 241).

[margin: Pp. 196–197. Note and references concerning the expulsion of the Jews.]

The number of Jewish exiles is stated to have been 16,511 in the ' Flores Hist.' attributed to Matthew of Westminster, anno 1290 (p. 414).

Edward's promise to devote the proceeds of the Jews' houses to pious uses appears on the Patent Roll, 19 Ed. I., m. 20. His actual grant of synagogues and burial-grounds to the clergy is established by a document preserved in the Tower of London and now in the Public Record Office. Its description is 'Tower Records Miscell.' No. 74. It is headed ' Littere Patentes de concessionibus factis de domibus que fuerunt Judeorum in Anglia.' These Letters Patent, bearing date 19 and 20 Edward I., were also enrolled on the Originalia Roll, 20 Ed. I., from which they have been printed, not quite accurately, in the ' Rotulorum Originalium Abbreviatio,' vol. i. p. 73. The debts of the clergy to the Caursins, and the bitter complaints excited, are mentioned at length in Matth. Paris (Ed. Wats.), pp. 417–419, anno 1235.

[margin: Pp. 197–198. Reco ds concerning the appropriation of the Jews' goods, &c.]

Some data for estimating the value of £100,000—the loss sustained through the robbery of the Treasury in the reign of Edward I.—are to be found in Matthew Paris, anno 1245, where the amount of the national revenue is stated to have been less than 60,000 marks or £40,000, and in the Patent Roll 5 Edward III., part 3, m. 4, according to which the

P. 199. Note and references concerning the value of £100,000 (stolen from the Royal Treasury, Ed. I.)

Merchants' company of the 'Bardi' are to have (with certain limitations) the customs of London, Boston, Hull, Lynn, Newcastle-on-Tyne, Hartlepool, and Southampton, for which they are to give the king 1000 marks per month. Compare also Matt. Par. anno 1252, where the 'reditus merus Regis' is said to be less than a third of 70,000 marks. It is, however, impossible to fix definitely the value of the pound sterling at any period of the middle ages, though many writers on prices have grappled with the problem. The whole of the conditions of life are so completely altered that it is impossible to exclude false assumptions in attempting to make the calculation. The most useful collection of facts relating to the subject, is, perhaps, to be found in the 'History of Prices,' by Mr. J. E. T. Rogers. The Treasury liberally granted aid from the Public Record Office for the compilation of the work, and the materials brought together by Mr. F. S. Haydon of that office are of the highest value.

The particulars of the robbery of the Royal Treasury have been collected from the following sources. The first commission to enquire,

Pp. 199–203. Note and references to Records, &c., concerning the proceedings after the great robbery at the Royal Treasury.

dated June 6, is printed in Rymer's 'Fœdera' (Record Com. Edition), vol. i. part 2, p. 956, from the Patent Roll, 31 Edward I., m. 21, đ. The functions of the juries under this commission were somewhat analogous to those of grand juries. Their finding was not to be final, but the persons declared guilty by them were to be imprisoned until the king gave further commands. The second commission, dated October 10 (Rymer, p. 959, from the same Roll, m. 12, đ.), appoints justices to hear and determine the case, and refers to the assertion of the accused abbot and monks that they were wholly innocent; the juries are to be selected from Surrey and Middlesex. A third and amended commission issued on November 10 (Rymer, p. 960, from the same Roll, m. 9, đ.). It is there mentioned that juries are to be summoned from the City of London as well as from Surrey and Middlesex. Both in the second and in the third commission the value of the treasure stolen is estimated at £100,000. The information laid before the justices and the verdicts of the juries under the first commission of enquiry, and under the final commission of November 10 to try the accused, as well as Podelicote's confession, are recorded in rolls which were found among the 'County Bags,' and which are now known as 'Exchequer, Treasury of Receipt, Miscellanea, $\frac{25}{42}$.' From these have been extracted the details which throw suspicion on the abbot and monks, and indicate a conspiracy in which they were concerned with some officials at the Palace. The attempts of the monks who wrote annals to exculpate the men of their own order are excessively feeble.   There are two different though very brief accounts of the affair in the ' Chronica et Annales' of one house. In one place it is stated that the robbery was effected by a single thief, in another that most atrocious traitors and thieves were the culprits. (William Rishanger, Ed. Riley, M.R. series, p. 222 and p. 420.) The judges are, of course, described as perverse, and their conduct as iniquitous in the ' Chronicle of the Monk of Rochester' (Cotton, Nero, D. ii. fo. 192, b., 193) and in Rishanger, p. 225, in the latter of which passages the liberation of the monks is mentioned.   But the scandalous discord between the abbot and his monks after they were restored to the Abbey, and the charges brought by one against the other seem to be a sufficient justification of the verdicts given by the juries and of the sentences pronounced by the justices. (Rishanger, p. 420.)

The account of the ordeal in the reign of John, and of the hanging of a prisoner who was convicted by it, is from the ' Placita Assisarum et Corone,' held at Lichfield in the fifth, and at Lincoln in other years of John's reign, which are fully transcribed in the Petyt MSS. in the Inner Temple Library.

P. 204. References concerning the later ordeal and its abolition.

The abolition of the ordeal in England (A.D. 1219) appears in a document printed in Rymer's ' Fœdera ' (Record Com. Ed.), vol. i. part 1, p. 154, from the Patent Roll, 3 Henry III., m. 5. The difficulty of substituting another form of trial is there almost ludicrously manifest.

The interrupted duel to try the right to an advowson, and the decision of the king and council concerning recreancy, are the subjects of an instrument on the Patent Roll, 55 Hen. III., m. 3. The reference was found in the Hale MSS. With the exception that the parties could fight in person in the duel which decided a criminal charge, it does not appear that there was any difference between it and the duel which decided a civil cause. In the document to which reference has been made, each champion is designated by a term which implies the use of the fists, ' pugil.' It is generally believed, however, that in the ordinary duel sticks were used. The battle of treason was a very different proceeding, and a full account of it is given at p. 389 from a treatise of the reign of Henry V. written by the King's Armourer and Sergeant.

Pp. 204-206. References concerning the Trial by Battle.

Bracton, lib. iii. c. 22 (fo. 143), is the authority for the examination of the accusing jury by the judges, and for the fact that after examination and challenge the same jury delivered a second verdict, which was final.   He also shows, lib. iii. c. 19 (fo. 138, b.), that in the time of Henry III. a person ' appealed' could throw himself upon ' the country,' which would then pronounce

Pp. 206-208. References concerning the growth of the petty jury.

only *one* verdict. The distinction between the two forms of accusation should be well borne in mind by any one who wishes to understand the growth of trial by jury in criminal cases.

Fortescue's 'Laudes Legum Angliæ' (temp. Hen. VI.), chapter 26, shows that jurors were still regarded as witnesses, but that, in civil cases, and apparently in them only, other witnesses were sworn in court and examined before the jury.

Pp. 208–209. For the difficulty or impossibility of obtaining a conviction by appeal, *see* pp. 289 and 481 of the present volume.

Instances in which persons standing mute (but found by juries to be of ill fame) were hanged in the fifth year of Henry III. are printed,

Pp. 210–211. Records, &c., concerning the 'prison forte et dure,' and standing mute.
from the Roll of 'Placita Coron. coram Justic. Itin. Com. Warwic.,' in Emlyn's note to his edition of Hale's 'Pleas of the Crown,' vol. ii. p. 321–323. On the 'Liberate' Roll (Chancery), 3 Edward I., m. 12, is an account of the expenses incurred by the Sheriff of Yorkshire in his attack upon malefactors, 'in quo idem Walterus [the leader of the gang] et quidam fautores sui predicti se secundum legem et consuetudinem regni nostri justiciari non permittentes decapitati fuerant.' The reference to this passage (not correctly given) was found in the Hale MSS. with the meaning attached to it in the text.

The statute relating to the 'prison forte et dure' for those who refused to stand to the law is 3 Edward I. (Westminster the First), c. 12 (Statutes of the Realm, vol. i. p. 29). The curious case by which the operation of the law is illustrated, and in which, as alleged, a woman was saved from death by starvation through a miracle, is recorded on the Patent Roll, 31 Edward III., Part i. m. 11. Reference has been made to this also in the Hale MSS., and the document has been printed in the 'Fœdera.'

The case of maihem cited in illustration of the brutality of manners, which was at once an effect and a cause of punishment by mutilation, is from

Pp. 211–213. Evidence concerning mutilation, &c. (Edward I.— Edward III.)
'King's Bench, Mich., 7 and 8 Edward I., Ro. 13,' printed in Emlyn's notes to Hale's 'Pleas of the Crown,' vol. ii. p. 325. The instance of mutilation to which a man was condemned for an offence committed in the presence of King Edward III. is from the 'Rotulus Calisie, 21 Edward III., No. 22,' to which a reference was found among the Hale MSS. The proper description for reference in the Public Record Office is Patent Roll, 21 Edward III., Part iv. m. 22. The Roll consists of instruments dated at Calais, whence its ancient name.

For an indication of the state of the Forest Laws under Canute, *see* the 'Laws of King Cnut,' Secular, c. 81. The statement that the Forest Laws were of a growth earlier than the Conquest is confirmed by such terms as 'Swain-mote,' which seems to have been a court of inferior jurisdiction to that of the Justices in Eyre for forest-pleas, precisely as the ancient shire-moot was, under the Normans, a court of inferior jurisdiction to that of the Justices in Eyre commonly so called.

Pp. 213-215.
References
concerning the
Forest Laws.

For mention of the swain-mote *see* the Forest-Charter of Henry III., Statutes of the Realm, vol. i., Charters of Liberties, p. 20.

For the provision that none shall in future lose life or limb for taking the king's venison *see* the same Charter, p. 21. *See* also p. 20 for the expedition of dogs, which is the subject of a clause in the 'Assisa de Foresta' of Henry II., Benedict Abbas, ii. clxi.–clxiv., and Hoveden, ii. 245–247 (both Ed. Stubbs).

The remarks upon the nature of the courts and prisons of the barons, and of the manner in which the barons abused their privileges in the time of Henry III., are founded on Bracton, lib. 3, c. 8. fo. 123, b., and on the 'Statutum de Marleberge,' 52 Henry III., c. 1 (Statutes of the Realm, vol. i, p. 19). This subject is further illustrated by the 'Placita de Quo Warranto,' and 'Rotuli Hundredorum' (published by Record Com.), *passim.*

Pp. 217-218.
Evidence
concerning the
privileges of
the Barons.

A writ (of the time of Henry III., A.D. 1233) for the conservation of the Peace is printed in Rymer's 'Fœdera,' vol. i. part i. p. 209, from Close Roll, 17 Henry III., m. 9, d.

Another writ, showing the connection of the Watch and Ward with the Assise of Arms, is printed in the 1640 edition of Matthew Paris, four pages before the index, and at the end of the Adversaria. The clause relating to an escort for merchants is also in the same volume (in the 'Auctarium Additamentorum'), p. 1145.

Pp. 218-223.
References
concerning the
'Conservation
of the Peace,'
the Division of
the Courts, the
Justices of
Trailbaston,
the origin of
Justices of the
Peace, &c.

The Statute of Winchester (13 Ed. I.) is printed in the Statutes of the Realm, vol. i. p. 96. The parallel clause referring to perjuries in civil actions is in the Statute of Westminster the First (3 Edward I.), c. 38 (Statutes of the Realm, vol. i. p. 36).

For provisions relating to Justices of Assise, or Nisi Prius, *see* the Statute of Westminster the Second, 13 Edward I., c. 30 (Statutes of the Realm, vol. i. pp. 85-6). For those relating specially to Justices of Gaol Delivery, *see* 27 Edward I., c. 3, and the Statute of Northampton, 2 Edward III., c. 2 (Statutes of the Realm, vol. i. pp. 129-30, and p. 258).

An instance of a special commission to try cases not pending elsewhere occurs in the so-called Statute of Rageman, 4 Edward I. (Statutes of the Realm, vol. i. p. 44). An ordinance respecting 'Trailbastons' is entered on the 'Rotuli Parliamentorum,' 33 Edward I., No. 10 (Printed, vol. i. p. 178). The word Trailbaston appears only in the margin, but the offences described are as nearly as possible those which are the subject of special commissions in later years, and of which a full account is given in Chapter IV. An indication of the feeling against special commissions in general may be detected in the Statute 18 Edward III., St. 2. cc. 1 and 2, Statutes of the Realm, vol. i. pp. 300–1, in which latter the powers of Guardians of the Peace are defined. See also 34 Edward III., c. 1, Statutes of the Realm, vol. i. p. 364, and 42 Edward III., c. 4. A Petition in Parliament concerning persons convicted before Justices of Trailbaston, and afterwards placed on Juries and Inquests to injure their accusers, appears in the 'Rotuli Parliamentorum,' 35 Edward I., No. 63 (vol. i. p. 201). The recommendation of Parliament that there should be elected in each county six Guardians of the Peace, rather than Justices of Trailbaston coming from a distance, was made in 21 Edward III., No. 70 ('Rotuli Parliamentorum,' vol. ii. p. 174).

It is to chapters 3 and 7 of the Statute of Northampton (2 Edward III.), that reference seems to be made in the special commissions mentioned in Chapter IV., and in the later Commissions of the Peace. In the reign of Henry VI., the Justices of the Peace are required to enforce the provisions of the older Statutes of Winchester, Northampton, Cambridge, and others relating to labourers and liveries.

Pp. 223–224.
Statute of
Treasons.

The Statute of Treasons, in part, no doubt, declaratory, is 25 Edward III., Stat. 5, c. 2 (Statutes of the Realm, vol. i. pp. 319–20).

Pp. 224–225.
Records, &c.,
concerning the
cases of
Gavaston and
the De-
spensers.

On the 'Rotuli Parliamentorum,' 5 Edward II., No. 20 (vol. i. p. 283), will be found the accusation and sentence against Piers Gavaston. An error which appears in the State Trials has been copied from history into history. It is commonly stated that Gavaston was to be declared a public enemy only *if he returned from exile.* In the original it is stated explicitly that it is *as* a public enemy he is banished, and that as a public enemy he will be treated should he return. His execution is mentioned in Trokelowe, 'Annales,' p. 77 (Ed. Riley, M.R. Series).

The case of the Despensers is illustrated by the Close Roll, 15 Edward II., m. 14, by Trokelowe, 'Annales' (Ed. Riley, M.R. Series), p. 108, and by the Close Roll, 20 Edward II., m. 3, đ., which shows that the barons at Bristol claimed the authority of a Parliament to execute whom they pleased. For the executions, *see* De la Moor (Camden's 'Anglica, Normannica,' &c., pp. 599, 600).

P. 226.
Early Record
concerning the
punishment for
High Treason.

The form of sentence in high treason, with the reasons for disembowelling, is from the 'Coram Rege' Roll (Queen's Bench, Crown Side), 18 Edward II., Hilary, 'Rex,' m. 34, đ. The reference to this passage was found in the Petyt MSS.

in the Inner Temple Library, 'Theatrum Criminalium.' It appears from other parts of the same Roll that some criminals were *drawn* for treason, and *hanged* for other offences. It is at this time apparently that the full punishment for treason was invented.

The proceedings in the deposition of Edward II. are recorded on the Close Roll, 20 Edward II., m. 3, d̶., in the ' Apologia Adæ Orleton,' ('Decem Scriptores,' col. 2765), and in De la Moor's 'Life and Death of Edward II.' (printed in Camden's ' Anglica, Normannica,' &c., p. 603). The condemnation of Roger Mortimer appears on the ' Rotuli Parliamentorum,' 4 Edward III., No. 1 (vol. ii. p. 52). The judgment against him was annulled in Parliament, and the lands restored to his heir. *See* ' Rotuli Parliamentorum,' 28 Edward III., Nos. 8–12 (vol. ii. pp. 255–6).

Pp. 226–227. Records, &c., concerning the deposition and murder of Edward II.

Mortimer's confession that the Earl of Kent had been wrongfully put to death, and a statement that the Earl had been induced by means of a conspiracy to believe Edward II. still alive, appear on the ' Rotuli Parliamentorum,' 4 Edward III., Nos. 11-12 (vol. ii. p. 55). The story of the Earl, the Friar, and the Spirit is given in a letter from Edward III. to the Pope, ' Roman Roll,' 4 Edward III., m. 5, the reference to which was found in the Hale MSS.

Pp. 228–229. Records concerning the Earl, the Friar, and the Spirit.

Commissions to enquire concerning maladministration and oppression are so numerous that it is unnecessary to give a catalogue of them. The great commission of 14 Edward III., relating to all officers, legal, military, naval, ecclesiastical, and financial, is enrolled on the Patent Roll, 14 Edward III., m. 8, d̶. *See* also the same roll, m. 3. The reference to this most important instrument was found in the Hale MSS. The Ordinance and Oath of the Justices are printed in the Statutes of the Realm (vol. i. pp. 303–306).

Pp. 229–231. Records concerning corruption and attempts to check it.

CHAPTER IV.

MOST of the incidents mentioned as being brought to the notice of a
P. 232.   foreign traveller landing at Dover are described from evi-
Evidence
concerning the   dence given in a later page of this chapter. The widow-
scene at Dover. pilgrim with her attendants is from Close Roll, 22 Edward
III., part i. m. 29, d.

In the various records which relate to criminal matters instances are
frequent in which the offender takes sanctuary in a church, stays there
Pp. 232-233.   a considerable time, is, no doubt, fed by sympathising friends,
Records con-
cerning Sanc-   and at length confesses his crime before the coroner, who
tuary and ab-
juration of the attends for the purpose of hearing his statement. The
realm.   coroner, after the criminal has taken the oath of abjuration,
assigns him a port, and gives him a definite number of days in which
he is to reach it. The time allowed for travelling from Yorkshire to
Dover is mentioned in a passage which is in other respects illustrative
of the whole subject, and is to be found on the ' Placita Corone,' 22
Ed. III., County of York. A jury presents that one William of Coventry
took sanctuary in the church of Thweng, and remained there from
Sunday the 9th to Friday the 21st of December, when he confessed
various robberies before the coroner, and abjured the realm. ' Et dati
sunt ei novem dies usque portum de Dovoř. ad transfretandum mare.'
Other ports are of course mentioned sometimes, but Dover was certainly
the chief place of embarkation for the Continent.

For the attack by the seamen of the Cinque Ports upon the ship
sent as a present to Edward, son of Henry III., *see* Matt. Par., ' Hist.'
Pp. 233-234.   Major and Minor, anno 1254. Winchelsea was the port
Records, &c.,
concerning the   chiefly, if not wholly, concerned in the outrage. For subse-
seamen of the
Cinque Ports,   quent piracies, *see* Close Roll, 11 Edw. II., m. 21, d. : ' De
&c.   Discordiis inter Barones Quinque Portuum et Flandrenses
reformandis,' which seems to show that the Cinque Port men had been
acting without orders. *See* also Patent Roll, 15 Edw. III., pt. i. m. 44 :
' De Fœdere et amicitia inter Quinque Portus et Civitatem Baionæ.'
These with many other documents, showing the prevalence of piracy,
are printed in Rymer's ' Fœdera.'

It is hardly necessary to cite a number of passages for the purpose of showing that saddle-horses and pack-horses carried travellers and much of the merchandise of the fourteenth century. The carriage of the Chancery Rolls on horseback is mentioned on the Close Roll, 22 Ed. III., part ii. memb. 16, dors. The authority for the famine in Kent, which was at this time caused by the war (and which must have been chronic, like war itself), is the Close Roll, 22 Ed. III., part i. memb. 29, dors.

Pp. 234-235. Records concerning a journey from Dover to London in the 14th century.

The description of a traveller's reception upon his arrival at a walled town in the evening is founded on the Statute of Winchester, which was confirmed in all points by the Statute of Northampton in the reign of Edward III., and was long afterwards enforced.

The sketch of Southwark and of the City of London is from the text of the 'Liber Albus' (Munimenta Gildhallæ Londoniensis), which has been edited for the Rolls Series by Mr. Riley, in whose Introduction all the most important points have been very clearly arranged. There seems to have been no important change in City crimes and City punishments from the time of Edward I. to that which is now under consideration.

Pp. 235-238. Evidence concerning scenes in London.

The account of the lepers on the road from London to Westminster and the royal proclamation concerning them are from the Close Roll, 22 Ed. III., part i. memb. 25, dors.

Pp. 238-240. Records concerning the road from London to Westminster, Westminster Abbey, and scenes there.

For the incident of waxing the body of Edward I. the authority is the Close Roll, 22 Ed. III., part i. memb. 19.

The state of the highway near Westminster Abbey is described in the Controlment Roll, King's Bench, 22 Ed. III., memb. 13, Middlesex. The 'Almorigate' was the Almonry Gate, afterwards still further corrupted into the Ambrygate, as mentioned by Stow.

The order for the repair of all bridges between Stratford and Hertford will be found on the Close Roll, 22 Ed. III., memb. 6, dors. It is so worded as to imply that they had not only become faulty, but had in some cases altogether disappeared. The sheriffs are to have as many bridges made as there used to be.

Pp. 240-242. Records showing the state of the Roads, &c.

For instances of liability to repair bridges, &c., disputed by the clergy, reference may be made to the Controlment Roll (King's Bench), 22 Ed. III., memb. 16 and memb. 19, dors., which show that the Abbot of Eynsham refused to maintain the town bridge of Cambridge, then broken and in ruins, and memb. 17 and memb. 21, which show that the Abbot of Westminster refused to maintain Pershore Bridge. For the abundance of pools, fish-ponds, and other waters, *see* the Patent Roll of the year, *passim.*

A den of robbers on the highway is thus described in the 'Placita Corone,' 22 Ed. III. : 'Quidam latrones ignoti in campo de Denyngton, in quodam loco vocato le Covyng, qui est spelunca latronum in

Regia Strata noctanter interfecerunt . . . et eum de bonis et catallis,

&c., ad valenciam vi. *s* viii. *d* depredaverunt. Sed Juratores dicunt quod nulli de personis latronum habuerunt noticiam.' For ordinary robberies of merchants on the road, *see* also the Gaol Delivery Rolls, 22 Ed. III., Lynn, Aylesbury, &c.

Acts of brigandage, or similar acts, are the subject of no inconsiderable portion of the Roll of Letters Patent of 22 Edward III.

Commissions of enquiry for almost every county are there enrolled, and usually contain a description of the offences committed. The injury done to the Abbot of Abingdon at the time of his fair is mentioned in part i. memb. 38, đ. A favourite place of attack during fair-time was Boston. In the year 1288 a gang of robbers clad as monks set fire to the whole town, and committed murder and robbery as they pleased. It was said by the imaginative chroniclers that streams of molten gold flowed from the burning town to the sea. In the year before the Black Death there had apparently been a similar riot, for there is on the Patent Roll, 22 Edw. III., m. 8, a pardon to forty-three persons who had been guilty of assuming the royal power, confederacies, conspiracies, &c., at Boston. The offenders are described as men of Boston, but there were commonly traitors in the camp. A minor nocturnal disturbance at Yarmouth during market time appears on the Controlment Roll (King's Bench), memb. 76, Norfolk. The successful attack upon Bristol and its shipping is recorded partly in the Patent Roll, 22 Ed. III., part i. memb. 44, đ., and partly in the Patent Roll, 21 Ed. III., part i. memb. 19, and part ii. memb. 28, đ. The truth, however, of the general statements in the text is better established by the whole tenour of the various commissions of enquiry, &c., enrolled on the back of the three parts of the Patent Roll for the year, than even by the particular passages to which reference has been made.

The capture of a prisoner of war by a gang of robbers from the knights who were guarding him is the subject of an entry on the Patent Roll, 22 Edw. III., part i. memb. 43, đ. ; the taking of Queen Isabella's horses and wine, and the attack upon the ship of the envoy returning from Spain, appear on the same part, membrane 14, đ. On the Patent Roll of the same year, but on the second part, membrane 37, đ., is an account of the loss of the Black Prince's horses and carts, and on membrane 20, đ., an account of the assault on 'Queen Philippa's Merchant,' of the burning of his house, and of the robbery of her jewels. The onslaught upon her collector of rents, the restitution of the £500 taken, and the consequent stay of proceedings, are recorded on the third part of the Patent Roll, membrane 37, đ.

The murder of the King's Serjeant-at-Arms is described in the Controlment Roll, (K.B.), 22 Edward III. memb. 72, Ebor. Offences in the northern forests are also mentioned in the Patent Roll, 22 Edward III., part ii, memb. 29, đ. The destitution of the king's tenants who were unable to pay their rents, and wandering about the country homeless, appears in the Close Roll, 22 Ed. III., memb. 5.

Pp. 245–246. Records concerning the state of the Marches, &c.

The predatory band from Great Yarmouth, and the pardon to its leader and the whole of its members, are mentioned in the Patent Roll, 18 Edward III., part ii. memb. 36.

The removal of the timber from the Free Warren and Chace of the Countess of Lincoln, and the accusation against two abbots and a prior as leaders in the offence, are the subjects of a commission on the Patent Roll, 22 Edward III., part i. membrane 43, đ. The pillage of a close belonging to the Archbishop of Canterbury by knights and chaplains is the subject of a commission on membrane 35, đ. The illustrations given in the same paragraph are from the same Roll, part i. membranes 19, 13, 11, and 12, and part ii. membranes 36, 30, 28 (bis), 24, 23, and in every case from the back of the membranes. Any critic who wishes to verify the particular statements in the text, and to learn for himself that they are in accordance with the actual state of society, has only to consult the Roll at the Public Record Office. The back of any one of the parts will probably satisfy him.

Pp. 246–253. Records concerning the acts of private war, brigandage, &c., committed by the townsmen, knights, and clergy.

An instance in which an attacking party broke a house open and carried off the title-deeds as well as timber, &c., is recorded on the Patent Roll, 22 Edward III., part iii. membrane 28, đ. Many others might be mentioned.

The case of forcible entry in Worcestershire is from the same Roll and part, membrane 31, đ. The forcible entry on a manor of the Bishop of Exeter, which was mistaken for a foreign invasion in force, is described on the same Roll, part ii, memb. 26, đ. The forcible entry in Wiltshire, followed by murder, rape, and brigandage, appears on the same Roll, part iii, memb. 15, and on the Controlment Roll, m. 2, đ., Wilts ; m. 12, đ., Lancashire; and m. 28, Wilts. The account of Ercedecne, knight and outlaw, is from the Patent Roll, part i., membranes 41, đ., and 30, đ., and part ii., membrane 42, đ. Part iii., membrane 26, đ., contains the commission of enquiry concerning the engagement between the Under-sheriff of Cambridgeshire with an escort, and another armed force at Cambridge ; membranes 13 and 20, đ., the commission concerning the attack upon the cemetery, cathedral, and priory of Worcester by the ' duo ballivi dicte ville Wygorniæ, et communitas dicte ville.'

The total of murders (*i.e.* of persons feloniously slain) in Yorkshire, either by one person or at any rate not by a gang of brigands, has been ascertained from the 'Coroners' Rolls,' which are mm. 39 to 56, d. of the Controlment Roll. The numbers appearing in the Rolls of the various coroners cannot, when added together, be made less than 88 for the year 22 Edward III. The numbers, however, from year's end to year's end must have been considerably greater, as some of the lists (*e. g.* that for the North Riding) obviously extend over only a part of the year. These rolls contain lists of felonious homicides for earlier years, which fully confirm the inferences drawn from the year 22 Edward III. alone. The Coroners' Rolls exist, in part only, in duplicate in the Assise Series, but are not equally complete for any other county. The best authority for the population of England shortly after the Black Death is the Subsidy Roll, 51 Edward III. It has been printed in the ' Archæologia,' vol. vii. pp. 337–347. The persons taxed were those above fourteen years of age, and the total population has been found by calculation. *See* McPherson, 'History of Commerce,' *sub anno.* The total is not, of course, absolutely correct, but cannot be very far from the truth. The evidence for 'Verdicts of Murder on Coroners' Inquests,' from 1860 to 1869, is the Parliamentary Paper No. 109, Session 1871. (Mr. Lambton). This does not include verdicts of manslaughter, but does include cases of infanticide, and may very fairly be compared with the Roll of 1348.

Pp. 253–255. Records concerning the proportion of homicides to population in 1348.

It is well known that *estre* was a feminine affix before the Low German dialects in England began to lose their grammatical vitality—that ' webbestre' was a female weaver, and 'bæcestre' a female baker. In the Controlment Roll, however, of 22 Edward III., m. 34, Lincoln, two men are described as websters, and distinction of sex could not, therefore, have been at that time indicated by the old termination. It has already been mentioned that the punishment for a female brewer of bad ale in Chester appears among the customs recorded in Domesday Book. The ' Munimenta Gildhallæ Londoniensis' do not show that women were occupied in London in baking and brewing at the period now under consideration, but the Statute 37 Edward III., c. 6, shows that there were still female brewers and bakers in England. The case in which a woman strangled her husband and placed the dead body in an oven is from ' Placita Corone,' Derbyshire, M. $\frac{1}{34}$, in the Public Record Office. A somewhat similar case will be found on the Gaol Delivery Roll, Town of Great Yarmouth, Friday after the Feast of St. Margaret. For instances in which women took part in the riotous doings of the time a general reference to the back of the Patent Roll will suffice.

Pp. 255–256. Records concerning the character and position of women in 1348.

The words in which the common obstruction of the justices by armed bands is described, will be found on the Patent Roll, 22 Ed. III., part i. membrane 32, dors., and elsewhere. The attack upon the Mayor in the presence of the sitting justices, at Cambridge, is related upon the authority of the Gaol Delivery Roll, 22 Edward III., Cambridge Castle, Michaelmas. The imprisonment of the sheriff's retainers by the trades-men or working men of York appears on the Patent Roll, 22 Edward III., part ii, membrane 23, dors. The riot and the use of swords and knives in the presence of the Justices of Assise at Somerton are recorded in the Controlment Roll (King's Bench), 22 Edward III., membrane 2, Somerset.

Pp. 256–257. Records concerning attacks upon Justices, and brawls in Court.

The cases of intimidation of indictors and appellors have been selected from the Patent Roll, 22 Edward III., part ii. membrane 33, dors., and part iii. membrane 32, dors.

Resistance to the king's officers in the collection of tenths, &c., and rescue from bailiffs after distraint, are the subjects of commissions on the Patent Roll, 22 Edward III., part i. membranes 32, 31, 28, 18, 14; part ii. membrane 2; part iii. membrane 36, and especially membrane 38. These matters will be found, in each case, on the back of the membrane.

Pp. 257–259. Records concerning intimidation of suitors, resistance to tax-collectors, &c.

The case in which burglary and the threat of rape are employed to force a woman to promise marriage will be found on the Controlment Roll (King's Bench), 22 Edward III., m. 4, Somerset. An instance of abduction occurs on the same Roll, mm. 27, and 29. The Statute forbidding the forcible marriage of women against their will is 3 Henry VII., c. 2 [iii].

Pp. 260–261. Records concerning forcible marriage and abduction.

The frauds committed by the Keeper or Master of the Horse (Custos Equicii et Magnorum equorum) and his subordinates, appear on the Patent Roll, 22 Edward III., part i. m. 3, dors., and part ii. m. 5, dors. Instances of corruption, and complaints against the king's collectors of taxes, escheators, and other ministers, may be seen on the Patent Roll, part ii. m. 10, ð., and part iii. m. 25, ð., and 26, ð., on the Close Roll, part ii., m. 16, and on the Controlment Roll, m. 63, ð., Yorkshire. An instance of a 'chivaler' shipping a cargo of wool and evading the duty will be found on the same Roll, part ii. m. 33, ð. ; the complaint of the merchants that their money was taken, and the convoy for which it was given not supplied, on part i. m. 15, ð.

Pp. 261–262. Records concerning peculation by the Master of the Horse and other knights.

For instances in which the French, when at war with the English, were supplied with provisions from England, *see* the Patent Roll, part ii. m. 26, ð. ; for the supply of food and arms to the Scots when at war with the English, *see* the Controlment Roll, m. 38, Somerset, and m. 17, ð., on which membrane will also be found (Sussex) the case of the Arrayer of Archers, who embezzled the sums levied in the king's name.

Pp. 264–265. Records concerning the treachery of merchants and knights.

There are five commissions to enquire concerning merchants who defrauded the king of his export dues, on the Patent Roll, 22 Edward III.,

Pp. 265–267.
Records concerning evasion of duties, the importation of false coin, and the manufacture of it in England.
part i. m. 43, đ., and others on part ii. m. 30, đ., and part iii. m. 30, đ. The same subject is illustrated by the Controlment Roll (King's Bench), 22 Edward III., m. 23, Northumberland. An instance of evading customs by false declaration of port appears on the Patent Roll, 22 Edward III., part i. m. 31, đ. ; an instance of collusion with the collectors, on the Close Roll of the same year, part i. m. 21. The commissions to discover who had exported good and imported bad money are in the same form for the various counties, and it may suffice to refer to one (for the county of Gloucester) on the Patent Roll, 22 Edward III., part ii. m. 21, đ.

There were successive debasements of the coinage by royal authority in the years 1300, 1344, and 1346. The effect is made apparent in an Appendix to McPherson's ' History of Commerce.'

In the Gaol Delivery Roll, 22 Edward III., Aylesbury, Trin., two coiners are mentioned. The manufacture of false plate and coin at Scarborough is described in the Controlment Roll of the same year, m. 67, Yorkshire. It also appears on m. 12, London, that a coiner was sent to the Tower before his trial. A case of unlawful possession of false money by four persons will be found on the same Roll, m. 34, Suffolk.

Pp. 267–268.
Record concerning false accusation of importing base coin.
The case of false accusation made by the Examiner of the port of Hull as a pretext for seizing good coin appears on the Controlment Roll, m. 66, Yorkshire.

P. 268.
Record concerning the Mints.
The case of the Lombard merchants who entrusted silver to a mint-master to be coined, and could not recover it, is the subject of a commission on the Patent Roll, part i. m. 5, đ.

Accusations of counterfeiting letters and seals may be seen in the Gaol Delivery Roll, 22 Edward III., Bedford, Michaelmas, and

Pp. 269–270.
Records concerning counterfeit seals, forged letters, writs, returns, &c.
Aylesbury, Trinity. A form of enquiry concerning the misdeeds of purveyors, and persons falsely representing themselves to be purveyors, occurs on the Patent Roll of the same year, part i. m. 16, đ. The case of personation of the Lord Chancellor's kinsman and purveyor, is taken from the Controlment Roll, m. 37, Middlesex.

Forgery as applied to writs, counterfeit seals attached to them, and the losses incurred by the Bishop of Exeter and others from sham

Pp. 271–272.
Record concerning forgery as an aid to brigandage.
legal proceedings, are the subjects of a commission on the Patent Roll, part i. m. 17, đ.

The doings of the Suffolk gang, which united the ordinary acts of brigandage with counterfeiting, forgery, and other crimes of the kind generally considered more ignoble than crimes of violence, are recorded on the Controlment Roll, m. 14, Suffolk.

On the same Roll, m. 8, Norfolk, is the case in which a man was brought to trial for forging Letters Patent of pardon.

P. 272. Record concerning forged pardons.

The commission to enquire into corruption at the Exchequer, payments without warrant, counterfeit seals, and false bills, is enrolled on the Patent Roll, part i. m. 35, đ.   The writ to the Treasurer and Barons of the Exchequer respecting an extension of time to merchants who were afraid of presenting false bills purporting to have issued from the Wardrobe, is on the Close Roll, part ii. m. 8, đ.   The case in which a 'king's minister' is convicted of forging bills on the Wardrobe to the amount of more than 6000*l.* of ancient money, appears on the Controlment Roll, m. 24, London.

Pp. 273–274. Records concerning the forgery of Exchequer Bills.

Particulars of the falsification of a charter in the monastery of Bruerne are given on the Close Roll, 42 Edward III., m. 8, đ., the reference to which is given in the Hale MSS.   The extent to which forgery of this kind was practised may be inferred from an inspection of the charters in Kemble's 'Codex Diplomaticus,' to which the mark of spuriousness has been most freely, though by no means too freely, attached.

Pp. 275–276. Evidence concerning the forgeries of Charters.

Falsification of a writ while in the hands of the Sheriff of Norfolk is the subject of a case recorded on the Controlment Roll, 22 Edward III., m. 3, Norfolk.

Pp. 276–279. Records concerning forgery by sheriffs, packing of juries, &c.

The instance in which the Court of King's Bench held that the Sheriff of Hampshire had sent an insufficient return to a writ, for the purpose of shielding a person accused of homicide, appears on the same roll, m. 81, đ., Suth[t].

The refusal of the Sheriff of Hampshire to execute the judgment of the Court of King's Bench, and the attempt of the coroners to support him, appear on the same roll, m. 31, Suth[t].

Packing a jury is a charge brought against the Sheriff of Sussex, and established, according to Controlment Roll, m. 34, Sussex.   On m. 22, Suffolk, is a record of an inquisition annulled because the Sheriff had placed outlaws upon the jury.

An instance in which accused persons were to be tried at the Gaol Delivery of Newgate, because they were too powerful in their own district, appears on the Gaol Delivery Roll, 25 Edward III., Huntingdon, where there is a writ to that effect, directed to the Sheriff of Cambridge.

The accusation of bribery against the Chief Clerk of the King's Bench, and the subsequent threat of violence, are recorded on the

Pp. 279–280.
Records showing corruption in the Court of King's Bench.

Controlment Roll, 22 Edward III., m. 29, đ., Middlesex. The commission to enquire into misdeeds in the Court of King's Bench is enrolled on the Patent Roll of the same year, part iii. m. 28, đ.

Pp. 280–281.
Record concerning forgery and double-dealing by Counsel.

On the Controlment Roll of this year, m. 21, Middlesex, are the curious prosecution and conviction of a counsel for taking fees from both parties to a suit, and for being concerned in the forgery of a panel of jurors.

Pp. 281–282.
Record concerning an Archdeacon's Court.

The conspiracy by which a man was excommunicated without notice, in the Archdeacon's Court in London, is recorded on m. 20 of the Controlment Roll, Middlesex.

The paragraph in the text which relates to the corruption of Chief Justice Thorpe is founded on the following authorities :—

Pp. 282–284.
Records concerning the acceptance of bribes by Chief Justice Thorpe, &c.

The ordinance for the Justices, and the oath exacted from them on appointment, as printed in the Statutes of the Realm, anno 20 Edw. III. ; the exemplification of process, sentence, and stay of execution, against Thorpe, enrolled on the Patent Roll, 24 Edward III., part iii. m. 3, đ. (printed in Rymer's ' Fœdera,' Record Commission Edition, vol. iii., part i., pp. 208–210), and referred to in the ' Rotuli Parliamentorum,' 25 Edward III. (vol. ii., p. 227) ; the pardon and restitution of lands on the Patent Roll, 25 Edward III., part i. m. 17. References to this subject were first collected in the Hale MSS., partly, as it seems, from an old calendar of the Patent Rolls since published.

Instances in which corn, timber, and hay were carried off without interference on the part of the local authorities may be seen in abundance on the Patent Roll, 22 Edward III. It may suffice to refer to part ii., m. 2, đ., and part iii. mm. 16, đ., 22 đ., 32 đ., 35 đ.

The statement in the text that criminals, even when brought to trial, were but rarely convicted, is justified by reference to as many of the

Pp. 284–285.
Records showing the reluctance of jurors to convict.

Gaol Delivery Rolls of the 22nd year of the reign of Edward III. as have been preserved. They include the Deliveries of the Gaols of Norwich Castle, Bury St. Edmunds, Cambridge Castle, Huntingdon, Bedford, Aylesbury, East Dereham, Great Yarmouth, Bishop's Lynn, Eye, Ipswich, Melton, Worcester Castle, Gloucester Castle, Old Sarum Castle, Old Sarum, and Winchester. Out of 337 persons accused (except clerks, of whom more hereafter) only 83 were convicted. Instances in which persons found in suspicious possession of goods were remanded by the judges for an Inquest of Fame, and afterwards declared to be of good repute, may be seen in the Gaol Deliveries of Cambridge, Easter Term, of Aylesbury, Trinity Term, of Melton, Easter Term, etc., etc.

For instances in which men and women are described as ' Common

Receivers' of felons and stolen goods, it is sufficient to refer to the Gaol Delivery Rolls, *passim.* Similar instances may also be found on the Controlment Roll, as well as notices of 'common peace-breakers,' common 'latrones,' common 'malefactores.'

Pp. 285-286. Records concerning receivers.

The statement that persons accused by approvers were almost always acquitted, and the approver almost always hanged, is founded on the Gaol Delivery Rolls, to which reference has already been made.

Pp. 286-289. Records concerning approvers, and appeals by them.

The commission of enquiry concerning tortures at Newgate, extortion of money, and appeals instituted by prisoners forced by duress to become approvers, appears on the Patent Roll 7 Edward III., part i., m. 22, đ. A reference to this was found in the Hale MSS. Deaths of approvers in prison are frequently mentioned in the Gaol Delivery Rolls, and the deaths of fifty in the prison of York Castle are mentioned in the Controlment Roll, 22 Edward III., mm. 59 to 61, đ., inclusive.

The approver who accepted the wager of battle, withdrew his charge, and was hanged, appears in a case in the Gaol Delivery Roll, 22 Edward III., Trinity Term, Aylesbury.

Common appeals, other than by approvers, are to be seen in such numbers on the Controlment Roll that it is unnecessary to give more than that general reference. The particular instance to which attention has been drawn in the text occurs on m. 36, Suffolk.

Pp. 289-292. Records concerning other appeals.

A writ to apprehend the Keeper of the Marshalsea Prison for permitting the escape of prisoners is enrolled on the Patent Roll, 22 Edward III., part i., m. 37, đ. Instances of gaol-breaking, and cases in which the accused were sent back to prison untried, 'pro defectu patrie,' may be found on the Gaol Delivery and Controlment Rolls, *passim.*

P. 292. Records concerning the escape of criminals by gaol-breaking and collusion.

The two first instances adduced in illustration of the difficulty of identifying a prisoner by his name are from the Chancery Roll 'A,' of Thomas Hatfield, Bishop of Durham, of which a calendar, by the author of the present work, is printed in the 31st Report of the Deputy Keeper of Public Records. *See* p. 143 'Litster William,'

Pp. 293-294. Evidence concerning difficulty of identification of name.

and p. 155 'Robertservant, Nicholas, of the Woghes.' Of the other instances, the first two are from the Controlment Roll, m. 1, the third from the same roll, m. 12, Kent. For numerous similar cases reference may be made to the Controlment Roll, *passim* ; but *see* especially m. 22, Suffolk, m. 27, Norfolk, m. 34, Lincoln, m. 83, đ., Yorkshire. The Statutes which relate to this matter are 37 Edward III., c. 2, 'De

Idemptitate Nominis,' 1 Henry V., c. 5 (the Statute of Additions), and 9 Henry VI., c. 4.

Among the genuine instances of pardon for service in war may be mentioned one to a ' communis latro' on the Controlment Roll, m. 72, đ.,

Pp. 294–297.
Records concerning pardons, false and genuine.

Lincoln, and m. 84, Yorkshire. Pardons granted at the request of men who had influence with the king appear on m. 83, đ., Yorkshire, and (to one of the actors in the affair related at pp. 250–251), on m. 3, đ., Wiltshire. The detection of John Mast in the offence of obtaining a pardon for a brother by personating him at the battle of Crécy is recorded on m. 65, đ., Yorkshire. Proceedings in Parliament relating to the evils brought about by the facility with which pardons could be obtained will be found in the ' Rotuli Parliamentorum ' for the reign of Edward III., *passim.* (Printed vol. ii. *See* especially pp. 161, 167, 171, 172, *annis* 20 and 21 Edward III.). Instances in which the accused are detained in prison without trial until a year and a day have passed are common on the Rolls of Gaol Delivery. *See, e.g.,* the Roll 22 Edward III., Bedford, Trinity.

The pardon for burial of a body in a false name, during the life of the person represented to be dead, and the particulars given in the text, are found on the Controlment Roll, m. 17, đ., Norfolk, and on the Patent Roll, part iii. m. 35.

Instances in which Benefit of Clergy is claimed may be seen in abundance on the Rolls of Gaol Delivery in the Public Record Office,

Pp. 297–302.
Note and references to records concerning Benefit of Clergy, the manner of claiming it, and its effects.

which illustrate the mode of proceeding better than any other documents. It is perhaps hardly necessary to give particular references, but a case in which a clerk was given up to the Ordinary before trial occurs in the Gaol Delivery of Bury St. Edmund's, 22 Edward III., Easter, where also are cases in which clerks are given up as convicts. By Statute 3 of 18 Edward III., c. 2, the decision whether a person claiming clergy was disqualified by bigamy was declared to be within the ecclesiastical jurisdiction ; but at the Gaol Delivery of Old Sarum Castle (Monday after the Feast of St. Matthew the Apostle) the right was waived by the Ordinary, and a jury gave a verdict upon the point. The Ordinary probably had reasons for not wishing to save the accused, who was hanged as a receiver of felons. A case in which a trial by jury was held after clergy had been claimed, in order that it might be known in what character the clerk was to be given up, may be seen in the Gaol Delivery of Gloucester Castle (Wednesday after the Nativity of the Virgin). Compurgation was recognised by the canon law as a ceremony through which a clerk should pass after delivery to the Ordinary. The abuses to which it led are faintly indicated in the promise of the Archbishop of

Canterbury, that, in future, clerks convict should receive a fitting punishment. This is recited in Statute 6 of 25 Edward III., which relates to benefit of clergy, and which, in referring to extortions by Ordinaries (c. 4), indicates that compurgation was to some extent at least a matter of purchase.

The paragraph in the text which relates to the definition of a clerk, and the classes protected by Benefit of Clergy, is founded on the following evidence :—The Statute of Bigamy, 4 Edward I., c. 5, which deprives the bigamist (in the ecclesiastical sense) of his clergy ; the ' Liber Assisarum,' 26 Edward III., p. 122, in the series of Year Books, in which it appears that the tonsure was held to be essential for privilege of clergy, by Justice Shard at the Gaol Delivery of Newgate ; the same book, p. 138, where the judges are instructed (Article 11) to enquire what gaolers had aided their prisoners to learn letters ; and the Year Book for 34 Henry VI., p. 49, a. b., which shows that at the later period the judges could insist on knowledge of letters being held sufficient, though they were somewhat doubtful, for a time, of their own power against the Bishop's deputy.

Sir Matthew Hale discovered the curious case in which the son of a ' clerk ' convicted of felony was declared his father's heir, though the father died without purgation. There is a short reference to it in the Hale MSS. The document is in the Public Record Office, and its description is ' Inquisitions *post mortem*, Chancery, 13 Edward III., Southampton, Johannes de Valoignes.' The expression in it ' quatenus clericus convinci potuit convictus ' is well worthy of remark.

For the invariable conviction of clerks, when accused in secular courts, of the offences with which they were charged, and for their escape when they became approvers, it is sufficient to refer to the Gaol Delivery Rolls of the year, *passim*. *Pp. 302–304. Records concerning the conviction of clerks, and the unpopularity of the clergy.*

For instances of burglary at parsonages and churches, *see* the Gaol Delivery Rolls of the year, *passim*—especially those of Bury St. Edmunds and Melton, and the Patent Roll, Part i. m. 41, đ. *See* also the Gaol Delivery Rolls, *passim*, for instances in which persons described as common receivers are also described as clerks ; for an instance in which a vicar was accused of receiving a box of jewels taken from two murdered merchants, *see* Aylesbury, Trinity Term. The Controlment Roll, m. 62, Southampton, shows that another vicar was outlawed after having received certain offenders. The offence of obtaining papal provisions was first mentioned in a Statute in 35 Edward I. Upon this apparently were founded all the later Statutes of Premunire. The matter excited great commotion during the whole reign of Edward III. It is only necessary to refer to the Patent Roll, 22 Edward III., *passim*,

for instructions concerning those who usurped the king's privileges, and
denied the authority of his laws, and those who introduced into the
realm 'bullas et instrumenta prejudicialia.' *See*, however, especially part ii.
m. 41, đ., where each offence is mentioned in a separate instrument.
Cases in which the offenders had to answer in the Court of King's
Bench will be found on the Controlment Roll, m. 15, đ., Devon, m. 27,
đ., London, &c. On the Close Roll, part ii. m. 2, đ., may be seen the
form of oath in which the Archbishop elect of Canterbury had to renounce all those words in papal bulls which might be to the prejudice
of the king with respect to the temporalities of the See.

Cases in which forcible entry was made into rectories and prębends
P. 304.   both by clerks and by laymen are recorded on the Control-
Records con-   ment Roll, m. 6, London, &c., and on the Patent Roll, part
cerning for-
cible entries ii. mm. 24, đ., 19 đ., &c., and part iii. m. 16, and the forcible
upon Rec-
tories, &c.   collection of tithes, on the Patent Roll, part ii. m. 7, đ.

P. 305.   The excommunication of the Under-sheriff and the
Record con-   Sheriff's men by the Bishop of Exeter, because they had
cerning the
excommunica- seized his cattle in execution, is mentioned in the Control-
tion of sheriff's
officers.   ment Roll, m. 6, đ., Devon.

Mismanagement of charities by religious persons—the diversion of
land and revenues from the charitable purposes for which they had been
Pp. 305–306.   given—is the subject of complaint in instruments on the
Records con-   Patent Roll, part ii. m. 4, đ., and part iii. m. 24, đ. A recom-
cerning mis-
management   mendation by the Commons that the Alien Priories should be
of charities,
&c.   taken into the king's hand appears on the ' Rotuli Parliamentorum,' vol. ii. (p. 162), as early as the 20th year of the reign of Edward III.
Their final suppression, with the absorption of their lands by the Crown
under Henry V., was the precedent according to which monasteries were
dissolved in the reign of Henry VIII., and affords a valuable indication
of the temper of the people, with respect to religion, during successive
generations.

Instances of homicide by parsons of churches will be found, in the
P. 307.   same order as in the text, on the Controlment Roll, m. 81,
Records con-   Salop; m. 77, Leicestershire; m. 27, đ., Wiltshire; and
cerning homi-
cide, &c., by m. 21, đ., Suffolk; by a Prior and monk, m. 5, đ., Warwick-
parsons.
shire; and many of the same character elsewhere. The case of the
parson of Trent is from m. 2, Somerset.

Writs for the arrest of apostate monks will be found on the Patent
Roll, part ii. m. 44, đ., and part iii. m. 23, đ. The deeds of the robber-
P. 308.   monks of Ramsey Abbey are recorded on the Controlment
Records con-   Roll, m. 7, Hunts; m. 19, Hunts; and m. 67, Yorkshire.
cerning fugi-
tive monks.   Similar cases were by no means uncommon; *see* the Gaol
Delivery Roll, Bury St. Edmunds, Friday after the Feast of St. Matthew

the Apostle, for an instance in which two clerks were convicted of church-breaking.

The case of sacrilege at Scarborough is recorded on the Controlment Roll, m. 65, d., Yorkshire. For another case, *see* Gaol Delivery Roll, Melton, Easter.

P. 309.
Records concerning sacrilege.

The lines quoted from Chaucer in illustration of the manners of the clergy are from the well-known prologue to the 'Canterbury Tales.'

The lines from the 'Vision of Piers Plowman' are within a few of the beginning of the work. The language has been so far modernised in the text as to make it generally intelligible.

Pp. 309-312.
Chaucer and the 'Vision.'

The assertions made (in illustration of the state of education) with respect to the languages in which the Year Books or Legal Reports of Cases, the Treatises on Law, and the Public Records were written, are founded on actual inspection of the documents mentioned. The Statute which provides that pleadings shall be in English is 36 Edward III., c. 15. The Statute by which the distinction between Norman and Englishman was abolished, in the abolition of the Presentment of Englishry, is 14 Edward III., Stat. i. c. 4. The proclamation in English, of the reign of Henry III., is enrolled on the Patent Roll, 43 Henry III., m. 15; the proclamation in French, of which it is a translation, on the Patent Roll, 42 Henry III., m. 1.

Pp. 312-316.
Records, &c., concerning the state of education in the 14th century.

French of the school of Stratford-atte-Bow is mentioned, as spoken by the Prioress, in the prologue to the 'Canterbury Tales.' The inability of the common people to understand any language but English is established by the 'Rotuli Parliamentorum,' 21 Edward III., No. 64 (vol. ii. p. 173), as well as by the statute 36 Edward III., c. 15.

The account of the Black Death and of its immediate effects is principally from the 'Chronicle of Knighton,' *sub ann.* This is confirmed by the absence of certain records belonging to an otherwise continuous series. Mr. Seebohm has found additional evidence in the records of institutions to livings after the plague, and has given the proportion of deaths among parsons in the 'Fortnightly Review,' vol. ii. p. 149. To him also is due the credit of being the first to point out the great importance of this plague in the social history of England.

Pp. 316-321.
Note and evidence concerning the Black Death and its importance.

NOTE.—Wherever, in the references to Chapter IV., a roll is mentioned without date, it is to be understood that the 22nd of Edward III. is the year to which the roll belongs.

CHAPTER V.

THE Statute of Labourers is the title usually given to the Statute i. of 23

P. 323.
The Statute
of Labourers.
Edward III., cc. 1–4, by which also innkeepers and dealers in provisions are required to sell their goods at prices fixed in the Act.

Pp. 324–327.
Evidence for
the history of
slavery and
villenage: a
deed of sale
in full.
The authorities for the condition of slaves and churls before the Norman Conquest are given in Chapter I. (References and Notes, pp. 437–438, 445).

In Domesday Book 'servi' and 'villani' are mentioned, *passim.*

Exportation of slaves is forbidden in the ' Laws of the Conqueror,' iii., 15, to which reference has already been made (C. I.).

Deeds relating to the sale of villeins may be seen in Madox's ' Formulare Anglicanum,' Nos. 314, 315, 399, 410, 556, 756, 757–762. Subjoined is a specimen (with full details) from another source :—

(Extended according to the contemporaneous spelling.)

Miscellanea, Duchy of Lancaster, London, 825. Public Record Office.

[*Endorsed.*]

Carta Galfridi de Scalariis de Johanne filio Roberti nativo suo empto apud Corneye.

'Sciant presentes et futuri quod Ego Galfridus de Scalariis filius Hugonis dedi et concessi et quieteclamavi et presenti carta confirmavi Deo et Ecclesie Sancte Trinitatis, Londonie, et Ricardo Priori et Canonicis ibidem Deo servientibus, Johannem filium Roberti de Wydyhale, nativum meum, cum tota sequela sua, que de eo exiit, vel exibit, inperpetuum, cum omnibus catallis eorum, que habent vel habituri sunt— scilicet quicquid juris in dictis Johanne, et tota sequela sua, et catallis eorum, habui, vel habere potui, sine aliquo retenemento—Habendum dictis Priori et Canonicis et eorum successoribus, extra me et heredibus meis inperpetuum. Pro hac autem donatione, concessione, quietaclama- tione, et presentis carte confirmatione, memorati Prior et Canonici dederunt mihi Galfrido sex marcas argenti. Hiis testibus,' etc.

The value of the 'nativus' varied probably with the number of his 'sequela.' A man without any family was sometimes not worth more than a pound.

In the 'Formulare' (Nos. 750, 751, 752) are deeds of enfranchisement anterior to the Conquest. The commission to receive fines for manumission from the king's villeins (Ed. III.) is printed in Rymer's 'Fœdera,' Record Com. Edn., vol. ii., pt. ii., p. 1038, from the Patent Roll, 12 Edward III., part ii., m. 29. Instances in which 'nativi' were manumitted upon payment of money to other lords are given in the 'Formulare' (Nos. 754 and 755.

Pp. 327-329. Records showing the beginning of free labour.

The Statute of Labourers was re-enacted, with little alteration, in 25 Edward III., and subsequently, and commissions to enforce it and to punish those who violated it are of frequent occurrence on the later Patent Rolls. In the end it became usual to mention the Statute in the commissions to Justices of the Peace.

It appears by the Close Roll, 35 Edward III., m. 30, and m. 21, printed in Rymer's 'Fœdera' (Rec. Com. Edn.), vol. iii. pp. 616 and 621, that there was a return of the plague in the year 1361.

For the doctrine of equality taught by the unorthodox preachers of the period, *see* Froissart, ii., 73, and Walsingham, 'Hist. Angl.,' vol. ii., pp. 32–34 (M.R. Series). For the Apostate Monks, *see* Chapter IV. of the present work, pp. 308, 484.

P. 329. Doctrine of equality : unorthodox preachers.

For the claim of the villeins to freedom, asserted on the faith of transcripts from Domesday Book, *see* the Statute 1 Richard II., c. 6, which was repealed by 2 Richard II., Stat. ii., c. 2.

Pp. 329-331. Records illustrating the claim of the villeins to be free.

The case in which the condition of a recognisance (made in the time of Henry VI.) was that the collector of the Bishop of Durham should become a 'nativus' if he failed to pay his arrears, occurs on the Cursitor's Roll, No. 4 [BB.] of Bishop Neville [Public Record Office], memb. 12, d.

The outline of Wat Tyler's rebellion is from Knighton ('Decem Scriptores'), 2633 et seq., and from Walsingham's 'Historia Anglicana' (M.R. Series, Ed. Riley), vol. i., p. 453 et seq., and vol. ii., pp. 1–34. The connection of the movement with ecclesiastical questions is made sufficiently clear by the release of John Ball from the Archbishop's prison, and by a reference to Piers Plowman in the words attributed to Jack Carter, one of the leaders, by Knighton. The subsequent petition of landholders, incidentally mentioned, that no villein should be taught to read, appears on the 'Rotuli Parliamentorum,' 15 Ric. II., No. 39 (printed

Pp. 331-337. Evidence of Records, Chronicles, Songs, &c., for the details of Wat Tyler's Rebellion.

vol. iii., p. 294). The particulars relating to the Duke of Lancaster are from the Patent Roll, 6 Ric. II., part ii. m. 6 : Pardon of John Cote. The reference to this passage was found in the Hale MSS. The particulars relating to Richard Lyons are from the 'Rotuli Parliamentorum,' 50 Edward III., Nos. 17 and 31 (printed vol. ii., pp. 323-4 and 327). The restitution of his goods through the alleged influence of Alice Perers, is mentioned in the 'R. P.,' Richard II., No. 41 (printed vol. iii., p. 12). Some of the details of Sudbury's death, together with a lament on the want of heart shown by the gentlemen on this occasion, are to be found in a song of the period, published in the M.R. Series ('Political Poems, &c.,' Ed. Wright), vol. i., pp. 227-230. The bitter animosity between the Lollards or Wycliffites and the orthodox clergy is well illustrated by other poems in the same volume—some written on one side, and some on the other. *See* pp. 231-250, 263-268, &c. The general coarseness of the age appears here as elsewhere.

The word impeachment has assumed a restricted and technical signification only in later times. William of Wykeham was 'impetitus,' as

Pp. 338-340. Note on 'Impeachment.' Records concerning the charges against William of Wykeham, the Bishop of Norwich, &c.

an ordinary criminal might have been in his day for an ordinary offence before an inferior tribunal. The charges brought against him, and the subsequent transactions, are recorded in the Patent Roll, 1 Richard II., part i., mm. 23 and 24. There is an 'Inspeximus' of the same documents in part ii., mm. 1 and 2, where it is stated that the pardon was confirmed with the unanimous consent of the Great Council. The references to those documents were found in the Hale MSS. Similar charges against the Bishop of Norwich, who was condemned, appear in 'Rotuli Parliamentorum,' 7 Richard II., No. 15 (Printed vol. iii., p. 152.) An inspection of these Rolls of Parliament will suffice to convince anyone that accusations and counter-accusations, attainders and reversals of attainder, were the ordinary events of public life at the period.

The general pardon of felonies, granted in the fiftieth year of the reign of Edward III., with the express declaration that William of Wykeham 'should nothing enjoy of the said graces,' appears among the Statutes of the Realm, 50 Ed. III., c. 3 (Vol. i., p. 397).

The diversion of tithes from one of their proper objects—the support of the poor—is mentioned in the Statute 15 Richard II., c. 6, by which

Pp. 340-342. References concerning Appropriations, misapplication of tithes, and general dissatisfaction with the clergy.

it is enacted that in future no licence for Appropriation shall be given except when a fitting sum has been set aside to be distributed yearly among the poor, and when a fitting provision has been made for the Vicar. The Statute of 1388, concerning beggars and vagrants, is known as 12 Richard II., c. 7.

Among the political songs and poems of the period, to which reference is made in the text, may be mentioned : ' The Complaint of the Ploughman,' Ed. Wright, M.R. Series, vol i., pp. 324–346, and the three pieces which follow it, pp. 346–362, ' The Corruptions of the Age,' ' On the Vices of the different Orders of Society,' and ' On King Richard II.' *See* also vol. ii., pp. 1–114, the Complaint of ' Jacke Upland,' a Lollard, the Reply of Friar Daw, and the Rejoinder of Jacke. In the last appears the charge, made against the friars, of kidnapping children, which is the subject of complaint and redress in the ' Rotuli Parliamentorum,' 4 Henry IV., No. 62 (vol. iii., p. 502).

The suggestion of the Commons that the money required by the king should be taken from the alien priories appears in the ' Rot. Parl.,' 4 Henry IV., No. 48 (vol. iii., p. 499), as well as earlier. There was an ordinance against them in 13 Ric. II., and they were finally suppressed by the Statute 1 Hen. V., c. 7. An important Statute against papal provisions was 2 Hen. IV., c. 3. The petition of the Commons that in cases of appropriation a secular vicar should be appointed, and the king's consent, appear on the ' Rot. Parl.,' 2 Hen. IV., No. 52 (vol. iii., pp. 499–500).

P. 343. Statutes, &c., showing the policy of Henry IV. and Henry V.

It is laid down in the later law-books that the writ ' de heretico comburendo ' existed at the common law before the Statute 2 Henry IV., c. 15, gave authority to the sheriff to burn heretics without a special writ ; and this opinion is to a certain extent confirmed by Bracton, &c. *See* Hale, ' Historia Placitorum Coronæ,' vol. i., pp. 383–395 ; Coke, ' Instit.,' part iii., pp. 39–43. Both Hale (' P. C.,' vol. i., p. 397) and Fox (' Acts and Monuments,' i., 773) discuss the question whether the Statute had the assent of the Commons, Hale taking one side, Fox the other. Bacon, in the concluding paragraph of ' A Preparation for the Union of Laws,' denies the existence of any Statute for the burning of heretics, but admits the king's writ ' de heretico comburendo ' as part of the common law. It seems, however, difficult to explain away the thanks offered by the Commons to the king at the end of the session for the remedy ordained in destruction of the heretical doctrines and sects, ' Rot. Parl.,' 2 Hen. IV., No. 47 (Printed vol. iii., p. 466).

Pp. 343–344. References concerning the writ and statute for burning heretics.

The writ for the execution of Sautre, dated before the passing of the General Act for the punishment of heretics, appears on the ' Rotuli Parliamentorum,' 2 Henry IV., No. 29 (vol. iii., p. 459). It issued by authority of the king and council in Parliament.

Writs ' De Lolardis arestandis ' in the various counties will be found on the Patent Roll, 9 Henry IV., part i. and 10 Henry IV., part i., and probably also elsewhere. An execution

Pp. 344–346. Records concerning the execution of Sautre, and the persecution of other Lollards.

by fire, possibly that of John Badby, is mentioned in the 'Eulogium Historiarum sive Temporis,' a contemporary chronicle (Ed. Haydon, M.R. series), vol. iii., pp. 416-417. The writ for Badby's execution is in the 'Fœdera,' Original Edition, vol. viii., p. 627, from the Close Roll, 11 Henry IV., m. 18.

The documents which relate the sentence upon Oldcastle are the indictment on the 'Coram Rege' Roll (King's Bench, Crown Side), 1 Henry V., Hilary, Rex, Ro. 7, the outlawry of Oldcastle and many others, on the same Roll, Ro. 13, and the Proceedings in Parliament, 5 Henry V. The Proceedings in Parliament are printed, 'Rotuli Parliamentorum,' vol. iv., pp. 107-110, and seem to be the only documentary evidence on the subject

Pp. 346-351. Records of the proceedings against Sir John Oldcastle, Blake, and Acton.

seen either by Fox, who deals with the matter in his 'Acts and Monuments,' or by the editors of the 'State Trials,' who make in words the accusation of forgery implied by Fox. The arguments of Fox from the internal evidence of the indictment as it appears in the 'Rot. Parl.' are of no great weight, nor indeed would it be possible to establish such a charge as forgery except by reference to the original on the King's Bench Roll. In support, therefore, of what has been said in the text the indictment has been transcribed in full from the 'Coram Rege' Roll, and is now printed, it is believed, for the first time. The points in which it differs from the Parliamentary transcripts and the erasure are also indicated.

Extract from the 'Coram Rege' Roll, 1 Henry V. (King's Bench, Crown Side), Rex, Hilary, Ro 7.

(The contracted Latin of the original has been extended, but no other alterations have been made in the spelling).

'Adhuc de Termino Sancti Hillarii. Rex. Middlesex. Alias coram Willelmo Roos de Hamelak, Henrico Lescrop Willelmo Crowemere, Maiore Civitatis Londonie, Hugone Huls, et sociis suis, Justiciariis domini Regis ad inquirendum per sacramentum proborum et legalium hominum de civitate domini Regis Londonie et suburbiis ejusdem ac de comitatu Middlesex, tam infra libertates quam extra, de omnibus et singulis prodicionibus et insurreccionibus per quamplures subditos domini Regis Lollardos vulgariter nuncupatos et alios in civitate, suburbiis, et comitatu predictis, factis et perpetratis, necnon de omnibus prodicionibus insurreccionibus, rebellionibus et feloniis in civitate, suburbiis, et comitatu predictis per quoscumque et qualitercumque factis sive perpetratis et ad easdem prodiciones, insurrecciones, rebelliones, et felonias audiendum et terminandum

Pp. 346-351. The Indictment of Oldcastle, Blake, and Acton, copied verbatim from the 'Coram Rege' Roll, and compared with the transcript exhibited in Parliament.

secundum legem et consuetudinem regni domini Regis Anglie [¹ per
literas ipsius domini Regis patentes assignatis, apud Westmonasterium,
die Mercurii proxima post festum Epiphanie Domini, anno regni Regis
Henrici quinti post Conquestum primo, per sacramentum xii juratorum
extitit presentatum quod Johannes Oldecastell de Coulyng in Comitatu
Kancie, Chivaler, (² dominus] Walterus Blake de Bristoll capellanus,
Rogerus Acton de Salopia in comitatu Salopie, Chivaler), et alii,
Lollardi vulgariter nuncupati, qui contra fidem catholicam diversas
oppiniones hereticas et alios errores manifestos legi catholice repug-
nantes, a diu est, temerarie tenuerunt, oppiniones et errores predictos
manutenere aut in facto minime perimplere valentes quam diu regia
potestas et tam status regalis domini nostri Regis quam status et officium
prelacie dignitatis infra regnum Anglie in prosperitate perseverarent,
falso et proditorie machinando tam statum regium quam statum et
officium prelatorum necnon ordines religiosorum infra dictum regnum
Anglie penitus adnullare, ac dominum nostrum Regem, fratres suos,
prelatos, et alios magnates ejusdem regni interficere, necnon viros
religiosos, relictis cultibus divinis et religiosis observanciis, ad occu-
paciones mundanas provocare, et tam ecclesias cathedrales quam alias
ecclesias et domos religiosas de reliquiis et aliis bonis ecclesiasticis
totaliter spoliare ac funditus ad terram prosternere, et [dictum³] Johannem
Oldecastell regentem ejusdem regni constituere, et quamplura regimina
secundum eorum voluntatem infra regnum predictum quasi gens sine
capite in finalem destruccionem tam fidei catholice et cleri quam status
et majestatis dignitatis regalis infra idem regnum ordinare falso et
proditorie ordinaverunt, et proposuerunt quod ipsi insimul cum quam-
pluribus rebellibus domini Regis ignotis ad numerum viginti millium
hominum de diversis partibus regni Anglie modo guerrino arraiatis
privatim insurgerent, et die Mercurii proxima post festum Epiphanie
Domini, anno regni regis predicti predicto, apud villam et parochiam
Sancti Egidii extra Barram veteris Templi Londonie in quodam magno
campo ibidem unanimiter convenirent et insimul obviarent pro nephando
proposito suo in premissis perimplendo Quo quidem die Mercurii apud
villam et parochiam predictas predicti (Walterus, Rogerus ⁴) et alii in
hujusmodi proposito proditorie perseverantes predictum dominum
nostrum Regem, fratres suos videlicet Thomam Ducem Clarencie, Johannem de Lancastre, et Humfridum de Lancastre, necnon prelatos et

---

¹ The passage in brackets is written on an erasure, in a different hand, and with
lighter ink.

² The passage in a parenthesis is omitted from the Roll of Parliament.

³ The word ' *dictum* ' is interlined in a different hand, with lighter ink.

⁴ For the two names in a parenthesis the one name ' Johannes Oldecastell ' is
substituted in the Roll of Parliament.

magnates predictos interficere, necnon ipsum dominum nostrum Regem
et heredes suos de regno suo predicto exheredare, et premissa
omnia et singula necnon quam plura alia mala et intollerabilia facere et
perimplere falso et proditorie proposuerunt et imaginaverunt, et ibidem
versus campum predictum modo guerrino arraiati proditorie modo insur-
reccionis contra ligeancias suas equitaverunt ad debellandum dictum
dominum nostrum Regem nisi per ipsum manu forti gratiose impediti
fuissent. Quod quidem indictamentum dominus Rex nunc certis de
causis coram eo venire fecit terminandum. Per quod preceptum fuit
Vicecomiti quod non omitteret quin caperet (eos [1]) si etc. (Et [2] modo,
scilicet die Mercurii proxima post Octabas Sancti Hillarii isto eodem
termino, coram domino Rege apud Westmonasterium venit predictus
Walterus in custodia Marescalli ductus, in cujus custodiam perantea
occasionibus predictis per consilium domini Regis commissus fuit. Et
super premissis allocutus qualiter se velit inde acquietare dicit quod ipse
in nullo est inde culpabilis. Et inde de bono et malo ponit se super
patriam. Ideo venit inde jurata coram domino Rege apud Westmonasterium die Sabbati in quindena Sancti Hillarii. Et qui etc. Ad ˚recogñ,
etc. Et interim predictus Walterus committitur Marescalcie etc. Ad quos
diem et locum coram domino Rege venit predictus Walterus in custodia
Marescalli. Et juratores exacti similiter venerunt, qui, ad veritatem de
et super premissis dicendum electi, triati, et jurati, dicunt super sacramentum suum quod predictus Walterus culpabilis est de premissis
superius sibi impositis et quod ipse nulla habet bona seu catalla, terras
seu tenementa. Ideo consideratum est quod predictus Walterus Blake
distrahatur et suspendatur. Postea, scilicet die Veneris in Octabis
Purificacionis beate Marie Virginis, isto eodem termino, coram domino
Rege apud Westmonasterium, venit predictus Rogerus Acton per
Thomam, Comitem Arundell, et Thesaurarium Anglie, de precepto
domini Regis personaliter ductus, qui instanter allocutus est qualiter de
prodicionibus et feloniis predictis superius sibi impositis se velit acquietare, qui dicit quod ipse in nullo est inde culpabilis. Et inde de bono et
malo ponit se super patriam. Ideo venit inde jurata coram domino Rege
apud Westmonasterium die Sabbati proxima post Octabas Purificacionis
beate Marie Virginis. Et qui etc. Et ad recogñ etc. Et interim predictus Rogerus Acton committitur Turri Londonie per breve domini Regis
de recordo hic in Curia etc. Ad quos diem et locum coram domino Rege
hic venit predictus Rogerus per Constabularium Turris predicti ductus.
Et Juratores exacti similiter venerunt qui ad veritatem de et super pre-

---

[1] For this word, the words 'prefatum Johannem Oldecastell' are substituted in
the Roll of Parliament.

[2] The whole of the long passage in a parenthesis is omitted from the Roll of
Parliament.

missis dicendum electi, triati, et jurati dicunt super sacramentum suum quod predictus Rogerus Acton culpabilis est de premissis superius sibi impositis et quod ipse nulla habet bona seu catalla terras seu tenementa. Ideo consideratum est quod predictus Rogerus Acton ducatur abinde usque Turrim domini Regis Londonie et quod ipse ab eadem Turre distrahatur per medium Civitatis predicte usque novas Furcas in campo Sancti Egidii factas et quod ibidem suspendatur. Et sic suspensus pendeat ad voluntatem domini Regis. [1] Et, quia predictus Johannes Oldecastell se coram domino Rege occasione predicta non reddidit, preceptum fuit Vicecomiti quod non omitteret etc. quin caperet eum si etc."), and the usual proceedings in outlawry follow. At the foot of the skin are the words : ' Memorandum quod Willelmus Hankeford, miles, Capitalis Justiciarius Anglie, die Martis proxima post festum Sancte Lucie Virginis anno regni regis Henrici Quinti quinto, de precepto domini Johannis Ducis Bedford Custodis Anglie detulit coram ipso Custode et magnatibus Anglie in pleno parliamento apud West-monasterium tunc tento recordum et processum predicta *quo ad dictum Johannem Oldecastell* in parliamento predicto auctoritate ejusdem parliamenti ad tunc ibidem exequend. et terminand.'

Little more light is thrown upon the matter by a document of the next reign (Patent Roll, 7 Henry VI., part i. m. 19, d.), by which an enquiry is directed concerning some of Oldcastle's lands claimed by his son as having been entailed, and therefore, *per formam doni*, not forfeited for treason. The words, however, in which the authority for Oldcastle's execution is there described show how the matter was regarded in the reign of Henry VI. : 'auctoritate ejusdem parliamenti, ibidem, et virtute utlagarie predicte.'

The contemporary song in which there is an allusion to Oldcastle, and a contempt expressed for persons who study to gain the approbation of Lollards, is printed in the ' Political Poems and Songs,' Ed. Wright, vol. ii. p. 245. It is possible, indeed, that the word ' study ' is used merely as a synonym for ' strive,' and has no reference to the study of letters, but the prejudice against independent investigation is sufficiently established by the persecutions of the time. *(Pp. 352–353. Note and reference concerning the 'unchivalrousness' of Lollardism.)*

The form of commission directed to a bishop for the arrest of sorcerers, &c., within his diocese is printed in Rymer, vol. viii. p. 427 (Original Edition), from the Patent Roll 7 Henry IV., part i. m. 22. *(Pp. 353–356. Records, &c., concerning the Maid of Orleans, and the search for Witches under Henry IV. and Henry VI.)*

The terror excited in the English troops by the supposed incantations of the Maid of Orleans is the subject of documents printed in Rymer, vol. x. pp. 459, 472, from the Close Rolls, 8

[1] The outlawry process against Oldcastle is in a different hand, and written with lighter ink. That fact, however, considered alone, would not be of any importance,

Henry VI., m. 11 d., and 9 Henry VI., m. 23. Some particulars are also given in Fabyan, *anno* 8 Henry VI.

A writ for the arrest of Northfeld, suspected of sorcery, is printed in Rymer, vol. x. p. 505, from the Patent Roll, 10 Henry VI., part ii. m. 13 d. In the same volume and page is a document (Bib. Cott., Cleop., F. 4) relating to the appearance of accused persons before the Council. *See* also Proceedings and Ordinances of the Privy Council (Ed. Sir Harris Nicolas, Record Commission), vol. iv. p. 114. The reward for witchfinders (1441), (printed from the Pell Rolls) appears in the same volume of Rymer, p. 852.

The account of the trial of the Duchess of Gloucester for witchcraft is from the Patent Roll, 19 Henry VI., part ii. m. 16, printed in

Pp. 356–358.
Records, &c., concerning the Trial and Penance of the Duchess of Gloucester.

Rymer, vol. x. p. 851, from Fabyan, *annis* 19 and 20 Henry VI., and from the contemporary song quoted in the text, 'Lament of the Duchess of Gloucester' ('Political Poems and Songs,' vol. ii. pp. 205–208), a composition not devoid of a certain pathos.

The imputations against the Duchess of Bedford and her daughter are from the Patent Roll, 9 Edward IV., part ii. m. 5 (in which the ex-

Pp. 358–360.
The Duchess of Bedford and her daughter.

emplification of. the Privy Council Proceedings is enrolled). The document is printed in the 'Rotuli Parliamentorum,' vol. vi. p. 232. The renewal of the charge when the throne was offered to Richard appears in the same volume, p. 241.

Pp. 360–362.
Burdett and Clarence.

Particulars of the trial of Burdett and his accomplices for Constructive Treason, in calculating the time of the king's death by forbidden arts, appear in the Records of the King's Bench.

The particulars of Clarence's attainder are from the 'Rotuli Parliamentorum,' 17 Ed. IV. (vol. vi. p. 193). Fabyan p. 266 tells of the butt of wine.

The well-known story of Jane Shore is from the well-known source

Pp. 362–363.
Jane Shore.

Sir Thomas More's 'Historia Ricardi Tertii,' p. 18 (Frankfort Edition of 1689).

Some of the remarks concerning the development of the art of printing were suggested by an exhibition of early specimens of printed

Pp. 363–367.
Note and references concerning the introduction of Printing, its relation to ancient seals, the growth of paper manufacture, &c.

books at the rooms of the Archæological Institute.

The increase in the demand for parchment will be apparent to any one who compares the records of any of the courts at. the end of the fourteenth century with the same classes of records as they were made up a century or two earlier. Their bulk is many times multiplied, and there is

as there would have been no irregularity in entering the outlawry process (which required a considerable time) after the earlier enrolment of the indictment. There is no doubt that the outlawry considered alone was effected in due course, as shown by m. 13 of this Roll, but the facts relating to the indictment speak for themselves.

no doubt that the demand elsewhere corresponded with the demand apparent in the English law courts.

The exact date at which paper was first made from cotton is not known.   There are instances of its use at the beginning of the fourteenth century.   The earliest known specimen of linen paper in England seems to have been used in the year 1337.   (*See* Rogers' ' History of Prices,' preface to vol. ii. p. xviii., where there is a description of a piece used for the accounts of Merton College.)   This was of the rudest possible fabric. Before the year 1388 the art was developed so far that its utility could no longer be doubted.   The paper made in imitation of parchment is described in Toulmin Smith's ' English Gilds' (published by the Early English Text Society), p. 132, and Preface, p. xliv.   In the same work, p. 44, will be found the description of the piece of ruled vellum taken out of a book and used for a return to Parliament.   Mr. Smith went through the whole of the original writs and returns made in obedience to the order of Parliament in 1388, and now in the Public Record Office. The details given by him, throwing light as they do upon the very period at which the art of paper-making was developed, are, therefore, of very considerable value.

It matters little whether we regard the printer's type as a number of frag- ments of seals or as a number of small seals each complete in itself. The fact remains, that when printing was invented there was nothing new in it except the manner of arranging the letters and the manner of taking the im- pression. Stereotyping on wax had been known from time immemorial.

The remarks concerning the use of a seal alone, on occasions when according to modern custom a name would be signed, need no justification to those who are familiar with the most ancient deeds. The use of the seal, which was really equivalent to a signature, has not, indeed, even yet died out, for ancient practices remain when they have become meaningless. But many binding contracts can now be made without the use of any seal at all.   The ancient equivalent for the modern felony known as forgery, and the difficulties to which its definition gave rise, are illustrated by the cases of ' Johannes de Bosco,' who transferred a seal by means of a heated knife (' Coram Rege ' Roll, 6 Ed. II., Easter, Ro. 2, Essex—Emlyn's Hale, Note, p. 180); of Huntynton and Clinton, which was similar ('Coram Rege' Roll, 11 Ed. II., Mich., Ro. 156, Hereford—Emlyn's Hale, ib.); of Redynges, who counterfeited a seal and suffered as a traitor (Patent Roll, 6 Ed. II., part ii. m. 18) ; and of Clement Peytevin, who not having actually coun- terfeited the Great Seal, but having transferred it from one document to another, was judged (in the opinion of lawyers, wrongfully) to be a traitor (' Coram Rege ' Roll, 2 Henry IV., Hil., Ro. 16, Midd.—Emlyn's Hale, p. 81, note).

Pp. 367–368. References concerning the ancient use of seal and pen.

It would be out of place in this history to discuss the question whether the invention of printing should be attributed to a native of Holland

Pp. 368–371. References concerning printing and commerce in the reign of Edward IV. : Caxton, the Poles, &c.

or to a native of Germany. Block-printing, at any rate, which was the first step, seems to have come from Holland.

The attention paid to commerce in the time of Edward IV. is evident not only in the well-known commission to Caxton to negotiate a commercial treaty with Burgundy, but also in the numerous statutes of the reign which refer to trade and manufactures. The assertion that Edward was himself a trader is made in the ' Continuation of the History of Croyland Abbey' (Fulman), p. 559. The rise of wealthy merchants had already excited the surprise of a foreigner (Poggio Bracciolini, ' Opera,' p. 69). There seems to be little doubt that the aggrandisement of the Poles was effected by the wealth gained in mercantile transactions. The father of Michael de la Pole was named William ('Rot. Parl.,' 5 Ric. II., No. 3 ; vol. iii. p. 127). A William de la Pole is distinctly mentioned as a merchant in 'Rot. Parl.,' vol. ii. p. 457, and a William de la Pole, who was evidently a person of some influence, at pp. 114, 118, 121, 154, all of which passages are consistent with the supposition that there were not two persons of the same name living at the same time, but that there was only one William de la Pole, at once land-holder and merchant. William, however, though probably in one sense the founder of the family, himself inherited some lands, as shown by 'Rot. Parl.,' vol. i. p. 356 ; but he had the wisdom to disregard the prejudices of his class. The ordinary contempt of the nobles for city life, appearing in many forms, is mentioned by Bracciolini, who was in England when Cardinal Beaufort was Bishop of Winchester. (' Opera,' p. 69).

The sale of cloth good at the end but faulty in the middle called forth the Statutes 13 Rich. II., St. i. c. 11 ; 4 Edward IV., c. 1 ; 8

Pp. 371–372. Statutes showing the frauds practised in the 15th century.

Edward IV., c. 1, and various others. It was the object of 5 Henry IV., c. 13, to prevent the common trick of selling vessels and ornaments of copper or latten as gold or silver. Frauds by means of casks of deficient capacity are mentioned in 2 Henry VI., c. 11 ; frauds by means of barrels of fish, in 22 Ed. IV., c. 2. The discredit of English woollen exports in foreign countries through deceptions in weight or quality appears from 8 Henry VI., cc. 22 and 23 ; from 20 Henry VI., c. 10 ; from 4 Ed. IV., c. 1, and from subsequent statutes. The tricks of smugglers are mentioned in 4 Ed. IV., cc. 2–4, and in 12 Ed. IV., c. 3. There are provisions against tampering with the coinage in 3 Henry V., Stat. 2, cc. 6, 7, and a provision that gold coin is to be taken by weight only, in 9 Henry V., Stat. i. c. 11.

Pp. 373–376. Note on town life and country life.

It is hardly necessary to cite passages from the later classics in order to show how great an appreciation the civilised Romans had of town life, how they regarded the country-house as a place of relaxation, and made even the country house as much like a town as possible in its extent and in its luxurious appliances.   Their contempt for the man who had never lived in a town could not be better expressed than in the famous words in which Horace refers to an old fable : —

' Rusticus expectat dum defluat amnis.'

This is a curious contrast to the remark of the Italian that the English gentleman of the fifteenth century thought town life beneath his dignity.

It will hardly be supposed that the history of every art can be given in these pages to justify the statement in the text that we owe almost every art directly or indirectly to towns.   The Church, no doubt, did much to hand down various arts, and Roger Bacon is a familiar instance, if not of a monkish inventor, at least of a monk who took interest in inventions (*See* 'Works' of Roger Bacon, edited by Mr. J. S. Brewer for the M.R. Series).   As many men were living in monasteries with the means of study at hand, it would be strange if they had not con-tributed something to the knowledge of mankind.   But as a matter of fact they contributed little that was new ; their intellects worked in a deep groove, and they were, upon principle, opposed to innovations.   We owe them many thanks for having preserved to us a few fragments of Roman literature and Roman art, which Rome had borrowed in part from Greece, and for not having frowned upon Caxton ; but as a class they had no wish that mankind should become more enlightened.

For the text of a great number of the Ordinances of the Craft-Guilds, *see* Toulmin Smith's ' English Gilds.'   They seem to bear out the opinion expressed by Herr Brentano, in his Introduction to the volume, that each craftsman, though a worker with his own' hands, had a little stock in trade.   The greatest light upon that period of transition, during which the wealthier craftsman'was becoming a capitalist, and the poorer a mere working-man, is afforded by the ' Political Poems and Songs' published in the M.R. Series by Mr. Wright.   In *(margin note: Pp. 376-380. References concerning trade-guilds, the relations of capital and labour, and the progress of commerce in the 15th cen-tury.)*

vol. ii. pp. 157–205, will be found the ' Libel of English Policy,' and at pp. 282–287 another poem on ' England's Commercial Policy.'   In these two documents appear the complaints of the workmen who were still partly retail-dealers, and who sighed for a golden age, which they believed to have existed in the past, when each man received his wage in coin.   (The Statute 4 Edward IV., c. i., provides that workmen shall be paid in money and not in goods).   Many other curious details are also given in the Songs.   A safe-conduct granted in 1452 to some foreign miners brought into England, shows, as well as the Poems, the attention which was now being given to metal-work. *See* Rymer, vol. xi. p. 317, from the French Roll, 31 Henry VI., m. 13. An instance of the export of ship's guns occurs as early as 1411. Rymer, viii., 694, from the French Roll, 12 Henry IV., m. 5.

In 1463 Parliament prohibited the importation of a great number of manufactures, which the artificers asserted could be made better in England than elsewhere (Stat. 3 Edward IV., c. 4).

The Ordinances of many religious or social guilds are, like those of craft-guilds, printed in Toulmin Smith's ' English Gilds.' Their most striking features are well put together in the Introduction.

Pp. 381–383. Records concerning the social or religious guilds. The statement that these guilds retained full vitality after 1388 (the date of the return of the Ordinances to Parliament), is founded on the best authority—the Public Records. Licences to reconstitute a guild, and for the guild to acquire land, are common enough. As instances may be mentioned the licences for the two guilds in the Parish Church of Houghton, for which *see* Roll No. 2 of Bishop Booth (Durham Cursitor's, No. 49), mem. 13, *temp.* Edward IV.

It is unnecessary to trace through its various stages a doctrine so well known to every lawyer as that of ' Uses.' The Statute which checked the abuse of this legal fiction by the clergy is

Pp. 384–385. Statutes relating to ' Uses.' 15 Ric. II., c. 5 ; that which gave it vitality as a legitimate aid to conveyancing is 27 Henry VIII., c. 10.

The best contemporary guide to the ordinary course of legal proceedings about the time of the Wars of the Roses, is Fortescue, ' De Laudibus Legum Angliæ.' The civil trial is described in cc.

Pp. 386–388. References concerning legal procedure, the 'peine forte et dure,' &c., in the 15th century. 25 and 26, the criminal in c. 27 ; the punishment following an attaint of perjured jurors in c. 26. The Statute 15 Henry VI., c. 5, relates to perjury, and in its preamble the prevalence of the offence is lamented. There appears to have been less restraint upon the practice of approving than in earlier times. The Stat. 5 Henry IV., c. 2, recites that ' divers notorious rogues, for the safeguard of their lives, had become provers, to the intent, in the mean time, by brocage and great gifts, to pursue and have their pardons, and then, after their deliverance, had become more notorious felons than before.' That torture was sometimes used to extort confessions is, as already stated, clear from the passage in the Pipe Roll, 34 Henry II., Ro. 10, and the Council Books of later date. It may also be inferred, perhaps, that the practice was not very common, from c. 22 of Fortescue's ' Laudes,' in which indeed, to his honour be it said, he most feelingly denounces the practice ; but although he reprobates torture as it existed in France, he does not expressly deny that it was used in England, as foreign and English authors have sometimes assumed. The form into which the 'peine forte et dure ' had developed in the fifteenth century will be found in the Year Book, 8 Henry IV., 1, 2. Trials of a later date, of which some minute details have been preserved, show that it was the custom of the judge to examine the prisoner in a manner by no means gentle. That, however, is a matter for future comment. The passage concerning English robbers and their 'hearts,' is from Fortescue on 'Monarchy,' pp. 99–100.

The description by John Hill, the royal armourer, of the formalities observed in a 'Battle of Treason,' has been preserved among the Hale MSS., vol. xii. (xi.) · Pp. 389–392. Treatise on the Battle of Treason.

In the Hale MSS. also was found the reference to an instrument entitled 'De certis requestis Karolo Adversario Francie ex parte Regis Anglie offerendis.' It occurs on the French Roll 7 Richard II., memb. 24, and is a very remarkable document. Richard addresses it to his uncle, John Duke of Lancaster, whom he desires to approach the French king with the propositions, described in the text, for settling all differences by one final combat. Pp. 393–394. Note on the challenge of Richard II. to the French king.

The Statute against forcible entry is known as 5 Richard II., Stat. i. c. 8. Upon the Patent Roll, 15 Richard II., m. 23, will be found the grant of Leonhale Castle, with an express mention of private jurisdiction. Pp. 394–396. Forcible entry, and private jurisdiction (Ric. II).

Against maintenance, liveries, retainers, conspiracy, &c., were directed the 'Ordinacio de Conspiratoribus,' 33 Ed. I., the Statutes 1 Ric. II., c. 7, 13 Ric. II., St. 3, 16 Ric. II., c. 4, 20 Ric. II., c. 1, 1 Hen. IV., c. 7, and others down to 8 Ed. IV., c. 2. The Ordinance relating to liberties into which the king's officers do not enter, appears in the 'Rotuli Parliamentorum,' vol. iv. pp. 421–2. It is also enrolled among the records of the Palatinate of Durham Pp. 396–397. Statutes and Records concerning liveries, retainers, &c. (*See* Cursitor's Records, Roll ' C,' of Bishop Langley, m. 8)—a proof that it reached one at least of the persons for whom it was intended. The deed by which Sir William Eure becomes the Bishop's retainer is enrolled on the Cursitor's Roll, No. 5, of Bishop Neville, m. 13.

The first Statute relating to *Scandalum Magnatum* is that of Westminster the First, 3 Ed. I., c. 34. It was followed after a long interval by 2 Ric. II., St. i. c. 5, and 12 Ric. II., c. 11. Walter Sibille's case is recorded on the ' Rotuli Parliamentorum,' 8 Ric. II., No. 12 (printed vol. iii. p. 186). Pp. 398–400. Statutes and Records concerning 'Scandalum Magnatum.'

John Cavendish's accusation against Michael de la Pole, and his punishment for having made it, are recorded on the 'Rot. Parl.,' 7 Richard II., Nos. 11–15 (printed vol. iii. pp. 168–170), and the subsequent judgment against Pole on the 'Rot. Parl.,' 10 Ric. II., Nos. 6–17 (printed vol. iii. pp. 216–220).

The case of Sir Ralph Ferriers and the beggar is from the ' Rot. Parl.,' 4 Ric. II., Nos. 17–26 (vol. iii. pp. 91–93).

Charges of surrendering fortresses to the enemy for a bribe will be found in the 'Rotuli Parliamentorum,' 1 Ric. II., Nos. 38–40 (against Weston and Gomenys), 7 Ric. II., No. 17 (against Cressingham), and 7 Ric. II., No. 24, (against Elingham and others), (printed vol. iii. pp. 10–12, 153 and 156).

The similar charges made against William de la Pole, Earl of Suffolk, in the reign of Henry VI., appear on the 'Rotuli Parliamentorum,' 28 Henry VI.. Nos. 14–51 (printed vol. v. pp. 176–183). Suffolk's murder is related in the 'Continuation of the History of Croyland Abbey,' p. 525 (Fulman).

Gloucester's murder, or private execution, with the religious ceremonies which accompanied it, is described in the 'Rotuli Parliamentorum,'
1 Henry IV., No. 11 (printed vol. iii., pp. 452-3). *See* also the 10 preceding Nos. The proceedings in which he was declared guilty of treason, at the end of the reign of Richard II., appear in the 'Rot. Parl.,' 21 Richard II., Nos. 1-13 (printed vol. iii., p. 347 -351). Attainder, as is well known, followed sentence of death in all cases of treason or felony. The proceeding in Parliament by Bill of Attainder, is, if not more common, more frequently recorded, after the time now under consideration.

For the supposed murder of another Duke of Gloucester in the reign of Henry VI., *see* Fabyan, p. 619.

The proceedings which relate to the deposition of Richard appear at great length on the 'Rotuli Parliamentorum,' 1 Henry IV., Nos. 10-60. (printed vol. iii., pp. 416-424), upon which the passage relating to the same subject in the text is founded. It is in No. 60 (p. 424) that Richard 'hoped that is cosyn wolde be goode Lord to hym.'

The Acts and Ordinances of the Privy Council, 4 Henry IV. (vol. i., p. 208) show that Henry Percy had proclaimed King Richard II. to be still alive. A general pardon, excepting Warde, the personator of Richard, appears on the Patent Roll, 5 Henry IV., pt. ii., m. 31, in the form of an exemplification. The view put forward in the text, that Richard lived a very short time after he had been deposed by Henry, seems most in accordance with the spirit of the age. There was, however, a very strong party, which from hatred of Henry, or belief in the survival of Richard, entered into a formidable conspiracy. This is apparent from documents preserved in the Chapter House, and printed, in part, in the 'Chronique de la Träison et Mort de Richart II. (Ed. Benj. Williams). The 'Coram Rege' Roll (King's Bench), 6 H. IV., m. 5, shows that a supposed Richard had a strong party in Essex and the neighbouring counties. Had he been alive, and in his senses, however, there is little doubt that he would have appeared at the head of an army, and the mention of Warde as a personator goes far to show that an impostor was exposed. Searle, the valet of King Richard, was taken, convicted of treason, dragged through Norwich, Colchester, and other towns, and from Colchester to London. *See* Foreign Account Roll, 1-6, H. IV.

The particulars relating to the proceedings against Alice Perers, are from the 'Rotuli Parliamentorum,' 1 Richard II., Nos. 41–43 (printed vol. iii. pp. 13–14). The opinion of a later Chief Justice of England upon her case is this :—'The record against the said Dame is long, and approveth no such heinous matter against her. . . . And these two suits, wherefore she was condemned, seemeth very honest. Her mishap was, that being friendly to many, she found not all in like sort affected towards her' (Sir M. Hale's MS., vol. vii.). The restitution of her lands after her marriage to William Windsor, appears by the Patent Roll, 3 Ric. II., part 3, m. 5, the reference to which was found in the Petyt MSS.

Pp. 409–412. References concerning the position of women in the 15th century.

The description of the chastisement inflicted on a young lady by her mother is from the 'Paston Letters' (Ed. Fenn), vol. iii., pp. 206-208. This curious collection of letters generally bears out the statement in the text, that the family life was hardly one of mutual confidence and affection.

Statute 33 Henry VI., c. 5, recites the complaint of the London silk-women, and provides a remedy.

The assault committed by Ralph Garneys in the presence of the Judges in Westminster Hall is thus described in the Inquisition :—

'Ad quod Damnum,' 16 Henry VI., No. 10.

(Spelling as in the original, but contractions extended.)

'Cum Radulfus Garneys, per nomen Radulfi Garneys de Gelston in comitatu Norfolk Armigeri, nuper coram nobis indictatus extiterit de eo quod ipse, sexto die Februarii ultimo preterito inter horam decimam et undecimam ante horam nonam ejusdem diei, apud Westmonasterium in Magna Aula Placitorum infra Palacium nostrum ibidem, apertis tunc et ibidem tam Curia Cancellarie nostre quam Curia nostra Coram Nobis ac Curia nostra de Communi Banco, in presencia tam Justiciariorum nostrorum ad Placita Coram Nobis tenenda assignatorum quam Justiciariorum nostrorum de Banco predicto tunc ibidem sedencium, in Edmundum Fitz-William Deputatum Johannis Ducis Norfolk Marescalli Marescalcie nostre Coram Nobis adtunc et ibidem quandam indenturam officium ejusdem Edmundi Marescalcie predicte tangentem inspicientem tunc ibidem affraiam et insultum fecit, ac ipsum Edmundum cum pugillo ipsius Radulfi manus

P. 412. Record (in full) of a brawl in Westminster Hall.

sue dextere super faciem ejusdem Edmundi tunc ibidem percussit, per quod tam Justiciarii et alii ministri nostri Curiarum predictarum quam Domini Spirituales et Temporales ex Consilio et circa Consilium nostrum tunc ibidem existentes et attendentes tunc et ibidem tam graviter pertur- bati extiterunt quod iidem Justiciarii et alii ministri Curiarum predic- tarum circa Placita nostra ac diversorum ligeorum nostrorum ac Domini dicti Spirituales et Temporales circa consilium nostrum tunc ibidem attendere non potuerunt '—a Commission issues to enquire what lands were held by Garneys.

A reference to this curious document, which illustrates the customs observed at Westminster, as well as Garneys' crime, was found in the Hale Collection.

The assault with a great armed company, in the king's presence in

Pp. 413-415.
Records con-
cerning armed
forces in law-
courts, mutila-
tion, misdeeds
of soldiers, &c.

the Star Chamber, is the subject of the 'Rotuli Parliamen- torum,' 28 Henry VI., No. 56 (printed vol. v., pp. 200-1).

The instance in which four hundred armed men rode to Walsingham to prevent justice being done is from the Paston Letters, vol. iii., p. 118.

Statute 5 Henry IV., c. 5, is that which relates to the cutting out of tongues, and the putting out of eyes. Statute 33 H. VI., c. 1, deals with the habit, which servants had, of scrambling for their master's goods as soon as he was dead.

The complaints of the misdeeds of English soldiers bound for France appear on the 'Rotuli Parliamentorum,' 20 Hen. VI., No. 34 (printed vol. v. p. 61). The account of similar practices under Edward IV., and of the King on circuit, is from the ' Continuation of the History of Croyland Abbey' (Fulman, p. 559).

A contemporary account of some of Jack Cade's doings is given in one of the Paston Letters, vol. i., pp. 54-62. It there appears that Sir

Pp. 415-417.
References
concerning the
Wars of the
Roses.

John Fastolf was suspected of having 'minished all the garrisons of Normandy and Manns, and Mayn, the which was the cause of the losing of all the king's title and right of an heritance that he had beyond sea.' The thoughts of a knight's wife for the defence of her home are expressed in vol. iii., pp. 314–316, her thoughts for bedchamber and malthouse in vol. iii., p. 324, the difficulty of communication in vol. ii., p. 72 (where the opportunity of sending a letter at the time of Bartholomew fair is mentioned as one too good to be lost). The thieves on the roads about London, and the impossibility of sending money, are described in vol. iii., p. 254, the unhealthy condition of the towns in vol. ii., pp. 74-76, and riots, routs, affrays, and forcible entries, in very many letters.

The description given in Parliament of the state of England during

the Wars of the Roses is from the ' Rotuli Parliamentorum,' 1 Richard III.,
No. 1 (Printed vol. vi., p. 238).

Preambles of statutes and statements made in Parliament have frequently been used in illustration of the condition of the country, and they
are very valuable where they describe the condition as existing
when a statute was made, or immediately before, but they
are of no value where they describe the condition as existing
in ages before the describers lived.   They then become
second-hand authorities, giving merely the historical opinions of peti-
tioners who wished to prove a case, but who were not recording the
events of their own time.   It would not be difficult to prove on such
evidence that the country had progressively lost population, wealth, and
good morals, for nothing more frequently occurs in the preamble of a
statute than a statement that the evil to be remedied is of quite recent
growth, and entirely unknown to previous generations.   The statement,
in some statutes of the Tudor period, that certain towns had become
less populous than in earlier times, is in all probability incorrect, even
as applied to the particular towns mentioned, and gives a wholly false
idea of the development of commerce and town life as a whole.   The
subject, however, is one which may be more appropriately touched in
another volume, though it seemed necessary to show in this that a possible objection had not been overlooked.

Note on the value of state-ments in the preambles of statutes.

A charge of peculation against a Chancellor was, as has been incidentally mentioned in the cases of the Poles, of very common occurrence.   Corruption of Judges is indicated in the Statute 8
Richard II., c. 4, but still more by the widespread maintenance and intimidation ; corruption of the ' Pincerna ' in
the Patent Roll 8 Richard II., part 2, m. 30, d. ; and of various
revenue officers, in the ' Rotuli Parliamentorum,' 11 Henry
IV., No. 25 (printed vol. iii. p. 625).   Bribery of sheriffs is the subject of
18 Henry VI., c. 14 ; and in the reign of Edward IV. there was a commission to enquire concerning neglect of duty and partiality on the
part of sheriffs, throughout the whole realm (Patent Roll, 13 Edward
IV., part ii., m. 8 d.).   The outcry against Empson and Dudley in the
reign of Henry VII. was no more than an expression of dissatisfaction
which had continued for centuries.   The mention of bloodshed by the
dagger, drawn in haste, is very common in the criminal proceedings of
the period, and was not then considered by any means ' un-English.'
The exposure of traitors' heads upon London Bridge was too frequent
to need special references in proof of it.   There is, however, a curious
collection in illustration of the subject among the Petyt MSS. ('Theatrum Criminalium,' vol. iv.).   The influence of royal blood is shown
by writs directed to sheriffs in favour of the widows of some traitors,

Pp. 420–421. Evidence of the state of society to-wards the end of the 15th century.

who are permitted to receive their husbands' heads and to bury them. Such writs are enrolled on the Close Roll, 1 Henry IV., part i. m. 9 (concerning the head of the Earl of Kent), and m. 12 (concerning the head of the Earl of Huntingdon). *See* also the same roll, m. 19 (concerning the head of Thomas le Despenser, sent from Bristol to London), and the Close Roll, 5 Henry IV., part i. mm. 1, 25, 28, for other instances, including one of a head set on the pillory at Cambridge (m. 1). The Close Roll of Henry IV., m. 10, illustrates the manner in which heads and quarters were distributed, and afterwards, sometimes, collected. The practice of quartering traitors of noble birth died out about the end of the fifteenth century, though the sentence was passed upon them as before, and persons of inferior birth suffered the full horrors of the judgment.

INDEX.

The References are, as far as possible, in accordance with the best known descriptions of the various matters, and, therefore, not always consistent, *e.g.* ' Patent Rolls' and ' Rotuli Curiæ Regis,' 'John of Salisbury' and 'Radulfus de Diceto.'

262–263. Connexion of, with force, 263–264 Various forms of, in the fourteenth century, 264–282, 477–480. Attributed to William of Wykeham and other public men, 338–340, 488. Forms of, in the fifteenth century, 371–372, 496

French, how long distinguished from English in England. *See* English, Normans

'French Rolls,' referred to, 497, 499

Froissart, referred to, 487

'GALANAS,' equivalent to 'murdrum,' 436

Gallows, an appurtenance of a Manor, 82, 442. The New, in St. Giles's Fields, 351, 493

Game-Laws, origin of the antipathy to, 214, 260

Games, the Roman sentence of condemnation to the. *See* Arena

Gaming, for liberty among the ancient Germans, 90, 445. With loaded dice in the twelfth century, 145–146, 456. With loaded dice in the fourteenth century, 237, 473

Gaols, treatment of accused in, by the Romans, 17, 427. Deficiency of, in England, before the Assise of Clarendon, 130, 450. Private, of the Barons, 217–218, 469. Intimidation and torture in, in the fourteenth century, to make prisoners become approvers, 287–288, 481. A Coroner's Inquest held on all persons who died in, 288. Breaking of, and escapes by connivance of the keepers of, 292, 481. Of Bishops, 299, 332, 482–483, 487. Letters taught in to secure Benefit of Clergy for prisoners, 300–301, 483. Broken during Wat Tyler's rebellion, 333, 487

Gaol Delivery, Justices of, 221, 469

Gaol Delivery Rolls, referred to, 474, 476, 477, 478, 479, 480, 481, 482, 483, 484, 485

'Gau,' the, compared with the shire, 72

Gaul and Britain, alleged execution by fire in, 10–12, 429

Gaunt, John of. *See* Lancaster

Gavaston, Piers, the Law of Treason illustrated by the case of, 224–225, 470

Gentlemen, unorthodoxy and superior learning thought disgraceful to, in the Middle Ages, 353, 493. Debt of, to towns and commerce, 373–374

Germans, } *See* Teutonic
Germany, }

Gervase, the Chronicle of, referred to, 452, 456, 457

'Gesta Dei per Francos,' referred to, 458

'Gesta Stephani Regis,' referred to, 449

Gibbon, the historian, his name incidentally mentioned, 68

Giles' Life and Letters of Becket, referred to, 449–450

Glanville, description of Trial by Battle, the Grand Assise, and the Inquest of Usury by, 124–127, 451. Division of criminal jurisdiction according to, 453. Definition of 'murdrum' by, 455. The guild or commune of towns and its privileges according to, 460–461. A passage in corrected by authority of the best MS., ib. Wager of Law mentioned by, 450. The Prologue of, compared with the Proœmium to Justinian's Institutes, 452

Gloucester, history of the name of, 67. Name given by the city of, to a shire, 72. The burgesses' guild at, and charter to, 173, 459–460, 462. Population of, under Edward II., 181, 462–463

Gloucester, a Duchess of, tried and sentenced for Witchcraft, 356–357, 494

Gloucester, a Duke of (uncle of Richard II.), murder of, 404–406, 500. Declared guilty of Treason after death, 406, 500

Gloucester, a Duke of, probable murder of, in the reign of Henry VI., 406, 500

Godwin, compared with Warwick, the King-maker, 82

Gold-workers in England before the Conquest, 65, 440

Goods and chattels, forfeited by flight, after charge of felony, till the reign of George IV., 19, 428

Government, value of settled, in diminishing crime, 94, 217, 419. Good, in the modern sense impossible in the Middle Ages, 109–110. No abstract theory of, existing in early times, 177, 224, 226–228. More settled under the Tudors than previously, 419

Gracechurch, or Graschirche, scenes in the Market at, 237, 473

Grand Assise. *See* Assise

Grantham, population of, under Edward II., 181, 462–463

Gray, Elizabeth. *See* Elizabeth

Great Seal, the, counterfeited, 273, 479. Fraudulent use of the, 368, 495

Greece, the fine for homicide in, 42, 436

Gregory VII., Pope, his letter to Lanfranc concerning wife-selling, 99–100, 447. Encroachments of, 104–105, 449

Guilds, Roman 'collegia' or, 23, 429. Existence of 'collegia' or, in Roman

536   *INDEX.*